NEW SOCIAL MOVEMENTS IN THE SOUTH

ABOUT THE EDITOR

The Editor, Dr Ponna Wignaraja, is a well-known development economist who worked originally with the Development Advisory Service of the World Bank. He is currently Vice Chairman of the Independent South Asian Commission on Poverty Alleviation appointed by the Heads of State of the SAARC Region and is also Adviser to the United Nations University on South Asian Perspectives. He is a former Secretary General of the Society for International Development and Chairman of the Participatory Institute for Development Alternatives (PIDA) in Sri Lanka. He is particularly renowned for the original perspectives on participatory development that he and a network of Asian scholars have pioneered in response to the current crisis of development paradigms and democratic formations; the lessons derived from realities on the ground are essential for moving forward both in thinking and action.

Also edited by Ponna Wignaraja:

TOWARDS A THEORY OF RURAL DEVELOPMENT
(Progressive Publishers, Karachi, 1988)

THE CHALLENGE OF SOUTH ASIA:
DEVELOPMENT, DEMOCRACY AND REGIONAL COOPERATION
(*with Akmal Hussain*; Sage Publishers, New Delhi, New York and London, 1988)

WOMEN, POVERTY AND RESOURCES
(Sage Publishers, New Delhi, Newbury Park and London, 1990)

PARTICIPATORY DEVELOPMENT:
LEARNING FROM SOUTH ASIA
(OUP, Karachi and Oxford, 1991)

NEW SOCIAL MOVEMENTS IN THE SOUTH

EMPOWERING THE PEOPLE

Edited by

PONNA WIGNARAJA

ZED BOOKS

London & New Jersey

New Social Movements in the South is published in South Asia by
Sage Publications, Post Box 4215, New Delhi, 110048,
India and in the rest of the world by
Zed Books Ltd, 7 Cynthia Street, London N1 9JF
and 165 First Avenue, Atlantic Highlands, NJ, 07716, USA in 1993.

Cover designed by Andrew Corbett
Typeset by Vijaya Enterprises, Madras, India
Printed and bound in the United Kingdom by
Biddles Ltd, Guildford and King's Lynn

A catalogue record for this book is available
from the British Library

US CIP is available from the Library of Congress

ISBN 1 85649 107 2 Hb
ISBN 1 85649 108 0 Pb

Contents

About the Contributors

Samir Amin is head of the research organization, Third World Forum, in Dakar. Africa's most illustrious economist, his recent books in English include *Delinking: Towards a Polycentric World* (1990), *Maldevelopment: Anatomy of a Global Failure* (1990) and *Eurocentrism* (1989).

Daniel Comacho is a senior faculty member of the University of Costa Rica.

Teresa S. Encarnacion is a Latin American social scientist associated with the United Nations University.

Orlando Fals Borda is Professor Emeritus of Sociology at the Institute of Political and International Studies, National University of Bogota and a former President of the Latin American Council for Adult Education (CEAAL). His most recent book in English is *Action and Knowledge: Breaking the Monopoly with Participatory Action Research (PAR)* (1991).

Rajni Kothari founded the Centre for the Study of Developing Societies in New Delhi in 1963. He is one of India's most eminent social scientists and author of, among other books, *Politics in India* (1970) and *State against Democracy: In Search of Human Governance*. He is widely regarded as one of India's premier voices of dissent against authoritarianism and anti-people development policies of the state.

Leilah Landim is a Senior Researcher with the Institute of Religious Studies in Rio de Janeiro, Brazil.

Mahmood Mamdani is Director of the Centre for Basic Research in Kampala, Uganda. A sociologist, he is particularly well-known for his work on the peasantry in Africa.

Thandika Mkandawire is Director of CODESRIA (the Council for the Development of Economic and Social Research in Africa), which is the leading independent social science research network in the Continent. His current work focuses specifically on the role of the state in Africa.

Ramashray Roy is a Senior Fellow at the Centre for the Study of Developing Societies in New Delhi.

Bassem Serhan is a Professor at the University of Kuwait.

Harsh Sethi is a leading Indian social scientist, closely associated with Lokayan—a forum of intellectuals, non-party activists and citizens involved in various movements in India. He is author of numerous works on new social movements in the Indian subcontinent.

Eduardo C. Tadem is a Latin American social scientist associated with the United Nations University.

E. Wamba-dia-Wamba teaches History at the University of Dar es Salaam in Tanzania.

Ponna Wignaraja is particularly well-known for the original perspectives on participatory development which he and a network of Asian scholars have pioneered, and which have been published in a series of recent books including *Participatory Development: Learning from South Asia* (1991). His most recent assignment has been as Vice-Chairman of the Independent South Asian Commission on Poverty Alleviation whose report is in press.

FOREWORD

Since the social movements in Eastern Europe brought about a drastic political change of the socialist regimes of the region, 'social movement' has become a key phrase used, sometimes overused, by political analysts and social scientists around the world. Dr Ponna Wignaraja has rightly decided to entitle this book *New Social Movements in the South* as this title also helps make a distinction between these new movements and older social movements such as the trade union movements and peasant movements. The book does blur the distinction between people's movements and social movements, but at this stage too precise definitions are premature. What is required for the present is a broad, pragmatically evolved concept with which the wide variety of people's responses to the multifaceted crises in their lives can be probed and collective efforts to bring about social change identified.

The United Nations University (UNU) Project on Third World and World Development began extensive research in 1986 on the role of social movements in different Third World regions: Africa, Asia, the Arab world and Latin America, long before the study of these movements became fashionable. The previous UNU projects in the early 1980s were called Regional Perspectives Projects. The UNU's interest in this subject did not represent any brilliant foresight by some genial political scientist predicting the coming 'boom' of social movements. This subject was in fact one of the major common themes of study jointly selected by the UNU regional research networks in the above-mentioned Third World regions.

Even as early as 1976, the UNU had been engaged in several international network projects, involving researchers of all regions of the world, which were looking into human and social development with a special emphasis on how the different regions of the world were conceiving their development and political processes. The UNU had been told by an international panel of development specialists that development theory was now in disarray, and that the UNU should create an inter-regional and inter-disciplinary dialogue involving the researchers of different world regions who were in search of 'alternative development', i.e. development that did not just emulate the Western industrial development model.

In 1981–82, a panel of other experts was called in to evaluate the result of the first five years of alternative development research. The panel was of the opinion that the UNU research had opened new perspectives in a futuristic manner. That was good, they stated, but not enough in the 1980s now that the hope for a New International Economic Order had faded away in the face of a worldwide crisis—not only economic but also political and cultural. The UNU should now study the complexity and reality of the crisis, while keeping in mind the objectives of development in wider human terms. These could not be identified solely with economic models, but involved human and social aspects as well. It has to be an endogenous, participatory and ecologically sound process.

Some of the experts already involved in the first-phase research networks and some new researchers were mobilized to conduct in-depth interdisciplinary research on the regional perspectives in which economic growth, human and social development were regarded as complementary goals. They were not given a rigid research agenda by the UNU, but were asked first to identify in each region their respective research priorities. Only after such a choice was made did the regional project teams' coordinators meet to identify the common themes regarding Third World and world development, cutting across Africa, Asia (South, Southeast and East), the Arab world and Latin America.

After a careful discussion, the regional networks of these four Third World regions arrived at a common understanding that the impact of the world crisis on each region should be studied, taking into account the socio-cultural specificities of each region. They also decided to study the pattern of conflict and cooperation in each of them, and among the different actors involved in the social-economic and political processes triggered off by the world crisis.

The researchers of all the Third World regions were in agreement on two premisses:

(a) The regions' states were in deep crisis and were unable to cope with the impact of the world crisis on their internal crises.

(b) There was a great variety of social movements, which were becoming increasingly important as people's responses to the deepening crises. Some of these responses were in nascent, experimental stages, others had matured into movements of significant proportions with clear ideologies, objectives, programmes, leadership and organisation. There were many of variable quality, as categorised by Ponna Wignaraja's 'seeds' and 'bubbles' in Chapter 1.

It is within this context of collective reflection that the UNU discovered the importance and variety of these movements and experiments in the different Third World regions, responding to the impact of the contemporary world crisis.

The editor of the present volume, Dr Wignaraja, has attempted to put together the quintessence of the research conducted by so many highly qualified Southern researchers in different Third World regions. Some of the chapters represent the result of long theoretical debates engaged in during regional and inter-regional meetings organized by the UNU. Others are based on action research in the field and case studies involving, beside the authors of the chapters, many unmentioned young scholars and researchers. All the chapters have been contributed by Third World researchers studying the reality from their own perspectives and from inside their own respective regions. No attempt has been made to claim comprehensiveness, or to claim elegance of formulation of an alternative theory.

The reader should not expect to find a single point of view advocated by this book, be it a 'Third Worldist' view or a single Southern point of view. Nor should he or she hope to find a unified theory on social movements or, as they are also known, people's movements and experiments. Rather, the reader is invited to learn from this volume the richness of Third World social scientific reasoning regarding social movements, a theme so far studied mostly in the industrialized North and somewhat less in Eastern Europe, but not prioritized, let alone studied in an inter-disciplinary fashion, even by the area study specialists studying the different Third World regions from the outside. For them, it would rather be a specific social movement of a given region which would be studied in its specific environment. To look at people's movements and experiments as actors and processes caught up in the global and the regional crisis is not an approach adopted even by these area study specialists.

Without entering into details, one may identify in the different chapters of this book at least three viewpoints that Third World researchers adopt when studying social movements.

First, that people's movements and experiments are in effect new social movements and are manifesting the true nature of the contemporary world crisis. According to this standpoint, there was a time when all social movements in Third World countries were engaged in common struggle, namely the anti-colonial fight. They were competing among themselves to assume power in the post-colonial states. Now, it is these very states that are in deep crisis. Therefore the myriad of social movements in the Third World regions do not fight to assume state power. They constitute in this sense an integral part of the present crisis and response.

A second viewpoint looks at the social movements as new actors, performing multiple functions—political, economic, social and cultural. The new actors are not fighting to assume state power, not because they do not know what to do with state power, but rather because they represent a new breed of actors, interested not in state power but rather in creating a free space from where a democratic society can emerge. The term 'civil society' is often used to represent this space that is not dominated by the state. A corollary is that, whether or not power is an objective, these movements do represent a form of countervailing power.

A third viewpoint sees, in the social movements, social experiments preparing a future desirable society. The role of these people's movements and experiments thus transcends not only state power, but also wants to go beyond the new existing civil societies with their built-in inequality and unauthenticity hidden behind the window-dressing of 'democracy' or 'development'.

The above-mentioned three points of view reflect all aspects of the experience of the authors of this book as Third World researchers who live the multifaceted crisis in the Third World. Some put an emphasis on the lost historical opportunity that the national liberation movements represented. They see the proliferation of social movements without a national/state project as a symptom of the crisis of the post-colonial states. Others are disillusioned by these states and hence hope to see a new type of civil society emerge. For them, the social movements are the carriers of this message of hope. Still others have been disillusioned not only by the state, but also by the modern/industrial society as it is proposed to and imposed on them by the industrialized North. For them the people's movements represent more endogenous, more participatory and more authentic experiments of an alternative society. Yet another perspective goes beyond a critique of the past to identify elements in alternative processes that could become the basis of a new social contract yet to be forged.

One common belief is shared by practically all the contributors to this volume, namely, that the present world is in deep crisis and the Third World is reacting to this crisis through the people's movements and experiments. There is also a shared hope: that the present crisis will be overcome by the combined efforts of the peoples of the Third World, represented by these movements and experiments. The contributors all, too, want to share their points of view with whoever is concerned with the contemporary world crisis, both in the Third World and in the industrialized North, as well as in Eastern Europe and the former USSR which are in even greater disarray than the industrial North or the South. There are lessons to be learned by everyone, as Dr Ponna Wignaraja indicates in his Preface.

Therefore, we hope that the reader will find all the chapters of this book directly relevant to his or her scientific and social interest, irrespective of his or her regional context. This is because the combination of the above three points of view is the only broad conceptual framework within which the role of the different social and people's movements and experiments can be correctly defined in their full complexity.

We hope that the UNU efforts to present these multifaceted perspectives on social movements will provide the occasion for all the readers of this book to participate in this continuing international research endeavour. If they find in this book an entry point into Third World research and reflection on the present world crisis, and if they decide that people's responses undogmatically presented in the Third World deserve special attention in view of their rich potential, they have already joined the international community of scholars of the UN University in their search for solutions to pressing global problems.

Kinhide Mushakoji
Former Vice-Rector
United Nations University

PREFACE

This book is one product of the United Nations University's Third World and World Development Project. In 1987, this project brought together an inter-disciplinary group of scholars from Third World countries in Asia, Africa, the Arab region and Latin America to reflect on their own socio-political reality and understand the changes underway. It was also an attempt to understand the implications of these changes for the theory and practice of human development and participatory democracy, as well as for the strategic options open to national policy.

This particular book, however, did not emerge from a specific research design. It represents a selection of papers written by various scholars in the network, individually, who were searching for alternatives to Western paradigms of development and democratic notions and institutions. In this search they identified various social movements and people's responses, which exhibited sustainable characteristics and which promoted both development and democracy in new terms. In this sense, the papers in this book provide some overview of the new thinking, and the nuances within it, that is emerging under different socio-political circumstances. It is not an exaggeration to say they reflect an emerging school of thought, albeit rudimentary, a set of ideas whose time has come. The South Commission in its recent Report, *The Challenge to the South,* stated:

> Three and a half billion people, three quarters of all humanity, live in the developing countries. By the year 2000, the proportion will probably have risen to four fifths. Together the developing countries—accounting for more than two thirds of the earth's land surface area—are often called the Third World.
>
> We refer to them as the South. Largely bypassed by the benefits of prosperity and progress, they exist on the periphery of the developed countries of the North. While most of the people of the North are affluent, most of the people of the South are poor; while the economies of the North are generally strong and resilient, those of the South are mostly weak and defenceless; while the countries in the North are, by and large, in control of their destinies, those in the South are very vulnerable to external factors and lacking in functional sovereignty.

> The countries of the South vary greatly in size, in natural resource endowment, in the structure of their economies, in the level of economic, social, and technological development. They also differ in their cultures, in their political systems, and in the ideologies they profess. Their economic and technological diversity has become more marked in recent years, making the South of today even less homogeneous than the South of yesterday.
>
> Yet in this diversity there is a basic unity. What the countries of the South have in common transcends their differences; it gives them a shared identity and a reason to work together for common objectives. And their economic diversity offers opportunities for cooperation that can benefit them all.

This unity needs to be reinforced. Its peoples, cultures, natural resources and knowledge systems are the South's greatest assets. One thing shared common that has become increasingly noticeable, that transcends the differences in the South, is the tendency towards political democratization and economic decentralization.

The multifaceted crises that are affecting these countries—poverty reproducing itself, the ecological crisis, gender conflicts, human rights conflicts and the inability of state structures to mediate these tensions—are creating new responses from the people, particularly the poor and vulnerable. These people's responses also attempt to protect the South from penetration by external forces which further intensify these internal tensions. These people's responses are taking the form of new social movements, people's movements and experiments.

No attempt has been made in this book to define these movements and experiments with precision. They range from large collective protest movements to small-scale development actions. Some have clear organization, others are 'processes' which may not have any organization to begin with. But they are all part of a continuing process of political, economic and social change and exhibit both temporal and cultural specificity. The limited theoretical frameworks available, and the unfinished debates among scholars of all persuasions on both theoretical and methodological issues, can only permit some rudimentary concepts to be identified from the experience on the ground. A recent survey, *New Social Movements in India: A Review of the Literature* by Ghanshyam Shah (Sage Publications, 1990) reinforces the view that it would be premature to go much beyond drawing some practical conclusions, advancing a simple set of hypotheses and introducing some new categories of analysis. All the authors in this book have done this—which is what sets them apart and links their thinking.

These responses by ordinary people are providing a number of lessons for rethinking past approaches to development and democracy and the paradigms that informed these approaches. This book attempts to highlight some of these lessons and some of the experience on the ground and raises some basic issues in relation to sustainable development and democracy. In this process the analysis also discounts the possibility of reproducing in the South Western capitalist democracy, let alone former Eastern European socialist practice. It reflects dissent from more conventional orthodoxies—neo-classical and Marxist. It is in this sense that it also contributes to the search for new paradigms of democracy and development that are relevant and sustainable in the South.

The papers included in Part One were selected from the ongoing work of various scholars within the UNU's Third World and World Development Project. Chapter 1 gives an overview of the new approach and how it evolved from the efforts of a particular group of South Asian scholars engaged in participatory action research at the grassroots. Chapter 2 indicates the multiplicity of new social movements which have arisen in the complicated structure of Latin American societies. Chapter 3 argues that the state has been transformed from an instrument of liberation of the masses into a key source of their oppression. Chapter 4 is a critique of capitalism. And Chapter 5 is primarily a literature survey of emerging new thinking in Africa on social movements—which is complementary to the work by Ghanshyam Shah for India.

Similarly the case profiles in Part Two are also only illustrative of the issues that Southern researchers are addressing and indicate the range of people's processes, raising of mass consciousness and new institutions being built. Additional case profiles are available in two other publications edited by Ponna Wignaraja entitled *Women, Poverty and Resources* (Sage Publications, 1990) and *Participatory Development: learning from South Asia* (Oxford University Press, 1991).

A great deal more work needs to be done and many new questions need to be asked to deepen our understanding of these social movements and experiments. The rudimentary conceptualisation that is emerging needs to be refined further. The present volume's 'thoughts in progress' are presented as a modest input into the ongoing process of thinking and action on social change within countries of the South. It can, we believe, also have wider implications for thinking on the larger global changes currently taking place, with the collapse of the Eastern bloc countries and the social disarray in Western capitalist societies. Further, there are elements in the rudimentary concepts that are emerging from the grassroots that could upset any simplistic notion that the answer to the failure of the cruder forms of socialism and statism lies in the cruder forms of capitalism and market forces.

This was not an easy book to edit. The issues being raised by the new social movements, and their implications for social change, are both vast and complex. The challenge was how to continue to introduce some order into the understanding of this complexity. There is no pretence at elegance and synthesis. Even terms like 'social movements' and 'people's movements' are sometimes used interchangeably, sometimes with different nuances. Eventually, a new terminology may even have to be coined.

The accumulation of a large volume of philosophical material in the South, some of it more than 2,500 years old, requires that this philosophical and intellectual tradition informs our strategic responses today. But this begs the question of what methodology to use and where to begin. In these turbulent times, we cannot merely continue to do 'more of the same' of what we have been doing in the past 40 years, only more efficiently. Nor can we go on accepting institutions from other cultures and environments without conscious adaptation. We in the South are like flotsam and jetsam in someone else's political game. The myths that have become a part of the imposed paradigms—the intellectual and elite thinking that has been transferred to the South—have to be demystified. The only way to do this is to look on the ground and begin the long road to rethinking.

Deeply conscious of my personal limitations, I have simply tried to prepare a work in progress that can provoke discussion, particularly among those like-minded intellectual companions who are searching for alternatives to the more conventional and dominant neo-classical and Marxist modes of thought and action. If this discussion provokes a new research agenda in the South, the publication of this book would have been amply justified for such research could lead in turn to further coherence in thinking and action.

A special word of thanks is due to my colleagues in the UNU Third World and World Development Project who contributed papers to this volume. These pioneering efforts were undoubtedly undertaken in interaction with other network members, whose collective contribution is also acknowledged. As editor, I owe a special word of thanks to Kinhide Mushakoji, former Vice-Rector of the UNU and George Aseniero, Programme Officer of the UNU, for their support of our attempts to generate these first efforts at individual and collective rethinking and reconceptualization.The Foreword by Kinhide Mushakoji also helps to situate this book in the current discourse on development and democracy. Harsh Sethi of the Centre for Study of Developing Societies, India, read the first drafts of some of the papers and helped in the preliminary selection. Susil Sirivardana, Sri Lanka's Janasaviya Commissioner, read some of the papers, particularly my own, and his comments are deeply appreciated. Jayadeva Uyangoda of the University of Colombo and Secretary of the Sri Lanka Social Scientists' Association worked closely with me in pulling the final manuscript together and in the arduous task of shaping some of the contributions to give the book coherence. Without his help this manuscript might not have been completed. A final word of thanks is due to Romesh Fernando of the University of Sri Lanka who assisted with the editing and proof-reading of the manuscript and to Naleer Lantra of the UNU South Asian Perspectives Project who painstakingly did the insertion into the word processor. The IRDC Canada and the CIDA through its Management for Change Programme carried some of these costs. To the United Nations University itself goes the credit for having sponsored and supported this kind of pioneering research and provided the opportunity for scholars from Third World countries to interact. It is expected that this will be a part of the continuing task of the United Nations University, in keeping with its mandate.

Ponna Wignaraja
Adviser on South Asian Perspectives
United Nations University

PART ONE

Conceptual Issues

INTRODUCTION

In recent years millions of people in the South have shared a common experience: the failure of conventional models of develeopment and paths to modernity to benefit them. Whether the model is some variant of capitalism or an image of socialism, many negative consequences have occurred when the South has attempted to imitate the development paths of industrialized societies.

Along with the failure of conventional development paths, there has also been an inability to establish a democratic polity. Both these factors have led to the erosion of the very fabric of society and an inability of state structures, even with increasing centralization and militarization, to manage the multifaceted crises in the South.

The realization that the conventional and dominant paradigms—both neo-classical and Marxist—have failed, as far as the South is concerned, leads not only to an examination of the why of the failures, but also to an attempt to identify, in however rudimentary a fashion, elements in a conceptual framework that can inform both the process of development and democracy in the South. The five chapters included in Part One represent recent attempts by Southern scholars to rethink both the development and the democratic processes as they pertain to the South.

What is new about this emerging paradigm of fresh thinking is the attempt to conceptualize a positive synthesis of ideas with social praxis. It views the process of social change in its totality, when development and democracy are integral components. It also introduces to the debate the missing elements in conventional paradigms: culture, values, democracy, participation and people's mobilization.

The chapters by Wignaraja, Comacho, Kothari and Amin are by no means comprehensive. They are, however, illustrative of the ideas, analysis and concepts inherent in the new thinking on development and social change. They are indicative of how scholars in the South have in recent years been making a conscious attempt to address themselves to some fundamental issues concerning the transition to the twenty-first century.

Chapter 5 contains an illustrative survey of the literature on Africa. This is intended to draw the attention of readers to the emerging body of writers on social movements there and the need for a new research agenda for the South.

1. Rethinking Development and Democracy

Ponna Wignaraja

This chapter is a personal reflection on some of the new thinking that is emerging among scholars in the South in their search for relevant new paradigms of human development and participatory democracy.[1] This thinking has evolved over the past 15 years or so as a result of experiential learning. It has gained legitimacy as the older, Eurocentric paradigms that were at the core of post-independence practice in most of the countries of the South failed to result there in forms of development or democracy that were sustainable. The disarray in the workings of these conventional models in both the industrialized Western capitalist societies and the socialist East has given further legitimacy to the new thinking in the South.

Selected elements in this recent thinking can be found at the periphery of Marxist thinking in the writings of Rosa Luxemburg, Gramsci and a few others, and in the evolution of the welfare state inspired by liberal philosophies and Fabian socialism in the capitalist West. Others are implicit in Gandhian philosophy and in the cultural milieu of most of the South. However, two of the basic values—human development and participatory democracy in their widest connotations—which are at the core of the new thinking, were not at the centre of the Western-imitative models of development and democracy that were translated into nearly half a century of Southern efforts to establish viable nation states. Neither were they part of the mainstream development economics that dominated development thinking and practice.

The two dominant frameworks of thinking and action—both borrowed—were Marxism (mainly Leninism) and neo-classicism. Their failure to set in motion processes of social change in the South that ensured material well-being to large numbers and were both participatory and humane, is producing a grassroots response in the form of people's movements and experiments. The variety and richness of the cultural and socio-political context in which these movements are emerging, particularly at the micro level, will be considered below. This popular experience provides a basis for some initial, though rudimentary, generalizations and some broad guidelines for the continuing search for relevant new paradigms of development and democracy.

This chapter does not attempt to identify a single paradigm or dogma as an alternative to Eurocentric models. Nor does it presuppose that the new macro and micro social processes in the South are homogeneous or monolithic. But it will attempt to identify several positive elements in the changes in social formations, consciousness and organizations that are beginning to emerge on the ground.[2] People can be manipulated at lower levels of consciousness, but such manipulation, leading often to the emergence of highly centralized and repressive organizations, is not the direct concern of this chapter.

The positive elements analysed here stem mainly from the release of the creative energies of the people at the micro level, as they struggle to survive and respond to the multifaceted crises in their lives. The central concern here is to clarify how the praxis, that is the action–reflection–action process inherent in these people's movements and experiments, can be refocused. This continuous process is itself an instrument for reinforcing the positive changes underway. The proposition stated here is that, as the poor and vulnerable groups in the South deepen their understanding of their reality, they also, through greater consciousness-raising and awareness, action and organization, can bring about changes both in their lives and in society that will lead to human development and participatory democracy. They can at the same time contribute to economic growth. The deepening of their understanding can begin with collective protest against some form of social injustice or with a positive development action undertaken by a group.

To deepen our understanding of the above processes on the ground, and to see where they may lead, two fundamental issues have to be clarified. First, a clearer vision and perspective on social change, whose values are explicitly stated, is an essential prerequisite. Southern cultures abound with visions of a good society. Second, a different intellectual framework, emanating from within the Southern cultures and knowledge systems, must be used in analysing the complex realities of, and transitional pathways to, social change. The values to be used emanate from philosophical underpinnings that are holistic and not characterized by narrow and rigid ideologies. The associated methodology of analysis needs to be interdisciplinary. This in turn requires questioning of the narrow intellectual framework, the single-discipline analysis, a priori theorizing and methodology of Western so-called scientific enquiry, which have for the most part informed attempts to analyse social change. A corollary is that we need to take stock of both the wide range of analytical tools and the knowledge systems that are now available in the South.

In other words, to understand in depth the new people's movements, which are manifestations of a new pluralistic paradigm of development and democracy, a re-evaluation of some of the fundamental values in our own cultures and of the intellectual tools and resources at our disposal must be made. The biases and inadequacies for understanding complex inter-related social phenomena by means of conventional intellectual processes, must be questioned and criticized. To assist in this task, there is now a sufficient body of new critical literature on the structure of social action and the relationship between theory and practice.[3] The essence of this literature will not be repeated here. It is taken as axiomatic that intellectual frameworks borrowed from other historical, cultural and political environments can no longer be effective in understanding the complex realities of other, fundamentally different cultures and contexts, or in giving direction to social changes underway in them. The additional question is how to use the total knowledge systems that are available in the South to facilitate this understanding. Here, both the holistic and cognitive approaches to the generation of knowledge, as well as the much wider range of technological choices that can result, are critically important instruments.[4]

Another aspect in the search for new paradigms is to identify the fundamental nature of the process of social change itself. Is it one that results from a sharpening of contradictions leading to a 'big bang' type of revolution, which then automatically ushers in a good society? Or is it one that more commonly proceeds through marginal reforms and incremental changes? Both processes can be observed in reality, as can their varying consequences. But other intermediate processes and transitional pathways to social change may also exist, as the new movements operate in the various political spaces available in their given historical contexts. These latter transitions themselves may be considered revolutionary in that they involve in-depth structural changes in limited situations and within available political spaces. Through raising mass consciousness, building countervailing power and initiating equal access to resources for the poor, for instance, the old dominant structures could be modified and changed. The process might or might not be bloody. The question then is, can the structural changes within limited political spaces be multiplied in a comprehensive and systematic way, with political commitment and support from new coalitions within the structures and with the participation of the poor and other vulnerable groups, under a variety of socio-political circumstances?

One last point that needs to be made here is that in looking at the specificity of the new people's movements and experiments in the South for culturally relevant and sustainable social change, the need for linkages between them across the globe should not be ignored. Such links would enrich the pluralism that is implicit on the ground in people's movements both in the South and in the North. They could also help to build countervailing power at the global level. This chapter will not, however, elaborate on the global aspect. It is mentioned because of its relevance to even larger global paradigms.

The points of departure

The people's movements in the South not only express dissent, they also are providing some basis for a developmental and democratic alternative to the system as it now works. There is a qualitative difference between the new people's struggles and earlier liberation movements against colonialism, the peasant movements for land reform, and trade union movements. The point of departure is the discrediting of the conventional paradigm of national liberation, socialism and economic development itself. Conventional notions of capitalism, socialism and the sovereign nation state also have changed with the emergence of multinational corporations and various new philosophical 'mixes'. Without delinking from some of the conventional paradigms, the doctrines associated with them and purely legalistic formations, it is impossible to understand and learn from the emerging reality on the ground.

A fundamental departure from the conventional paradigms is also justifiable because of their failure both to initiate action leading to new accumulation processes and viable economic growth, and to establish appropriate new democratic state structures. They also failed to provide sustainable social formations in wider human and ecological terms. People were treated in the praxis of the old paradigms as objects of history rather than as its subjects. They were non-participant observers and fell victim to hierarchical, centralized bureaucratic processes in both the development and the political processes. In addition, they were, and are, frequently victims of repressive militarized state structures and what amounts to state terrorism.

The whole process negated the diversity, humaneness and freedom that were fundamental to Southern cultures. It attempted to impose a monolithicness and homogenization that were alien and alienating. The tensions that were created resulted in mindless violence and anarchy rather than in positive social change. The centralization achieved through repression created increased violence and militarization of state structures. The processes of poverty creation, youth alienation and environmental degradation reproduced themselves.[5] The human and material resource base available to reverse past processes itself began to be eroded. The state could no longer function as mediator and consensus maker.

Growth, human development and equity: no trade-offs

As this multifaceted crisis deepened, the accumulation process set in motion either by means of private capitalism or of state capitalism, a process that was basic to the old concept of economic development, turned out to be insufficient, and the pressures mounted for an alternative accumulation process. It was not a matter of growth first and equity afterwards, but, equally, redistributive justice and 'trickle-down' were simply not the issues.

Most Southern countries were predominantly rural, peasant societies, with traditional knowledge systems and non-predatory relations with nature. And yet, nearly four decades ago, when Southern countries began to emerge as politically independent nations from centuries of colonial rule, they adopted a development model that was indifferent if not inimical to the large numbers who live in rural areas.[6] Support for this model, which essentially permitted the continuation of existing international economic relationships, came from two external sources: the industrialized countries of the West and the industrialized, centrally planned countries of the Eastern bloc.

The framework that has influenced this development process in the past half-century assumed that there were 'developed' countries and 'developing' countries and that if the experience of the former, along with some capital and technology, was transferred to the latter the gap would be narrowed. The objectives and processes were viewed in economic terms and great reliance was placed on economic factors and centralized decision-making to achieve results. This framework assumed that rapid economic growth could take place if there was central planning and control of the economy (by the state or the private sector) as a 'top-down' process, with emphasis on industrialization, modernization and urbanization. Capital, the factor in short supply in the so-called developing countries, was seen as the main input into the process. Internal capital accumulation, it was assumed, would be assisted by free and massive inflows of foreign capital and technology. The cumulative benefits of growth in the modern sector were expected eventually either to 'trickle down' automatically or at best to be handed down in an administrative fashion or 'delivered'. Material accumulation either in public or private forms was expected to solve other human problems.

The widening gap between the industrialized and the Souther countries, the results of the so-called green revolution which helped the rich get richer and made the poor poorer within Southern countries, the massive transfer of resources from poor countries to rich, illustrated both the dangers and the irrelevance of this framework to the majority of people in the South. They confirmed the limitations of the narrow, techno-economic model of development, even in its own terms.

Apart from the model's narrow orientation and its lack of relevance to Southern countries, the realities of the quantity and quality of foreign aid, of transfers of technology, and of the weak internal mobilization efforts ensured that the prevailing assumptions regarding the possibilities for rapid growth were of little operational value. There is sufficient evidence even from studies carried out by the United Nations (UN), World Bank and other institutions operating within the system to confirm that, by any standards, neither the quantity of aid nor its quality nor the kinds of technology transferred were sufficient or appropriate to transform these societies, let alone to lift them out of the poverty trap into modernization and industrialization. Even as there is general apathy towards aid and capital flows to the South in most industrialized countries today, there is also a growing body of opinion which supports the view that the earlier methods of aid-giving and technology transfer are things of the past. They have created impoverished rural areas in the South and increased the dependence of Southern countries within an inequitable global order. This is not an argument against aid or international development cooperation as such, but a critique of the manner in which things have worked.

Furthermore, the transnational corporations that control the stock of modern technology, and are still the main instruments for its transfer, extract high prices for their knowhow and equipment. The highly capital-intensive and import-substituting technology that continues to be implanted into the South with little social control or social conscience bears insufficient relation either to real factor endowment, particularly of labour, or to the existing knowledge system, or to the wide range of technological choices available to the South. The entire process has been wasteful and the contradictions too sharp and numerous for any orderly form of management of the process as a whole for the real benefit of poor countries. Under these circumstances, for the South to keep asking for more of the same kind of aid is an irrational option. In terms of the old paradigm, a massive inflow of resources from external sources and reversal of the outflow of resources from the South would be required. Neither precondition has materialized.

Throughout the 1960s and early 1970s some token attempts were made to modify the narrow techno-economic notions of development and to effect some reforms. The reformists argued that a modified framework of economic development could still be made to work 'efficiently' if (a) redistribution or social justice were built into the objectives; (b) elements of popular participation (mainly some consultation with the people or manipulation of the people) in an essentially top-down planning process were allowed; and (c) a continuous process of transfer of a proportion of the income and technology from industrialized to Southern countries could be ensured, particularly through the UN system and its specialized agencies such as the World Bank, the International Monetary Fund (IMF) and the regional banks. More recently, a 'human face' has been added to the reformist option.

But the reformist position continues to be based on conventional development thinking and practice.[7] Even with greater social justice and safety nets built into it and with greater human capital formation, the development process is still considered mainly as an economic exercise, subject to allocation of scarce resources by governments and big private sector corporations. Furthermore, a conflict-free social framework for change is assumed. The vision of 'one world' continues to pervade the international rhetoric, along with the assumption that these changes—brought about under existing conditions and within unchanged structures—will result in an orderly and continuous transfer of resources from industrialized countries to the South. Underlying all this are further assumptions: that the problem of development is still mainly in the poor countries; and that a consistent set of policy packages based on technocratic considerations can be evolved and carried out from the top, both internationally and within individual countries. The basic assumption continues to be that the modernization/industrialization process, with some consultation with the people and the goodwill and assistance of 'developed' countries and the international community, will bring about positive social change. The poor are still considered to be the objects and the targets of the process and are at best to be provided with a safety net, while adjusting to an inequitable global system and a national system devoid of vision or capacity.

What, then, is the alternative development pathway for the South? As mentioned earlier, a sustainable development strategy for the present needs to search for alternative driving forces for a self-sustaining accumulation. It also seems necessary for Southern countries to adopt a development strategy that combines human development, growth, equity and technological change with a wiser and more creative use of local resources and knowledge. In such a strategy, the people, locally available resources and local knowledge systems become critical instruments. Imported capital and technology, the factors in short supply, can be supplementary. The new strategy, moreover, does not have to be reflected in a single, replicable model; each country has its own socio-cultural specificity and will have to chart its own social transition. In this transition all countries, however, will need to pursue internally a basically two-pronged strategy that will permit them to maintain the gains from past attempts at modernization and industrialization—with appropriate damage limitation—and to make a direct attack on poverty in all its manifestations, an attack in which the poor themselves are the subjects and not the objects of the process.

Initially, the two prongs of the strategy may have some contradictions, but over time they can be harmonized. Regional cooperation can reinforce national efforts. This kind of regional cooperation will also permit Southern countries to adjust to the global system on more favourable terms.

Recent studies, referred to in this chapter, by South Asian scholars confirm that human development, growth and equity need not be trade-offs in the South Asian socio-cultural setting. Studies by international commissions of enquiry such as the South Commission have endorsed the concepts of people-centred development, wise resource use and building technological capability in a step-by-step manner by widening the availability of technological choices. The 1990 United Nations Development Programme (UNDP) report on the concept of human development demonstrates that it is possible to achieve a high level of human development and quality of life even at initially low levels of income. The World Bank in its 1990 report on poverty drew attention to the importance of participation by the poor in poverty alleviation and their contribution to development. It also drew attention to several successful micro-level people's movements and experiments in the South that, from small beginnings, have grown larger, increasing the savings, incomes and assets of the poor. In these experiments poor people's creativity, local resources and local knowledge were critical elements. The UN Conference on Environment and Development and its forerunner, the Brundtland Commission, have increased awareness of the need for a wiser and more equitable use of natural resources. No longer can 20 per cent of the world's people use 80 per cent of the world's resources and also erode the resource base needed to sustain future generations.

Countervailing power: a critical element in the transition

Another point of departure in rethinking past paradigms of development and democracy relates to the question of participatory democracy. In this regard, devolution of power and empowerment of the poor and vulnerable groups, as opposed to representative democracy and highly centralized elite power, requires clarification. There is little need to criticize the dangers of centralized power, repressive state structures and absolute power that corrupts. What needs to be elaborated is the concept of participatory democracy and the building of countervailing power, initially within the political spaces that are already available.

Conventional thinking on both development and democracy was based on a harmony model. This needs to be demystified. The assumption of harmonious communities in a conflict-free social framework for change has no basis in reality, whether at local, national or global levels.

At the local level, for instance, rural communities in the South in today's historical conditions are not homogeneous entities. Sometimes, where land reform has occurred or in a tribal society in which land is communally owned and traditional social values continue to exist, the situation may be comparatively harmonious. But even there, the degree of harmony will have been reduced by colonial penetration and other forms of external intervention. These interventions themselves have generated further local, national and global contradictions. They have also contributed to the erosion of traditional communal bonds and values and disrupted the traditional system that assured a more equitable access to resources by the poor and vulnerable groups.

In most Southern villages, deep-seated contradictions exist between different groups with conflicts of interests. There are sharp relationships of dominance and dependence. These relationships give power to the dominant (the landlord, the trader, the moneylender, the bureaucrat, etc.), bringing about a crisis of immediate survival for the poor. Serious divisions exist among the poor themselves, based on caste, religion, gender, age, etc. These divisions, the people's resultant reluctance to take economic, social and political initiatives collectively to improve their lives, and their inability to change their lives individually, further compound their difficulties. These factors also prevent them from benefiting from technocratically evolved development packages. The same conflict syndrome, between those who have power and those who do not, can be identified in the actual working of the national and global systems. Therefore, the rhetoric of harmony and interdependence at all levels cannot be a point of departure from which to rethink the question of transition to participatory democracy and devolved power. Sometimes class differentiations are blurred by caste or clan loyalties. This makes analysis in conventional social categories irrelevant.

Any meaningful approach to social change that will not benefit the rich at the expense of the poor, or the powerful at the expense of the powerless, must be both political and social. It should not be a purely technocratic, fragmented sectoral or economic project approach. The political space for a political–social approach exists already in some countries, while in others it needs to be created.

Participation is of central concern in any discussion of development in wider human terms, and vice versa. Here it must be emphasized that participatory development and democracy are identical concepts. It is sheer pretension to think that the multifaceted crisis of Southern countries can easily be overcome or that the reshaping and development of these societies in a more balanced and sustainable way can be undertaken without the participation of the people, particularly the large numbers who are poor and vulnerable.

If participation means democracy, representative democracy as now practised is a singularly limited form. People participate in elections. But such formal participation is a mere token, unless power is shared, particularly at the local level. Participation also means trusting the people and commitment to a more egalitarian society, that would ensure equal access to resources, not only to land but also to education, food and health. Where formal power is in the hands of a few and power is not shared but grossly misused, participation in the first instance results in building countervailing forms of power, leading ultimately to a healthier democracy.

Furthermore, if development results from releasing the creative energies of the people, particularly the poor and the vulnerable, then *they* must be the final arbiters of their lives. Participation and self-reliance are thus interrelated. This form of development goes beyond merely meeting the material needs of the people and beyond considerations of equity. To participate people need to form their own organizations. The poor need, through their own organizations, to counter the socio-economic reality around them and the forces that keep them in poverty. Such participation then opens up possibilities for people to bring about changes in their conditions through their own reflections and collective actions. This constitutes a learning process, a process of further consciousness-raising and self-transformation. In this sense participation is also a basic human need.

The extent of participation will depend initially on the political space that is available for the participatory processes to start, particularly at the local level, and on the opportunities for an intervention in the existing socio-economic system by those who have a higher consciousness and commitment. In many Southern countries there is great potential energy and will to change. This energy needs to be harnessed, and agents for change can be found in many areas to initiate the process of mobilization. There is strong support for people's causes from such groups as the radical church, various professions, students, non-governmental organizations (NGOs) and even members of the bureaucracy and the judiciary. New coalitions between these groups and the poor and vulnerable are necessary.

The very nature of participatory, self-reliant development activities is such that they will eventually attract the attention of the power structure, still working within the confines of the failed paradigm. Some of these new participatory activities will then be co-opted by the system, others exterminated. While some are repressed, many still survive. Those which survive, existing in isolation, do not add up to much in terms of social transformation. But if they are properly linked and multiply themselves through the processes of mobilization, conscientization and organization, they can become a countervailing power in the social context and help to widen the political space for change even further. Countervailing power is necessary to retain the vitality of the people. It is a living, collective consciousness of the people and a vigilance of the people against the abuse of formal power. It is the capability to resist such abuse and to assert the people's will whenever formal power deviates at the macro, as well as the micro, level. It is critical for ensuring accountability by those who wield power. They must be held accountable for its proper use to the people, and not merely for its abuse. Thus, building of countervailing power at all levels becomes a necessary component in a participatory democratic process, and constitutes a critical point of departure for rethinking development and democracy.

Positive lessons from the new movements[8]

The recent search for new and relevant Southern paradigms of development and democracy has been inhibited by many factors. Primacy of place must, however, be given to the unquestioning adoption by the majority of intellectuals of crude and simplistic versions of the neo-classical or Marxist paradigms, or very marginal reformist options to these. These dominant paradigms have guided not only the intellectual approach to development and democracy, but also practice in the South. That these paradigms had evolved in other (Western) contexts and had resulted in many variations was often ignored when they were transmitted to Southern environments.

These two paradigms were not only rendered more simplistic and reductionist as they were transmitted to the South, they also were often mystified beyond comprehension. When made explicit, they were theoretically stated more often than not in narrow power and/or economistic terms and practised with even greater narrowness and fragmentation. The Marxist paradigm claimed to be critical of the neo-classical, and to have elements of social justice and equity built into it. It is only belatedly that intellectuals and practitioners are beginning to recognize the basic similarities between the two paradigms in practice. Private capitalism and state capitalism, which come from the two different ideological orientations, have structural similarities. Their highly centralized decision-making power is one. Another relates to the industrialization model, a third to the exploitative process and transfer of resources from rural to urban areas.

Both paradigms are now proving too simple to relate to the crises—of poverty, ethnic conflicts, ecological conflicts, etc.—that have emerged in Southern societies. Though Marxist theory was a little more explicit about issues of social justice and equity, issues such as participation, culture, gender and equity, and ecology were central to neither paradigm.

In both, formal decentralization of state structures was confused with real devolution of power and democracy. Representative democracy and party politics in the Western paradigm were confused with participation of the people as subjects in matters which affect their lives. In the former socialist countries there was a high degree of centralization and little participation. Development in both cases was confused with modernization and industrialization, with capital and not people seen as the major factor in the transformation. Putting capital, the scarce factor, as the major input into development created further distortions in environments where people were the greatest asset. This emphasis on capital gave greater power to owners of capital.

Though one conventional paradigm relied mainly on the market and getting prices right and the other mainly on a directed command decision process, both in reality depended on centralized decision-making—in one by the boardroom, in the other by the state.

The real issues relating to profitability, efficiency and the accumulation process also need to be demystified. Private capitalism or state capitalism were insufficient options, when there were strong compulsions for seeking alternative driving forces for accumulation, even in its narrower economic conception. In the South, where 30–40 per cent of the economy is informal, to ignore the people's sector was unrealistic. It could also be that for most countries of the South a more sophisticated mix of state, private and other (people-oriented) forms of accumulation are required, along with the sharing of political power with the poor and vulnerable. Conventional planning looked at the private sector and the public sector as dichotomies, ignoring completely the mainly informal people's sector, which was not sufficiently captured in the paradigms either conceptually or statistically.

Social transitions at the macro–national level

In the past four decades, attempts at social transition in Southern countries have resulted in industrialized societies, post-revolutionary societies, and societies with some interpenetration of capitalist and socialist modes of production and accumulation. Some of these societies have been authoritarian, others semi-authoritarian and paternalistic. A few have been more democratic and participatory. Some have taken a predominantly 'capitalistic' transitional pathway, some have taken a 'socialistic' pathway from their feudal or semi-feudal origins.

A few of these countries have some distinctive features that set them apart: they have taken what may be called a non-classical approach. They have attempted to put greater emphasis on people and their participation.

These non-classical approaches have tried to address the basic human needs of the large mass of people and their participation, whereas the more classical and cruder versions have concentrated wealth and power in the hands of the few, at the expense of the large majority of people.

South Korea, in the dominant capitalist category, illustrates a non-classical approach. It can be contrasted with Brazil, which attempted a more orthodox capitalist transformation. The UNDP's *Human Development Report* of 1990 characterizes Brazil as a high GNP-per-capita country with modest human development and little equity, whereas South Korea has achieved a higher level of human development with both fast and equitable growth. Brazil represents the cruder type of capitalist transformation, which has resulted in a massive polarization of the people and a very deep debt crisis, having been incorporated into a global system without any safeguards in terms of the equity of internal structural changes. South Korea on the other hand has instituted a capitalist transformation with land reform, human resource development, the building of technological capabilities and a rapid transformation of rural society. This rural transformation was effected through a social mobilization effort called the Saemaul Undong Movement (the 'new village movement'), not only to increase rural incomes and quality of life, but also to prevent migration from the country to the towns and the kind of inequalities that Brazil suffers from. South Korea had the benefit of massive inflows of external resources, but development was not left to market forces alone and was coupled with very detailed state planning, controls and monitoring. It was deeply rooted in the Korean culture. Alongside the land reform, secondary education was expanded and an elaborate network of rural cooperative marketing and banking institutions was established in support of the process of rural mobilization. In contrast to Brazil, the relative equality of the villages has produced a fairly homogeneous rural society with no sharp class conflicts. The planning system was oriented towards providing a sensitive support system for rural mobilization and keeping rural surpluses in rural areas.

In some countries that attempted a socialist transition, wide variations from the classical model were also in evidence. China in the first 30 years after the revolution, under Mao, represented a major variation in the socialist model, with a greater degree of decentralization and people's participation. The Chinese experience also included a new accumulation process based on mass mobilization and total resource use.

Without romanticizing the process, it is possible to identify some of the essential features in the Chinese experience: mutual aid teams in this participatory decentralized system, a limited division of labour, an attempt to evolve conscious and purposeful people, some community cohesion and a production process that was symbiotic with nature. The Chinese experience drew a great deal from the people's culture and the people's knowledge systems. The process of total mobilization included the use of the people's creativity, local resources and local knowledge. There was an attempt to combine the material transformation of economic production with political, philosophical and aesthetic concerns. In other words, there was an ideological and valuational framework which attempted to be culturally relevant, more human, participatory, and people-centred; and it was leading to a new accumulation process that was economically sustainable, at least in the rural areas.

This was clearly an attempt at socialism under non-classical conditions. It was expected that the new relations of production that evolved would generate new social, political and ideological processes and a new mass consciousness appropriate to them. This, in turn, would help to sustain the new accumulation process. That the situation has not developed entirely as expected should not prevent us from drawing the relevant lessons for social mobilization from the successes of the first 30 years of the Chinese experience in terms of both human development, growth and equity on the one hand, and people's participation on the other.

A third illustration can be drawn from those Southern societies that have hardly moved either towards capitalism or socialism. They are in semi-feudal stages with interpenetration of socialist or capitalist formations. Some are at a stage of primitive accumulation, or of simple commodity production, or of a kind of state capitalism, and getting locked into consumerism. Examples range from Tanzania to Burma, Bangladesh and Sri Lanka. In each, some interesting social experiments have been half-heartedly tried, which resulted in a dissipation of efforts. But with the stasis of these societies, other social conflicts and tensions have mounted and have led to unmanageable situations and, in some cases, to near social collapse.

The Tanzanian experience is worth elaborating in this context. Tanzania did not undergo a revolution as in the case of China, nor a significant transition to capitalism aided by external capital as happened in South

Korea. It attempted, after an orderly attainment of independence in 1961, to search for an alternative development strategy based on self-reliance and participation, and tried to move directly into a new society. The political leadership also took a bold step in re-examining the inherited nomadic tribal society and colonial political system, instead of allowing itself to follow the conventional pathway adopted by most former colonies. The Arusha Declaration enunciated in 1967 emphasized equity, mass participation, decentralization and rural self-reliance.

The necessary structural changes were, however, conceived and implemented from above. The bureaucracy was the main instrument for mobilization; the real participation of the people as envisaged at Arusha did not occur. This was an insufficient basis for a development strategy with people at the centre. After an initial experiment with people's participation, the villagization programme was made compulsory by the government and party. This alienated the peasantry and thus increased the need for further state intervention. The fact that participation implied both structural and cultural change and a raising of mass consciousness was ignored; what resulted was merely an extension of bureaucratic control to the village level. This result was inevitable if the strategy was to move merely from mobilization directly to bureaucratic organization. Without an intermediary stage of conscientization of the masses, new educational processes and a remoulding of the elite, it was inevitable that only a weak top-down process, with people geared for the most part to the delivery of resources and expertise from outside, could result.

An important cultural dimension was missing from the Tanzanian villagization programme. Africa's traditional forms of communal land ownership had ensured the existence of commons, to which the community had access. This had helped to avoid extremes of poverty, landlessness and polarization of the communities. The traditional system also provided secure land tenure and encouraged farmers to invest in the land. Common pasture and forest resources are important for the rural poor. They provide food, fodder, fuelwood and work. Community management systems of the commons were democratic, based on consensus, and ensured greater equity in the distribution of assets. A great deal more research and study would have been necessary to incorporate these and other cultural dimensions into the process of social change contemplated at Arusha through the Ujama villagization programme.

This synoptic presentation of some recent attempts at macro social changes suggests some important lessons for the South in ordering future social transitions. It also suggests that if political space can be provided at the macro level, the people's creative energy waiting to be released at the micro level can be tapped for a more orderly social transition and a new social contract between people and the state.

Micro-level experiments: seeds and bubbles

Action at the micro level may help to reinforce macro efforts and vice versa, and in addition to social changes at the macro level, experiences at another level in most countries of the South also need to be analysed. These are the thousands of people's responses, movements and experiments. Many of these movements, having come through independence struggles, then attemped to consolidate the basic creativity of the people that had been released in that process of change. A rich body of experience of grass-roots mobilization was evolved through innovative experimentation and was used in many areas of activity: for alleviating poverty, achieving social justice or preserving the environment. Some of the micro-level activities involve larger social movements, some are movements with considerable significance since they involve large numbers of people and cover a significant geographical space; others are small-scale grassroots experiments. Some of the grassroots experiments are confined to a particular locality and a few villages, some operate in several localities and are multiplying. Sharp distinctions, and precise definitions would be premature. It is sufficient to say that both the movements and experiments are mobilizing people for social change in one form or another on particular levels. The people's responses and experiments, even if they may not always achieve the proportions of a movement, have a varied mix of activities, ideologies, operational methodologies and scales. They also have things in common in that they attempt to empower the poor and vulnerable in one way or another. Some start with protests against the system, others start with small development activities.

Several positive lessons may be drawn from the wide variety of new people's movements and micro-level grassroots experiments. The people's movements are the result of broader-based people's responses to ecological, ethnic or gender conflicts. The micro-level experiments are not homogeneous and differ in their origins. Some are the result of romantic and idealistic approaches taken by charitable institutions, religious organizations, the 'small is beautiful' advocates, etc., which have tried to teach the people to do 'good' things, often treating the village as a harmonious entity or 'community'. These groups then may link together to form a movement or to reinforce a protest action. Then there are ideas introduced by radical political parties looking for a political constituency. They have been able to move poor people locally to anger at the workings of the exploitative system. Some of the people's movements have been sustained over time, others are eruptions and die down after a while. Similarly, some of the grassroots experiments represent seeds of change, others are mere bubbles.

At this stage, it is important to make a distinction between a 'seed' and a 'bubble'. A seed can be identified with such broad aims as equality of access to resources; equality of social, political, cultural rights; real participation in all social decisions affecting work, welfare, politics, etc.; the end of the division between mental and manual labour and the use of technology appropriate for this purpose. It is not, however, merely a matter of stating these objectives: genuine participation, awareness creation and the effort to change social relations must be built into the process. One can keep adding to this list: local orientation, self-production and self-management, autonomy, solidarity and innovativeness. A bubble, on the other hand, is a soft process and may not last, for a variety of reasons. However, bubbles should not be dismissed too hurriedly; they may represent entry points to change and some can be transformed into seeds through additional sensitization and conscientization programmes, training of facilitators and change agents. The essential point about a seed is that it is the outcome of a process of mobilization, conscientization and organization at the micro level, which under certain social and political conditions can expand and lead to structural and social change.

The studies referred to in this chapter are replete with analysis, reviews and attempts to learn from a variety of people's responses at the micro level. The Deeder Cooperative for landless labourers in Bangladesh, the tribal Bhoomi Sena in India, the Attock peasants' struggle in Pakistan, the Peasants' Association in Ethiopia, and the Anta Community in Peru are illustrative of the first generation of projects. Second-generation experiments that are now firmly established include the Grameen Bank and BRAC in Bangladesh, the Working Women's Forum, SEWA, the Chipko movement and the Kerala Science movement in India, the PDP in Mexico, and the Six S movement in Burkina Faso. There are thousands of others. All represent varying degrees of mobilization, conscientization and organization for development and democracy. These processes may not always proceed in a linear fashion. Within the political space available, there have been interventions into the socio-economic system. In the case of smaller experiments, someone with an advanced consciousness initiates dialogue and a group activity involving, for example, landless labourers, poor women or a youth group trying to do something as a means of living, or a social activity, such as a health or environmental sanitation programme; the process can move forward to become a seed or stay as a bubble until it bursts.

What further needs to be done to reinforce the new people's movements and experiments when they arise and to help the micro-level seeds to multiply and go to scale? A well-articulated and coherent people-oriented strategy, even if pluralistic and rudimentary in theory, would be a progressive response to the new compulsions for social change and the crises that affect all Southern countries. Such a strategy would of course have to recognize the contradictions that exist in reality and make a distinction between the rich and the poor and the powerful and the powerless. Harmony cannot be assumed. The strategy would also need to recognize that industrialization, modernization and the creation of new levels of technological capability are also a part of the longer-term process, and that countries of the South must move 'on their own two legs' and at the same time attempt to link into the global system on better terms. These are tasks of considerable magnitude.

Some common features of the new people's response

Larger and larger numbers of people are no longer willing to accept, fatalistically, exploitative or repressive regimes and state structures, or a development paradigm that excludes them. They may not be concerned with the capture of state power and 'big bang' revolutions. Yet they may in reality be building, consciously or unconsciously, a countervailing power to the dominant state power. In the new people's movements, the actors may also be demonstrating ways to humanize the larger macro processes, whilst showing that the terms of incorporation into the modern world at all levels can be changed.

In recent times, new democracy movements and people's struggles in the Philippines, Pakistan, Bangladesh and some Latin American countries have been dramatic responses to repressive regimes and military dictatorships. Ecological movements such as Chipko or the Narmada Andolen in India and people's movements against the commercial destruction of rainforests in Brazil and other kinds of economic development that are predatory on nature build countervailing power. The women's movements in nearly all Southern countries and their impact on gender and equity issues are equally significant. These movements differ sharply from feminist movements in the West and cannot be understood purely in terms of the generalized paradigm of 'Women in Development' into which the analysis of women's issues has recently been locked. Smaller development experiments that demonstrate how people cope simultaneously with the multiple crises in their lives locally, survive and move on, through their own efforts, to improve their quality of life are also increasingly evident.

People's movements and experiments may arise spontaneously or be initiated and multiplied by sensitive external facilitators and local change agents. Sometimes they have a charismatic leader. They may be protest and/or damage-limiting responses, or they may be positive development actions. In some instances, these two types of activity link to build new coalitions. Some processes may be coopted or even smashed by the system. The fragile twenty-month democracy in Pakistan eroded rapidly. When such reversals happen, if the movement for people's power is deeply rooted in society, it may re-emerge. Macro-level democracy movements need to be reinforced with micro-level development actions and deeply rooted in people's lives. Some movements evolve in a zigzag fashion. But the fact is that these people's movements and experiments, as a new social phenomenon and a new social force, have come to stay and can no longer be ignored. The question is, can they achieve greater coherence and sustainability?

The elements mentioned above essentially relate to aspects of social change in the South: these new movements are emerging out of the peculiar contradictions within societies and cultures in transition. They also emanate from contradictions and weaknesses that are appearing in the role of the state and/or in the particular division of labour resulting from the intervention of transnational capital. In many countries, these contradictions have weakened the legitimacy of the nation state, its claims to sovereignty and its ability to be a protector and mediator. There is enough evidence of the fragility of state power and of the system undermining itself. Parallel with this weakening is the endless conventional accumulation process by the private sector and the public sector as currently established polarizes people, marginalizes larger and larger numbers and undermines people's harmonious relations with nature. Cultural cohesion consequently also disintegrates.

In the new movements and experiments where the level of people's awareness and assertion is high, evidence is accumulating not of hierarchical social formations, but of a horizontal integration of people and groups associated with new values and a system that could be sustainable over a historical period. People are no longer tolerating polarization and inequity and are seeking means to satisfy human needs in a humane way. The people's movements are rooted in their own reality and demonstrate how the people themselves have emerged as the chief actors through participatory processes.

People themselves are seeing the futility of merely moving intellectually or in practice between the two conventional options of state and market forces. And in the large informal economy of most countries of the South there is considerable scope for a new form of accumulation involving people's creativity, a form of accumulation that is outside the scope of the private and public accumulation process. This new accumulation process itself will be part of the alternative paradigms.

Moving from lessons towards new concepts and processes

From the processes on the ground—macro and micro—outlined synoptically above, I turn now to discuss some elements in a framework for rethinking development and democracy that are beginning to emerge. What follows are 'thoughts in progress', a basis for discussion of propositions to be evolved further.

Perspectives and values

The changes at the macro and micro levels outlined above start with a clear vision and perspective. This is essential for correct action. Before action is taken, the underlying values need to be made explicit. It is then that praxis, the action–reflection–action process, becomes an instrument for initiating and reinforcing the positive macro or micro changes desired or underway.

A basic assumption from which the search for the underlying paradigms begins is that democracy and development are two sides of the same holistic vision that has inspired human endeavour in different Southern socio-cultural settings over the past 2,000 years and more of recorded history.[9] The values and ideologies that have emanated from this deeper interpretation of the vision have implicitly incorporated, in one way or another, these two fundamental cornerstones. Several fundamental values which existed in traditional societies must be identified and re-examined. Some critical values relate to looking at life in its totality and all its richness; participation of the people in decisions that affected their lives; sharing and caring for the community beyond individual self-interest; trust, innocence, simplicity, thrift; a work ethic with a fine-tuned balance between work and leisure; harmony with nature and a rational use of resources; communal ownership of the commons; and complementarity between men and women.

Highly evolved social norms balanced the crude use of power in Southern cultures. There were elements of paternalism, as well as wisdom in leadership. Where social injustice threatened the fabric of society it could be corrected by a 'just' war. In many Southern cultures there was provision for the emergence of non-antagonistic countervailing power to check and control the abuse of power and manipulation by the wielders of dominant power. Women were able to secure their rights and establish a complementary role with men in social processes.[10] This list could be elaborated and illustrated, but it is not my intention here to define either development or democracy narrowly or with precision, but instead to indicate some of the focal values by which these twin interrelated processes were identified historically in Southern cultures. It is also to assert that democracy was not interpreted in these cultures in terms of democracy for the few based on slavery, as the Greeks interpreted it, or in terms of representative democracy on the Westminster model; nor was development understood in terms of the commonly accepted conventional economic models—neo-classical or Marxist.

To elaborate further, in all historical Southern cultures there were built-in methods of consensus-making. One example is the republican tradition of the Lichchavis in ancient India, elaborated in classical Buddhist texts.[11] Another is the Krishna–Arjuna dialogue in the *Mahabharata*, which also illustrates correct decision-making at a higher level of consciousness and provides the intellectual underpinnings for a 'just' war against a repressive and undemocratic regime.[12] A recent study of the Hindu *Vedas* reveals that women in Hindu society asserted their rights throughout history against male domination. It also shows, through the concept of Ardhinarishwara, the complementarity of men and women in Hindu society.[13] The literature is full of instances of people's participation and democratic practices at the base of the system alongside wise and compassionate leadership at the top. Democratic consensus-making was very much a part of African tribal mode of governance. Peer pressure was a major deterrent to corrupt practices. This also extended to the taking of loans and credits, where peer pressure ensured repayment. There was an open information system at the level of the community, which further reinforced principles of equity and checks and balances. Democracy in labour relations, exchange labour, common ownership of land and other productive assets further reinforced cooperative values, mutual aid and equity.

The knowledge system that evolved in these cultures and from these valuational frameworks, by intuition as well as by trial and error, propelled the process with its own rationality and mediated various tensions in the process. It bears repetition that this knowledge system was scientific in any terms.[14] The technology that resulted provided the material basis for a sustainable, basic needs-oriented development and for predominantly self-managed societies aware of their reality. The knowledge system also helped to resolve some of the sharper contradictions whenever they arose, providing a wide range of technological choices in keeping with the fundamental human values, and cultural norms and lifestyles.

Having said this, I believe intellectuals and activists alike have a long way to go in clarifying some of the fundamental features of the culturally rooted historical paradigms, processes, instrumentalities and organizational forms. The task is made very complex because of both the historical contradictions that have existed in these societies and the distortions in the modes of production, community spirit and consensus-making that set in as colonialism, modernization, industrialization, Westernization and other external interventions and penetrations occurred.

Any further interventions designed to build on the lessons of the new people's movements to create new societies, where the historical Southern values become dominant also requires, in the present historical context, an analysis of the process designed to identify operational guidelines for action. To be sustainable, these guidelines must be culturally relevant in a dynamic sense. A vision and a perspective for change cannot be laid down in political cultural terms while the operational guidelines are technocratically orchestrated and bureaucratically imposed.

In many cases with colonialism and the attempts at Westernisation and the cultural homogenization that went with it, not only was the holistic view of life distorted, but the value system, the knowledge system, the institutions and the cultures themselves were delegitimized and downgraded. Southern elites, many of them alienated from their cultural roots, compounded these distortions and helped sharpen contradictions. The bureaucratic systems imposed for 'law and order' and 'systems maintenance' were hardly instruments of social change, when a political approach to action and devolution of power was called for (a political approach does not mean 'party politics'). Instead of decentralization the tendency was towards greater centralization. When people's creativity needed to be released and supported, the in-built bureaucratic tendency was for the process to be controlled from above. In the dependent and soft societies that resulted, it was possible to encourage the easy acceptance of ever greater centralization and manipulation of the people and some charity or delivered inputs to the poor in the name of growth and redistribution, which were the stated objectives of the borrowed 'economic' development paradigm.

In the new people's movements and experiments, one sees glimpses of an older civilizational rhythm in their relationships of people to people and people to nature. Some of these relationships as they now exist are fragile, while in other cases they still remain only at the levels of experiment or of the desirable. Whatever their degree of manifestation in reality, these relationships need to be further reinforced as part of an ongoing process of social change towards real democracy and development.[15]

Understanding these people's responses and relating them to the earlier civilizational rhythm are not easy tasks. The objective of the exercise is not to go back to the past, viewed with romanticism, but to understand the contradictions and the praxis, and then to observe the seeds of change that reflect some of the democratic and wider development values. The hard lessons learned can then point towards a more humane and qualitatively better society for larger numbers, building on the sustainable processes already initiated in the people's movements.

A new reading of indigenous value systems and traditions, both from written and unwritten sources, is essential for a deeper understanding of the nature of democracy and the human development and accumulation process in the Southern context. This is a matter of research, research methodology and scientific validation of history.

The long revolution

Not only to avoid social collapse, which seems to result when contradictions sharpen and lead to bloody conflicts, but also to move in the direction of positive social change requires more than marginal tinkering with the system and the kinds of damage limitation strategies that are part of the current reformist option. It requires a holistic intellectual perspective and participatory action of a more comprehensive kind. This participatory practice itself needs to evolve and cannot be predetermined in a prescriptive fashion.

A corollary question to be addressed is whether past processes that are resulting in crises, anarchy and social collapse in the South can be reversed partially or fully by means of the new people's movement and experiments and the people's creativity they release, by multiplying them, linking them further, building the capacity for sustainability and giving them coherence. Such a process would also mean providing political space and a sensitive support system for such a process to grow and mature. These twin requirements are part and parcel of the long revolution for social change. The long revolution implies structural change. It is neither a once-for-all bloody revolution, nor is it marginal tinkering with the system.

Although there will be a great deal of variations in detailed practice in different socio-political circumstances, depending on the depth of the contradictions resulting from the industrialization–modernization process and the centralization of power that has taken place previously, some broad generalizations are possible. It is clear that a protest movement on a single issue alone is insufficient to reverse the complex processes of the past. Single-issue movements can merely be eruptions or the first mobilization. Movements must acquire greater depth through continuous processes of mobilization, conscientization and organization-building. Furthermore, the economic base of the poor and vulnerable groups must be improved simultaneously with raising their awareness.

To facilitate the analysis, it is necessary to start with a somewhat narrower frame of reference. There are in most of the South, variations of capitalist or socialist transformations, as well as stagnant societies, and societies displaying some interpenetration of both types of social formations and modes of production. When new people's movements arise spontaneously or are initiated under these circumstances, the question must be asked, how the surplus generated under the new conditions is being used and distributed. A corollary would be: is there both a qualitative and a quantitative difference in relation to the accumulation process in the new people's movements and experiments that can make them sustainable? Every society needs an economic base. Even when a people's movement is initiated by a religious group (for example, Swadhyaya in India or a church group oriented towards Liberation Theology as in many Latin American countries), a new accumulation process is required.

It is possible to elaborate this point further. In the new processes underway it is possible to see varying elements of equitable distribution and human development. They range from elements such as safety nets under the poor, food subsidies and health and welfare schemes, to harder processes of income generation, saving and asset-creation for meeting the basic needs of the poor. The concern here is not with mere redistributive justice, but also whether self-reliance and a sustainable process have been set in motion, starting with human development, where the benefits are enjoyed by the large numbers who are poor and vulnerable. As such a process evolves, the poor begin to save, invest in income and human development activities and create some assets for themselves. The full impact depends on the extent to which beneficiaries use their share of the surplus so that a new accumulation process that is not consumerist or predatory on nature is set in motion. Values such as thrift and equity, sharing and caring, and the requirement to use natural resources wisely, which are part of the cultural tradition, have to be built into the process right from the outset.

Another aspect of the same question is, will the surpluses be used in an exploitative manner or will new values inform the actions of the poor as they begin to increase their incomes? The surplus must be used in a manner different from that of the past, that is, only partly consumed, so that the surplus may be in part shared with the community, in part saved and in part used for productive purposes, etc. If it is used for the latter, the processes generated become a new social force facilitating the seeds of change. If the poor become the new exploiters as their incomes increase, or if, on the other hand, consumerism becomes rampant, particularly the purchase of imported consumer items unrelated to basic needs, then the development process will not be sustainable. Communicating this fact is part of the consciousness-raising process that must accompany the initial mobilization of the people in development action. Consciousness-raising is not a once-for-all process.

Whether the seeds of change germinate and multiply depends on the economic and political space available. As the development process gains pace, the existing economic and political space can be widened. Wherever sufficient economic and political space exists not only can seeds of change be planted, but also a whole new critical mass of mobilized, conscientized and organized people can perform an objectively historical role in relation to development. The continuous multiplication of the process with a conscientized group of people then becomes countervailing power in opposition to the crude dominant power. This is also where participation and real political democracy come into their own, and where democracy and development in wider human terms become two sides of the same coin.

Countervailing power can be non-antagonistic or antagonistic depending on the nature of its relationship to the dominant power. Even non-antagonistic countervailing power can help to reduce exploitation, check corruption, check and control the abuse of dominant power, take over and manage more efficiently and perhaps even more equitably some of the institutions and available resources in this complex situation. This is a part of the more democratic checks and balances system that results from empowering the people. The institutions themselves evolve as the process evolves. Just as the process cannot be predetermined, it cannot be prematurely institutionalized.

At some point, non-antagonistic power can become antagonistic and go on to capture dominant power.[16] On the other hand, if the surplus is reinvested locally and a new consciousness and new values prevail by virtue of the widespread sowing of seeds for change, then the extreme conflicts that normally accompany this process need not arise. Thus social change does not necessarily mean 'big bang', once-for-all revolution and a unidirectional movement.

The long revolution can proceed slowly or faster, and even in a zigzag fashion, depending on a number of unforeseeable factors. There is also no single starting point for the process. It does not preclude industrialization, the move to new levels of technological capability and selective modernization, provided they begin with labour-intensive processes, agro-industries, decentralized micro-level enterprises feeding into larger industrial capacities and moving with forward and backward linkages in a less alienating process.

In most countries, whatever the current social formation, economic and political space exists or can be found for this kind of systematic change to occur. The historical conditions also exist for the sowing of seeds of change. Further space can be created through single-issue or limited struggles. An ecological movement or a protest against large dams, or penetration of transnational capital and technology without social control or social conscience, can provide greater political space and begin to create popular awareness. Solidarity also begins in this way.

As stated earlier, where there has been a measure of land reform or in a tribal society where land is communally owned, as for instance in most of Africa, there is a great deal of space for mobilizing, conscientizing and organizing the people. These processes may arise spontaneously or a committed individual or group of persons may initiate them. The starting point can be economic or social. A small savings movement or a pre-school programme or a community health programme can result in a wider social movement. The Gandhian liberation movement in South Asia, the culture of '*animation rurale*' in Francophone Africa or experiments resulting from Liberation Theology in Latin America may all move in this direction.

Thus seeds of change moving together or dialectically through praxis can generate positive social changes, which go beyond conventional redistributive justice. To thrive, this strategy requires a continuous search for space and the creation of space for the seeds that are sown. It is not possible to predict deterministically how and when each social group or process will move. This will depend on internal social formations, external factors, fortuitous circumstances and the quality of leadership. A charismatic leader can further build on existing seeds of change, and so on.

This emerging theory of social change, even in its rudimentary form, tends to be interpreted as purely 'economistic' or 'reformist' by conventional Marxists and as 'revolutionary' or 'radical' by neo-classicists. The conventional Sarvodaya Gandhians working on a harmony model are put off by the use of the terms 'power' and 'political space', even though Gandhi was himself an adherent of Kautilya (the Indian Machiavelli) and used the power of mass struggle against the British in the movement for Indian independence.[17] This was the only effective political instrument he had and he used it. As a corollary he tried to articulate a development strategy that could complement mass political mobilization. Some of his concepts still inform the people's movements in India, although in some cases they have gone beyond his original concepts.[18] His basic concept was not 'Sarvodaya' but 'Antodaya', which meant starting with the poorest.

The inescapable conclusion is that if a long revolution is a meaningful transitional pathway to a form of social change that is more humane and sustainable, then one-sided conceptions of complex social processes are irrelevant both to understand and intervene in the complex crises that face most countries of the South today. The narrow ideological theorizing of the past and attempts to force complex reality to fit simplistic theory have in most countries prevented the flowering of concepts and ideas relevant to a more pragmatic evolution of democracy or development. A historical pathway must be found to take us from the existing reality to a reality in which these societies can move in keeping with their own civilizational rhythms.

Refocusing praxis

Another element that requires further elaboration is the methodology of praxis. Whilst many Southern intellectuals are still locked into conventional ideologies and theories borrowed from the West and are afraid to abandon these theories and the practices that follow from them, some small but systematic efforts are being made to break out of this trap by groups of Southern scholars and activists working together. Beginning in the 1960s and 1970s some new thinking was initiated, which analysed the interrelated processes of democracy and development from essentially two perspectives.

The first line of thinking was organized around the Latin American 'dependency' thesis and the 'centre–periphery' thesis. Raul Prebisch originated this thinking. The theme of unequal exchange also played a key role in the analysis of the deteriorating terms of trade. This thinking has been developed and deepened by Samir Amin and others. It examines development at the global level in very broad terms and represents a useful tool of analysis of the dominance versus dependence syndrome into which the South is locked. It calls for a new international division of labour. Samir Amin has recently extended the argument to include the possibility of recompradorization of the South and sees in popular movements the possibility of a new social force.

The second line of research, still in its infancy, takes off from the cultural and historical schools of thought in the South. It criticizes a predetermined universalism and stresses pluralism, including geo-cultural specificity. As has been stated in the past, social sciences have evolved through the study of Western societies. Hypotheses and value judgements have emerged from that historical cultural world and continue to influence a major part of the academic community and through it the educational, technical and administrative systems. Some social scientists have begun to break out of this mould. The writings of Orlando Fals Borda and Rajni Kothari have initiated some new thinking on new social movements.[19]

In the 1970s in their book *Towards a Theory of Rural Development,*

Wahidul Haque, Niranjan Mehta, Anisur Rahman and Ponna Wignaraja elaborated a basic premise in this line of research. Development, they indicated, is simultaneously a 'top-down' and a 'bottom-up' process.[20] There are the national macro perspectives and the constituent micro grassroots contradictions. Successful development is viewed as a process of human development, a process of social transformation in which the people are both the subject and the object. In such a process the people participate at all levels of decision-making in matters affecting the totality of their lives and through this process of empowerment a more democratic process is initiated.

Self-reliance is both a means and an end in this process. It is a process that releases the creative energy of people, assures equal access to resources for all, tends to eliminate the difference between mental and manual labour, and uses technology appropriate to these social goals. This research, though giving some space to micro–macro linkages, was primarily concerned with the grassroots micro problematic. It saw the issues of people's participation, conscientization, and the building of countervailing power as part of an ongoing social process: the long revolution towards social and structural change.

The beginning of this alternative thinking was based not on a priori theorizing or on purely borrowed thinking from Western social sciences. It was based on looking at the South Asian reality and attempting to formulate a more rational intellectual framework for the eradication of rural mass poverty, rooted in a more scientific approach to South Asian history and culture than the conventional paradigms. It also went beyond the 'Asiatic mode of production' thinking that was at the periphery of Marxist thought. The material basis for the generalizations on alternatives was provided both by the negative impact of a quarter-century of development on large numbers of people in South Asia and by the first generation of people's experiments at the grassroots level.

This analysis demonstrated the possibilities of incorporating social justice and participation into a process of accumulation and economic growth that would involve and benefit the poor and the vulnerable in the all-round development of their lives. The methodology was praxis. In particular, there was increasing evidence that such processes were sustainable at the micro level. While the process of refocusing praxis has gone far in South Asia, African intellectuals are also beginning to see popular national power, involving a participatory approach, as a new social force. In Latin America, Liberation Theology and movements for human rights and cultural autonomy, particularly for indigenous people, began to influence the thinking of the dependency school of thought.

Two critical instrumentalities that are at the core of the methodology are now apparent. One is the knowledge system inherent in the culture, which must inform the whole process. The other is the role of the initiators/animators without whom the process cannot multiply and go to scale during the foreseeable time horizon. These initiators/animators are different from the conventional vanguard.

Discussion of the knowledge system starts at a philosophical level where the dominant paradigm of positivist knowledge has influenced development action and legitimized one type of social action and delegitimized another. The corollary of this paradigm is the premise that there existed 'one stock of knowledge', whose operational tool for economic development was the transfer of technology from industrialized to poor countries, which was considered as indispensable. Even this technology transfer was conceived in a fragmented Cartesian mould and provided an insufficient knowledge base to allow adequate response to the complex set of problems it was supposed to address.

Praxis and Participatory Action Research (PAR) were located outside this knowledge system. Therefore, it was necessary to demystify both the nature of this knowledge and the premises and method of this knowledge transfer, before proceeding to the concept of cognitive knowledge and to the many stocks of knowledge and technology that can be drawn on for praxis, PAR and sustainable development. The framework then can be elaborated in relation to the relationship between knowledge, action and power on which PAR is premised. This then helps to bridge the gap between real knowledge and wisdom, and development action and social change. Praxis and PAR must be premised on the wider alternative knowledge system that is available, in which the knowledge system provides the power to bring about a change in the condition of the knower and generates the new social process. It also gives a wider range of technological choices.

The second issue relates to the role of the animator. In order to initiate praxis and enable the people to bring out their creativity with a spirit of self-reliance and self-involvement, and also to assert their right to participate in development as subjects in the process, an appropriate stimulation is required. Sometimes an independence struggle or a violent protest movement against oppression, exploitation and repression can spontaneously conscientize and help organize a people, as happened in India in 1947 or Bangladesh in 1972. But the point here is how this creativity may be released under less dramatic conditions and prevailing socio-political circumstances. The creative spirit exists in all human beings and does not always manifest itself spontaneously. The challenge is to bring out this quality and the strength and the dignity of the people that goes with it.

A growing body of experience shows how an animator can initiate and catalyse this process. It also deals with dialogue as a mode of promoting participation, the training of animators through participatory methodology and identifies steps for initiating Participatory Action Research (PAR). Finally, the question of the progressive redundancy of the external animator as the sustainable and self-reliant process gets underway is analysed.

Fundamental to this new methodology is the epistemological proposition that development theory and practice develop in a dialectic relationship with each other, that at each stage the lessons of practice will form the basis for further theory, just as a deeper theory will then feed back into a deeper practice. For this reason the formulation of the alternative theory must be rudimentary. However, specific elements of the process in place can be clearly identified, and inform a variety of micro-level actions. As actions are taken through praxis, more explicit theorizing can follow.

It is the nature of the alternative theory that it develops not through a priori formulations, but through the comprehension of its application to practice at each stage of praxis. Thus the rudimentary state of the alternative theory should not be taken as reflecting a rudimentary state of understanding of either the Southern reality or the alternative social processes that are emerging.

Towards the emergence of a relevant 'school of thought'

It is clear that research bearing on values, the long revolution and praxis at the global level, at the national, macro level and at the grassroots, micro level must be not only integrated but also expanded and refined for different cultural settings. Some still preliminary conceptual work is going on, but much more needs to be done in which micro–macro–global (local–national–international) issues of development are organically linked and integrated. At the same time, some innovative rethinking is being initiated throughout the South which needs to be synthesized as far as possible.

The emergence of a school of thought, though in a rudimentary form, can be observed in the context of South Asia, where the new processes of development appear to have gone furthest on the ground. There is now a significant material basis for generalization.[21] In practice, however, in South Asia many people's movement development experiments exist in isolation. Protest movements may link temporarily to overthrow military dictatorships or highly authoritarian regimes. They have even, on occasion, captured state power, but often do not know how to use this power effectively in a complex macro reality.

Both macro political movements and micro development experiments need to be further identified, analysed and linked as part of an ongoing praxis and for mutual reinforcement. But even this limited task requires a more coherent conceptual framework. If coherent but flexible paradigms are not evolved, what results is a great deal of protest at how the system works, a rhetoric of social change and development for people, and a great deal of isolated and fragmented activities. In Pakistan, the re-establishment of democracy after continuous military dictatorship could not be sustained for the most part, because the larger movement for democracy could not organize a development base at the micro level. This kind of movement turns out to be an eruption rather than an exercise in real people's power . It then ends in the same kind of marginally representative democracy as in Pakistan. Even after several years of non-military government, there was little evidence that a participatory development strategy and democracy that responded to the people's needs had been articulated. In Sri Lanka, after ten years of an 'open economy' and its consequences, which have resulted in greater social polarization and near anarchy, the Janasaviya Programme of recent years is attempting a strategic response to enable the poor to participate in development as subjects in the process. This provides the political space for initiating praxis at the grassroots level and for reorienting the macro support system. It is too early to tell whether a new social contract can be forged between the large numbers of poor and vulnerable and the state.

In the 1980s as the countries of South Asia began to face an even more critical crisis of development, with the global system itself in disarray and the existing structures and institutions of the nation state incapable of coping with the twin crises of development and democracy, several issues became clearer. It was possible to understand more clearly the steady slide of these societies into varying degrees of anarchy and destabilization. A deeper look at the emerging reality and the crisis in all South Asian countries revealed that the crisis threatened to destroy the national resource base, caused further erosion of native cultures and increased the tendency towards militarization.[22] The case of Sri Lanka illustrates how a country which was said to be the best bet for democracy and development in Asia, slid into a 'Lebanon' syndrome. If the Janasaviya Programme as a strategic thrust had not been articulated, the long slow task of systematically reversing this slide could not have been attempted. In other words, if in 1988 some strategic thrust like the Janasaviya Programme had not been articulated, some strategy on those lines would have had to be invented.

The crises that are sparked by acute inequities resulting from the development process generally impact on the internal political process and democracy. Significant sections of the people are denied participation, and alienation increases. Minorities are tyrannized and political power is increasingly wielded by military bureaucratic oligarchies. The tendency for growing militarization and fragmentation of states along ethnic, religious or linguistic lines creates internal conditions for further external intervention. While Sri Lanka epitomized the crisis in extreme form from the early 1980s, the writing on the wall for other countries was clear.

In this context, with women's concerns and the women's movement assuming greater importance, the gender and equity crisis—another facet of South Asia's growing economic, social and political problems—came to be highlighted. In an attempt to further refine the thinking in *Towards a Theory of Rural Development,* some scholars and activists in South Asia began collaborating on these issues.[23] Here again it was observable that there was an increasing body of positive evidence from women's movements and development experiments indicating that poor women contributed significantly to economic and social development, particularly in the informal sector and represented a social response at the micro level to the crises in their lives. Furthermore, they could overcome their double burden of being women and poor through better organization, and by using local resources and knowledge and their own creativity through the methodology of praxis. In Latin America the way in which many social movements operate was learned from the women's movements there, in particular non-hierarchical ways of organization. Such non-hierarchical forms differentiated these methods from the organizational forms of traditional political parties.

Moreover, where women's small development actions initiated through praxis had support from sensitive macro institutions, they could go to scale and be sustainable. This revealed that the energy released through the women's movement in South Asia was being harnessed for a different kind of accumulation and sustainable development. Stronger links are necessary between the macro women's movement and micro grassroots experiments, and a greater clarity in concepts and institution-building is required.

Ongoing empirical research and conceptual work by a group of South Asian scholars and activists has recently attempted to refine further the methodology of praxis. This is important not only for attempts partially to reverse the negative aspects of past development processes, but also for initiating the transition to a new complementary strategy of democracy and development beginning at the micro level.[24] This strategy does not preclude attempts to maintain the gains from past industrialization with suitable modifications and damage limitation policies, so that in effect a more complex 'walking on two legs' strategy is effected.

Four issues can be highlighted, as far as action at the macro level is concerned, for reversing past processes and reinforcing the new processes at the micro level. The crisis that is already upon South Asia makes it imperative for these countries to adopt a different and more complex development pathway, which is more democratic and equitable. Second, a strong critique of the dominant development paradigm shows that neither in its own narrow ideological and socio-economic terms nor as a political response to the wider crisis is it sufficient. Therefore, this paradigm cannot be followed uncritically. Third, it is possible to articulate in an unambiguous manner elements in a micro-level strategy (one of course based on participatory development and praxis), which can both limit some of the damage of past strategies and go a long way towards alleviating the worst forms of poverty and dehumanization in South Asia. It can be demonstrated that this process, once initiated at the micro level, can at the same time provide a significant element in a transition to a more complex sustainable development strategy moving on two fronts—macro and micro. But such a micro-level strategy must be supported sensitively by the macro support system. As the process unfolds it could help to refine some of the methodological and analytical tools indispensable for reinforcing the alternative micro-level processes already underway, and could also refocus praxis and identify the new capacities and institutions that need to be evolved.

The crises that South Asian countries face—no longer only the poverty crisis, but also now the ecological crisis, ethnic violence, gender conflict, militarization and external destabilization—are not isolated phenomena. They are inter-related both to each other and to the fundamental developmental intervention that was initiated after decolonization. Taken together, they have deep consequences for the fragile democratic processes at work and for the tasks of nation-building and regional cooperation.

The emerging alternative school does not pretend to substitute a comprehensive and elegant alternative theory as such to the dominant classical, neoclassical or Marxist theories. Rather it proposes that the methodology of praxis and the instrumentality of participatory action research that goes with it can help in moving the development intervention, initially at the micro level, towards development in wider human terms and in a more democratic manner, thus making both processes more sustainable. A great deal more coherence will be able to be given to the rudimentary theorizing as the process of learning on the ground continues.

Development is a political process. Without a relevant pluralistic theory of political economy with which to understand the reality on the ground or the strategic options, only an intellectually and operationally fragile development process can be achieved. It is not, however, a matter of substituting a new, elegant theory for the old.

This chapter has attempted to identify several new elements in a conceptual framework and raise several issues that require further clarification through action research. To reinforce the positive processes, a new, more coherent conceptual framework and interdisciplinary analytical tools are required on the one hand, as well as a collective rethinking by those engaged in social praxis on the other. Social praxis can be achieved only by further releasing the creative energies of the people who are now being marginalized, and by mobilizing them, along with local resources and knowledge, for the all-round development of their lives.

The Southern scholars discussed above have located the methodology of praxis and PAR instrumentality unambiguously in the context of the development theory and practice. They have also identified development as a political process and not merely a technocratic exercise. For the past 15 years, since the methodology was first identified in the contemporary South Asian context in *Towards a Theory of Rural Development* and later in Latin America and Africa, it had been considered a maverick methodology by the development establishment. The rhetoric of participation has been widely used by scholars and practitioners all over the world, both in theory and practice,without their making explicit its methodological basis or its point of departure from existing development theory.

Neither have the implications of participation for more democratic political formations been fully analysed. Today, with the mounting crisis of development, the crisis of the state and civil society, past attempts at development theory are also in disarray. This restatement of the emerging new premises for development thinking and action, as they are manifested in the positive experience of new people's movements and participatory micro level development experiments, may therefore be timely.

From the critique of conventional thinking and the negative experience of the past forty years, it is not a major step towards new premises of action. People who are impoverished and marginalized by current growth processes are seen in the methodology of praxis as the prime movers of history in future. Further refinements are necessary to generalize the basis of action that has been taken on possible ways to reinforce ongoing people's action. If the release of the creative energies of the people is a critical factor, the question is, what is needed to initiate a process to enable them to use their full creativity and realize their true self-worth?

Once this is achieved the further task of building organizations to sustain and multiply the process could be left to the internal dynamics of the process itself. The essence of it is the mobilization, conscientization and organization of the people, in that order. This process could proceed from being a countervailing force to ensuring both material benefits and greater social justice and equality.

This chapter has attempted to reinforce the possibilities of finding some points of commonality in the diverse people's movements that are emerging in the South. One clear message is that with the wide range of social processes on the ground and the cultural variation in countries of the South, mechanistic approaches to the study of social processes are misplaced. Similarly, an unconscious application of Western standards and value judgements to non-Western situations has little relevance. Today, even among Western intellectuals, there are fundamental differences as to what is development and what is democracy, and the connections between the two. In the present uncertain intellectual climate there are hazards in evaluating societies in transition and the emerging social processes without agreeing on some broad new valuational framework, methodology of analysis and institutional basis. This chapter is a small contribution to the discourse among Southern scholars and practitioners in this regard. It seeks to understand people's movements and experiments, and through these, the larger issues of rethinking development and democracy in the South.

Notes

1. For convenience the term 'South', rather than the more reductionist term 'Third World', has been used to categorize broadly those countries in Asia, Africa and Latin America that contain three-quarters of the world's peoples, more than three-quarters of the world's resources, and have deep-rooted cultural traditions that should permit them to have a good life. Yet the majority of the peoples of these countries have not shared in the benefits of global trends towards freedom, prosperity and progress. These countries are diverse, with varied cultural, political and economic systems, but they also have several commonalities, not least their great potential.

2. Not all new social movements are positive. Some, like the movements arising from the cruder compulsions of religious fundamentalism, are left out of my analysis even though they too provide a critique of Western notions of development and democracy—and of imperialism—and play a crucial role in identity formation, whilst providing the ideological underpinnings for ethnic conflict. As the anarchy in their lives deepens, alienated people tend to withdraw into the safe ground of the familiar. This withdrawal is then used by vested interests and immature political leaders to manipulate the people. The processes analysed in this book, however, are the more spontaneous and positive social movements, people's movements and experiments.

3. See Talcott Parsons, *The Structure of Social Action,* Free Press, Illinois, 1949; and R. Sudarshan, 'Theory, Ideology and Action in Economics and Law', *Lokayan Bulletin,* 5.5, New Delhi, 1988.

4. See P. Wignaraja, 'The Knowledge System', in P. Wignaraja, A. Hussain, H. Sethi, and G. Wignaraja, *Participatory Development: learning from South Asia,* Oxford University Press, Karachi/Oxford (forthcoming).

5 See P. Wignaraja, 'Towards a New Praxis for Sustainable Development in South Asia', in P. Wignaraja and A. Hussain (eds.), *The Challenge in South Asia: development, democracy and regional cooperation*; 1st edition: Sage Publications, New Delhi/Newbury Park/London, 1989; 2nd edition: Oxford University Press, Karachi/Oxford, 1989.

6. See G.V.S. de Silva, W. Haque, N. Mehta, A. Rahman, and P. Wignaraja, *Towards a Theory of Rural Development,* Progressive Publishers, Lahore, 1988.

7. Today, the World Bank's *Development Report* (1990) on poverty and the UNDP Human Development *Report* (1990) accept unambiguously the failure of past paradigms of development and democracy, but continue to make a strong case for the marginally

reformist option, which amounts for the most part to conventional developments, more efficiently delivered from the top with some consultation with the people. Instead of GDP and per capita income as measures of living standards and well-being, now a slightly broader indicator, the Human Development Index, is used. This shift still hardly addresses the more fundamental issues.

8. Throughout this chapter references will be made to various case studies and analyses that illustrate the material basis for new forms of social change. The Chipko movement in India has been mentioned and references will be made to the Bhoomi Sena ('land army') movement. In South Asia, the Grameen Bank in Bangladesh, the Working Women's Forum Credit Society in India, the Small Farmer Development Programme in Nepal and the Aga Khan Rural Support Programme in Pakistan are some of the better known. In Africa, the Six S Programme in Burkina Faso is deeply rooted and going to scale. In Latin America, several experiments have been spawned by the new democracy movements and Liberation Theology within the Catholic Church. These are but illustrative of thousands of possible examples, not all of which can be documented or referred to here.

9. This recorded history is not only confined to printed history books from the Western world. It is also increasingly available in manuscripts, written on *ola* leaves or inscribed in stone, which even predate recorded Greek and Roman history. They complement the oral transmission of history, intuitively recognized and communicated through mythological stories and anecdotally handed down over a long period of time. In addition, cognitive knowledge was itself part of the knowledge system in most Southern countries, particularly in Asia. It gave depth to the understanding of the Southern cultures and civilizations they were interpreting. Much of this cognitive knowledge can be subjected to modern scientific validation. See Chattaopadhya Debiprasad, *What is Living and What is Dead in Indian Philosophy,* People's Publishing House, New Delhi, 1976.

10. See Gowrie Ponniah, 'Ideology and the Status of Women in Indian Society', in P. Wignaraja and A. Hussain (eds.), *The Challenge in South Asia*, 1989.

11. See Trevor Ling, *Buddha,* Sharma, Jagdish.

12. See C. Rajagopalachari, *Mahabharata,* Bharatiya Vidya Bhavan, Bombay, 1968. The *Mahabharata* further states: 'The knowledge, that is merely so much indigested information crammed into the mind, cannot instil virtue' (p.122).

13. See Gowrie Ponniah, 'Ideology and the Status', 1989.

14. See P. Wignaraja, 'The Knowledge System', forthcoming; and D.L. Sheth, 'Catalyzing Alternative Development: Values, The Knowledge System, Power', in P. Wignaraja and A. Hussain (eds.), *The Challenge in South Asia,* 1989.

15. What is reflected in emerging people's movements and experiments in South Asia has been analysed in a few recent studies with a degree of sensitivity. Some of these movements are merely damage-limiting, or are of a temporary nature and confined to a single issue. Some are more positive and incorporate a range of basic democratic values and processes. They also demonstrate the possibility of development in wider human terms.

The case studies presented in Part Two of this book have attempted to capture some part of this experience. Other case studies are available in G.V.S. de Silva et al., *Towards a Theory of Rural Development,* 1988; P. Wignaraja, *Women, Poverty and Resources,* Sage Publications, New Delhi/Newbury Park/London, 1990; Martha Alter Chen, *A Quiet Revolution,* BRAC Prokshana, Dhaka, Bangladesh, 1986; A. Fuglesang, and D. Chandler, *Participation as Process* (a case study of Grameen Bank), NORAD, Norway, 1986; Vandana Shiva, *Staying Alive*, Zed Books, London/New Jersey/New Delhi, 1989.

16. As the Tiru-Kural says: 'The king who oppresses and rules by frightfulness will find a speedy and certain end.' In K.K. Munshi and R.R. Widakar, *Kural, The Great Book of Tiru-Valluvar,* Bharatiya Vidya Bhawan, Bombay, 1965.

17. See Mahatma Gandhi, *Non-violence in Peace and War* (two volumes), Navajivan Publishing House, Ahmedabad, 1962.

18. See *Economic and Industrial Life and Relations* (two volumes), Navajivan Publishing House, Ahmedabad, 1962.

19. See O.Fals Borda, *Knowledge and People's Power,* Indian Social Institute, 1988; and R. Kothari, *Masses, Classes and the State,* 1990.

20. See *Development Dialogue,* 1977:2, and the follow-up study published in *Development Dialogue,* 1979:2, under the title 'Bhoomi Sena—A Struggle For People's Power'. These were later published in de Silva et al., *Towards a Theory of Rural Development,* 1988.

21. See R. Sudarshan, 'Theory, Ideology and Action', 1988.

22. See P. Wignaraja and A. Hussain, *The Challenge in South Asia,* 1989, in which the crisis of state power was examined along with the problems and prospects of regional cooperation.

23. See P. Wignaraja, *Women, Poverty and Resources,* 1990.

24. See P. Wignaraja et al., *Participatory Development,* forthcoming.

2. Latin America: A Society in Motion

Daniel Comacho

In Huehuetenango, Quiche and Zolala we kidnapped the leaders of the Indians, we raped their women and hit their children; I only hit them, I did not kill, but if I hit them it was because I had to obey orders....

My job consisted of robbing people, taking them out of their houses, under the protection of the night and our weapons. We were disguised, we were dressed up as civilians. [Ricardo Fuentes's declarations to the newspaper *La Jornada*. Fuentes is an ex-member of the Guatemalan military police.]

Two years ago some leaders and I began to change our opinions in order to create a single idea, a single action, which would allow us to confront and fight the abuse and exploitation we were suffering. It was then that the necessity to become one, to create a large organization was born. [Alberto Andrago, indigenous peasant from Cotacachi, Ecuador.]

Prologue: some reflections on liberation struggles in Latin America*

In Latin America today, the word liberation is used less than the words democracy or revolution. Democracy, as the object of the liberation and revolutionary struggle today, is perhaps the most extensively used concept. As distinguished from conservative definitions of democracy, which remain within the realm of liberal thought, progressive definitions refer to a democracy in which power belongs to majorities, especially the working people. The idea of a true revolution—the establishment of a popular-based revolutionary democracy through a radical change in the role of the ruling oligarchies and bourgeoisie—is widespread in several Latin American countries. The ideas of socialism and of working-class rule are used less commonly than the ideas of a struggle for revolutionary democracy and for the hegemony of the working people. Revolution is put forward as a simultaneous liberation from both imperialism and the local oligarchic bourgeoisie; but there is no talk of

* This section was written by Pablo Gonzalez Casanova.

liberation from imperialism without liberation from the local oligarchic bourgeoisie, or of liberation or revolution in order directly to achieve socialism. Democracy with 'people power' is the great objective.

In many countries, political and civic movements predominate. Indeed, they are the only types of movements that exist in Argentina, Uruguay, Brazil, Paraguay, Panama, Costa Rica, Mexico and the Dominican Republic, to name the main instances. However, in Central America—and especially in Guatemala and El Salvador—and in the Andean region stretching from Colombia through Ecuador, Peru and Chile, there are revolutionary and insurrectional movements which at times operate in considerable areas of the national territory.

The richest and most developed thinking about liberation is found in the Caribbean, Central America and some Andean countries. It is worth highlighting a few of the current theses.

Today's revolutionary movements see themselves as the heirs and the continuation of the movements that began in the 1960s. In analysing the historical conjuncture and tendencies, they stress a score of objective facts about the hegemonic crisis of imperialism. Unlike the majority of analyses of the economic crisis, they pay careful attention to the hegemonic crisis. They think that 'the moment is ever more favourable for the Revolution' (FMLN of El Salvador). They see the crisis as a revolutionary situation.

Having experienced defeats and aware of their weakness, they are interested in rethinking the role of the working class in the revolutionary processes, the role of class and vanguard, the role of the material base, the urban base, the rural base, and the production and reproduction of life itself as key to the revolutionary struggle.

Distinct from the great quantity of Marxist literature that tends towards a structural analysis, their fundamental goal is to identify the contradictions into which the ruling classes and groups will fall. Even if these revolutionaries recognize the existence of primitivism and dogmatism within the revolutionary organization, they still consider the enemy's weaknesses and crisis to be more serious.

Whilst in the process of abandoning or raising the banner of one cause or another, today's Latin American revolutionaries choose to take up and deepen struggles. Thus it has been with the banners of democratization and moralization. Democracy and morals become necessarily radical. But these revolutionaries distinguish themselves clearly from those who turn the logic of contradiction into the logic of accommodation.

From the practice of criticism and self-criticism, which sought to place the blame on someone else (or on oneself), they have moved on to a practical proposition: if the problem is how to take power and how to defend it, then errors should be studied in order to improve the possibilities of effective action. By centring on this goal, false problems are discarded. For example, building unity among the popular forces does not mean harmonizing the interests of various parties, but rather creating an emerging or broadened popular power. And on that basis, it is possible to pursue the politics of alliances. In this way, politics appears as necessity; for example, the necessity of policy toward the regular armed forces. With the regular armed forces there is not only the war problem; there is the political and diplomatic problem as well.

The politics of alliances implies taking up the banners of different causes. If the Left struggled for socialism until the 1950s, for revolution since the 1960s, and for democracy since the 1980s, and each time other goals were forgotten, now the Left brings together the struggles and those who struggle; it internalizes values and does not simply amass forces. Unlike the politics of alliances in the past, when various issues were raised superficially in order to attract the largest possible number of groups into the alliance, today the Left is working for something more coherent and integrated. If socialism and revolution are an ultimate goal, so is democracy.

The demise of reformism is manifested in the revolutionary potential of reforms. Today reforms create confrontations and struggles for power that they did not before. At the same time, many former social reformers are such no longer, and many social democrats have turned into neo-liberals without even a minimal alternative programme of social reform. Now even the minimal alternative is left to be carried out by revolutionaries, some of whom are of reformist origins.

Even in those countries where the struggle is more developed, the search for the 'alternative of the people' needs to be carried out through a deepening of the struggle for democracy. In countries like Haiti, the so-called democratic revolution shows that there is no room within the system for democracy or for the most elemental necessities. The following is an example of the deepening of the struggle for democracy: in Haiti the people rose up shouting 'long live the army!' in reaction to the *tontons macoutes,* the thugs who acted as the Duvaliers' private police force; now contradictions within the army put it in conflict with the people.

Democracy and liberation

Some clarifications must be made about democracy as an anti-ideal and as an ideal. Democracy of the minorities is not democracy, nor can it be sovereign. The most liberal capitalist regime is profoundly anti-democratic if one considers the masses and their lack of influence on decisions and information. At most there is a repressed representative democracy. The structure of production in the nations of Latin America is not designed to serve more than 30 or 40 per cent of the population. If an attempt is made to serve more of the population, then immediately there are problems of shortages, hoarding, speculation and inflation. Consequently, an electoral victory is not a victory of the Left.

The problem is to heighten the consciousness of the working people, that is to say, to organize them in pursuit of their immediate and strategic goal: democracy as their democracy, with the power necessary to achieve it and defend it. In this situation—as well as in the sense that the masses do not always do what the bourgeoisie has planned—the intermediate battles are significant. In Uruguay, for example, the mass organizations won rights for the communists and the Frente Amplio. This is reformism by the masses and consequently it is not opposed by those who call for revolution, as it would have been in the 1960s. Nor are political struggles in Uruguay today opposed by those few who are involved in armed struggle. The education and organization of the masses is the fundamental issue.

By the degree to which popular power is built, the social movements express their specificity and their solidarity. Liberal democracy atomizes the subjects as citizens. Popular democracy—or democracy of the people—seeks the solidarity of social movements that dominate, deliberate, and govern.

Structural social heterogeneity provokes solidarity accompanied by a very rich pluralism. It influences the formation of the vanguard in such a way that its members (groups, parties) see themselves not as property owners or bosses but as articulators, coordinators of the social movements within a perspective of power. The vanguard cannot predetermine the subject of the movement, but rather can integrate forces and occasionally help to create a protagonist from various actors. Democracy has to recognize ethnic autonomy, as in Nicaragua.

Liberation thought

In Latin America, Marxism's close relationship and fraternal integration with Christianity has permitted revolutionaries to use religious symbols previously used by tyrants and the Spanish empire. It also has helped to make both Christian politics and Marxist politics less sacred, even whilst respecting the beliefs of those who exercise their faith through Christian celebrations and of those associated with a pedagogy of the oppressed. According to revolutionaries, new beliefs and pedagogy are to prepare for liberation by re-educating the religious and the Marxists. When it comes to an analysis of the kingdom on earth, Marxism enriched by concepts and words from different cultures and ideologies has no rival.

The change in revolutionary thought has occurred as a rupture with the authoritarian Hispanic or Caribbean culture and with the culture of a certain Marxism-Leninism (not simply Stalinism). The rupture is not a general fact, however. Of the current movements in Latin America, Peru's Sendero Luminoso guerrillas are a product of an authoritarian culture—a combination of the authoritarianism of the Peruvian highlands, of that of the Chinese Gang of Four, and of that which, in the name of Jose Carlos Mariategui, a leading Marxist intellectual in Peru in the 1920s, evolved in Lima. The latter was related to the heritage of a communist party in which some members, upon becoming radicalized, sustained their political beliefs with tension and roughness. This tendency was accentuated and hardened in the peasant struggle against an army that widened its nets by seeking recruits among the population itself and organized that population for use in the 'internal war', a policy carried out today in the form of 'low intensity' conflict. To control the peasants, *Senderistas* reinforced authoritarian measures within their own ranks and in their relations with the people.

Popular movements: a single, multiple and varied process

The presence of a multiple and varied phenomenon known by the generic name 'social movements' has been widespread throughout Latin America.

Within this category one can include processes as varied as the following: the struggle of the inhabitants of a Caracas barrio trying to prevent the removal of a tree; the decision by Guatemalan ethnic groups to rise up in arms to defend their millenarian culture; the coming together of tens of thousands of students in Mexico City seeking to eliminate obstacles to university entry and study; the accusing presence in the Plaza de Mayo in Buenos Aires of grandmothers and mothers distressed by the disappearance of their sons and grandsons; the metamorphosis of religious contemplation into social and political action as a new way of exercising love for one's fellow man in important sectors of the Christian population; and the founding of political organizations which, after having exhausted all other possible means to bring about transformations within society, find themselves compelled to bring about these changes through force, as has been the case in the agitated history of E1 Salvador.

Only a brief description of these and other processes will make clear the diversity of subjects, historical situations, objectives, forms of organization and leadership, political concepts, self-definitions and projects that exist within social movements. What then allows us to consider them as a single phenomenon?

In the first place, these movements are popular in character. There are, however, social movements which are not popular. They belong to hegemonic groups and include managerial cadres and associations of big businessmen, financiers and industrialists. Landowners, in general, do not try to transform a form of society that benefits them. They merely seek partial adjustments. The sectors of society that share conditions of exploitation and domination are the basis of the popular movements.[1]

These movements' importance in creating history is enormous. One finds a utopian vision of what might constitute a new society in these popular movements, a point of obvious interest for a reflection on Latin American perspectives.

It is true that popular movements are sometimes reduced to defending specific interests of certain sectors in society. Examples are peasant movements, whose principal objectives concern land, credit, ploughs and other instruments of cultivation. But there can also be much wider interests, as in popular religious movements, whose motivation is the defence of general interests rather than the specific interests of its members.

As an expression of civil society, social movements represent a distinct dimension in the sphere of politics. They are not a part of the state apparatus. Nevertheless, they propose transformation of the state which can be either partial or total. It is partial when the movements seek the adoption or modification of a policy in reference to a specific issue. This is the case with the ecological movements, which attempt to modify policies concerning the exploitation of nature. The transformation is total when the movements unify their struggles, generate a shared project for the structural transformation of society and constitute themselves into movements representing the entire population. This occurred in Nicaragua in 1979 and subsequently in El Salvador. It also happened in Bolivia in 1952, in Mexico in 1910, in Cuba in 1959, in Grenada in 1979 and to some extent in Peru in 1972. They turned into what came to be called the Popular Movement.

Another context of popular movements relates to social classes. The confrontation between classes in today's world has acquired complex, varied and subtle characteristics. He who sees in today's Latin America a clear confrontation between the bourgeoisie and the working class is as mistaken as he who sees such a class confrontation nowhere. The bourgeoisie, local as well as international, is in a permanent process of constitution, transformation and diversification: in this process of searching for new and more efficient mechanisms of accumulation, the bourgeoisie directly or indirectly runs roughshod over any social sector that might oppose it. Events apparently as far removed from this process as the knocking down of trees in a neighbourhood have to do, undoubtedly, with the way in which the needs of accumulation impose upon man's relation with nature: if the value of urban land goes up, the presence of trees and green areas obstructs landowners' accumulation. In Latin America, genocide, the double working day for women, restriction of university matriculation, violation of human rights, falling real wages, industrial unemployment and so on are the causes of the emergence and struggles of social movements. They are responses to the processes of capital accumulation by various factions of the bourgeoisie. If one wants to understand social movements, one has to place them in direct relation to classes and class struggles.

Yet another common characteristic of social movements is their lack of organizational coherence. In the first place, a movement does not always generate a structure or an organization, and when it does, it does not fuse with it. The organization is a mediation which may or may not help in the attainment of the movement's objectives. In fact it has been said of some organizations that they obstruct the movement's objectives. This is the case with certain trade unions accused of acting against the workers' movement. On the other hand, some social movements may go from movements with a high degree of organization to phases in which a coherent structure hardly exists.

To sum up, social movements in Latin America share five main characteristics: 1. they are located in civil society; 2. they constitute a dynamic process; 3. they are not always organizationally structured; 4. they defend the interests of specific sectors of society; and 5. they are tightly linked with classes and class struggle.

The indigenous movement

In Latin America, from the beginning of political independence, or what happened at the same time, the beginning of capitalism, a contradiction occurred between the forms of indigenous social organization, based on joint property and the needs of capitalist accumulation which were to convert the land into a commodity to extend the area of large-scale agricultural production for the market and to release large numbers of rural people for work in the city. Capitalism's development demands a 'free' labour force which can be hired by nascent capitalist enterprises and a surplus of labour freed from its obligations to the land. In addition, it necessitates the control of vast areas of land incorporated into capitalist agriculture. Capitalist control of the land presupposes that land become a commodity in the market subject to free buying and selling. Capitalist expansion also results in the eviction of indigenous populations from communal land, reducing them to the status of wage workers, increasing the reserve army of labour and linking communal land to the circuit of capitalist production.

Capitalism's advance, while robbing indigenous communities of their land, also destroys their cultures, particularly the collectivist elements of traditional cultures. Popular responses to these processes have taken the form of social movements. Indigenous ethnic movements in Guatemala, Mexico, El Salvador and Colombia are illustrative of this kind of social movement in Latin America.

In El Salvador, for example, (Menjivar, 1981, p.85) the establishment of large haciendas by the emergent bourgeoisie brought about the plunder of indigenous communal lands or common land. This plunder acquired gigantic proportions during the last third of the nineteenth century, a time during which many indigenous people and peasants were forced off their land. Although land and workers were incorporated into the capitalist sector of the economy, great numbers of indigenous peasants were thrown into unemployment and displaced from their lands. The expulsion of the indigenous people, the destruction of their culture and the formation of a highly repressive state explain in great part the reason for the uprising and massacre of 30,000 Indian peasants in 1932 in El Salvador and the civil war which continued in that country until 1992.

As the capitalist mode of production expanded and changed its form, the indigenous culture suffered corresponding transformations. In Guatemala, a contributory factor in the struggle of the indigenous population was the ethnic problem, and in Mexico it was a community movement (Mejia and Sarmiento, p.24). But what is common to all indigenous movements throughout Latin America is the struggle for land and culture.

In Mexico, the declarations and aims of peasant and indigenous congresses have had land as one of their main concerns. For example, in the aims of the National Coordination Ayala Plan Congresses, demands for land appeared repeatedly as a central theme. Their Declaration of Principles emphasized the struggle to:

> recuperate the poor peasantry's land and liquidate the latifundia; to rescue natural resources which historically belong to the communities; to organize production and commercialization of the countryside collectively and independently; to rescue, preserve, defend and develop the cultural manifestations of ethnic groups and demand the full recognition of peasant women's rights. [Mejia and Sarmiento, p.82]

The generality of declarations of the majority of indigenous organizations in Mexico are of this nature. According to Mejia and Sarmiento (p.221ff.), the indigenous movements' demands, which are primarily of an ethnic and cultural character, do not stop there, but rather respond to many other motivations. Moreover, these authors find that the development of ethnic consciousness is derived from the struggles of the peasant communities. This shows, once again, the fusion of land and culture in the indigenous movement.

In Colombia (Suarez, p.23) the ethnic populations were wiped out by imposing on them a type of education alien to their forms of social and productive organization. A foreign language and a foreign religion broke their system of thought. But the most profound imposition has been the plundering of their lands, since these are not only the means of their livelihood but also what gives sense to their community.

> According to Law. No. 89 of 1980 and other indigenous rights, the lands they occupy belong to them, but in practice, this right has been violated by landowners, settlers and state or private enterprises which exploit natural resources. Today, there exist only a few shelters and reserves, which do not correspond in quality and size to the needs of the indigenous population. [Suarez, p.35]

All this has laid the basis for the development of an increasingly strong and active indigenous movement. In Colombia, the whole of the indigenous movement, allied with the lowest levels of the peasantry, has made the recuperation of their land the most influential factor for the unification of their forces.

In Guatemala (Arias, 1985, pp.62–119) the indigenous population has developed in the course of centuries a resistance—sometimes active and sometimes passive—to the plundering of their lands, destruction of their culture, language and religion, exploitation of their labour, forced migration, forced conscription by the army, and social prostration. Indigenous people show the lowest indices in Guatemala in terms of health, literacy, housing, school attendance, nutrition, and per capita income.

The earthquake on 4 February 1976 disrupted the army's communication inside the country, allowing room for the indigenous population's own autonomous organization. They found new, trustworthy leaders, established contact between the twenty-two existing groups in Guatemala and found allies among the poor *ladinos* (white peasants) in the South, and among students and priests' groups.

In this way, the movement became stronger, at first with little structure, then extending itself slowly up to the point of forming the Committee of United Peasants (CUC) in April 1978. The CUC united for the first time all the Guatemalan ethnic groups, and formed an alliance with the worker's and peasant's movement.

The CUS's work, which was at first clandestine because of previous experiences of repression, provoked a violent response from the army. On 29 May 1978 soldiers occupied the indigenous village of Panzos, killing men, women, elders and children, and raping women. In a calculated move, they allowed a few individuals to escape so that their terrified reports of the incident should spread all over the country.

The attack on Panzos was to become the model for the army's repression of hundreds of indigenous villages. Meanwhile, the CUC organized massive demonstration and strikes in which almost all the ethnic groups and peasant organizations participated. In this struggle ecclesiastical communities played a leading role.

The formation of the CUC and the march of the Ixtahuacan miners (they travelled 351 kilometres in search of better working conditions) were landmark events in this process. In their march, the miners crossed the indigenous area of the western high plateau.

Faced with the strength of the CUC, the army occupied the area and conducted a ruthless campaign against the indigenous population. An example of their conduct was the burning alive of twenty-seven indigenous activists who had taken over the Spanish embassy to protest against repression. Against this backdrop, a massive campaign was launched to draw the indigenous population to the guerrilla movement. The propaganda base of the guerrillas was the Iximche Declaration. This declaration, entitled 'The Guatemalan Indigenous People in Front of the World', was approved on 14 February 1980, a few days after the Spanish embassy massacre, by representatives of all ethnic groups. The declaration stated:

> May the blood of our indigenous brothers and their example of firm and brave struggle give strength to all the indigenous people to go on ahead and attain a life with justice.
>
> For a society of equality and respect. For our Indian people, that they may develop their culture that has been broken by criminal intruders. For a just economy in which no one exploits the others. For the land, that it be common as was that of our ancestors. For a people without discrimination, that all repression, torture, abduction, murder and massacre may end, that the 'fights for the barracks' may end, that we may have the same rights to work, that we no longer be used as tourist objects. For the just distribution and use of our wealth as it was used and distributed in the days of our ancestors, when their life and culture bloomed.

The document ended with the following phrase which later became a slogan:

> Rise all of you, call everyone, that no one nor any group among us remain behind the others. [Quoted in Arias, 1985, pp.102–3]

There then began one of the most dramatic struggles that has ever taken place in Latin America, and one of the most appalling genocides ever known.

As far as the indigenous population is concerned, Arias notes (p.104) that from that moment on, the situation changed dramatically:

> Effectively, guerrilla and people became one. The entire population participates in the war and the partisan effort, although only those adequately armed are integrated into permanent units. Others, with less sophisticated weapons, become part of the local irregular forces and self-defence units. The entire indigenous population feeds the permanent partisans, provides constant information and fulfils a great number of tasks, all of them indispensable.

The army's answer, inspired by the advice of the governments of the USA, Israel and Argentina, was brutal. Arias (p.114) describes it as follows:

> [The repression] centred on the high plateau which covers almost the whole western part of the country, where the great majority of the indigenous population lives.... [The army decided that] it was necessary to act against this population in order to cut any kind of supply to the guerrillas and punish 'subversion'.... This is how the most ignominious genocide since the extermination of the North American Indian population in the last century was carried out in the American continent.
>
> The genocidal action of the army destroyed entire villages and all the produce that belonged to the inhabitants. This is known as the policy of 'land clearing'. Many inhabitants—especially pregnant women, and children—were killed, houses as well as harvests and grain reserves were burned, belongings stolen, and domestic animals slaughtered.

The fleeing population and even those who hid themselves in the mountains were captured and forcibly settled in strategic villages, which in effect became virtual concentration camps. The great indigenous guerrilla mobilization was thus contained. Nevertheless, the struggle is not over. In the collective memory of the indigenous people, there remains the unforgettable memory of this episode.

To reiterate, land and culture are simple yet complex demands of the indigenous movement throughout Latin America. For a greater understanding of social movements in Latin America, it is useful to compare this indigenous movement with an urban social movement.

The city, a battlefield

Capitalist society has its own characteristics. Within it, the profit motive—the urge to accumulate—plays an important role in the construction of the infrastructure of cities. A garden, a park, a historical relic have, from the investment point of view, a very low yield. For this reason, capital for the construction of buildings, infrastructure and communication is unevenly distributed between the elegant neighbourhoods and commercial centres on the one hand, and the neighbourhoods of the masses on the other.

One way in which capital secures a financial return on its investment in urban infrastructure is to charge very high prices. As a result, members of low income groups are compelled to move away. These were the factors at the root of the struggle of the inhabitants of Fernando de Mora, in Asuncion, Paraguay, who according to Luis A. Galeano's study (1986) were forced to abandon their neighbourhood because of the high prices they had to pay for the installation of a sewage system, paving of the streets and piped water once their area was swallowed up by the expansion of the city.

Often, the building of new infrastructure by displaced inhabitants adds to their difficulties and suffering. Kowarick and Bounduky (1987, p.45), referring to the city of Sao Paulo in Brazil, pointed out that 'the [displaced] workers resigned themselves to live in remote areas, difficult to reach and practically without any urban facility.' As was noted in the *Correo Paustano* of Sao Paulo (No.11, August 1946):

> A manual worker acquires a piece of land, he himself digs a well after working hours, buys bricks.... In a few Sundays the house is built on the cliffs of Villa Matilde, Villa Esperanza, Villa Guillermina. They are the 'Sunday houses', the ones which tremble in the gusts of wind.

In his excellent study on urban popular movements in Mexico, Juan Manuel Ramirez Saiz (1986) concludes that 'the goals which give rise to the struggles of the urban popular movements revolve around the issue of the consumption or reproduction of the workforce' (p.29).

The problems endured by the social groups displaced from the city are the product of the logic of urban development in Latin American cities. They are not a rectifiable, marginal by-product, but an essential and integral part of urban capitalism.

The problem of housing and habitat is so central that it rapidly exceeds the specifically economic and places itself within the cultural plane. It is for this reason that the urban popular movement acquires such significance. Its struggle embraces almost all aspects of social life. In Mexico, for example, its demands relate not only to the right to housing and the use of barren land. They include defence of civil liberties, democratization of daily life and organization of production cooperatives (Ramirez Saiz, p.15). The urban popular movement has succeeded in Mexico in generating its own original symbols such as Superbarrio, a street theatre character inspired by Superman, the mythical protagonist of the comic strip. A closer look at Superbarrio deepens our understanding of what the Mexican movement represents. In the first place, he is a contestant in the sport known as free wrestling. The allusion to the spirit of combat is obvious. His opponent is Catalino Creel, a greedy landlord. But Superbarrio says that his adversaries are also the laws that go against tenants and the authoritarianism of the administration. He affirms that his strength comes from the union and organization of all his neighbours and that, like Samson, who becomes weak if his hair is cut, what weakens him is lack of organization and discouragement of the neighbours. For Superbarrio, 'the struggle for housing translates itself into a struggle for love. It is necessary to have some privacy to nourish love.... Male chauvinism is a cultural phenomenon, learned and transmitted. It can and it must change... the settlers are not only fighting for housing or cheaper tortillas and dairy products.'

From the housing problem, this cartoon character, who represents the collective feelings of the movement, turns his attention to the recovery of the rights of women, the right to adequate nutrition, democracy and love *(Excelsior, La Jornada, Doble Jornada)*.

In Brazil (Diaz Coelho, p.8), urban movements have proceeded rapidly to develop forms of struggle against the high price of basic products. In 1973, in Sao Paulo, it was the clubs of mothers of the south of the city that initiated the great movement against the high cost of living which had important political consequences.

In Rio de Janeiro, in 1975, Copacabana's inhabitants started a campaign 'for a more humane Rio', denouncing the high levels of contamination and in 1976 the inhabitants of the Alto Leblon neighbourhood opposed, although unsuccessfully, the construction of highways, bridges and flyovers within the narrow confines of their district.

In 1977, as a first phase of a common initiative by all the Rio neighbourhoods, the popular Campaign for the Defence of Nature developed, through which the people blocked a project to build nine 16-floor buildings in the area known as Copacabana Fort (Diaz Coelho, p.11).

In Peru (Tovar, pp. 83 and 121) the urban movement organized popular kitchens. In Lima 625 existed in 1986. The Glass of Milk Programme, imposed upon the municipality by the urban popular movement, employed 50,000 women organized in 7,500 committees. In the same city, the inhabitants organized and participated in popular libraries and health teams.

In all these struggles, there is an underlying theme of great importance, a struggle for dignity. In Peru, according to Tovar (p.75), in the 1970s under General Velasco, the recognition of certain rights of the citizen was accompanied by an anti-oligarchic discourse and the recovery of Quechua and the national culture which supported the migrant, defended the dignity of the *cholo (mestizo)* and undermined the society's authoritarian behaviour towards urban migrants from the countryside. In this way, the 'invader' became the 'settler'; he felt defended and recognized as a human being and as a legitimate inhabitant of the city and the country, with proper opportunities to defend his rights.

The above examples illustrate the comprehensive character and goals of the *barrios* (neighbourhood) struggles for housing, clean air, recreation, love, a decent environment, education, democracy, solidarity and dignity.

In such a multifaceted struggle, the adversary is also varied. In general, the enemy that appears in the front line as visible adversary is the state. Nevertheless, behind this facade is the real enemy made up of the sectors of society that profit from the status quo. In particular, these are the owners of real estate capital, clandestine dealers in urban land, and owners of transport systems (Ramirez Saiz, p.32).

Through their struggles, urban movements have developed alliances with other sectors. In Mexico, the neighbourhood organizations 'accompany almost systematically in the city the independent workers', peasants' and teachers' marches, making class consciousness grow in the process' (Ramirez Saiz, p.15).

Under conditions of repression, the neighbourhood associations have served as substitutes for trade union organizations. When communications between union members have been suppressed in factories, they have taken place instead in homes, taking advantage of the neighbourhoods' struggles. It is in this way that people responded to the cutting off of normal institutional channels for expression which occurred in Brazil following the coup of 1964. In 1978, when the struggle for a return to democracy was going on, and there were difficulties in reorganizing the trade union movement, it was the neighbourhood movement that eventually obtained the greatest political expression. These movements occurred in Rio de Janeiro and also in Sao Paulo, where the struggle against the high cost of living initiated by a letter of the mothers' clubs mobilized 20,000 people—in the midst of a dictatorship—in a street demonstration which remained a landmark in the struggle for democracy.

In the recent history of Latin America, the neighbourhood movements have repeatedly formed alliances with the workers' movement, as was the case in Peru between 1975 and 1980 (Tovar, pp.72 and 75) and with the women's movements, as occurred in the same country, where public kitchens and Glass of Milk Committees became intimately integrated with the neighbourhood organizations (Tovar, p.112).

In this sense, descriptions of Mexico City's 'Mrs Superneighbour ' is significant. She, according to her companion Superbarrio, has all the power because it is the Mrs Superneighbours who are building the entire neighbourhood movements, thereby increasing the self-confidence of everybody constantly *(Doble Jornada,* p.2).

The alliance of the neighbourhood movements with the religious popular movement is also fundamental. Among the activists of the latter we often find priests and other leaders of religious organizations.

The urban popular movement is not exempt from internal conflicts. I mention this lest any excessively optimistic picture might be imagined from what has been said previously.

Ramirez Saiz (p.24) mentions the problem of political bosses whose activities can destroy a movement. A movement's influence may also decline (Unda, p.7) and even disappear when it has successfully obtained a specific demand. In Ecuador (Unda, p.7) housing cooperatives turned into businesses operated by the manager and his colleagues, a situation which may lead to a failure to honour contracts, collection of money under whatever excuse, the multiple awarding of a single site to two or three different people, etc.

In many cases, the internal conflicts within popular movements reproduce the general exploitation of society, that is to say, they are the manifestation of class exploitation; in other instances, they are examples of the exploitation of the poor by the poor.

The indigenous and urban popular movements of Latin America are clearly constituted by individuals belonging to popular sectors. Another type of movement, in spite of developing its struggles on the side of the people, can be constituted by people coming from various social origins. This is the religious popular movement.

Beyond class: the priests opt for the poor

It is said that Benedita Cypriano Gomes, called Dica, a peasant girl from Goias, Brazil, suffered from convulsions at the age of fifteen. The convulsions kept her apparently dead for five years, after which she 'resurrected' herself with miraculous powers. These extraordinary events resulted in the coming together of a crowd of followers, a great number of whom abandoned their property and worldly life to live in a community at the side of the saint. Many more came in pilgrimages to pray for favours from her and the saints of her devotion.

According to Lia Zanotta Machado and Custodia Selma S. de Amaral, who tell this story in their work on religious movements in central west Brazil (1986, p.29), Santa Dica taught that the earth belonged to God and for this reason could not be appropriated by man. She formed a commune in Villa de Anjos, where work was communal and the products were distributed according to the needs of each individual. She became the highest authority in the community, establishing the norms of life, the prohibition on alcoholic drinks, the sacrament of marriage and baptism, and meting out justice and settling conflicts. She preached against private ownership of land, poor working conditions on private farms, and the payment of taxes. She also recruited adepts to constitute a city independent from the laws of men. The Church hierarchy and the landlords were the first to denounce her movement, whose activists were, in their majority, workers on the neighbouring farms in dispute with their employers.

The popular religious movement has had its martyrs, but this has not weakened it; rather, it has given it more strength. One of the most dramatic martyrdoms was that of Monsignor Arturo Romero, Archbishop of San Salvador, who was murdered while celebrating Mass by an ultra right-wing death squad under the protection of the army (*The Nation*, 24 September 1987).

The archbishop's homilies had become the only medium in El Salvador where one could publicly hear a free voice in favour of the poor, and where political life was discussed objectively without sparing criticism of the Left or the Right. Crowds met to hear their pastor's voice, but in El Salvador, objectivity became subversive in the eyes of those who arranged for the assassination of the archbishop.

Priests who have become involved in the religious popular movements reached such profound personal decisions after having gone through various stages in their exploration of commitment. One early realization was the repressive role played by the Church itself. In the words of Father Sosa (pp.20–1), this realization is arrived at through reaching a breaking point:

> From confidence in pre-established order, one goes on to the discovery that it is not order, but established violence.... One discovers oneself as a representative of this 'order'. It is no longer possible to play such a role—one has been used unwittingly as an agent by those above to implant in the minds of those below the lie that society is a continuous whole in which, through efforts and talent, one can move up without more restraints than that of the law and acquired advantages. These agents [pastors] go from a sympathetic generosity to the realization that they are living a sinful situation. They must choose—either stay in a situation which creates, maintains and deepens this social breach—or go with those oppressed by it. This option is understood as a conversion.

The popular religious movement derives its strength from the support of wide sections of the population. In the past, people who joined revolutionary parties or movements faced the dilemma of whether or not to abandon their religious beliefs, or at least their religious practices.

Religious social movements are sometimes referred to as the Popular Church, or the Church of the Poor. The popular religious movement has meanwhile generated a theory—the so-called Liberation Theology. It also has its own organizations known as 'grassroots or basic ecclesiastical communities'. Other organizations which emerged from the movement are the 'Word Delegates.'

Grassroots ecclesiastical communities emerged as a religious necessity derived from the scarcity of priests. One of their most immediate antecedents, found in Honduras in the early 1960s, was the group called Word Delegates.

As a consequence of Vatican Council II, some functions previously restricted to priests were entrusted to the faithful within the collective organizations called grassroots ecclesiastical communities in countries such as Brazil, Panama, Guatemala, Argentina and Peru. In order to alleviate the scarcity of priests, these institutions provided legitimate space for members from the poorest levels of the population. As a consequence, the acute social problems of the people also came to light.

These ecclesiastical organizations still remain within the Church. They are a particular form of putting into practice Jesus's teachings which do not conform with the practices of the dominant sectors of the Church. However, they are not a separate church, nor are they an underground or parallel one.

They define themselves as basic because their members belong to the poorest sections of the rural and urban populations. They do not exclude the participation of better-off people, provided their intention is to remain part of the grassroots, without trying to use the movement for their own benefit.

These characteristics give the movement its greatest potential. Being from the base, the organizations take care of the whole of human life, its spiritual as well as worldly aspects, providing radical explanations of people's problems.

Meanwhile, Protestent sects have also developed. Their interest lies in taking away popular sectors from their struggles and conditioning them in favour of the dominant social forces. In general, this role is played by the so-called Pentecostal sects found in almost all Latin American countries.

In Brazil, for example, Pentecostal sects are gaining many followers, while the Catholic Church loses them. Zanotta Machado and Selma S. de Amaral (1986, p.1) say that, according to demographic censuses:

> In 1940 Protestants represented 2.6% of all Brazilians. In 1970, 5.2% and in 1980, 6.6%.... If in 1930, from all Protestants, a mere 9.5% were Pentecostalist (Braga and Grubb, 1932), in 1960 they represented 65% of all Protestants (Souza, 1968), and were expanding rapidly.

The expansion of Pentecostal sects represents a tendency opposed to the Popular Church, because Pentecostal sects impart to their faithful an attitude totally opposed to any form of social struggle or demands. They submerge them in conformism, in a scale of values which prevents them from perceiving exploitation and makes them accept existing social relations as a sacrifice. In a study of Pentecostal sects in the banana-producing area of Guapiles in Costa Rica, Jaime Valverde (p.24) establishes a relation between the sectarian religious affiliation of the workers and their submissive and obedient attitude. The bourgeoisie that controls the banana plantations has developed a policy of making use of Pentecostal sects in order to keep and secure their power in the area. To achieve this, they cultivate good relations with the ministers of these churches, collaborate economically with them in order to strengthen them and transform them into seekers of favours and put pressure on the workers to join these sects by discriminating against those who do not belong. This is obviously an effective manoeuvre in an area of high unemployment.

A similar phenomenon occurs in the Caribbean. For Armando Lampe (p.518), the penetration of Pentecostal sects in all the islands of the Caribbean is impressive: the Mahikari movement, coming from Japan, which is not even Christian and even less Pentecostal, but which has some similarities, has prospered in Guadeloupe and Martinique. The Adventist movement has prospered in Martinique. Some other examples are the Apostle of Infinite Love sect in Guadeloupe and the charismatic movement in Curacao.

Lampe (p.520) suggests that these movements gain their support on the one hand from a rebellious attitude towards the Catholic Church, which is seen as an instrument of domination, and on the other, from the regeneration of symbols of the Afro-Antillan religions opposed to the culture of the colonialists. This group of beliefs removes the people from political activity of any kind. The world is corrupt and only God will be able to change it.

In Costa Rica too, Pentecostal sects have grown a great deal. According to Valverde (p.275), the number of sites dedicated to Pentecostal sects rose from 215 in the whole country in 1974 to 1,088 in 1985. During the last three years alone the number has doubled.

In Central America, the popular religious movement has committed itself to the struggle of the people. In Nicaragua (Opaza, 1985, pp.187 ff.), during the Somoza dictatorship, the Popular Church emerged against the Church hierarchy, which had compromised itself by its support for the Anastasio Somoza Garcia regime. The 1972 earthquake represented a step forward in the development of the popular religious movement. This was evident in the Word Delegates, organized by the Zelaya Capuchins and the community of Solentiname Island, led by Father Ernesto Cardenal, who later became Minister of Culture in the Sandinista government. In the principal cities also, Christian communities were organized, and channelled popular interests and developed an increasingly radical opposition to the regime. When repression became more severe because of the growing Sandinista struggle, members of Christian communities, priests and nuns gave protection and assistance to the fighters and allowed them to use churches for the insurrection and supported the struggle in their sermons. A similar process occurred in the countryside. The FSLN (Sandinista National Liberation Front) not only recognized and encouraged the role of Christians in the struggle against the dictatorship, but took them within its ranks as militants without making any distinction between them and the fighters; consequently, many Christians reached high-ranking posts in the movement's leadership.

After the triumph of the revolution, the grassroots Christian communities became stronger and had to confront the opposition of the Church hierarchy. Christians continued to join the FSLN, the government and the army at all levels. Protestant voluntary workers in development projects and Catholic institutions such as the Universidad Centroamericana, administered by Jesuits, were involved in the construction of a more just society, in the struggle against external US aggression and in the formation of the technical and scientific cadres necessary for the realization of a more independent nation.

Turning to El Salvador, the Church there is also divided, since some bishops are allies of the army and even bless the weapons received by the army from the USA. But the majority of believers, priests and bishops, reject the regime's repression. Some go even further. The history of religious martyrs of the Popular Church in El Salvador is as extensive as its commitment to the people (Opazo, 1985, pp.179ff.). Father Ernesto Barrera, chaplain of the workers' union, was murdered by members of the police on 28 November 1978. Father Octavio Ortiz Luna, chaplain of the youth organizations, was murdered by the National Guard on 20 January 1979, when he was with a group of young people.

In Guatemala (Opazo, pp.172ff.), the institution of the Word Delegates includes also the indigenous population, mostly the young. Priests go to the countryside and through Catholic Action change traditional practice and link religious teachings with economic and social activities such as cooperatives, health centres, literacy campaigns and schools. These centres are a focus of enlightenment for the indigenous population, who thereby see themselves valued. The state's response is severe repression, sometimes with the help of the Church hierarchy, which in turn stimulates the radicalization of the indigenous people who, allied with other sectors, make up and organize the guerrilla movement.

In Haiti the Church of the Poor played an important role in the struggle against Duvalier's dictatorship. At a symposium held in December 1982 with the participation of bishops, priests, and lay people, the participants called for an 'identification with today's Haiti characterized by division, injustice, poverty, hunger, fear, unemployment, lack of land for the peasant, splitting up of families and insufficiencies in the educational system' (Lampe, p.550). Grassroots communities have developed a great deal, more so in the country than in the city, and according to Lampe (p.554), the Haitian Church of the Poor constitutes a popular movement and asserts its legitimacy within the Haitian Church.

In short, the popular religious movement has offered to the Latin American people, in exchange for many sacrifices, an environment that gives direction to their struggles, an opportunity to reconcile their material with their spiritual needs, a way to boost their own often trampled dignity and a space in which to establish alliances between various sectors of the people.

Having examined some of the most important popular movements present today in Latin America, it is important to consider under what circumstances they can become a superior, united movement, with a common project.

The workers' movement

The role of the working class in the formation of the popular movement has been discussed many times. Often, theoretical or political positions determine the analyst's attitude on the issue. Nevertheless, until now, the workers' broad objectives and forms of struggle have been much more radical than those found in other social sectors. The conditions under which the workers perform their work contributes to this situation: the presence of large groups of workers within the same factory, the division of labour which accustoms them to coordinate their individual actions with those of others, the discipline this implies, the fact that it is the manual workers who directly transform the raw material, their relatively high educational level as compared with workers in other sectors, the fact that manual workers work in the most clearly capitalist sector, a situation which provokes a clash between these contradictions and the very foundation of the system, and above all, the so visible and elemental fight between workers and capitalists for the distribution of the fruit of labour.

The involvement of the working classes in popular struggles in Latin America implies that these struggles adopt a more global and radical vision. Even in countries like Peru, where the working class was still not very big by the mid-twentieth century, the working class had much influence in the popular struggle of the mid-seventies. Syndicalism's impressive activity was let loose during the second period of the military regime, when not only were workers' demands for political citizenship denied, but also their social gains were beginning to be curtailed (Nieto Montesinos, p.57).

In Chile, Bolivia and Brazil, the participation of the industrial working classes in the struggles for democracy was unquestionable. In Chile, the participation of the miners was crucial in the confrontation with the dictatorship. The miners' leader Segel, in spite of his political affiliation with a centre-right party, was the well-known leader of the copper mine workers in their fight against the dictatorship. Segel became symbolic because he represented the presence of the working class in the front line of the struggle for democracy.

In Latin America, nevertheless, the industrial working class does not constitute the entirety of the proletariat. But the development of its organization in industrial branches increases its range of action to agriculture, the mining industry, services, etc. As Marini (1985) notes, working-class struggle expands in conjunction with that of other professional groups. In whatever manner, the petty bourgeoisie's reaction in the face of its expulsion from the paradise created by the 'economic miracle' has consisted in getting closer to the working class in its forms of organization and in its methods of struggle. Its trade unions, particularly the banking, medical, civil service and teachers' unions, especially in the universities, are today very active, and the strikes they have supported during recent years stand out for their number and combativeness. This process in turn strengthens the organized workers' movement.

In Brazil, within a different context and with different origins, we also find a working class which goes further than simple trade union demands. Ruy Mauro Marini (1985, p.185) confirms this possibility of a class alliance:

> It opens the possibility of effectively uniting, if not all, at least a significant part of the middle classes in the form of a service sector proletariat. That is to say, service sector salaried people, with a proletarian conscience. In fact, only class struggle allows for this sort of permutation, which cannot be given or denied by decree.

Marini argues that the proletariat is much larger than the working class. The members of the proletariat are, in general, those who do not have access to the means of production. These sectors can acquire a proletarian conscience because classes are formed in the process of class struggle and are not a direct expression of the mode of production.

In my view, this is a consideration which must be noted in order to solve the always discussed question of social transformation in Latin American society.

When the whole people moves

As we delve deeper into the study of social movements, the idea that each one of them, on their own, lacks the necessary conditions to change the roots of domination, which produce states of inequality, becomes stronger.

The recent experience of social movements in Latin America confirms this hypothesis because it shows that popular movements have succeeded in achieving their specific goals and in changing power relations only when they have generated a political front, part or movement, that is to say, a vanguard, able to outline its objectives in general and global terms. An opposite thesis exists, according to which political parties, and especially the revolutionary ones, have lost prestige and influence among popular movements and that the latter have constituted themselves into the dynamic element, the new motor of history. Neither recent history nor concrete research have confirmed this point of view.

The clearest examples are Cuba, Nicaragua, Guatemala and El Salvador. In the first of these countries, the July 26th Movement emerged from the student movement allied with important sectors of the working class. The long struggles of the Cuban workers' and students' movements did not gain the strength to bring about an overall transformation of society until these movements converged with the political movement that led the revolution. In El Salvador, it was only when workers, peasants, teachers' unions and students' organizations were able to generate political and military fronts that a fundamental change in society became possible.

In Guatemala, the indigenous movement began to see a change in the relations of oppression when it was able to generate its own guerrilla movement. In Guatemala, El Salvador and Nicaragua, the priests, consistent with their Option for the Poor, have participated in the political and military organizations as the only feasible way to social justice.

History does not give a single example in which the urban movement alone, or the religious movement on its own, or the workers' movement without alliances succeeded in changing fundamentally the existing system of domination. With the exception of the ecological movement (and this occurred outside the continent), none of these movements on their own have even been able to launch an electoral political party.

Nevertheless, all their transformatory possibilities gain strength when they succeed in constituting what Pease and Ballon (1982, p.23) call a 'Popular Movement'. For these authors, the Popular Movement is a process of confluence of individual popular movements in a common project to transform society. In this common project, the individual movements' historical memories unite and they create a common history. Individual struggles become parts of the same struggle, a goal is generated and the area of action moves towards the political field.

But if one mentions a change in the relations of domination, it is because a sector of society exists that dominates the others. In Latin America, clearly inserted in the process of capitalism's global development, this dominant class is none other than the bourgeoisie, the dominant class in the capitalist mode of production. Obviously, other classes, such as the landowning oligarchy, reminiscent of other previous or still present modes of production, are also dominant, but secondarily. The bourgeoisie is at once one and multiple. It is one when its general interests are at stake. Some topics interest the bourgeoisie as a whole, all its factions and sectors. One such topic is the principle of private property. But there is also a great diversity within the bourgeoisie. For example, the transnational bourgeoisie, the owners of large world monopolies, seems to be the most dynamic in Latin America, and therefore is able to influence in a determining way the course of the other factions. Able to operate across national boundaries, the bourgeoisie is differentiated according to the activities it controls: finance, industrial concerns, agriculture and within the latter, export of farm produce, etc.

The bourgeoisie could not exist, however, without the proletariat and wherever that class exists, it is the class antagonist of the bourgeoisie.

The category 'proletariat' is dynamic and changing. Latin America's proletariat, although similar in essence to the one that made the Russian Revolution of 1917, is substantially different. To characterize the proletariat one has to begin with the process that gave birth to it. A useful guide is to focus on its constitution and reproduction from the point of view of the constitution and reproduction of the bourgeoisie, which is its class antagonist. In Latin America, the transnational bourgeoisie is the most dynamic dominant sector. It produces great concentrations of proletarians in the principal Latin American metropolises such as Mexico City, Sao Paulo, Rio de Janeiro and Caracas. Agricultural production becomes increasingly capitalized, giving rise to a concentration of the rural proletariat. Although dependent, the local bourgeoisies control parts of the industrial, commercial and agricultural economic sectors for which they establish typically capitalist work relations. These are the clearest aspects of the creation of the proletariat. On the other hand, there exist other processes which are not so direct, but which also proletarianize important sectors of society:

> The subordination of Latin American economies to the world market, and at the same time, to capitalist production; the existence of an uninterrupted capitalization process since the beginning of the twentieth century; a permanent process of uprooting workers from their means of production; the existence of great numbers of workers who have no other means of survival than their ability to work; subordination—direct or indirect—of increasing numbers of workers of the country to capital and capitalists; the development of an ever greater division of labour and increasing opportunities for collective organization at places of work and where people live. [Orlando Nunez, 1986, p.6]

The above conditions objectively lead masses of workers into direct opposition to capital and the state which represents it. However, we must not miss the subjective element, the realization of one's situation as a member of an exploited class and of one's ability to fight against exploitation.

This chapter has considered Latin America as a whole, viewing the development of popular movements as a single, cumulative process. Although there are profound differences between countries, and even within regions of the country, there exist powerful integrating factors. One of the strongest is constituted by the dominant economic processes. Darcy Ribeira once said that the real integration of Latin America is carried out by the transnational companies. In my opinion, these entities, and the processes of capitalist development which generate them, are the most dynamic elements of social domination and they have a determining influence over individual societies. For this reason, there does exist a real relationship between ecologists in Venezuela, the mothers of the Plaza de Mayo in Argentina and settlers in the marginal areas of Mexico. All fight against the same method of organizing society, one which uses the same logic, that of capital.

Notes

1. This concept of 'the people' has been developed by Pablo Gonzalez Casanova in *The Hegemony of the People*, EDUCA, San Jose, 1984.

References

Alas, Higinio, *El Salvador, por que la insurreccion?,* first edition, Secretariado Permanente de la Comision para la Defensa de los Derechos Humanos en Centroamerica, San Jose, Costa Rica, 1982.

Arias, Arturo, 'E1 movimiento indigena en Guatemala 1970–1983', in Daniel Camacho and Rafeal Menjivar (eds.), *Movimientos populares en Centroamerica,* Editorial Universitaria Centroamericana (EDUCA), San Jose, Costa Rica, 1985.

Calla Ortega, Ricado, 'La encrucijada de la COB', mimeo, La Paz, Bolivia.

Camacho, Daniel and Menjivar, Rafeal (eds.), *Movimientos populares en Centroamerica,* Editorial Universitaria Centroamericana (EDUCA), San Jose, Costa Rica, 1985.

Castells, Manuel, *Movimientos sociales y urbanos,* sixth edition, Siglo XXI Editores, Mexico, DF, 1980.

Cezar, Maria do Ceu, 'As organizacoes populares do Recife: trajectoria e articulacao politica (1955–1964)', *Cadernos de Estudos Sociais,* Vol.1, No.2, July/December 1985.

Chiriboga, Manuel, 'Crisis economica y movimiento campesino e indigena', unpublished mimeo.

Concha Malo, Miguel et al., *La participacion de los cristianos en el proceso popular de liberacion en Mexico (1968–1983),* Siglo XXI Editores, Mexico, DF, 1986.

Diaz Coelho, F., 'Identidade e' diferencas. O movimiento de barrios no Rio de Janeiro,' unpublished mimeo.

Doble Jornada (supplement to the periodical *La Jornada*), Mexico DF, August 1987.

Excelsior (periodical), Mexico DF, 4 September 1987.

Flores, Graciela, Luisa Pane and Sergio Sarmiento, 'Muto Campesino y politica agraria. 1976–1984. Tendencias actuales y perspectivas', unpublished mimeo.

Galeano, Luis A., 'Entre la protesta y la lucha urbana. Dos estudios de casos', in Domingo Rivarola (ed.), *Los movimientos sociales en Paraguay,* Centro Paraguayo de Estudios Sociologicos, Asuncion, 1986.

Kowarick, Lucio and Bounduky, Nabil, 'Sao Paulo. Espacio urbano y espacio polatico: del populismo a la redemocratizacion', *Estudios Sociales Centroamericanos,* No. 44, May–August 1987.

Kries, Rafael, 'Confiar en si mismos. Las organizaciones de base en Chile', *Nueva Sociedad,* No. 64, Editorial Nueva Sociedad, San Jose, Costa Rica, January–February 1983.

La Jornada (periodical), 6 September 1987, Mexico, DF.

La Jornada (periodical), 12 June 1987, Mexico, DF.

La Nacion (periodical), 24 November 1987, San Jose, Costa Rica.

Lampe, Armando, 'Los nuevos movimientos religiosos en el Caribe', unpublished mimeo.

Leon, S. and I. Marvan, 'Movimientos sociales en Mexico (1968–1983): panorama y perspectivas', mimeo, Mexico, DF.

Marini, Ruy Mauro, 'O movimiento operario no Brasil', in *Movimientos Sociais no Brasil,* Politica e Administracauo, No. 2, Edicion especial FESP, Rio de Janeiro, 1985.

Marx, K., *El Capital,* Vol. 1, Editorial Cartago, Buenos Aires, 1965.

Mejia, M.C. and S. Sarmiento, *La lucha indigena: un reto a la ortodixia,* Siglo XXI Editores, Mexico, DF, 1987.

Mejia, M.C. and S. Sarmiento, 'La lucha indigena en Mexico 1970–1983', Mexico, unpublished mimeo.

Menjivar, Rafeal, *Acumulacion originaria y desarrollo del capitalismo en El Salvador,* Editorial Universitaria Centroamericana (EDUCA), San Jose, Costa Rica, 1981.

Nieto Montesinos, Jorge, 'El sindicalismo obrero industrial', mimeo, Lima, Peru.

Nunez, Orlando, 'Los sujetos de la revolucion', unpublished original, Managua, September 1986.

Opaza, Andres, 'El movimiento religioso en Centroamerica, 1970–1983', in D. Camacho and R. Menjivar (eds.), *Movimiento populares en Centroamerica,* Editorial Universitaria Centroamericana (EDUCA), San Jose, Costa Rica, 1985.

Oxhorn, Philip, 'Organizaciones poblacionales, la reconstitucion de la sociedad y la interaccion elite–base', unpublished mimeo, Santiago de Chile.

Pease, H. and E. Ballon, 'Limites y posibilidades de los movimientos populares: impacto politico', in *Dialogo sobre la participacion,* Geneva, UNRISD, No.2, April 1982.

Ramirez Saiz, Juan Manuel, *El movimiento urbano popular en Mexico,* first edition, Siglo XXI Editores, Mexico, DF, 1986.

Sectas Protestantes en Centroamerica, 'La Santa contra-insurgencia', in *El Parcial,* April 1984, No.12.

Sosa, Arturo, *Communidades eclesiales de base en Venezuela,* Centro Gumilla, Caracas, February 1985.

Suarez, Isauro,'Trayectoria y actualidad de las luchas agrarias en Colombia', unpublished mimeo.

Tovar, T., 'Barrios, ciudad, democracia y politica', mimeo.

Unda, Mario, 'Que hay de nuevo bajo el sol? Barrios Populares y sistema politico en El Ecuador', mimeo, Quito.

Valverde, Jaime, 'Sectarismo religioso y conflicto social en Costa Rica', unpublished mimeo.

Vargas, J., 'Movimientos barriales', in *Movimientos sociales y participacion communitaria,* Nuevos cuadernos CELATS, Lima, 1985.

Vives, Cristian,'El Pueblo Napuche: elementos para comprenderlo como movimiento social', unpublished article, Santiago, December 1984, mimeo.

Zanotta Machado, Lia and Custodia Selma S. d Amaral, *Movimientos religiosos no centro oeste,* Centro Latino de Altos Estudos (CLAE), Brasilia, 1986.

3. Masses, Classes and the State

Rajni Kothari

The paradox of transformation

It is commonplace these days to say that we live in an age of turbulence. What is not clear are the sources of this turbulence and the reasons why, despite so much of it, it is not able to change the world we live in and those who wield power and authority are still able to thwart, divert or suppress it. What I propose to do in this chapter is to explore precisely this relationship—between an increasingly defensive status quo, desperate to retain its power, and the forces of change and transformation that are getting increasingly restive and restless, conscious of the shackles that bind them and the need to escape them, yet frustrated and disorganised and unable to cope with the growing repression and terror from the status quo.

There is nothing new in this undertaking. All social commentators, at least since the middle of the nineteenth century, who have cared to look at the larger dynamics that lie behind the myriad expressions of the human condition, have sought to deal with this very problem: the encounter between the forces of status quo and those of change. What is new in examining the same problem in our time is the deep confusion and uncertainty about what really is underway on both sides of the equation—on the side of the global, regional and local status quos, and on the side of agents of change and transformation from the very local and micro to the global and planetary macro.

It is by seeking to unravel this deep uncertainty about the direction in which the world is moving—both the dominant structures and those opposed to the dominant structures—that we may be able to at least begin to understand what is at work, what new factors have emerged or are emerging, how these are likely to shape the future and what, if any, counter-trends may be in the offing and may perhaps succeed. At present no clear framework of understanding, far less of explaining, reality exists, nor even a method of coming to grips with it. The old ideological frameworks, the old grand theories, have become obsolete, no clear guide exists for formulating a praxis. There is a striking decline of confidence among all but the most naive dogmatists. And this pervading sense of uncertainty has given rise to insecurity, helplessness, bewilderment, withdrawal, cynicism and apathy.

Now, to a large extent periods of uncertainty in history are occasioned by major changes in the structure of reality, changes at so many levels of human organization and so simultaneous that their impact on consciousness leaves the latter adrift and without any firm anchor.

In the contemporary situation we see these changes at many levels of human endeavour and organization. At the larger political level of the world power structure, both the rise of the Third World in the post-colonial period and the replacement of a world structured around the European balance of power by a bipolar world structured around the two superpowers (at least until the end of the 1980s), have unsettled all earlier understanding of international relations. While each of these two facts is recognized, the two have not been considered together in an adequate manner. Once one does that, one can immediately see how a colonial kind of bondage was replaced by a much greater and stronger integration into either the global capitalist market or into the world strategic straitjacket fashioned until now by the struggle for world hegemony by the two superpowers. Our existing conceptual categories of historical analysis are somehow ill-equipped to grasp the full implications of this split in the human community occasioned precisely by its greater integration, globalization and homogenization. Most existing ideologies—and their offshoots—were born in the typical European setting of nation states, the setting of first-generation industrialization and of essentially class-based identities. They seem ill-equipped to deal with a transnationalized world in which the dominant currency is technological as distinct from economic and political. It is a totally different human setting.

Second, this change is also reflected at the level of the organization of the productive forces. We are confronted with a completely different model of world capitalism, a switch from the European to the American model, in which technology as a system, propelled on the one hand by the communication and information order conditioning the minds of men and on the other by the corporate form of organization conditioning the behaviour of states, makes all other relations of production subsidiary. This has generally forced all other systems—the socialist system (now apparently in its last throes), the Third World, the Japanese system—to fall in line and measure success on terms laid out by the American cultural syndrome, with its overriding emphasis on technology.

Third, this growing autonomy of the technological estate has found its greatest manifestation in the military field and the field of military–civilian relationships. We live in an age not just of growing militarization of the whole globe—from the powerful nuclear to the powerless Third World countries—but a model of militarization that is essentially technological. Nation states are at the mercy of the growing menace of military research and development, which develops inexorably and forces every major and even minor country to discard existing weapons systems and adopt ever-newer ones, at escalating costs no doubt and with increasingly hazardous effects on social and ecological systems. It is a new version of militarism, to an extent autonomous of the will of the rulers and of course, of the people.

Fourth, this dominion of technology and its pervasive impact on the political, economic and security domains—each of which has come to become vulnerable to its design—has in turn produced a massive erosion of the ecological basis of human civilization, destroying the resource base of the people and especially of the millions of rural, tribal and 'ethnic' poor who have not just been made into surplus and therefore dispensable populations by the aggressive march of high-tech capitalism but whose traditional access to natural resources and non-commercial produce has also been taken away from them. The usual situation facing even the most remote hill people is one in which the military builds roads, urban and tourist traffic moves in with its artifacts and consumerism, modern communications hard-sell these products and then modern technology and its commercial arteries come, drawing away all the resources of nature and heritage of history that were traditionally given free to these people.

All these forces have impinged on traditional societies, forcing them to fall in line and accept the dominant mode and the ideology of forced modernization. And as supposedly independent states too are forced to fall in line instead of providing new lines of defence for civil society, a deep sociocultural crisis has ensued, especially in older civilizations. As the state in effect withdraws from its responsibility and surrenders its autonomy, civil society in these lands is thrown on its own resources. And this happens precisely when these societies are experiencing deep convulsions thanks to the powerful twin impacts, first, of the modernizing juggernaut immanent in the aggressive thrust of ruthless technologism which is the form that world capitalism has assumed and, second, of the social and ethnic conflicts generated by formal electoral democracy in which somehow wresting a majority at the time of elections has become the main stuff of politics. This formal apparatus of democracy as a vehicle of modernization worked somewhat smoothly so long as it was controlled by an alliance of feudal and bourgeois elements. With the rise and self-assertion of the masses, who in good faith believed in the formal pretensions of bourgeois democracy, a big backlash arose from both the feudal landed interests and the industrial bourgeoisie, which found expression in massive repression of the poor on the one hand and the promulgation of a depoliticized technocratic state impervious to the social and political aspirations of the masses on the other.

It is the bewildering interface between these powerful trends—each heralding a strong current of domination and destruction—that we need to come to grips with if we are to comprehend, assess and, it is to be hoped, steer the counter-trends that are emerging on behalf of the affected masses and peoples of the world. Crucial to such an understanding are two prerequisites. First, we should give up the specialized, single-issue-oriented approach to problems and crises that has characterized the dominant method of both the physical and social sciences. And, second, we need to identify the emerging ideological elements in the current praxis of the counter-movements and to relate them into some sort of whole which, while drawing upon the best in earlier ideologies, empowers the masses towards a liberating process of their own creation and volition. If this is an 'age of the masses' it is the masses and their leaders that have to evolve a relevant ideology, not some highbrow intellectuals (except perhaps as aides), nor the wielders of state power who, as all indications suggest, have a declining interest in the masses except to 'mobilize' them from time to time for their own perpetuation and glorification. Hitherto, ideological claims or pretences have been made either by intellectuals in their role of being 'vanguards' or by government or party leaders in control of the state (or by 'planners') in consequence of which the masses have been treated as mindless followers with no ideas of their own, indeed no capacity for cognition. At least in our age this presumption must go. For all the elites, including those claiming to be revolutionary, have failed to grasp the reality on the ground. On the other hand, one notices some refreshing and original ways of thinking among the masses from which we can all learn.

The changing nature of the state

Both the need to consider the multiple dimensions of domination, exploitation and marginalization in their interrelated manifestations and the need similarly to interrelate and integrate the large variety of counter-trends and their new ideological underpinnings can be best done by working on one central issue of our time. This is the changing nature of the state and its role in civil society, especially as it impinges on the masses and the peoples of the world and of the Third World in particular. We need to re-examine our assumptions about the state and its presumed role as liberator, equalizer, modernizer and mobilizer. As we do this—and I propose to go into its role in some detail in this chapter—we shall be able to uncover a series of simultaneous dimensions. The state and its relationship to the people emerges as a relationship not just between classes and the masses, but also between the principal carrier of modern capitalism (and technology) and the social order (marginalizing a large part of the latter); between the military and the civil order; between the development policies of the state and its transnational sponsors and the economic and ecological catastrophes that are affecting the masses and the sheer survival of large numbers of people; between the global information order and the citizen reduced to a package of consumption, social prejudice and dazzling circuses organized by the state and corporate intelligence; and finally between dominant races and ethnic communities that have control of the state and those at the periphery, presumably still members of the civil order but progressively being pushed out of it by repressive and genocidal policies. It is this capture of the state by a convergence of class, ethnic, technological and military actors, by developmentalists, communicators and managers—including managers of votes—that has set the stage for the contemporary confrontation between the 'classes' (by which I mean the upper and middle classes) and the 'masses'.

There has been, especially in the post-colonial world, a presumption that the state was a mediator in ameliorating the harshness of traditional social structures for the purpose of ensuring justice and equality, a protector of vulnerable peoples and liberator of oppressed and colonized populations, and an engine of growth and development that would usher in a new civil order based on progress and prosperity and confer rights to life and liberty, equality and dignity, on the people at large. There was a further presumption of the relative autonomy of the state from entrenched interests and classes, of the state as an independent actor with preponderant powers to influence, discipline and, where need be, coerce established interests and estates to accept state policies aimed at transforming—either incrementally or through rapid strides—the status quo. And for a while it did seem that the bearers of power in the new states meant to act as autonomous actors and use their authority for the pursuit of declared policies. Not only the written constitutions and fundamental statutes that were enacted and the wide array of social legislation that followed were designed to do this. The vigorous pursuit of economic models that then ensued, whether in achieving greater self-reliance through import substitution and the building of a substantial infrastructure for industrialization (as for instance was the case in India) or in achieving greater welfare through provision of social minima in the field of food, health and education (as for instance was the case in Sri Lanka), also suggested that the state meant to be a positive state in the interests of clearly laid-out policies, in turn based on a given social and economic philosophy.

During the same period the opening up of the political arena, either through exercise of adult franchise as in the liberal polities, or through involvement in party structures and at production sites as in more socialist polities, or through a combination of competitive politics, local self-government and co-operatives in the rural areas as in mixed economies, also meant that leaders of these states were keen on involving the masses and seeking legitimacy from them. And, in fact, large segments of the masses accepted this new benevolent form of paternalistic state, and hoped to use it to improve both their life chances and their status in society, and indeed in the course of time to challenge the hegemony of the dominant classes in society. In short, though not always stated in that manner, built into the positive thrust and progressivist creed of the post-colonial state was an eventual encounter between the 'classes' and the masses, with the state providing a framework for mediation through which a confrontation of contending interests was translated into a series of transformative policies.

Now such a promise of the liberal polity through a mixture of faith in 'development', a degree of zeal in 'doing good' to the people and the availability of a credible and exemplary leadership that was on the whole not a prisoner of a particular class or estate was not without failings, or serious critics. Many compromises were effected along the way, as for instance in the implementation of land reforms or in putting on the ground truly effective public distribution systems. Concessions were made when entrenched groups and interests put up a tough resistance to intended changes. There was too much dependence on the bureaucracy, which was in most of these states a direct continuation of the colonial civil service. There was not a little corruption in high office and there were the inevitable compulsions of the middle-class base of the leadership and the social milieu in which both ministers and their secretaries and technocrats moved. All this was there and all along we were told about this. We had also been warned that the state was an instrument of class or of colonial power or simply of bureaucrats and policemen and soldiers. And yet whether it was Lenin or Mao, Nehru or Nkrumah, Nyerere or Nasser, the people all pinned their visions of transformation on state power. Only Gandhi did not, but even before India became independent he was rendered impotent and irrelevant. Leaving aside the Gandhian current (and most Gandhians also went for a model of voluntarism and 'constructive work' which heavily depended on state patronage), there was consensus across the board, from the industrialists to left-of-centre politicians to the radicals including the Marxists, on a positive and interventionist role of the state on behalf of the masses.

It is now clear that expectations of such a role of the state, and the presumed alliance between the state and the masses in such an expectation, have been belied. Today the state is seen to have betrayed the masses, as having become the prisoner of the dominant classes and their transnational patrons and as having increasingly turned anti-people. Nor has it provided the sinews for a radical bourgeois transformation from the dynamics of which a revolutionary alternative would emerge. The state in the Third World, despite some valiant efforts by dedicated leaders in a few countries, has degenerated into a technocratic machine serving a narrow power group that is kept in power by hordes of security men at the top and a regime of repression and terror at the bottom, kept going by millions of hard-working people who must go on producing goods and services for the system, for if they did not, everything would collapse. The fact of the matter is that without landless labourers and sharecroppers and without the unrelieved drudgery of women and children, the rural economy would collapse, and without slum and pavement dwellers the urban economy would collapse, but there is no chance of any of these people rising above their levels of penury and destitution—no chance either of the landless acquiring land or the homeless city-dwellers getting homes. The chances on the contrary are the opposite: of sinking below existing levels as a consequence of still greater increases in unemployment flowing from still further modernization, and as a consequence too of the growing sentiment against migrant labourers without whom the cities cannot be built but who are becoming eyesores to the affluent middle classes, who bulldoze them whenever they get somewhat settled.

The decline of the state and rise of the classes

Such a transformation in the role of the state in the post-colonial world, from being an instrument of liberation of the masses to being a source of so much oppression for them, is a result of a number of factors. Some of these were foreseen by theoretical models of historical change but many others are a result of developments that were not foreseen, at least not adequately.

One set of factors has to do with the very model of development that was adopted in most former colonial countries. Based on the urge to emulate and catch up with the countries that had once colonized them and from where their intellectuals continued to derive their main stimulus and sustenance after independence, this model of development produced a structure of opportunities that was inherently inequitable and pitched against the masses. The emphasis on capital accumulation for rapid industrialization and the understanding of industrialization and associated patterns of urbanization and modernization as being outward-oriented (from the village to the metropolitan centres) inevitably distributed resources unevenly, to the detriment of the poor. And this uneven distribution was not just of resources that were created by planned economic development but also of the resources that originally belonged to the people or to which they had free and easy access. Initially it was thought that these inequalities and disparities—between classes or regions—were transitory, largely due to the inevitable lag between accumulation and distribution, and would not only disappear with further development but would be reversed in favour of the poor and a more egalitarian society. In fact, despite a degree of welfare measures and despite a mixed technological package that included schemes for rural development meant to benefit the poor and the unemployed, the pattern of inequalities and of increases therein has acquired a structure that has more or less become permanent and in which a great many vested interests have been created.

The reasons for this are many. There is the greed of the classes that controlled or had access to state power and the administration at different levels and who were unwilling to make the so-called sacrifices which in fact meant allowing the poorer classes access to a part of the surplus that they had created in the first place, so that the whole society could move forward and develop even more rapidly, benefiting all classes. This latter notion was the typical liberal bourgeois 'democratic' assumption that has not worked in these highly divided societies, where the 'classes', upper and middle, and the masses constitute two worlds apart.

But inequalities were not simply a matter of greed and selfishness, of a lack not just of empathy for others but also of perspective on how better distribution leads to even greater enlargement of the cake (instead of the narrow view that says: there isn't enough to distribute and let us first simply enlarge the cake; in such a view there will in fact never be enough). The very lack of empathy on the one hand and perspective on the other was caused by other pressures. At the level of individuals and groups—of the owning classes—there was the snare of an imported package of consumption, amenities and lifestyle, a highly seductive consumerism that has had a powerful pull through the global outreach of a particular culture of consumption, namely the American mass culture which in the case of our societies has become an elite culture that has kept the masses out.

In terms of the role of the state in this, what has happened is that having created an adequate industrial infrastructure or enough exportable surpluses to satisfy the consumer needs of the owning classes and their middle-class cohorts, and all this through the institutions of the state, these classes lost interest in continuing to operate an interventionist state for that would have meant responding to the demands for redistribution, welfare and a more participatory framework of economic management. The result has been an emphasis simultaneously on liberalization and lowering of taxes on the rich, presumably to increase incentives and replace the role of the state by that of the market, and on modernization and computerization of the technological base in which, of course, the state is expected to play a big role. The 'classes' will wallow in the imported mass culture of consumption and comforts, while the masses will be left as the plaything of the market, and that too largely in the unorganized sector. And the organized sector of the economy will be modernized for effective competition in the export-led development to which all developing countries have of late been led, again by a global mind-set launched by international financial institutions and an international academic and policy elite that is at once client and consultant to these world bodies. It is all part of the 'catching up' syndrome—in consumption patterns, in technology, in the ruling doctrine as regards the best path to economic affluence.

This is one set of factors. The other and, to my mind, more powerful set has to do with a still bigger process of 'catching up' that is at work. This is the very strong drive at building an efficient, strong, hard state, heavily industrialized after the high-tech model and sufficiently militarized—in which too the latest, sophisticated armaments are acquired. Once this drive takes shape, both the transnational salesmen and experts in the latest civilian technologies and the merchants of violence, war and repressive technologies and intelligence systems come in and lay out both their hardware and their software. This mirage of greatness in a world increasingly dominated by one or two superpowers and the multinationals only serves to drain away resources from the countryside to the urban areas, and from there to overseas in return for both civilian and military high-tech, to increase areas of tensions as the phenomenon of regional overlordship takes shape as part of a global management structure, and to harden the very arteries of the state which finds it necessary to suppress local challenges as part of dealing with external challenges. All this is part of the logic of a global order based on technocratic and militarizing states. As far as the masses of these states are concerned, all this only draws away economic resources that could have been available for their well-being and, what is worse, drains away natural resources to which they hitherto had access and of which the new technologies are particularly destructive.

Third, as a consequence of these factors—the greed of the classes, particularly under the impact of modern consumerism, the 'catching up' syndrome, the drive towards a hard, efficient and militarized state, and above all the growing faith in market economies—we are witness to another important development that is still underway but is bound to grow: the collapse of the welfare state and of those components of development that were directed to the amelioration and welfare of the underprivileged. We need to remember that one of the more progressive streams in modern economic thought, still within the broad bourgeois–liberal framework, has been the effort to temper the harshness of modern capitalism and technology through the rise of the welfare state. In fact it has been said that the welfare state has proved to be a major defence of the capitalist order against radical and revolutionary forces. When the post-colonial states designed their models of development basing them on the experience of the West, they also took on the welfare components of the West's states. Now with the welfare state under attack everywhere (including the West) those components have been the first to suffer in the Third World too. Belief in the market and in technological solutions to basically social and political problems has taken their place. The fact is that, unlike in highly urban societies that were industrialized over time where the growth of a strong class-consciousness permitted the demands for equity and justice to emanate from the social sphere in the form of pressures on the state, in predominantly rural and tribal societies the state becomes a direct, unmediated presence, and whether it treats its citizenry in a humane way or becomes oppressive depends largely on the model of development in use as well as the balance of socio-political considerations that informs the model. This depends to a large extent on the ruling elite. When such an elite makes a direct jump to high-tech without having gone through the dynamics of capitalist growth, and when it allows the military, the tourist, the television and the computer full play, welfare goes out of the window.

Once this happens both capitalism and the state get hardened, the latter becoming an instrument of the former in place of softening its excesses. Thus it gives in to the compulsions of this computerized phase of capitalism, namely automation in the organized sector and a new division of labour in the unorganized sector in which migrant and bonded labour and women and children become the targets of exploitation. Both compulsions destabilize the 'working class' and its organizations. Their capacity to combat poverty, marginalization and destitution—and slow death—declines as these become integral parts of the advance of the system, of science, of modern civilization. They are inherent in a dual economy which in turn is inherent in the wholly technocratic vision of capitalism.

Fourth, a new ideological crystallization has emerged of late, taking hold of the minds of leaders and intellectuals in all parts of the world (including, I am afraid, the socialist world). The crux of the new ideology is breathtakingly simple: replacement of the state by the market. Building mainly on the right-wing critique of the positive and interventionist state and of the phenomenon of bureaucracy but also drawing indirect support from the critique of the state from the left and from liberals (though of course distorting it), the new thought that is emerging gives full play to the market, which is euphemistically called a 'free market', to competition, to modernization, to technology and to the great catalysts of all this, namely the transnational corporate giants. In large part this is a doctrine promulgated by the state itself, or the new bearers of power in it (the post-Fabian generation, if you like). But here too it is important to catch the nuance. The idea is to dismantle the state apparatus in regard mainly to the distribution of the national product, in short, in the social sphere, and yet fully and systematically to use it for promoting the new technologies and the dual economy that goes with them. It is a state that somehow bears a human face, uses liberal symbols and invites everyone to come in, especially voluntary organizations and non-governmental organizations (NGOs), opposition groups and the liberal intelligentsia. 'We want to reduce the role of the bureaucracy, depoliticize government and the administration and to draw motivated and highly educated people into this great march into the twenty-first century', as we are told by our new-look leaders in India. In this development, the state is still central for it is the state that will drive us all like a homogeneous mass into the future. It is a grand strategy of class collaboration away from the masses which are also, of course, being asked to look after themselves. That behind the state lurks the structure of corporate capitalism is true. But we are also witness to the rise of a new model of the state, the corporate capitalist state. All over the ASEAN (Association of South East Asian Nations) world, elsewhere too where the so-called NICs (newly industrialized countries) are to be found, there is a direct marriage of the state and corporate capitalism, not between the local bourgeoisie and foreign capital as was the case earlier. In fact, the local businesses are being wiped out.

There is one final and most dangerous element in this growing crystallization of the ruling class. Aware that the dual economy and the social consequences thereof are likely to generate restlessness and revolt from the bottom and lower middle tiers of society, as also from the politicized elements of the middle classes, the ruling class has set in motion a completely new canard that is meant to distract attention from the socio-economic sphere to the highly volatile communal and ethnic spheres, releasing strong religious, linguistic and cultural sentiments, pitching people against people, using mafia-like operations and unleashing a reign of terror on vulnerable castes, communities and regions. Obscurantist sentiments and fundamentalist ideologies are mobilized for this purpose, the state acquires still more firepower, this time legitimized in the name of national unity and threats to it, undermining in the process all the politics of struggle and social movements that had challenged the hegemony of the upper classes earlier. Draconian laws against 'terrorism' are enacted in the same vein, which are then used to deal with popular unrest and suppress social movements. This is an extremely serious development that has been a direct consequence of the ruling elite wanting somehow to hang on to power and, to this end, bringing into the political process a strong dose of violence and civil strife. As it succeeds in undermining the caste and class basis of social interactions, and in communalizing that too, it threatens to tear the social fabric apart, or at any rate the social fabric below the technocratic superstructure. In fact we are witness to the rise of not one but two ideologies, of technologism and of fundamentalism, and the two coalesce as the exercise of power becomes increasingly cynical. The result is civil wars, the ethnicization of civil society, and the collapse of secularism as a mode of organizing plural societies. This process undermines the conception of pluralism as such, of a unity that not only respects diversity but draws its resilience and strength from it. In countries where a large majority is able to steam-roller the whole society into a monolithic whole, the process goes hand in hand with the homogenizing drive of the modern corporate capitalist state. For the masses, it is a double steam-roller.

The rise of the masses

The obverse of this is the masses, and the question is: how did the masses allow the 'classes' and the state to stampede them into what looks like abject surrender? And, especially, how did this happen in this supposed 'age of the masses', which has led major observers of the human condition to pronounce the final arrival on the scene of the masses, the 'revolt of the masses', as Ortega y Gasset termed it some decades ago. The actual situation we face is 'fascinating' as Americans would say, 'excruciating' as we would say (for most Americans, all suffering is fascinating, as is all sport). It is like this. There is a flurry of mass action, in various social settings, at a veriety of sites, at many levels. There is also a spurt of state repression, usually at local and para-local levels but often escalating upwards to the urban metropolitan areas, including national capitals. There is at the same time an increase in exploitation in the economic sense, not just in the wage–capital relationship but also in terms of new production relations that have given rise to new structures of exploitation, and there is wanton distortion and undermining of whatever laws and allocations there are for the poor, the backward and the destitute.

It is against this matching of opposite forces, this deadlock, this tension, this peculiar state of stagnation and exhaustion arising precisely out of so much action from so many opposing segments and sites, that we have to evaluate the actual condition in which the mass of the people are placed. There is the continuing drudgery of so-called 'work' that must go on for the system demands it, even under deteriorating conditions of which everyone, including those who drudge, is aware, though perhaps not always so consciously aware. There is, second, the capacity of the ruling class to divide the labouring classes and the people generally—to break their strikes, to bring in outsiders and count on scab labour, to be certain that when one set of people walks out or protests, another will walk in or in any case incapacitate the protesters, to know that scarcity and poverty are the best conditions for demobilization (rather than of mobilization, as radical theory would have it). In rural areas and tribal belts even these methods are unnecessary; the feudal order in league with the centralized bourgeois state ensures the full success of the exploitative chain—all the way up and all the way down. The masses 'survive' precisely by surrendering. And there is, third, beyond the drudgery and the divisions and the chain of exploitation, a deep and pervasive conditioning of the mind of the masses by the powerful impact of modern communications media on the one hand and the deep schism and scare caused by fundamentalist drives on the other hand. The unfortunate fact is that the masses are more duped by both than the dominant classes, having little information on which to base a more discerning structure of appraisal and choice. The moot point, of course, is that such conditioning perpetuates the other characteristics of mass behaviour—from continuing drudgery to systemic exploitation.

And yet we know that the masses are on the march—despite the drudgery, the exploitation and the conditioning. There is a great spurt in consciousness, in willingness to challenge hegemonies and unearned privilege, to protest against injustice, to mobilize horizontally to deal with oppression of a vertical kind. There is no doubt that all this is there, and growing. What is it then that prevents this from crystallizing into an effective counter-force against dead drudgery, inhuman exploitation and involuntary conditions?

Here we come to the crux of the problem. The masses in the post-colonial world are unorganized, they lack politicization, they are unable to withstand cooption and conditioning despite constant struggle and growing consciousness. The poor, the minorities, those outside the stream of the main civil society—the tribal and forest peoples, large segments of the women—all suffer from this state of deep disorganization. This is largely because the typical avenues for mass mobilization and redress of disabilities and deprivation have given way before larger forces, or rather forces that are seductive and in a way corrupting. I have particularly in mind political parties on the one hand and trade unions on the other, two conventional channels and modes of mobilization and struggle. Unfortunately—and this observation applies almost across the board—political parties (not just ruling parties) have been so taken in by the compulsions of the electoral process that they have lost their capacity to serve the masses, in particular the more destitute and backward among them. As regards the trade unions, there has taken place a near collapse of the unions as catalyst of a working-class consciousness and a working-class movement. Even the press and the judiciary are found to fail in their appointed tasks; they too are found to be corrupted by the crumbs of 'development' on the one hand and the miasma of a national security and corrosive fundamentalism on the other. The masses are on the rise but the institutional channels through which they ought to have found expression and which were to provide a springboard of radical action are found to be wanting, coopted and corrupted.

It is in this state of vacuum in the traditional superstructure of the liberal polity, a superstructure that was supposed to render it humane despite powerful trends, that the real counter-trends are to be found—not in the party system, not in the arena of electoral politics and of state power, not in the typical confrontation between the so-called haves and have-nots within the conventional economic space dominated by trade unions. In their place there is emerging a new arena of counter-action, of countervailing tendencies, of counter-cultural movements and more generally of a challenge to existing models of thought and action.

It is necessary to understand the nature of this challenge. It is in many ways new and even unintended in the sense of some well-thought-out grand design. It is composed of a series of obvious and inevitable strands, of struggles against existing hegemonies, of organized resistance, of mainstream protest, of civil liberties and democratic rights. But it is much more than this. It is an effort to redefine the scope and the range of politics. It is an effort to open up new spaces in both the arena of the state and in several other spheres of civil society outside it. And it is based on new spurts in consciousness—beyond economism, beyond confined definitions of the political process, beyond the facile (and false) dichotomy of state versus market, beyond both dehumanizing religiosity and dehumanizing modernity, discovering new indigenous roots and sustenance and strength, based not so much on either the fractured old or the mediocre and insipid new as on genuine possibilities of alternatives that can in fact work. In generating these twin processes of 'conscientization' and engaging in actual struggles as well as in searching for new alternatives, there has emerged a whole new class of people known as activists, essentially drawn from the conscious and enlightened and troubled streams of the middle class, engaged in a wide range of activities, from Sarvodaya-style 'constructive work' and NGO-type development projects to more struggle-oriented political work, but essentially settling in the latter mode of intervention. It is from this convergence of a conscious and restless people and a conscientious and equally restless class of volunteer politicians (to be distinguished from professional party politicians) that the new grassroots movements are taking shape. It is a convergence that is making it possible to conceive of the thousands of micro struggles and experiments in some kind of a macro perspective.

It is from such a convergence of new grassroots politics and new grassroots thinking that new definitions of the scope and range of politics are surfacing, and around these redefinitions new social movements are emerging. The environment, the rights and the role of women, health, food and nutrition, education, shelter and housing, the dispensation of justice, communications and the dissemination of information, culture and lifestyle, the achievement of peace and disarmament—none of these were considered to be subject matter for politics, at any rate not for domestic politics, and certainly not for mass politics in which ordinary people were involved. This has now changed.

Ecology is something that can no longer be left to experts in ecology or in economic development, nor even to departments of environment, though the establishment of such departments is itself a new development, a concession to popular political pressure. Nor can ecological considerations be left to be sorted out in the future on the presumption that if development and technology erode the environment in the short run, this can be remedied in the long run. The environment is something to be preserved here and now; it cannot be left to the good intentions and pious declarations of governments but must become part of people's own concern, an organized concern at that, including agitation and movements to restrain the state and corporate interests from running amok and ruining the life chances of both present and even more of future generations, and indeed of non-human species and plants as well. Concern for nature and for reversing the rapacious approach to it that is inherent in modern science is becoming part of a political movement, both worldwide and within individual societies.

The same is the case with health, and with food and nutrition. These are matters that were hitherto left to specialists and experts and to ministries manned by them. Not any longer. It is increasingly being realized that the hazards to health, the new epidemics that are breaking out, the horrors created by modern drugs are in good part products precisely of the experts, the doctors, the medical profession and the multi-billion-dollar global drug industry in which millions are spent on the much-boasted-of research and development. They are also products of the kind of development that has been let loose on trusting people, of technology and the environmental hazards created by it. Modern civilization has created a whole new spectrum of diseases known as diseases of civilization, which in turn has produced a whole industry of specialists who are nowhere near curing either cancer or mental disorders, and will never be able to. All this is being confronted by various strands of the alternatives movement.

The same is the case with the access and entitlement to food, to minimum nutrition, to shelter and housing. These are among the most serious problems in distributive politics and the clearest refutation of the logic of development based on accumulation and production, with distribution to be taken care of at a later stage. Implied in this logic was also a view that treated people as beneficiaries of the process of development, not direct participants in it, thus without any real control over how things would go. And things have indeed gone awry. This is now being realized. The faith in the 'green' and 'white' revolutions, in the revolution in materials technology and in so-called cheap housing has been shattered with the realization of growing hunger and malnutrition and millions living in slums and on pavements, to be driven out and bulldozed from there too. It is realized that these are matters of empowerment and rights for which people will themselves have to fight. And that too not just at the level of securing more of the same goods but of devising alternative ways of attending to these needs, more often than not by the people themselves. The same is the case with lack of access to education, which is so clearly related to being underprivileged. Something that was supposed to be an instrument of liberation has turned out to be one of subjugation. Education cannot be left to the mercy of the so-called educationists. The whole perspective, applicable to many areas, about de-expertizing and de-bureaucratizing the provision of basic needs is seeping into the grassroots political process and generating a new agenda of concerns for it.

Even such presumably learned and technical matters as the dispensation of justice on the one hand and the communication of information on the other are being subjected not just to greater public gaze but to a large degree of direct involvement. Both the rise of public interest litigation and the growth of investigative journalism, in both of which human rights activists are getting deeply involved and which are together generating a substantial movement for civil liberties and democratic rights, provide ample testimony to my point about the politicization of issues that were hitherto considered beyond the pale of politics, especially of mass politics.

Nowhere is the enlargement and redefinition of the scope of politics brought out as vividly and dramatically as in what are called the women's movements and what I would prefer to think of as a feminist input into our whole thinking on politics. It is not just that the scope of politics has been enlarged by bringing into its ambit what was till recently considered a personal and private world. From the view that personal and political are polar opposites to the one that the personal is political and the political is personal is a massive shift not in just the position of women in politics but also in our whole understanding of politics itself. Also, in the process of this shift, new approaches and methods to deal with basic problems like the environment, health, drunkenness, sanitation and the choice of technology are gradually being evolved—and not just by women, by men too, for there is no necessarily exclusive overlap between feminism and womanhood. Above all, an unprecedented convergence is emerging—between the environment and feminist movements and between them both and the peace movement. This has already happened in Europe with the spectacular spread of the peace movement, with the affirmation that peace and disarmament are too important to be left to governments who, left to themselves, will in all likelihood blow up the world; in this movement women have played a major role. This convergence is yet to happen in our parts of the world, given the powerful hold of theories of threat from within and without. But it will happen here too; we just cannot afford to be prisoners of the arms race, and women will have to play a major role in changing this. But the more important point is one about the interrelationship of dimensions and movements, of a holistic approach to life, which goes against the grain of the modern scientific culture with its emphasis on specialization and fragmentation. As women come out of their presently narrow approach of catching up with men, and the more generalized that feminist values become, the faster a holistic approach will develop, a holistic approach that is also plural and based on complementarities. This is more likely to happen in the non-Western world than in the West.

This is all too brief a discussion of the grassroots orientation of mass politics—a vast terrain that is just opening up and still being shaped—but it does suggest one thing: the universe that mass politics seeks to build would be much more worth living in than the universe that the dominant tendencies seem to be building. The basic question is: can all this activity, all these movements produce a macro challenge, a general transformation (whether one calls it a revolution or not)? The analysis and prognosis of this chapter says that this cannot be achieved through the conventional channels of political parties, trade union activity, peasant organizations and capture of state power through electoral mobilizations. For this task we need new building blocks. Partly, a macro transformation will come through the non-party political process, partly through counter-cultural and alternative movements that are global in scope, and partly through 'nationality' types of movements for regional autonomy and for texturing a pluralist social order supported by a decentralized political order. It is a political convergence of class, culture, gender and environment that I have in mind on the basis of emerging counter-trends. These are possibilities that have not yet acquired high probability but which alone, it seems to me, can enable us to put an end to the 'two worlds' scenario based on a technocratic and militarized vision that we are fast moving towards. And all this change would of course happen in close alliance with the more economic forms of struggle for fair wages and dignity in treatment of the so-called lower rungs of society, the backward, the untouchables and the bonded, and of the social peripheries, the tribal people, the forest people and the aboriginals.

Let me end this chapter by saying that I do not conceive of the non-party political process as in any way hostile to the party political process. On the contrary, it is partly in order to revitalize the party political arena, partly to correct its inadequacies, but most of all to provide a constant grassroots infrastructural input, not just to act as watchdogs but also to intervene whenever necessary and, above all, to permit direct involvement of the people in both the non-party and the party political spheres that the whole conception of an autonomous grassroots politics (instead of one where grassroots politics is a derivative of elite politics) has been developed. Autonomous grassroots politics is not in any way opposed to or even deflecting from the party political process as is alleged by some party leaders jealous to occupy the entire political space and particularly suspicious of autonomous formations.

Where this conception of grassroots politics is new is that for it state power is not seen as the only or even predominant object of politics. It sees an equal and perhaps even greater necessity to keep struggling against injustices that are bound to occur no matter which party or coalition of parties is in power, experimenting with new modes of organizing social, economic and technological matters, insisting on norms in politics and keeping intellectual ferment alive so that the state-based politics do not become an orthodoxy. It believes that it is not enough to provide participation in the system, even if this could be made less formal and more substantial. The aim is also to create a just society. Participation is necessary but not sufficient for this to happen. For that what is needed is self-government, a decentralized order through which the masses are empowered, not decentralization in the sense of some territorial scheme of devolution of functions and resources to lower levels but decentralization in which the people are the centre. It is towards this end that the various social movements of the type discussed by me in this paper have a role to play, alongside, of course, the typical working class and peasant movements, in short a coalition of social movements and mass struggle. One without the other cannot bring about the necessary transformation.

There is, moreover, a socio-demographic reason why such a direct and dynamic role of mass politics of the grassroots variety becomes necessary, quite apart from being desirable. In a predominantly rural society with great diversity, party formations like the various social-democratic or labour parties that emerged in Western Europe and heralded the dawn of a mass age are not likely to emerge. We also know that without such formations and the pressure they generated, the phenomenon of the modern welfare state also would not have taken place. So on both these counts—the role of parties on the one hand and of the state on the other—we need to think wholly afresh, for ourselves, and transcending all that we imported which we had to, to begin with. And as we do this we will see that there is no alternative except to move towards a pluralist, decentralized polity with a humane technology and a relatively self-reliant economy, self-reliant for the people and not just for the state as has been the conceptualization of self-reliance till recently. The point is that in our kind of a context a just society cannot be built except by the people coming into their own and assuming responsibility for shaping their lives. We just cannot afford to hand over things to experts. This may be possible in centralized and homogeneous societies like the Western ones. To follow the same model here is of necessity to create dual societies with large masses left out of citizenship, left out really of civilisation.

Fundamentally, the vision that informs the grassroots model of mass politics (as against the parliamentary or presidential or party model of mass politics) is one in which the people are more important than the state. This is crucial and it is not as simple as it sounds. In fact, in the times we are living in, it is a revolutionary idea. The dominant tendency and mode of thought today is to place the state above the people, the security of the nation state above people's security, the removal of real or imaginary threats to the state more important than persisting threats to the people and their survival. On the other hand, to restore to the people their sovereignty is not to undermine the role of the state but to transform it.

This is to be achieved in four simple ways. The transformation of the state is to be achieved through the transformation of civil society, not the other way around, as formerly, in which the state was to be the author of social transformation: that was a real mismanagement of the processes and pitfalls of secular power. Second, the role of the centralized state must decline. It will be very much there—some functions will have to be carried out by a centralized apparatus—but it is basically to operate in concert with other centres as well as other institutional spaces in civil society. Third, the state should be enabled to regain its autonomy from dominant interests and classes; it should be made to gradually wither away as an instrument of class and ethnic oppression but enabled to survive, and survive effectively, as a mediator in the conflicts and stresses that will continue to take place in civil society. And, fourth, we will need to move beyond the nation state syndrome of statehood, in particular to move beyond the national security state syndrome which has been the source of both authoritarianism and hegemonism in our time. In any case, so long as the national security state rules the roost, the masses cannot and will not come into their own.

4. Social Movements at the Periphery

Samir Amin

The forms through which social movements express themselves have entered a phase of review. The outcome is largely unknown. This review appears to be universal, encompassing the West, the East and the South.

For a century or more we had become accustomed to particular forms of organization of the various currents running through society. In the developed capitalist societies this organization was articulated around two main themes. The first, the theme of class struggle, provided the rationale for the organization of the industrial working class (trade unions, labour, socialist and communist parties), the model of which sometimes inspired other popular classes (peasant or agrarian parties and unions, small business parties, etc.). The second, the theme of political ideology, justified the contrast between conservative right and reformist left. The 'communist' governments came out of this history, whose forms they retained, even though gradually putting an official end to the 'class struggle' by the party–state monopoly and changes through the ballot box had distorted its meaning.

In Africa and Asia, the history of the past century had been that of the polarization of the social movements around the struggle for national independence. Here the model was that of the unifying party, setting itself the objective of bringing together social classes and various communities in a vast movement that was disciplined (often behind more or less charismatic leaders) and effective in its action towards a single goal. The governments that emerged after independence became broadly fixed in this heritage, the single-party state deriving its legitimacy solely from the achievement of the goal of national independence.

Today, in the three parts of the world—West, East and South—the models of managing social life embedded in these organizational forms seem to have exhausted their historical effectiveness. This is most dramatically obvious in Eastern Europe and the former Soviet Union, but the crisis extends, albeit in different forms, to West and South as well.

In the West, the consensus is so broad that it has reduced the historical impact of the socialist movement and the right–left polarization, and is manifested today in a sort of 'depoliticization', that is, an abandonment of any ideological interest in a different global societal project. In the East, civil society has broken the straitjacket of the party state and, in doing so, has opened up a space for the real contradictions running through society to become visible. In the Third World, legitimacy based on having recovered independence is well and truly superseded in the eyes of the younger generation.

In these conditions, should we be surprised that the expression of unsatisfied social needs organizes itself in other ways? These new forms have already appeared: feminist movements, ecological movements, movements to defend local communities, ethnic and religious movements. Their rationalization in terms of great ideologies is perhaps still embryonic, but some of its outlines can already be made out, appealing to concepts which, if not truly new, have at least hitherto not really been spelled out (like ecology or the critique of sexism) or quite simply to the heritage of the past overlain by the 'modern' world (the religious revival and notably that of fundamentalist trends across various religions are to be explained by this need).

The general economic growth of the quarter-century that followed the Second World War not surprisingly created many illusions. In the West, people thought that they had found in Keynesianism the definitive solution to the problem of periodic economic crises and unemployment. They thought that the world had entered on an era of perpetual prosperity and definitive mastery of the business cycle. In the socialist world, it was also thought that a model formula for even higher growth had been discovered. This enabled Khrushchev to boast that by 1980 the USSR would have overtaken the United States 'in every domain'.

In the world of Africa and Asia, the national liberation movement that had seized political independence also had its battery of prescriptions which, in a mix of capitalist and socialist recipes, in doses that varied from case to case, would enable it to overcome 'underdevelopment' in 'interdependence' with the rest of the world economy (that is, without delinking in the sense that I have defined this term[1]). In Latin America the thesis of 'modernization' (in the form known as '*desarollismo*') fulfilled the same functions. The world economic order could as a result, it was thought, gradually be modified in favour of the Third World.

What was actually achieved was more modest than is often believed. Along with the 'miraculous' growth of the countries of Western Europe and Japan, the decline of Britain continued while the ideological malaise of the consumer societies developed apace. The denunciation of Stalinism in Eastern Europe and the USSR was not followed by the expected leap forward. In the Third World the social effects that accompanied development were often negative (growing inequality in income distribution, rural and urban marginalization, etc.). The rediscovery of 'external limits' to growth (in the shape of the globe's limited natural resources) was also a reminder of the fragility of the optimistic perspectives of the 1950s and 1960s.

In any event, the global crisis that began at the beginning of the 1970s (thus some twenty years ago) has put an end to these illusions. Does this crisis offer a new chance of reviewing the dominant ideas of the post-war years or is it just one more constraint?

New social movements: prospects for the future

Are the new forms of social expression the seeds of a future that will be very different from our contemporary world? Or are they simply the bubbles produced by the boiling up of a passing crisis that will burst and vanish when everything is restored to normal?

If the first view proves correct, will the development of new (or, when they build on old heritages, renewed) forms of expression make possible an advance for humanity, or on the contrary will it be the manifestation of a new collapse into barbarism?

Malraux, with his well-known intelligence and pessimism, said that the twenty-first century would be the century of religions, meaning thereby not a revival of tolerant faith but the violent conflicts of fanaticism. During the 1930s and 1940s Nazi barbarism had already caused it to be said that our epoch was one of intolerance, but the defeat of fascism had reawakened hopes: the nightmare was over, it had simply been a minor hiccup along the way.

I certainly share the view expressed by Immanuel Wallerstein that the 'old organizations' (trade unions, popular and labour parties, national liberation movements) were struggling to seize power from the monopolies of bourgeois classes and foreign imperialists. And they did indeed secure, in varying degrees—through reform or revolution, negotiation or war—much of what they strove for, even if it was not 'all': the welfare state, economic development and political power, national dignity, etc.

In this view, these movements, which were formerly anti-systemic in so far as they conflicted with the actually existing system, have today been coopted and are now systemic in the sense that they have become relatively conservative forces which are not very keen on anyone wanting to go beyond their achievements and, above all, to move forward without them.

Actually existing capitalism as a world system

My thoughts on the social movements in the Third World are organized around the following three themes:

1. The nature of 'actually existing capitalism', which is defined as a globalized system that reproduces and deepens polarization worldwide. The nature of the issues that emanate from this polarization is twofold: are we to see compradorization of the Third World or popular national power in the Third World?
2. The manner in which the 'old' national liberation movements responded to the historical challenge of unequal capitalist development, its historical limits and its contemporary crisis.
3. The nature of recent developments in the system and their prospects. Do these developments call into question, and to what extent, the issues in the conflict? Do contemporary social movements respond to these developments?

There are two ways of looking at the dominant social reality of our world, namely capitalism. The first stresses the fundamental relationship that defines the capitalist mode of production at its most abstract level, and from there focuses on the allegedly fundamental class struggle between the proletariat, in the narrowest sense of the term, and the bourgeoisie. The second stresses the other dimension of capitalist reality, its unequal development worldwide, and hence focuses its analysis on the consequences that polarization involves at every level, thus defining other issues in the political and social struggles that occupy the forefront of the historical stage. Here I opt for this second way of seeing what I call actually existing capitalism.

My analysis of the nature of the issues raised by social movements thus rests on two premisses: the unequal development of capitalism (an analytical thesis) and the need for delinking (a political strategy logically deduced from the first thesis).

By unequal development I mean something quite different from the banality of appearances (the ranking of per capita incomes and levels of industrialization). I mean that the capitalist system harbours within it an immanent tendency—operating from the very beginning—towards polarization into centres and peripheries; that this polarization has postponed the question of the eventual socialist transformation in the developed capitalist societies while in the periphery it has objectively required envisaging a 'different development' from the one that results—in these conditions—from the periphery's integration into the world capitalist system.

The object of this study is not to give the arguments—which I have developed elsewhere—that underpin these theses. Here I shall simply recall the conclusions necessary for understanding the analyses proposed below relating to the scope of the new social movements.

In this analytical framework, the development of the periphery has always been the history of a never-ending 'adjustment' to the demands and constraints of dominant capital. The centres 'restructure' themselves, the peripheries 'are adjusted' to these restructurings. Never the opposite.

But the violent effects of these successive adjustments are not equal in all phases in the history of capitalism. For its global expansion takes the form of a succession of long cycles (twenty to fifty years) in which phases of prosperity and accelerated growth alternate with phases of structural crisis of the global system. In phases of prosperity, adjustment seems less difficult, sometimes even easy for some countries: the demand for exports grows at high rates, capital is available, conflicts are attenuated (the period is often a prolonged period of peace, or at least relative peace), etc. This adjustment in general growth is of course unequal.

The periphery fulfils a variety of functions in the global system and this means that in fact there are several peripheries rather than a single periphery. There are 'rich' peripheries, important for the system at the stage we are looking at, which provide products whose worldwide marketing is today growing more strongly than others (because they are associated with the technological advances that provide the engine of growth) and which offer significant markets to the capital and products of the centre. The ease of their apparent adjustment then fuels many illusions, including the possibility of catching up and forming new 'centres'. The problematic of 'semi-peripheries', which we shall look at below, belongs in this context.

But there are also the write-offs, those areas of the world which in their present shape are of no importance to the structures of the system. These areas have sometimes fulfilled important functions at an earlier stage in the evolution of the global system, but have now lost their position. They now constitute the 'fourth world', delinked willy-nilly and passively suffering the fate that the system assigns them. But the 'fourth world', which is talked of as something new, is in reality a permanent product of capitalist expansion.

A fine but sad example of this old 'fourth world' is provided by the regions of slave exploitation in the Americas in the mercantilist period: the north-east of Brazil and the West Indies (Haiti among others). In that period these regions were considered prosperous and they constituted the heart of the periphery corresponding to the capitalist system of the time. Subsequently the new structures of capitalist development marginalized these regions, which today count among the most tragically impoverished of the Third World.

The history of capitalist expansion is, therefore, not only that of the so-called development that it has occasioned. It is also that of the savage destructions of societies and regions on which it was built. There is a destructive aspect in capitalism that is usually glossed over in the positive image presented of this system. Today a large part of Africa, truly part of the 'fourth world', suffers this type of marginalization, while the 'semi-industrialized' countries, contrary to popular belief, are not on the path to becoming new centres but precisely the real peripheries of today and tomorrow.

Recompradorization

The phases of serious restructuring through crisis constitute moments of truth in the evolution of the system. Illusions are broken. Difficulties—the danger of which had hitherto been denied—become the means by which the dominant capital imposes its *diktat*. Any fantasy of independence disappears. The law of profit reminds the 'underdeveloped' of the fate reserved for them: over-exploitation and subordination.

'Recompradorization' is now the order of the day—by any means, economic and financial (for example, today the pressure exercised through the external debt, the Uruguay Round of GATT negotiations and the food weapon) and political and military (*coups d'état* and interventions like that which Israel's presence in the Middle East represents).

Polarization within the world system is not the product of a sort of fate resulting from the implacable working of economic laws. The state fulfils central functions here. In the last analysis, the decisive criterion which makes it possible to classify the societies of the world capitalist system into centres and peripheries is that of the nature of their states.

The capitalist societies of the centre are characterized by the crystallization of a bourgeois nation state whose essential function (beyond the mere maintenance of the domination of capital) is to control the conditions of accumulation through the national control that it exercises over the reproduction of the labour force, the market, the centralization of the surplus, natural resources and technology.

Here the state fulfils the conditions that make possible what I have suggested calling 'autocentred accumulation', namely, the subordination of external (usually aggressive) relations to the logic of this accumulation. The bourgeois nation state is here an active actor modulating the evolution of the world system.

Conversely, the peripheral state (which like any state fulfils the function of maintaining internal class domination) does not control local accumulation. It is—objectively—the instrument of the 'adjustment' of the local society to the demands of worldwide accumulation, and how it evolves is mainly determined by how the centre evolves. Here, the state is by nature comprador.

This difference makes it possible to understand why the state in the centre is a strong state (and when it becomes democratic in the bourgeois sense of the word, that constitutes a further expression of that strength), while the peripheral state is a weak state (and that is why, *inter alia*, access to genuine bourgeois democratization is practically closed to it).

With regard to actually existing capitalism I shall make the following four comments.

First: the various social classes that constitute our present-day globalized capitalist society have their place on the world level, even though, in other respects, they belong to the logic of the various national formations. The bulk of the reserve army of labour available for capital is located geographically in the peripheries of the system. This reserve army is made up, of course, not only of what has become an enormous mass of urban unemployed and semi-employed (many times the number of jobless in the West even in times of crisis), but also of large numbers of unwaged workers, doomed, in line with advances in these areas of activity, to be driven off their land or out of the urban so-called informal activities that they are engaged in. Furthermore, liberalism has never managed to complete its programme of liberalizing trade and capital flows by a parallel and unfettered free movement of labour (by means of migration). It thus remains truncated. This reality dominates the scene of social struggles. The revolt of the 'victim' peoples in the context of the ongoing expansion of capitalism dominates world attention. The concept of 'people' here comprises the historical bloc of the oppressed, made up of both distinctly constituted classes and the reserve army I have been discussing.

Second: it is possible to recognize, in the long term, periods that are particularly marked by the functioning of an integrated world market and other periods marked by the break-up of that market. Arrighi has suggested a very convincing picture of this. I would add that these successive break-ups of the unity of the world system are the fruit, not of chance, but of necessity. For the unity at issue has never involved homogenization but rather the deepening of polarization precisely as a result of the always truncated, and hence inconsistent, character of the liberalism which constitutes its ideological legitimation. It is thus particularly intolerable for the peoples of the peripheries. No wonder that it is always being called into question. These challenges litter history with violent happenings even in periods when the unity of the system has predominated. At certain times they come together into a set of storms which account for the periods of global break-up of the system.

Third: this polarization does not look like a pyramid, in which semi-peripheries occupy intermediate places between peripheries and centres. The driving contradiction here is that which contrasts centres and so-called semi-peripheries (the true periphery in my view), while the 'fourth worlds' are cast away from the chief axis of capitalist expansion.

Fourth: at the level of ideology, politics and forms of social action, the system involved (actual capitalism) has been through a long prehistory—premodern times, from the Renaissance to the French Revolution—before entering on its modern history. With Wallerstein I attribute a qualitative importance to the break inaugurated by the French Revolution. This is because that revolution substituted for the old religious legitimization peculiar to what I have called the tributary ideologies a system of secular legitimacy for political and social action, and, in that sense, inaugurated many subsequent developments, both those of bourgeois democracy and those of socialism. The 1871 Paris Commune's slogan ('Neither God, Nor Caesar, Nor Tribune') is not accidental; it flows from—and extends farther—that of 1789 ('Liberty, Equality, Fraternity').

This creation as a result of polarization of the contrast between centres and peripheries is immanent in capitalism as it really operates. This conclusion calls into question the optimistic vision according to which capitalism is capable, by virtue of its dynamism, of 'homogenizing' the world, that is, of overcoming 'underdevelopment'. The thesis of unequal development involves fundamental consequences in identifying what questions are truly on the agenda of necessary and possible political changes in the contemporary world and consequently on the agenda of the social movement.

This thesis defines the system not only by its capitalist label (this label is obviously correct, but insufficient), but also by the inequality and polarizations inherent in capitalist expansion. Consequently, anti-systemic forces and movements are those that call into question this inequality, refuse to submit to its consequences and on this ground embark on a battle that is, as a result, objectively anti-capitalist, because it attacks that immanent nature of capitalist expansion.

All the major questions of our times—questions about the 'socialist transition' (in the East), the stability of the societies of central capitalism (the West) and the crisis of peripheral capitalist societies and the 'fourth world' (the South), must be situated in this framework.

Socialist transition or popular national reconstruction?

A challenging of the capitalist order from revolts in its periphery obliges us to rethink seriously the question of a socialist transition involving a move towards the abolition of classes. However many nuances are made, the Marxist tradition remains handicapped by its initial theoretical vision of workers' revolutions opening up, on the basis of advanced productive forces, a transition which is itself relatively rapid.

This transition is moreover seen by Marxism as being marked by democratic rule by the popular masses which, while it is still described as 'dictatorship over the bourgeoisie' (by means of a proletarian state of a new type which will rapidly begin to 'wither away'), is still considerably more democratic than the most democratic of bourgeois states.

Nevertheless, all the revolutions of our time (Russia, China, Vietnam, Cuba, Yugoslavia, etc.) that are unfailingly described as socialist (and which, in the intention of their actors did indeed set themselves the goal of socialism) are in reality anti-capitalist revolutions of a rather complicated character because they have been made in backward regions.

As a result, they have not inaugurated an era of 'socialist construction' that meets the criteria initially developed by Marxism. In the same way, and for the same reason, other attempts to 'move forward' initiated here and there in the capitalist Third World, based on the radicalization of the national liberation movement, may also describe themselves as socialist but scarcely meet the classic criteria of socialism.

In these conditions, history requires that we analyse the nature and perspective of the social issues 'beyond capitalism' initiated by the anti-capitalist revolutions in the peripheries and the radicalization of national liberation movements. To do so, it is necessary to go beyond ideological discourse whether of legitimation (depending on the discourse, these are indeed socialist societies whose achievements are 'globally positive', despite errors which are human) or of polemics (according to which discourse, these are 'deviations' from a theoretical socialist model that people have in their heads and is assumed to be possible). There are two other ways of proceeding intellectually.

The most common line of argument today is that these revolutions have in fact opened up an era of *capitalist* development pure and simple (and hence have in no way opened up an evolution 'beyond capitalism'), even if these societies are in (temporary) conflict with the dominant centres of world capitalism, and have, as is always the case, some specific features.

According to this thesis, in the last analysis, the prior passage through a phase of capitalist accumulation is inevitable. But is this not simply seeing only one aspect of the problem? For on the one hand, the bourgeois revolution is not essentially the product of a movement of the popular masses organized and led by political parties overtly anti-capitalist in their ideologies and vision of the future. On the other hand, capitalist expansion was and continues to be globalized, that is, it involves local developments open to the world system. Accepted by the local bourgeoisie broadly defined, this type of subordinate development is challenged by the popular masses whom it is crushing in the periphery.

The other line of argument, mine, is built around the observation that the unequal development immanent in capitalist expansion has placed on the agenda of history another type of revolution, that of the peoples (i.e. not specific classes) of the periphery. This revolution is anti-capitalist in the sense that it is against capitalist development as it actually exists because it is intolerable for these peoples. But that does not mean that these anti-capitalist revolutions are socialist.

By force of circumstances, they have a complex nature. The expression of their specific and new contradictions, which was not imagined in the classical perspective of the socialist transition as conceived by Marx, gives post-capitalist regimes their real content, which is that of a *popular national construction* in which the three tendencies of socialism, capitalism and statism combine and conflict.

For these societies are faced with the task of substantially developing the productive forces in order to meet their people's demands. But to do this, the technologies developed by capitalism are required; indeed there are no serious alternatives. And if one believes, as we do, that technologies are not neutral, it goes without saying that the development of the productive forces obtained on the basis of them implies certain forms of labour organization (and hence relations of production) that are at least partly analogous to those of capitalism.

That is indeed Marx's posthumous revenge and the message of Marxism: it will only be possible to build the classless society when the conditions of a sufficient development of the productive forces have been brought together. If nevertheless there are social tendencies that express a critique of the capitalist perspective, that is, living socialist forces in society, their existence must be located both at the level of the worker base and that of the organization of state power and the ideology that inspires it.

The sceptics will say that these forces are apparently weak at the base. Governments, moreover refuse them the means of expressing themselves, let alone letting them actually change reality. These governments, largely secretive and autocratic, manipulate the slogans of socialism and turn Marxism—perfectly instrumentalized—into an ideology legitimizing themselves as regimes.

Such a judgement, however, is one-sided precisely because it passes over without comment the popular national content of the regimes in question, that is, the relationship between the new government and the popular classes who have overthrown the capitalist order. This relationship is not the fruit of a passing conjuncture, that of just the moment of the revolution.

Naturally, in some bourgeois revolutions, too, the people were indeed mobilized against the old regime, but then under the undisputed leadership of a class—the bourgeoisie—already constituted and strong. In these conditions, the bourgeoisie effectively monopolized—and very quickly—control over the new government. On the other hand, in the anti-capitalist revolutions, the 'new class', for want of a better term, does not exist prior to the popular movement; it is rather a product of it.

To the extent that this new class attempts to crystallize into an autonomous force vis-à-vis the people, it operates precisely through the means of control of the state (whence statism). This crystallization thus works through a complex relationship—at once alliance and conflict—between the new class and the people.

At the same time, capitalist forces—in the ordinary sense of the word—continue to operate in these post-revolutionary societies, for the reason mentioned that the necessary development of the productive forces requires capitalism's permanent emergence. It is thus not a simple matter of 'vestiges of the past'.

Moreover, the opening up of a space for commodity relations—for small-scale production entrusted to capitalist enterprise, to which government is almost always spontaneously hostile but which often ends up having to accept—shows, almost unfailingly, its efficiency in the shape of a rapid improvement of production and living standards, and thereby achieves its popularity.

Why then this apparent superiority of capitalist forms over those of the state economy? I shall suggest an answer which turns the question round, and I shall thus ask it in the following terms: why the apparent inferiority of the state economy? My reply is based on the observation that the bourgeoisie remains in fact quite well organized, despite the blows it has received during the popular national revolution. It thus knows how to turn rapidly to account any opportunity that comes its way.

Conversely, the popular classes were only organized occasionally and in the popular national revolution. Subsequently, the government actually works to reduce their autonomy. They are thus ill-prepared to counter and argue for their own project effectively.

Here we come up face to face with the question of democracy. For the problems facing these post-revolutionary societies can only be overcome by a democratic development. This is so because democracy is an unavoidable condition, necessary in order to ensure the efficiency of a socialist social system. That is not the case with capitalism: here democracy only functions when its potentialities are emasculated by the 'majority consensus' produced by exploitation of dominant central positions in the capitalist system.

Conversely, social relations based on the cooperation of workers, and not on their subordination with a view to their exploitation, are unthinkable without the complete expression of democracy. Will the few remaining countries of 'actually existing socialism', as they are called, reach this stage? Or will they trap themselves in the impasse of rejecting it? That is an essential issue in modern social struggles, the answer to which looked increasingly clear by the early 1990s.

It is precisely here in these societies that we once again encounter the basic question of 'internal factors': here, and not in the capitalist peripheries where the autonomy of the internal factor, while it of course explains past history (peripheralization), today is very greatly attenuated by the weight of 'external' constraints. Conversely, in the popular national states, the internal factor has again become decisive. In this sense, it is being rediscovered that there is no historical inevitability. By 'internal factor', I mean of course the dialectic of the threefold contradiction mentioned above.

Governments often look upon democracy as a concession, to which it yields only if forced to. For these post-revolutionary governments also express the ambitions of the new class. That raises the question of statism and power fetishism. But does it mean that the anti-statist ideology that is currently riding high answers this question?

Not at all, since the state here fulfils specific functions different from those it fulfils in the capitalist centres and peripheries. It is the means of national protection and self-assertion, that is, the instrument of what we have called delinking, in the sense of the subordination of external relations to the logic of an internal development (which is not simply capitalist). It is the axis of the (conflict-laden) articulation of relations between the three tendencies identified.

Peripheral capitalist development, which is intrinsically extroverted (in the sense of being oriented to and dependent on the external world), breaks down the nations that are victims of it, while conversely capitalist crystallization in the centres of the system has given the nations composing it their modern content. Weakening of the nation as a collective actor really participating in shaping the modern world and economic peripheralization necessarily go together.

As a result, the rejection of peripheralization by the people who are its victims—their anti-capitalist revolution—necessarily assumes a national or even a nationalist dimension. The delinking that is required as a framework for an effective strategy of reconstruction reveals and accentuates this dimension. This national dimension is progressive since it expresses a basic demand for the abolition of inequality between peoples, inequality which is accentuated, reproduced and deepened by the very expansion of capitalism.

Whatever the value judgements based on the concepts of humanism, class liberation and internationalism that progressive bourgeois thought and later Marxism have forged, the fundamentally progressive character of national liberation and the national content of the post-capitalist popular society remains, in our opinion, undeniable. Of course, nationalism contains problems and includes its negative aspects, just as it will eventually experience its historical limits, like every stage of human history. But national liberation still remains an inescapable demand.

This attraction that the nation state model exercises on the ruling strata is not altogether negligible. Considerations of 'efficiency' (accepted too uncritically) might be the vehicles for a re-linking after the temporary delinking. The stress would then be transferred ever farther in the direction of making efficiency and international competitiveness synonymous, as is the rule in the West.

I still, however, suggest terming 'popular national' the post-capitalist societies we are discussing, which are engaged in a long historical phase whose task is essentially to erase the heritage of unequal development (knowing that that cannot be done by playing the game of 'adjustment' within the world system, but on the contrary can only be achieved by deciding to delink). I also suggest abandoning the ideological labels 'socialist societies' (they are not) or even 'societies engaged in the construction of socialism'.

Turning to the capitalist Third World countries, the problems they are facing following their political liberation are no different, except that the ambiguity of their strategies is even more marked than with post-revolutionary societies as a result of the fact that, even where the independence struggle was radicalized, the option in favour of a popular content and delinking is held back by bourgeois aspirations and illusions in the project that they nurture. Why, then, has most of the Third World not—or not yet—embarked on this path, the path of the construction of a popular national state?

If I had to label these two series of experiences, I should simply say that the socialist revolutions are popular national revolutions that looked as though they had attained their objective through a delinking based on a non-bourgeois power, while the national liberation movements, because they have remained under bourgeois leadership, have not yet realized that objective.

So, new popular national revoltuions are among the objective requirements in the contemporary Third World. Doubtless these revolutions will be no more socialist than the previous ones, but only popular national. No doubt, too, they will have their own new specificities determined both by internal conditions and external factors.

These popular national revolutions still to come may in turn modify possibly future North–South relations and constitute a fundamental dynamic element in the global evolution of our planet. What is at stake in these struggles that occupy the centre stage of modern history can thus be summed up in the alternative: the state embodying either popular national power or compradorized power.

Issues in popular social movements

Actually existing capitalism remains very much an obstacle to advances by peoples and there is no alternative to popular national transformation; but the transformations, initiated by the so-called socialist revolutions, have not exhausted the agenda of possible objectives.

That being the case it is difficult to say today whether the 'new' movements that are emerging in the periphery (like those of the centre indeed) are capable of responding to this objective challenge.

Some of these movements look to us like dead ends. This is the case with religious fundamentalist revivals or withdrawals into so-called ethnic communities. They are symptoms of the crisis, not solutions to it, and exclusively products of disillusionment. They will eventually lose steam as they reveal their powerlessness in the face of the real challenge. This view is, of course, the expression of an optimism which believes that reason must prevail!

Other movements, on the other hand, can find their place in the rebuilding of a societal project which, by going 'beyond capitalism', would resolve the contradictions that capitalism in reality cannot transcend, by learning the lessons from the first steps made in that direction. This is likely each time the 'new' movements (or the old ones!) take their stand not on the exclusive ground of 'conquering the state', but on that of a different conception of the social power to be conquered.

For the choice is not 'struggle for power or struggle for something else' (what else?), but what conception one has of the power for which one is struggling. The forms of organization built around the dominant, 'traditional' conception of power (power equals state) are doomed to lose a good part of their legitimacy as people come to appreciate the nature of this conservative state.

Conversely, the organization that stresses the many-sided social content of the power that has to be developed should experience growing successes. In this category, the theme of non-party politics might prove fruitful. The same is true of anti-authoritarianism in Latin America, which Pablo Casanova sees as the principal credential of the 'new' movements: rejection of authoritarianism in the state, in the party, in leadership, and rejection of doctrinaire expressions in ideology.

These are a reaction against the whole burdensome heritage of the historical formation of the continent, and doubtless a reaction that can be the harbinger of progress. But also, and for the same basic reason, feminism, through the objectives it sets of attacking at least some of the roots of autocracy, proceeds from the same logic of a different conception of social power.

In a way, the West is in the vanguard of new advances in the liberation of society. Whether these advances presuppose breakthroughs 'beyond capitalism' or are to be seen as remaining 'cooptable' ('recuperable') by that social system constitutes a new field of questioning. It seems that, in the medium term at least, the advantages of a central capitalist position are such that the movements in question will not shake the foundations of the capitalist management of society.

The future of the 'new' movements thus remains uncertain. That is why it cannot be ruled out that they may exhaust themselves in the present crisis.

Extrapolating the reflections set out by Frank and Fuentes, making explicit what is perhaps only implicit in what they write, it seems to me that the effectiveness of the social movement cannot be assessed by the same criteria in different periods. In periods of prosperity the movements easily adopt organized centralized forms. The reason for that is that they are functioning in a society where the rules of the game are known. They can then, depending on the conjuncture, effectively realize some of their objectives (a wage increase, for example). Conversely, periods of structural crisis are defined by uncertainty as to the rules of the game, and questionings without the 'new order' emerging from new international and internal balances, having still to crystallize.

Must the crisis of society not then necessarily involve that of ideologies, political practices and hence forms of organization? But is it not precisely in these periods that new ideological forces crystallize and the outlines of new social projects appear, which, to paraphrase a famous quotation, by seizing the imagination of the masses, become material forces?

The arguments developed above do not signify that the alternatives are either 'everything' (that is, delinking—which is moreover itself a relative concept and not absolutely synonymous with autarky)—or nothing (that is, recompradorization). Between the two extremes there is perhaps, but only perhaps, room for a 'mutual adjustment' (and not a unilateral one) in the context of a polycentric world. And it is worth struggling for that possibility.[2]

Unequal development engendered, reproduced and endlessly deepened by capitalist expansion, on the one hand, and the revolutions produced by the dramatic consequences of globalization in the periphery of the system, on the other hand, have shaped a world too diverse for a single recipe ('the market') to be acceptable. Critical thought should thus concern itself with looking for what might be the alternative social alliances likely to get out of the vicious circles imposed by the market.

From this angle the considerable differences between different regions of the world necessarily imply specific policies which cannot be derived simply from the rationality of the market. On top of these objective differences there are equally legitimate differences to do with culture and the ideological and political options arising from the diverse history of peoples.

The real imperatives of our time thus imply the reconstruction of the world system on the basis of polycentrism. But instead of seeing this in a political and strategic dimension merely composing the five Great Powers (the United States, the EC, Russia, China and Japan), replacing the military bipolarity of the two superpowers, it is vital to put forward a system which gives the countries and regions of the Third World their true place. Moreover, those countries and regions that can coordinate their visions must submit their mutual relations to the constraints of their *internal* development and not the other way around, that is, simply adjust their internal development to the global expansion of capitalism.

Could a mutual adjustment replace the one-sided adjustment proposed by the dominant liberal ideology? In a world threatened by the twin barbarism of an ever-worsening North–South contrast without hope for the peoples of the periphery (and that barbarism is already at work, if we see the true meaning of what amounts to the genocide of the peoples of the 'fourth world' now underway by means of famine; as it already is at work in the rise of racism), on the one hand, and the still continuing nuclear threat on the other, the idea of mutual adjustment ought to appear the most reasonable.

But it only has a chance if the objectives of the social movements in each of the three conventional parts of the world (West, East and South) begin to converge, which in turn implies progress towards an at least partly universalist culture (I shall return to this topic in the discussion of the cultural dimension of the problem before us).

I believe it necessary to state clearly, too, that this polycentric world in no way implies any weakening of states, as advocated by the now fashionable anti-statist ideology. On the contrary, an essential condition of what I propose is the strengthening of states—which in turn requires their democratization; without it capitalist globalization would inevitably impose compradorization on the weakest.

Finally, mutual adjustment, like delinking of which it is simply a particular aspect, implies a popular power that is anti-capitalist in the sense that it conflicts with the dominant capitalism but is driven by the numerous divergent interests (beyond their anti-systemic convergence) of the various fractions that make up the people concerned.

A social force is necessary to cement the popular alliance, overcome its internal conflicts, formulate an alternative popular national project, lead the popular bloc to enable it to achieve power, build the new state and arbitrate conflicts between the capitalist, socialist and statist tendencies that emerge in the long popular national transition. That is the proper role of the revolutionary intelligentsia, to which I shall also return.

The democratic dimension

In recent years, there has been a remarkable growth of the demand for democracy, both in the countries of the East and those of the South. This growth has been so great that some observers have concluded that the demand was now replacing demands for national liberation and socialism, whose final failure was said to have been consummated. The demand for democracy has indeed assumed proportions never before seen in the countries of the Third World: in many countries it has already won pride of place in the consciousness of the middle classes and is penetrating into the popular, especially urban, strata.

This phenomenon is new, since, until recently, the demand for democracy had remained limited to particular segments of the urban bourgeoisie and had only been expressed forcefully in the South at particular moments of radicalization of the anti-imperialist struggles (the case of the Egyptian Wafd is one of the best examples of this). Furthermore, this democratic consciousness was within the strict limits of bourgeois liberalism.

The key feature of the popular and radical movements for national liberation was more their progressive social content rather than the democratic conviction of the movements' militants, despite the use— sometimes ritualistic— of the term 'democracy' and despite the more advanced consciousness of some segments of the vanguard.

I do not think I am caricaturing reality in saying that the old peasant–soldier of the Chinese Liberation Army was thinking, as he entered Beijing in 1949, of agrarian reform, but was ignorant of the meaning of democracy. Today his son, worker or student, has new aspirations. It was the same with the Egyptian peasant, even one voting for the Wafd, and no doubt for many others.

That is an important and definite advance, which I believe to be irreversible. But that progress does not in my opinion mean that democratic conviction replaces national and social aspirations. On the contrary, the former reinforces the latter. Let us be clear: Marx's critique of bourgeois democracy, that it is formal and limited, remains, to my mind, wholly correct.

And let us remember this democracy was not offered by the bourgeoisie to its people but conquered, relatively late, by workers' struggles. For the capitalist mode itself, contrary to recent ideological rhetoric, does not require democracy. The spring behind its social dynamism is located at another level, that of competition among capitalists and individuals.

Moreover, capitalism separates economic and social management, governed by fundamentally undemocratic principles, from political management, governed today by the democratic principle of election. We would add that this form of democracy only functions when its social impact has been neutered by the exploitation carried out by the dominant forces of the core powers within the world capitalist system, that is, when the labour movement has renounced its own project of a classless society and accepts the rules of the capitalist game.

In the periphery this bourgeois democracy remains impossible and is scarcely more than the expression of the crisis of the despotic system normal in capitalism. Latin America, the Philippines, South Korea and others provided glaring examples of the violent political contradictions on this level afflicting a Third World in crisis.

It is well known that the theory of Latin American *desarollismo* claimed in the 1950s and 1960s that industrialization and modernization (along bourgeois lines and within the context of even closer integration into the world system) would automatically lead to an evolution toward democracy. Dictatorship was looked upon as a vestige of a supposedly pre-capitalist past. The facts have shown the error of this naive reasoning.

Industrialization and modernization have only brought about the modernization of dictatorship and have substituted an efficient and modern fascist-type violence for the old patriarchal, oligarchic systems. It was bound to be so, for this peripheral development implies, as we have seen, the aggravation of social inequalities, and not their reduction. In addition, the bourgeois project itself has failed to produce the promised results: the crisis has revealed the impossibility of the 'independence' which legitimated dictatorship in some countries.

By the same token, dictatorship itself has entered into crisis. But are not the more or less democratic systems that came into being in these conditions confronted with a formidable dilemma? For there are only two choices: either the democratic political system accepts subordination to the demands of 'adjustment' to the world system, and is thereafter incapable of effecting any major social reforms, soon precipitating a crisis for democracy itself; or else popular forces, seizing the means provided by democracy, impose these reforms.

The system will then enter into conflict with dominant world capitalism and inevitably move from being a bourgeois national project to being a popular national one. The dilemma of Brazil, Argentina and the Philippines can be located in this context.

The absence of political democracy in the radical experiences of the Third World has always operated in favour of capitalism, whether private or state, and caused the system to degenerate into a bureaucratic capitalism which, in the last analysis, opened the way to compradorization.

In the 'socialist' countries, this risk did not at one stage look so threatening, the popular national (although undemocratic) state apparently having solid historical bases. Either the situation would continue to stagnate in the deadlock in which statism had landed it, or society would succeed in resuming its forward march, by moving toward really advanced forms of democracy. In the event, as we now know, neither of these two possibilities came about.

It remains true that democracy is the only means of reinforcing the chances for socialism within popular national society, of isolating internal capitalist relations of production from the influence of their compradorized insertion into the world capitalist system, and of reducing their external vulnerability.

But what kind of democracy are we talking about? There is certainly no need to scorn the heritage of Western bourgeois democracy with its respect for rights and legality, freedom of expression for a diversity of opinions, the institutionalization of electoral processes and the separation of powers, the organization of countervailing powers, etc. But there is no reason to stop there.

To stop at Western democratic forms without taking into consideration the social transformations required by the anti-capitalist revolt in the periphery is to become trapped in a travesty of bourgeois democracy, which will remain alien to the people and consequently extremely vulnerable. In order to take root, democracy must from the outset inscribe itself in a perspective that transcends capitalism. In this area, as in others, the law of unequal development must operate.

Obviously it is this prospect that imperialism finds intolerable. That is why the campaign orchestrated by the West about democracy stresses only certain aspects of the problem and neglects others. For example, it identifies multi-partyism with democracy. No doubt the single party has more often than not become the expression of statist dominance. But often it has been the product of the effective achievement of popular national unity.

In these cases, the creation of other parties might be an artificial operation that is not really on the agenda of popular struggles. Making a clear distinction between state and civil society and opening up social organizations (truly independent trade unions, peasant cooperatives, etc.) to debate are the essential reforms.

These reflections on democracy in the service of national liberation and social progress (and not in opposition to them or ignoring them) should inspire us to go deeper into the concept of 'advanced democracy' or truly popular democracy.

In this respect, I believe that the topic of 'Jacobin democracy', to borrow a term from the French Revolution, remains astonishingly up to date. In each of the three great revolutions of modern times (the French, the Russian and the Chinese), in the moments of their radicalization, the movement of ideas and social forces succeeded in projecting itself far in advance of the demands for 'objectively historically necessary' social transformation.

Thus Jacobin democracy went beyond demands for the mere installation of a bourgeois power. Although functioning in a framework defined by private property, its concern to establish a power that was really in the service of the people came into conflict with the straightforward bourgeois demand.

This forward projection was the beginning of a socialist consciousness that was yet to be born (as evidence Babeufism). In the same way, the USSR in the 1920s and Maoist China launched themselves into a communist vision well beyond the demands of the popular national reform on the agenda.

Certainly, as a result, these moments of radicalization remained fragile, and limited conceptualizations that were in keeping with 'objective demands' ended up by carrying the day. But it would be very wrong to underestimate the importance of these moments of radicalization, because they are pointers in the direction that the necessary future movement must go.

Jacobin democracy, rejuvenated by the contribution of the moments of radicalization of the socialist revolutions of our time, is in fact the democracy to which the popular classes of the contemporary Third World aspire—however confusedly. It is marked off from bourgeois democracy, which ignores the dimension of the social reforms that are required, as it is from the sort of 'populist mobilizations' that we have seen in Latin America, in the Arab world (with Nasserism) and in Africa (in the 1960s) where contempt for democracy wore down the potential for renewal.

My proposal certainly does not seek to court popularity! The fashion today is to devalue the moments of revolutionary radicalization in the name of realism and to favour themes coming from another tradition, the tradition of local democracy familiar in the Anglo-Saxon countries.

Moves towards decentralization, the autonomy of a shattered and fragmented civil society, are often proposed in that spirit, as possible realistic advances, richer potentially even than the alleged illusion of statist popular democracy. Movements that go in that direction, often tinged with religiosity, appear to me to suggest a strategy that is too heavily biased by so-called anti-statism to be really capable of meeting the real historical challenge.

There is something to take from all of them, and here a true dialogue is called for—especially as the historical task of the democratic politicization of the popular classes remains a very long-haul task. The beginnings of action in that direction—through self-organization by the masses, self-development and self-defence—have not got beyond the embyronic stage.

I am thinking here of the experience of Thomas Sankara's Burkina Faso, and of others even more condemned by the dominant media in the West (Gaddafism, for example). No doubt these beginnings are a long way from having settled the fundamental questions of the relationship between power and the parties of the so-called traditional radical left, its relationship to populism, the military, etc.

The cultural dimension[3]

Our age is marked everywhere—in the West, the East (as was) and the South—by the emergence (or the resurgence) of social movements which express themselves in forms that one might have thought had been overtaken since the French Revolution. Here and there individuals are once again putting their communal (ethnic or religious) identity before their consciousness as citizens or their class consciousness.

We are ill-equipped to analyse systematically the cultural dimension of social reality. The economic dimension is certainly the best known. In this area, bourgeois economics has forged tools for close analysis and, with more or less success, for managing capitalist society. Historical materialism has gone deeper and, often successfully, throws light on the nature and scope of the social struggles that underlie economic choices.

The sphere of power and politics is less well understood and the eclecticism of theories proposed reflects the low mastery of reality. There is no conceptualization of power (modes of domination) as there is of economics (modes of production). There has been no effective analysis of the 'power fetish' (in line with that of the 'commodity fetish').

As for the cultural dimension, it remains even more unknown, empirical observation of phenomena in this sphere of reality having as yet barely done more than provide grist for intuitive essays. That is why the treatment of the cultural dimension of history continues to be imbued with culturalism. By that I mean a tendency to treat cultural characteristics as transhistorical constants. In addition, so long as major advances have not been made in this sphere, discussion will continue to be encumbered by emotional reactions and romantic visions.

The question posed by the emergence of culturalist movements is the following: do these movements show that (so-called cultural) specificity constitutes by itself not only a given (which is obvious) but an irreducible and irrepressible determinant (among others) that shapes particular futures in the contrast of interdependence? Or are they only the passing expression of a historical dead end that can be transcended (but will not necessarily be so)?

These movements are too heterogeneous for any global judgement to be made, as their definition is more negative (everything that does not express class- and citizen-consciousness) than positive; and the content of their proposals is no less different at one extreme than the other (but Liberation Theology cannot be confused with fundamentalism, on the pretext that both have to do with religion). I shall therefore suggest in what follows seven thoughts about this cultural dimension of the contemporary social movement.

First: If economistic alienation defines the essential content of the ideology of capitalism, pre-capitalist class societies are governed by politics that occupies directly centre stage, and other aspects of social life (*inter alia* economic life) seem to have to subordinate themselves to it. This fetishization of power—necessary for the social reproduction of the system—in turn implies an ideology dominated by metaphysical concerns.

Given that, the religions through which this concern is usually expressed are always flexible, so much so that they are capable, if the social circumstances so require, of adapting to the social, political and cultural revolution of both capitalism and eventually, one day, of socialism.

In Europe, the cradle of capitalism, Christianity did indeed make its bourgeois revolution and rediscovered a place in the new ideological construction of the modern (capitalist) world. Yet this construction remains ambiguous, associating the economistic alienation through which it defines itself in its essential content with a Eurocentric dimension, which in turn legitimates the world expansion of capitalism to the benefit of the centres (which, with the exception of Japan, are European in culture).

This Eurocentrism was built on a series of culturalist myths, including *inter alia* the one that I have described as the 'Christianophile myth', attributing to that religion a transhistorical specificity which is said to have predisposed Europe to the progress accomplished by the qualitative leap from feudalism to capitalism.

At the present time, in some regions of the Christian Third World (principally in Latin America) Christianity has perhaps begun another cultural revolution, in response to the demands of national liberation envisaged in a potentially socialist popular perspective. Liberation Theology, which expresses this reinterpretation, is thus not in conflict with the popular national revolution but on the contrary supports it.

Other 'revivals' of the social expression of religion, obviously, do not have this impact. That is so true of ultra-conservative fundamentalisms such as exist in the Western Catholic or Protestant worlds. Associated with racism directed against the Third World, many of these currents represent only one dimension of the current reaction in the West (particularly in the USA).

Religious revivals that sometimes occupy centre stage in the Third World are more complex. As regards the Islamic movements (which are in fact more diverse than the dominant media suggest), I have developed elsewhere analyses that have led me to the following two conclusions:

1. In the nineteenth century, the bourgeoisies of the Islamic–Arab world had initiated a reinterpretation of religion in keeping with the demands of 'modernization' (capitalism); but the Nahda—which is the name of that movement, which means 'Renaissance'—was aborted on this level as bourgeois evolution was aborted on the level of political and economic transformation.
2. Contemporary movements feed on the spontaneous popular revolt against the unacceptable conditions created by peripheral capitalism; they have so far, however, fallen short of making the demand for the double revolution by which modernization and popular enfranchisment must come together; as a result, their fundamentalist dimension, feeding on a backward-looking myth, continues to express itself in a language in which the metaphysical concern remains exclusive in the whole social vision.

Second: Movements making so-called ethnic demands including national, para-national or religious minorities are also largely the product of the failure to build a national state in the periphery of the capitalist system. Going beyond their diversity and analysing what I felt was the commonest cause of the emergence of these demands in Africa, I felt that I had to look for it in the behaviour of the ruling classes which, in order to create a base that peripheral capitalist development prohibits them from acquiring by other means, manipulate ethnicity.

Third: The contemporary social movement has other dimensions. Some of these, moreover, have a universal angle and are evidence of the universality of the problems, reinforced by the intensification of communications. Feminism is the best example of this. That its impact is supremely progressive—whatever the circumstances—cannot be denied.

Other dimensions are more ambiguous. Withdrawal into the 'small community'—the family, the village or the district—sometimes facilitates the mobilization of potentials that cannot be mobilized in the more classic frameworks of parties or trade unions, either because these have lost their credibility (or because the ruling autocracy banned their activity!) or because of the atomistic character of peripheral society, poorly structured into fully crystallized classes.

But such withdrawals may also reinforce negative attitudes towards popular national demands, like family-centredness (particulary powerful in the Confucian world), or the illusion of being able to do without the state level in the transformation of reality.

This latter type of illusion, which I call the 'cantonization' of consciousness, is common in the Anglo-Saxon cultural area, of which it is a negative aspect compared to its positive democratic contribution of the notion of civil society.

Fourth: It is erroneous to contrast the alleged rationality of classical ideologies on which modern politics is based to an alleged irrationality of other cultures. All cultures contain both rationality and irrationality, the meaning of which moreover is always relative and provisional. The commercial rationality of capitalism is certainly one such, but a devastating one, which not only eliminates the culture of the past, but also sets itself up as an obstacle to progress beyond capitalism.

Fifth: The unity of the world, despite the polarization between centres and peripheries on which it is built, requires that the core dimension of any culture, that wishes to build a better future based on the solution of the real problems of today, be universalist.

Diversity must serve the universalism that is to be built, not be contrasted with it as its polar opposite. It is true that peoples today are generally suspicious of universalist propositions. For, under cover of the Enlightenment, through Eurocentrism, universalist propositions have legitimized the subjection of Third World peoples or, under cover of socialism, Soviet praxis (the latter until, at least, the collapse of the Soviet system in 1991).

Today ecological neo-globalism calls for the same reservations. That said, to throw the baby out with the bath water by rejecting the universalist in the Anglo-Saxon tradition borders on racism through the appeal this argument makes to the irreducibility of cultures (is not apartheid built on this alleged irreducibility?).

Sixth: The resurgence of the cultural dimension in contemporary social movements obviously proves that the price of denying the reality of it was to be its return in strength. But it is also the simplest product of the exhaustion of the national bourgeois illusion and the inadequacies of the traditional left of the Third World, which helped perpetuate those illusions. Thus I do not feel that this resurgence—in its present form—is likely to continue for long or develop further. On the contrary, it seems to me that this resurgence has its origin in part as a reaction, a flight into the supposed certainties of the past.

Seventh: Transcending the current conflicts within the contradictory ideology of the social movement calls for democratic praxis.

The role of the intelligentsia

Here we come to the specific role of the intelligentsia in the popular national revolution. I will say straight away that this analysis is specific to the historical movement engendered by the attempt to escape from the dead end of peripheral capitalism.

The intelligentsia is not synonymous with either the petty bourgeoisie in general or even with 'educated circles' (or intellectuals, and even less, graduates, etc.). The petty bourgeoisie is a diverse and shifting amalgam of social strata engendered in all forms of capitalist development—central or peripheral. As a class, globally, it plays no decisive political role; the thesis that this class remains divided and vacillating, now leaning to the right, now to the left, seems to me to be fundamentally correct.

The particular strata constituted by intellectuals or graduates, bureaucrats and technocrats, etc. are no more than subgroups of the petty bourgeoisie, alongside others (petty producers, middle management, etc.). In this sense there is nothing particular to say about these strata as such that escapes the general rule regarding the vacillating character of the petty bourgeoisie and its non-decisive role in history.

When Gramsci made his well-known comments about the 'organic intellectual', he was assuming that each important class in history—be it dominant (the bourgeoisie in capitalism) or be it one which could aspire to become so (the working class)—produces by itself, collectively, its own ideology and culture, forms of organization and practices.

The organic intellectual is the catalyst of this production, to which he gives adequate expression to enable the ideology of the class that he represents to turn itself into the dominant ideology in society. Gramsci further assumed that the working class in the capitalist centres was revolutionary, and, on the basis of that hypothesis, reflected on the conditions under which the organic intellectual of the socialist revolution (the vanguard party) emerges.

If one believes that Gramsci's hypothesis is wrong, and that the working class in the capitalist centres also accepts the basic rules of the game in the system, then one must deduce from it that the working classes are not in a position, in the present state of things, to produce their own socialist organic intellectuals. Of course they produce cadres who organize their struggles, but these are cadres who have given up thinking in terms of the alternative project of the classless society.

There do indeed exist, in these societies, individuals who remain attached to that vision. But, as has already been said, the so-called Western Marxism is a Marxism of the debating chamber and the university, with no social impact. There also do indeed exist in these societies demands of a socialist nature which circulate and are expressed in various ways. But it is typical that these demands are not articulated in a global project (thus greens, feminists, etc. formally refuse to go beyond their own specific demands), and thus that they do not produce the organic intellectuals that Gramsci called for.

The situation in the periphery is totally different. Here the popular classes have nothing to expect from capitalist development. They are thus potentially anti-capitalist. Nevertheless, their situation does not correspond to that of the proletariat as envisaged by classical Marxism. For they make up a diverse amalgam of victims of capitalism.

These classes are not in a position to elaborate by themselves, and alone, a project for a classless society. They are capable—and prove it constantly—of refusing and even revolting, more generally of resisting (actively and passively). In these conditions, a historical space is opened up for the constitution of the social force capable of fulfilling this objectively necessary and possible function: that of the catalyst which formulates the alternative social project to capitalism, organizes the popular classes and guides their action against capitalism. This force is, precisely, the intelligentsia.

The intelligentsia—or the revolutionary intelligentsia if one wants to label it so—is then not globally the petty bourgeoisie of these societies as a class. The intelligentsia is largely drawn from this class—for simple and obvious reasons, but not exclusively: elements originating from the aristocracy and the people are also numerous among it.

The intelligentsia is not defined by the class origin of its members. It is defined by: (1) its anti-capitalism; (2) its openness to the universal dimension of the culture of our time and, by this means, its capacity to situate itself in this world, analyse its contradictions, understand its weak links, etc.; and (3) its simultaneous capacity to remain in living and close communion with the popular classes, to share their history and cultural expression.

It remains to know what are the conditions favourable to the crystallization of such an intelligentsia, and what are the obstacles to it. In my opinion, this question, on which there has been too little reflection, is the fundamental question facing the progressive movement of our time, the true question that history has objectively put on the agenda.

I shall not try to answer it hurriedly here. I shall simply say what seems to me obvious at the level of the cultural conditions for such crystallization. The refusal to accept and to grasp the universal dimension of culture which the real internationalization initiated by the capitalism has already imposed (despite the contradictory character of this internationalization, whose victims are the peoples in the periphery), this refusal and withdrawal into a negative culturalist nationalism (simply anti-Western—and often neurotic) do not constitute the possible yeast for an effective response. At the other extreme, Western-type alienation, which definitively separates one from popular reality, is also a dead end.

I think that Marxism offers the only intellectual means that makes possible the necessary successful synthesis, at least potentially. For, of course, there exists a 'Western Marxism', which the label 'Western-centred' would best suit in my opinion. That is why I have written elsewhere that Marxism has acquired an Afro-Asian vocation, which is perhaps its principal vocation.

I shall put forward the idea that, in the spirit of this proposed analysis, the Bolshevik Party and the Chinese Communist Party were perfect expressions of the crystallization of a revolutionary intelligentsia that effectively succeeded in organizing the popular classes and became its true vanguard. Perhaps, in the Russian case, being part of Europe was a favourable element, Marxism not appearing here as a foreign import.

Perhaps in China the secular (that is, non-religious) character of the traditional dominant ideology—Confucianism—was a lesser obstacle than elsewhere, in the sense that it could not offer strong resistance to the cultural import of Marxism in this case (moreover, in Japan an analogous culture did not reveal itself hostile to the import of capitalism). Conversely, perhaps, any totalitarian interpretation of religion (here Hinduism and Islam) constitutes a major obstacle to the necessary universalist openness, effective down to the present day at any event.

As regards the Third World, it would be interesting in my opinion to look more closely at the nature of this radical nationalist intelligentsia and its ideological and cultural vision of the challenge of modern times. No doubt one should—as always—avoid over-hasty generalizations and examine concrete situations case by case.

In the case of Egypt, I would suggest that the whole modern history of this ancient country has been largely activated by its intelligentsia. But this intelligentsia is nevertheless divided into three currents without them converging or any one of them succeeding in winning out in a decisive way. The 'modernist' currents have remained largely alienated culturally from the popular masses, both their 'Westernizing' liberal bourgeois branch in decline, and their radical branch which opened itself up to communism in the 1920s.

While the Islamizing current, ever present from the Nahda to the Muslim Brothers and fundamentalism, has always produced intellectuals whose message finds an easy echo among the people, it has never succeeded in making itself into a social force capable of leading the people and, as a result, has always in the end found itself manipulated by more powerful forces (local and regional reaction and, behind them, imperialism). It acts above all as a barrier to the spread of the ideas of the radical left. In these conditions, a third current of 'modernization', represented in recent history by the Free Officers, has succeeded in seizing the historical opportunity. For I hold that the Free Officers' organization, like the communist organizations, are essentially composed of would-be members of the intelligentsia who did not succeed, in the circumstances, in organizing the masses and unifying the anti-capitalist forces behind them.

This branch of the intelligentsia—which would give birth to Nasserism—is not the global expression of petty bourgeois ideology, despite certain superficial appearances. It turned out to be modernist, deeply anti-imperialist and nationalist, suspicious of the wealthy classes and making an appeal to the people, but nevertheless pragmatic, as Nasser himself acknowledged. But, to my mind, this character in reality conceals the global cultural poverty of Egyptian society and the failure to produce a creative synthesis of the universalist dimension of modern culture and the specific expression of the people's historic heritage.

In this situation, the movement 'beyond capitalism', initiated by the radicalization of national liberation, has found itself constantly hampered, both by the ambiguous and uncertain nature of its project and by the objective obstacles operating within society; these two elements reinforce each other and finally, combined with imperialist aggression, abort the hope for a popular national revolution.

Without wanting necessarily to generalize too quickly, it seems to me that all the attempts to go 'beyond capitalism' from the radicalization of national liberation have suffered from the same limitation and, for that reason, have shown the same fragility. But this history is still perhaps only just beginning, and it is because we are in a hurry that we are losing sight of all the future potential contained within the radicalization involved in the rejection of compradorization.

Notes

1. See S. Amin, *Delinking: Towards a Polycentric World* (Zed Books, 1990); *Maldevelopment: Anatomy of a Global Failure* (Zed Books, 1991); *Classe et nation dans l'histoire et la crise contemporaine,* Minuit, 1979.
2. *In Favour of a Polycentric World* , IFDA dossier No. 69 (Geneva), January 1989.
3. See S. Amin, *Eurocentrism* (Zed Books, 1989), chapters 1 and 2; 'La fin de la Nahda', *Revue des Etudes palestiniennes*, No. 19, 1987: also the works in Arabic cited in the References section.

References

Amin, S., *Eurocentrism* , Zed Books, 1989.

Amin, S. and F. Yachir, *La Méditerranée dans le système mondial*, La Découverte, 1988; preface in Y. Sertal, *Nord–Sud, crise et immigration, le case turc*, Publisud, 1987.

Amin, S., *L' Egypte nassérienne* , Minuit, 1964; *The Arab Nation*, Zed Books, 1978; in Arabic: *The Crisis of Arab Society*, Cairo, 1985; *The Arab Nation*, Cairo, 1988.

Amin, S., *Neocolonialism in West Africa,* Penguin, 1973; *Impérialisme et sous-développement en Afrique*, Anthropos-Economica, 1988; *The Maghreb, in the Modern World*, Penguin, 1970; *Maldevelopment: Anatomy of a Global Failure*, Zed Books, 1990.

'Il y a trente ans Bandoung' in *L'Echange inégal et la loi de la valeur*, Anthropos-Economica, 1988; *La Faillite du développement*, Harmattan, 1989, chapter 2.

Amin, S., *Delinking: Towards a Polycentric World*, Zed Books, 1990; 'The state and development', *Socialism in the World*, No. 58, Belgrade, 1987; 'Democracy and national strategy in the Third World', *Third World Quarterly*, October 1987; preface to the new edition of *L'Accumulation a l'échelle mondiale*, Anthropos-Economica, 1988; 'Intellectuais, libertacao e construcao do Estado', *Economia e Socialismo*, Lisbon, December 1987.

5. Social Movements and Democracy in Africa

Mahmood Mamdani, Thandika Mkandawire and *E. Wamba-dia-Wamba*

As the dawn of independence broke over the African continent in the late 1950s and 1960s, various schools of thought mushroomed, each with its own response to the question of the day: which way Africa? In time, the question was made more pressing by the defeat of the movements struggling for genuine national independence and by the performance of post-colonial African states. New and different perspectives developed on the same question. Today, as clouds of pessimism settle over the continent and consensus spreads that we are indeed in the midst of an 'African crisis', these same schools reflect over the experience of nearly three decades and ask the question: what went wrong?

An attempt to comprehend this crisis must take as its starting point these contending schools of thought, which have tried first to guide practice and now to conceptualize experience. Of these, three merit particular attention.

The first and the most prominent of these arose as a strictly intellectual tendency in African universities and universities in the USA specializing in the study of Africa. The development of this school of thought, like those that followed it, was of course closely linked to prevailing forms of domination, cultural hegemony and to forms of resistance against it. After the Second World War, part of the Pax Americana frontierist programme was the demand for the political independence of African colonies so they might become part of the USA's zone of influence. 'Africanism made in the USA' was part of a theoretical guideline and an ideological justification for the realization of that demand.

First efforts: the Africanist school

Baptized the Africanist school, this theoretical orientation grew as a direct counter to colonial social science and its claim that the 'Dark Continent' had no history worth recording. The school's front runners, mainly historians, dug into the African past and brought to the surface hitherto neglected facts about the glory of pre-colonial African kingdoms. For each historical period, they reconstructed what they dubbed 'the African initiative'.

But history for them was indeed a history of the ruling classes. They celebrated the process of state formation in African history. And they looked forward to the development of strong African states in the years to come. To be sure, there were voices which opposed 'this uncritical trend in the new African historiography' with its 'emphasis on the pre-eminence of political history'. Thus, Professor Afigbo (1977) protested:

> The point here is not just that, thus far, most of what passes for African history is a stupefying cavalcade of states great and small, ancient and modern, but that we write approvingly or even rapturously of these vanished imperial supremacies and their rulers.

But Afigbo's voice belonged to a small and isolated minority.

The programme of the Africanists for independent Africa could be summarized in one word: 'nation-building'. By nation-building, however, they meant no more than state-building, and at that really the building on the continent of strong bourgeoisies. Just as ideologically some of the most vocal proponents of the Africanist school were academics in African studies in the USA, in practice nation-building was understood as a project to be realized in partnership with erstwhile imperial powers.

Here then was the point of convergence between the Africanists and their erstwhile colonial protagonists. With independence, the contradiction between the two collapsed into a common programme: 'modernization'.

While modernization theory was the reigning perspective in the range of disciplines in the social sciences, its grand theory was produced in sociology. The dominant Parsonian view consciously sought to move away from the analysis of relations of exploitation; it defined the evolution from 'traditional' to 'modern' society as the result of a change in the structure of occupational roles and associated values.

At its core, modernism is the notion that history is finite, that it has a single line of development, a motive force and a common conclusion. Throughout the successive phases of bourgeois class rule, this unilinear conception of historical development has been central to bourgeois ideology. The emergence of post-colonial bourgeoisies led, in their specific circumstances, to variant forms of that ideology. In his widely celebrated general theory, Rostow (1960) employed a metaphor that cast these 'traditional' societies as so many airplanes gathering steam on the ground for a 'take-off'. In this metaphor, steam was analogous to capital. Scarcity of capital, like scarcity of steam, precluded a successful take-off. This scarcity could only be remedied in two ways. Capital had to be obtained through foreign investments and through local savings. To attract foreign investment required the guarantee of a cheap, docile and disciplined labour force, a guarantee that only a 'strong' state could provide. The Kuznet hypothesis further stated that accumulation not only required restraint on consumption but would in fact tend to aggravate inequality until a certain income level was reached. To impose the 'necessary sacrifice' and to sustain this growing inequality, a 'strong' state would be needed.

To ensure order in the face of growing disorder, to strengthen the state vis-à-vis civil society—so that it could successfully guarantee stability and carry out the task of modernization—became a central preoccupation of modernization theory. Order, the methodological assumption of the school at its outset, had in a decade been redefined as its supreme goal. What had begun as an attempt to explain change in the Third World turned into a recipe for how to contain that change.

Popular demands were seen as unrealistic, a combination of the atavistic and the utopian, the result of both traditional values (particularistic, tribal) and of a modern 'international demonstration effect' which created the anomaly of pre-industrial states burdened with 'post-industrial' values and demands (minimum wages, welfare demands). These popular demands—in one version theorized as the 'revolution of rising expectations'—were seen as undermining new and therefore precarious modern state structures. They were thus 'dysfunctional' or 'preatorian'.

Here, too, we must underline the historical/social context of such a theoretical/political orientation. It is not accidental that the reformist face of imperialism was visible only at home, not abroad. After all, were not the whole galaxy of reforms—parliamentarianism, syndicalism, welfarism—that went under the rubric of social democracy dependent on higher rates of profit in the colonies and neo-colonies? Did not the necessity to ensure the continued prevalence of such rates of profit require certain repressive forms of class rule in the dependent countries? Is not this why the same popular demands that were considered legitimate in the imperialist countries were viewed as unrealistic in the dependent countries?

What forces, then, had the capacity to achieve order and to propel society forward to modernization? These, not surprisingly, were said to be the modernizing elites. Theorists disagreed on their specific identification. But these were disagreements within the club. Some identified as the custodians of order and change the civil bureaucracy (Lapalombara), others the armed bureaucracy (Janowits) and yet others the political party (Huntington, Apter, Pye). As Gendzier (1985) has aptly commented, through its confrontation with reality and through its internal changes, modernization theory had produced a 'pedagogy against the oppressed'.

From such a point of view, social movements could only be identified and studied as a 'problem'. It is this tendency that became reinforced and consolidated as modernization theory turned from being simply one of the ideologies contending in the market place of academic ideas to an institutional ideology backed up by powerful government and foundation interests in the USA, beginning with the influential Social Science Research Council's Committee on Comparative Government in the 1950s. The history of this relationship between academic high priests and centres of power and privilege or, in other words, the history of the transformation of modernization theory into an institutional ideology has been carefully documented by Gendzier (1985).

The most notorious instance of this collaboration between the forces of law and order and the theoreticians of it was, of course, Project Camelot. Funded to the tune of an estimated $44 million by the Department of the

Army (US) and its contractor, Special Operations Research Office, this was to be a joint venture between US and Latin American scholars. Its purpose was plainly to identify social forces committed to change in Latin America and to predict their actions so as to contain them: in a word, counter-insurgency. No wonder the study of revolution and development became a growth industry in US universities by the late 1960s! 'Know thy enemy' was their first and only commandment. Thus, the University of Chicago's Center for Social Organisation Studies received the largest subcontract for a series of studies on military sociology under Professor Janowitz. And the Congress for Cultural Freedom (under Shills and Almond) was lavishly financed by the CIA as part of an elaborate international campaign to discredit left-wing politics among Third World intellectuals.

Noam Chomsky (1974) has recorded other cases where the 'New Mandarins' studied social movements in a similar vein. In practice, the suppression of democratic demands and of autonomous and popular movements in the name of development was a concern that went beyond the theoreticians of the modernization school. As we shall see, it became a central characteristic of a much wider 'ideology of developmentalism' (Shivji, 1985).

In the history of the production and spread of modernization as a school of thought, its African adherents took on a decidedly secondary and marginal role, more as catechists than as its principal ideologues. This reflected not only their distance from those imperial centres that provided the nourishment for this institutional ideology, it was also a telling comment on their position within African societies. It is no surprise that while by far the best works of African intellectuals in the 1960s had been on history and culture, they had precious little contribution to make by way of the analysis of contemporary African societies. As aptly observed by Jitendra Mohan (1968) in his review of the writings of Ali Mazrui:

> The African intelligentsia as a whole is far too deeply embedded in the post-colonial structures of power and privilege—or, to put it another way, is as yet not sufficiently detached or alienated from the whole system—to be able to undertake social analysis, which could prove uncannily and uncomfortably like self-analysis.

For the modernization school today, the African crisis is first and foremost the crisis of the African state. It is, on the one hand, the expression of the ugly fact that the ranks of the African bourgeoisies are riddled with factional differences, usually along nationality ('tribal') lines. And these differences are more often than not resolved through coups, no matter how 'bloodless', rather than through gentlemanly arrangements, electoral or otherwise. In other words, the African ruling classes have not only failed to create order in civil society; they have also failed to do so amongst themselves. The curse of Africa, it is said, is tribalism.

On the other hand, and from an economistic perspective, this same crisis is seen as the result of the failure of the state to create the conditions for a successful 'take-off'. On the contrary, through a maze of regulations and controls, well-oiled through official pork barrels, private initiative has been stifled. The problem with Africa, it is said, is official mismanagement or systemic bureaucratic corruption.

The dependency theorists' challenge

As signs of crisis loomed on the horizon like so many clouds gathering before a storm, the modernization thesis was vigorously challenged by the dependency school, strongly influenced by its Latin American formulators. In its Latin American setting particularly, dependency was also formulated as a critique of the vulgar Marxism of the dominant local parties. Vulgar Marxism, after all, was an outcome of the social democratic depoliticization of the working class movement on the one hand and the redefinition of Marxism as mainly the defence of 'socialism in one country' on the other.

Immediately, dependency theory made two positive contributions to the analysis of Third World societies. Central to modernization theory was the dualist model of the 'traditional' and the 'modern'. The theory had argued that the main obstacles to development were to be found in the inherent socio-cultural characteristics of traditional societies. Critics pointed out that the so-called traditional sectors had been analysed in isolation, thereby obscuring the history of their relations with modern centres of the world capitalist market since the fifteenth century. In fact, the main uniting conception of all dependency theorists was the claim that underdevelopment has causes that are principally external to the underdeveloped countries. In establishing this claim, dependency theorists reconstructed the history of the relations between the 'centre' and the 'periphery' of the world capitalist market since the fifteenth century. The theory's first great merit, then, was to direct attention to imperialism.

Dependency theory was at the same time a critique of the unilinear evolutionist perspective shared by both modernization theorists and vulgar Marxism. That perspective argued, explicitly or implicitly, that the underdeveloped countries were destined to go through the same stages of historical development as had the countries of Europe. For modernization theorists, this march was seen as a movement from traditional to modern society through a series of transitional stages. For vulgar Marxism, unilinear evolutionism inspired a supra-historical theory whereby every society must necessarily go through a succession of modes of production, from primitive communism to slavery to feudalism to capitalism to socialism.

The dependency critique or unilinear evolutionism was focused on the argument that underdevelopment was not a pre-modern or a pre-capitalist (feudal or otherwise) stage of development, mirroring a similar stage in the history of modern or developed capitalist societies, but that it was a special product of the very development of world capitalism since the fifteenth century. The economists among the dependency theorists thus analysed and underlined the structural distortions in the economy—for example, Samir Amin's analysis of the disarticulated and extroverted economy that is incapable of a sustained accumulation of capital—that were the result of the concrete history of underdevelopment. The second great merit of dependency theory, then, was that it directed attention to the need to study the concrete history of the so-called underdeveloped countries in order to understand the specific problems of 'underdevelopment'.

But from the point of view of the questions of democracy and development in Africa, three aspects of dependency theory were vital, and in fact summed up its analytical and political shortcomings. First, there was a strong tendency for dependency theorists to reconstruct the history of the centre–periphery relation in a one-sided and mechanical manner, whereby the centre was seen to represent the active side of the relationship and the periphery its passive side. Developments in the periphery were seen as an inevitable and direct outcome of the will of capital at the centre. The analysis obscured the entire history of the struggle of various classes and groups in the Third World against imperialist oppression and exploitation. Without reconstructing the history of this resistance, there could be no stocktaking of its strengths and weaknesses and therefore no concrete programme for liberation.

For those who believed that developments in the periphery were simply a result of the will of capital at the centre, dependency was simply incompatible with any form of democracy. The state was a state of foreign powers. As such, it was structurally alienated from the local civil society and could only relate to it in an authoritarian way. Only a radical 'delinking' from the centre could provide a framework for even posing the problem of development, let alone its democratization.

Even more fatalistic was the view of those who believed that transnationalization had blocked the emergence of those social movements that had played major roles in the democratization of the advanced countries. It had not only stifled the structural capacities of the popular classes to make democratic demands on the state, but also had denied them even the organizational capacity to do so. In the case of workers, transnationalization was said to have generated a 'labour aristocracy' (Arrighi and Saul, 1973) which had been more or less 'incorporated' by the transnationalization strategy of transnational corporations.

Neither did peasants fare much better. The nature of the incorporation of the peasantry into the world capitalist system had created a class that could not be expected to revolt as had peasants elsewhere. Writing about the land of the Mau Mau uprising, Leys (1975, p.352) had this to say:

> One cannot help feeling that in Kenya, at least, the character of politics will for some considerable time be determined by the fact that the peasantry as a class has not yet reached the limits of its development, and that the symbiosis between it and the urban-based classes is not yet fully developed either.

While it may be true that peasants in the imperialist epoch have different characteristics, everywhere a major social movement has developed peasants have indeed participated actively. Where they have failed to be active, other factors than the nature of the peasantry per se have to be studied to explain such a passivity.

In some of the radical versions of dependency theory, there was even a tendency to go beyond the assertion that dependency relations could not allow forms of democracy as practised in the centre economies. Even if they did, the argument went, such forms were 'bourgeois' anyway. The whole question of democratization was dismissed as a 'bourgeois' preoccupation. This could not be because the process of 'dis-engagement' was seen not as the goal of a social movement but as a problem internal to the ruling classes of the periphery.

And finally, without a concrete analysis of class relations within the periphery, related to contradictions at the centre, dependency theory could not explain the nature and the direction of change within Third World countries. As a result—and ironically, too—having correctly criticized the unilinear evolutionism of both modernization theory and vulgar Marxism, dependency theory in the final analysis capitulated to the same unilinear evolutionist mode of analysis. The very concept of 'underdevelopment' testified to this shortcoming. For it defined the dependent society in relation to the dominant 'core'—as not being what the latter was, without being able to define the internal character of the dependent society itself. Just as for modernization theory the 'traditional' was the 'non-modern', for dependency theory the 'underdeveloped' was the 'not-developed'.

The point is that without integrating the analysis of the dependency relation into a comprehensive analysis of social relations within the dependent country, dependency theory was unable to explain both how the relation of dependency was reproduced and how it could be transformed. The theory could neither identify those classes central to the reproduction of the relation, nor those classes that would have an interest in its transformation.

Today, from the point of view of dependency theory, the crisis of Africa is the crisis of centre–periphery relations. It is essentially an externally generated crisis. The solution is for the periphery to 'delink' itself from the centre. To be sure, there are those who speak of a 'popular delinking' as opposed to a simple 'delinking'. None the less, from such a perspective, it is not possible to discuss concretely the internal basis of such a delinking, the internal social transformations whose product would be a recasting of external relations.

Mode of production school

The origins of the third major school of thought, the 'mode of production' school, also lay in theoretical/historical debates outside Africa. These were, on the one hand, debates regarding the rise of Western capitalism (Hilton et al., 1976) and, on the other, attempts within French structuralism to counter the theoretical roots of economic determinism, unilinear evolutionism and humanistic idealism, which had infected the communist parties in the Third International. In the study of African societies, however, the mode of production school began with the dual critique, of both dependency and modernization theories. From this critique stemmed two major contributions of this school of thought.

In their critique of the dependency school's one-sided preoccupation with external relations, the mode of production theorists called for a more dialectical relation between external and internal processes. Their thrust was on an analysis of the 'articulation' of capitalist and pre-capitalist modes of production rather than on the link between central and peripheral economies (Wolpe, 1975; O'Meara, 1979; Depelchin, 1981). The first major contribution of this school was thus to shift the analytical emphasis from the state to society, from the bourgeoisie of the periphery to its producing classes.

And yet the mode of production school suffered from its attempt to negate dependency theory in a one-sided manner. It not only ended up reproducing some of the very shortcomings of dependency theory, it also failed to incorporate into its perspective some of the major strengths and contributions of the theory.

These mode of production school critics could not depart from the functionalist and objectivist orientation of the dependency school. They in turn succumbed to a new form of economism. Whether pre-capitalist forms were transformed, or whether aspects were retained, was a function of the needs of accumulation in the capitalist mode. Social reality, as it were, was deduced from the logic of capital accumulation.

At the same time, with the possible exception of Rey (1976), the mode of production theorists had a strong tendency to sidestep totally the central question raised by the dependency school: the question of dependency. They focused on relations between modes of production as if no states and state boundaries existed. They focused on the logic of economic structures as if no political relations existed. In fact, it would be no exaggeration to say that the writings of many of the mode of production theorists had a strong tendency to liquidate the very question of imperialism.

Even such an important study of working-class struggles as that by Shivji (1983) in Tanzania was marred by its single-minded focus on the relation between organized sectors of the working class and the state power, to the total exclusion of analysing their relation with the struggles of other producing classes, which formed the majority in a country like Tanzania. It is the absence of a focus on the specific question of a worker–peasant alliance, and on the general question of the relation of working-class struggles to the struggles of the non-proletarian masses, in an historical and social context where these masses formed the vast majority, that gave the resulting studies an exceedingly narrow political focus and a millenarian orientation.

And yet an important contribution of this school, as we have already pointed out, was to take as its point of departure African society and not the African state as the real subject of history. To that extent, it differed sharply from both the earlier Africanist historians and later dependency theorists. If anything, its emphasis coincided with that of Frantz Fanon, the most articulate spokesperson of the popular wing of anti-colonial nationalist movements. Fanon (1967), as is well known, had nothing but contempt for the 'decadent' and 'poverty-stricken' African bourgeoisie, which performed the role of a 'cheap-jack' for the Western bourgeoisie. Lacking any of the pioneering capacity of the latter during its youth, these African middlemen could aim at nothing more than to turn Africa into a pale reflection of Europe. Surely, for Fanon, the future did not rest in the hands of the African bourgeoisie, nor with the state it inherited; the future had to be wrested from it by the African masses through struggle.

For the mode of production school, as it would have been for Fanon, the crisis of Africa today is the crisis of the working people of Africa, the essence being their failure to transform the order forged during the colonial era. While the school's shifting of attention onto some sector of the popular masses (in this case, the working class) as the real subject of African history was undoubtedly an advance over dependency theory's preoccupation with the state, the school's tendency to isolate the struggles of the working class from the overall context of popular struggles gave its writings both too narrow a focus and a millenarian orientation.

Now, if dependency theorists were preoccupied with the objective side of relations and stayed an arm's length away from the study of social movements, and if the mode of production school was limited to a narrow concern with working-class struggles, does that mean that writers on contemporary Africa by and large simply ignored the movements of its non-proletarian masses? But for some notable exceptions like Joseph on Cameroon (1977), social protest was empirically studied by conventional scholars whose frame of analysis, as we shall soon see, was inspired by the assumptions of the modernization school. As Marx once commented, when materialism is mechanical, the human agency is portrayed by idealists!

Modernization theorists, as we have seen, had their own internal struggles as they tried to come to terms with the reality of social conflict and social contradictions in African societies. It took a protracted struggle before these theorists could even accept that such a reality indeed existed. While economists focused on the state and the modern economy, political scientists on the state and nation-building, and sociologists on urbanization, 'social anthropologists who pervaded the countryside maintained their traditional fixation on "tribes"'. As Mafeje (1985) has pointed out, the last place where 'peasant studies' made inroads was African studies, for cultivators in the African countryside were presumed to be tribesmen and women, not peasants! And why not, since prevailing assumptions held that land was relatively abundant throughout the continent, land tenure was communal, social relations were organized along cooperative, kinship lines generating and reproducing feelings of 'tribal' solidarity, and cities were relatively few and therefore absent (Welch, 1978). The African cultivator, from this point of view, lived more or less in a state of nature.

This 'noble savage' conception of African cultivators was effectively criticized by French economic anthropologists belonging to the mode of production school, who in the process established the need to study concretely the process of class formation in African societies. And yet, as if to underline that theories are not simply a product of rational discourse but also thrive in relation to prevailing interests, this same conception has subsequently been resurrected by Hyden (1979, 1981), with his assertion that the African peasant remains 'uncaptured' by dominant classes in society, or, to put it differently, that the African countryside (at least outside the labour reserve economies) remains classless and the African cultivators without any regularly reproduced relations of oppression/exploitation with dominant classes in control of state power. On the other hand, Hyden sees state power as suspended above society, held up from the outside by golden strings of aid, but helpless to penetrate African society, which is itself depicted as some kind of an unchanging leviathan with impenetrable scales knitted tightly together into an 'economy of affection'. Notwithstanding his entrepreneurial abilities—his capacity to incorporate Marxist terms into a modernization discourse—Hyden has really resurrected the 'primordial' and 'traditional' Africa of modernization theory, an Africa of the social anthropologists where social relations based on kinship ties preclude any internal social contradictions from developing.

It is not theoreticians of the modernization school, such as Hyden, but its practitioners in search of empirical facts who have been responsible in the main for concrete studies of social movements among the peasantry. But in spite of the richness of the empirical data uncovered by several of them, these studies have been marred by the assumptions of modernization theory, which have guided them in the very questions they have posed, and therefore in the very data they have sought. These empirical studies have reflected two different types of preoccupation.

On the one hand, researchers have investigated 'tribal' and 'nationalist' movements. Individual movements have been characterized as tribal or as nationalist depending, first of all, on the language in which their demands have been articulated and, second, on the geographical limits of their organization. Put in the unilinear evolutionist framework of modernization theory, tribalism was defined as pre-modern and backward, either hindering or at best preparing the ground for modern nationalist movements. Tribal movements were seen as examples of 'primary' resistance and nationalist movements as those of 'secondary' resistance, the latter seen as the outcome of the former (Ranger, 1968).

The teleological distinction between primary and secondary resistances is entirely based on the periodization of history centred around the colonial state: resistance against the establishment of the colonial state is said to be primary and that against the consolidation of functioning of the colonial state is said to be secondary. The simple fact of the continuation of the colonial state is taken as sufficient basis to establish these as two phases of a single movement, one primary and therefore primitive, the other secondary and therefore relatively advanced. Instances where such a distinction could not be established based on simple historical chronology, where 'tribally confined' movements arose but after the colonial state had consolidated, became the focal points of disagreement among scholars. This is why a central controversy in the literature focused on whether the Maji Maji or Mau Mau movement should be characterized as tribal or as nationalist. The former category became a label of disapproval, the latter of approval.

Democracy: the forgotten issue

In the process of such controversies, most issues important from the standpoint of democracy were bypassed. That all these movements arose in definite socio-political contexts was forgotten. Emphasis on ideology tended to preclude any serious investigation of the demands (content) of these movements, and even of which classes participated in them under the leadership of which class. As to whether these were movements for right or for privileges was a question seldom posed. The creative element in these movements, particularly in those defined as tribal—for example, in the invention of new democratic forms, whether on the plane of participation/ representation or of implementation—was seldom underlined.

On the other hand, a second body of studies developed that specialized on religious movements of peasants and migrant labourers. But this body of literature, too, to an extent reflecting the division of the social sciences into a variety of clear-cut disciplines—as if social reality could be similarly neatly divided—proceeded by way of entirely artificial dichotomies. Were these religious movements 'cultural' or 'political', researchers asked time and again? Were they 'counter-societies not aiming at conquest of political power but trying to escape from a hostile environment' or were they political movements that 'react first and foremost to political and economic oppression and (who) attempt to conquer political power?' (Buijtenhuijs, in Bisbergen and Schofeleers, 1985).

This false dichotomy between 'counter-society' and 'political protest', between fight and battle, suggested a simplistic and mechanical conception of struggle, one which robbed every political movement of its cultural dimension and every cultural movement of its political significance. And yet the empirical material unearthed by these same scholars tended to belie the same dichotomies. For example, the researches on the Nyabingi (Robins, 1974) and the Yakan (Sutten, 1968–69) cults in Uganda show that, much like Maji Maji, these strongly religious movements were simultaneously anti-colonial movements and movements for internal socio-cultural reform. They confronted both colonial and traditional authority. Any attempt to drive a wedge between the political and the cultural aspects of these movements, polarizing the two in sharp opposition in the process, would only produce a very one-sided understanding of these movements.

This, however, was not all. Other, similar rigid oppositions were drawn in the literature. Should religious experience be understood through a symbolic and literary analysis of syntaxes and texts which emphasize internal history or should it be understood through a contextual/structural analysis which emphasizes the social context of symbolic production? (Van Binsbergen and Schofeleers, 1985). A debate raged on whether religious experience must be understood symbolically or instrumentally, whether analysis should emphasize its intrinsic meaning or extrinsic effect—as if a social experience could be either wholly objective or wholly subjective, one to the exclusion of the other.

A pioneering study that did break through these absolute dichotomies and succeed in relativizing them was that by Fields (1985) on the Watchtower Movement in Central Africa. Whilst Fields brilliantly showed how 'millenial activists spoke the language of the institutions which ruled them directly', she never posed the question of which social groups and classes the movement succeeded in reaching and organizing and which ones it did not. Anxious to distance herself from the 'vulgar Marxist conception that social conditions "cause" religious ideology', she ended up simply detaching social consciousness (ideology) from social experience (class).

While field research inspired by the mode of production school carried out numerous studies of labour movements, and that inspired by the modernization perspective produced as many studies on tribal/nationalist and religious/cultural movements, there were social groups on whose social activity these schools of thought tended to remain relatively silent. These were primarily women and youth. But if democratic practice and democratic theory is to be popular, it must not only come to terms with the class principle—the rights of those who labour in society—it must also come to terms with the principle of the rights of political minorities in Africa, be these defined as the rights of nationalities (tribes), women or youth.

In sum then, the existence of a crisis in Africa demands that attention be directed to the subjective factor in African development. For whatever the roots of that crisis—external, internal, or a specific mix of the two—its solution can only be the result of initiatives by organized social forces inside Africa. Hitherto, all schools of thought have either focused one-sidedly on the African state as the subject of African development or, to the extent that they have shifted attention to some sector of the popular masses, this has been in a manner that has tended to isolate these movements from their overall social or historical context. As a result, our understanding—both of these movements and of the twin processes of democratization and development—has tended to remain partial.

Second, to focus on the question of popular movements and democracy should not lead to an exercise in abstract model-building. Its point is not to search for and devise institutions for popular participation in a manner reminiscent of the social engineering of the modernization school. Rather, the point is to underline actual forms of organization and participation, democratic or otherwise, that have actually emerged in the historical development of popular movements in Africa.

Finally, neither should the project be seen as a celebration of these movements. It is really more in the nature of an analytical study, a critical summing-up of the positive and negative aspects of these movements as reflected through actual historical experiences. It is in this sense a stock-taking exercise. For, after all, is not to understand the nature of the African crisis—to ask, which way Africa?—also to ask, what went wrong with popular movements in Africa?

References

Books

Afigbo, A.E., *The Poverty of African Historiography,* Nigeria Industrial Arts and Crafts, Lagos, 1977.

Amin, Samir, *Unequal Development,* Monthly Review Press, New York, 1976.

Arrighi, G. and J.S. Saul, *Essays on the Political Economy of East Africa,* Heinemann, London, 1973.

Babassana, Hilaire, *Travail force, expropriation et formation du salariat en Afrique Noire,* Presses Universitaires de Grenoble, Grenoble, 1978.

Badiou, Alain, *Théorie du sujet,* Seuil, Paris, 1982.

Beaud, Michel, *A History of Capitalism, 1500–1980,* Macmillan, London, 1984.

Benton, Ted, *The Rise and Fall of Structural Marxism: Althusser and his influence,* Macmillan, London, 1984.

Bernstein, Henry and Bonnie K. Campbell (eds.), *Contradictions of Accumulation in Africa: studies in economy and state,* Sage Publications, Beverly Hills and London, 1985.

Bisbergen, William Van and Schofeleers, Mattew (eds.), *Theoretical Explorations in African Religions,* KPI, London, 1985.

Blomstrom, Magnus and Bjorn Hettne, *Development Theory in Transition: the dependency debate and beyond, Third World responses,* Zed Press, London, 1984.

Chilcote, Ronald H., *Dependency and Marxism: toward a resolution of a debate,* Latin American Perspectives Series No. 1, Westview Press, Colorado and London, 1982.

Chilcote, Ronald H. and Dale L. Johnson, *Theories of Development: mode of production or dependency?,* Sage Publications, Beverly Hills, 1983.

Chomsky, Noam, *The New Mandarins,* Vintage Books, New York, 1974.

Crisp, Jeff, *The Story of an African Working Class: Ghanaian miners' struggles, 1970–1980,* Zed Press, London.

Fanon, Frantz, *The Wretched of the Earth*, Penguin, Harmondsworth, 1967.

Fields, Karen E., *Revival and Rebellion in Colonial Central Africa,* Princeton University Press, Princeton, 1985.

Fougeyrollas, Pierre, *Les processus sociaux contemporains,* Payot, Paris, 1980.

Fougeyrollas, Pierre, *Sciences sociales et marxisme,* Payot, Paris, 1980.

Freund, Bill, *The Making of Contemporary Africa: the development of African society since 1800,* Macmillan, London, 1984.

Gendzier, Irene L., *Managing Political Change: social scientists and the Third World,* Westview Press, Boulder, Colorado and London, 1985.

Gouldner, Alvin W., *The Coming Crisis of Western Sociology*, Hearst Corporation, Avon Books, New York, 1970.

Guha, Ranajit, *Elementary Aspects of Peasant Insurgency in Colonial India,* Oxford University Press, New Delhi, 1983.

Gutkind, Peter C.W., Robin Cohen, and Jean Copans, *African Labor History,* Sage Publications, Beverly Hills and London, 1978.

Gutkind, Peter C.W. and Immanuel Wallerstein, (eds.), *The Political Economy of Contemporary Africa,* Sage Publications, Beverly Hills and London, 1976.

Hilton, Rodney, et al. *The Transition from Feudalism to Capitalism,* New Left Books, London, 1976.

Huntington, S.P., *Political Order in Changing Societies,* Yale University Press, New Haven, Connecticut.

Jaffe, Hosea, *A History of Africa,* Zed Press, London, 1985.

Joseph, Richard, *Radical Nationalism in Cameroun: social origins of the UPC rebellion,* Clarendon Press, Oxford, 1977.

Lewis, John Wilson, *Peasant Rebellion and Communist Revolution in Asia,* Stanford University Press, Stanford, 1974.

Leys, Colin, *Under-development in Kenya: the political economy of neo-colonialism,* Heinemann, London, 1975.

Luke, David Fashola, *Labour and Parastatal Politics in Sierra Leone: a study of African working-class ambivalence,* University Press of America, Lanham, New York and London, 1984.

Meillassoux, Claude, *Maidens, Meal and Money: capitalism and the domestic community,* Cambridge University Press, Cambridge and New York, 1981.

Miller, Christopher L., *Blank Darkness, Africanist Discourse in French,* University of Chicago Press, Chicago and London, 1985.

Munslow, B. and H. Finch, *Proletarianisation in the Third World,* Croom Helm, London, 1984.
Oxaal, Ivan, Tony Barnett and David Booth, *Beyond the Sociology of Development: economy and society in Latin America and Africa,* Routledge and Kegan Paul, Boston and Henley, 1975.
Ranger, Terence, *Peasant Consciousness and Guerrilla War in Zimbabwe: a comparative study,* James Currey, London, 1985.
Rey, Pierre-Philippe, *Colonialisme, négrier: la marche des paysans vers le prolétariat,* Maspero, Paris, 1976.
Rey, Pierre-Philippe, *Colonialisme, néo-colonialisme et transition au capitalisme,* Maspero, Paris, 1971.
Rey, Pierre-Philippe, *Les Alliances de classes,* Maspero, Paris, 1973.
Rodney, Walter, *How Europe Underdeveloped Africa,* Bogle-L'Ouverture, London, 1972.
Rostow, W.W., *The Stages of Economic Growth: a non-communist manifesto,* Cambridge University Press, Cambridge, 1960.
Rweyemamu, Justinian, *Underdevelopment and Industrialisation in Tanzania,* Oxford University Press, Nairobi, 1973.
Said, Edward W., *Orientalism,* Vintage Books, Random House, New York, 1979.
Sandbrook, Richard and Robin Cohen, (eds.), *The Development of an African Working Class: studies in class formation and action,* University of Toronto Press, Toronto and Buffalo, 1975.
Shivji, Issa G. (ed.), *The State and the Working People in Tanzania,* CODESRIA, Dakar, 1985.
Smith, Alan K. and Claude E. Welch, *Peasants in Africa,* African Studies Association, USA, 1978.
Wolf, Eric, *Europe and the People Without History,* University of California Press, Berkeley, Los Angeles and London, 1982.

Articles

Adkin, Laurie and Catherine Hyett, 'The Chilean Left and the Question of Democratic Transition', *IDS Bulletin,* University of Sussex, April 1985.
Bodenheimer, Susanne J., 'The Ideology of Developmentalism: American political science's paradigm-surrogate for Latin American studies', *Berkeley Journal of Sociology,* 1970.
Chegge, Michael, 'The Revolution Betrayed', *Journal of Modern African Studies,* 17 (3), 1979.
Clayton, Anthony, 'The General Strike in Zanzibar, 1948', *Journal of African History,* XVII (3), 1976.
Cooke, Peter and Martin Doornbos, 'Ruwenzururu Protest Songs', *Africa,* 52 (1), 1982.
Davidson, Basil, 'On Revolutionary Nationalism: the legacy of Cabral', *Latin American Perspectives,* Vol. 11, Issue 41, No. 2, April 1984.
Depelchin, Jacques, 'The Transformation of the Petty Bourgeoisie and the State in Post-colonial Zaire', *Review of African Political Economy,* No. 22, 1981.
Doornbos, Martin, 'Land Tenure and Political Conflict in Ankole, Uganda', *Journal of Development Studies,* Vol. 12, No. 1, October 1975.
Drake, St Clair, 'Democracy on Trial in Africa', *Annals of the American Academy of Political and Social Sciences,* July 1964.
Elam, Yitzchak, 'Nomadism in Ankole as a Substitute for Rebellion', *Africa,* 49(2), 1979.
Ellis, Diana, 'The Nandi Protest of 1923 in the Context of African Resistance to Colonial Rule in Kenya', *Journal of African History,* XVII (4), 1976.
Eriksen, Tore Linne, 'Modern African History: some historiographical observations', *Scandinavian Journal of History,* No. 4, 1979.
Freund, Bill, 'Labour and Labour Studies in Africa: a review of the literature', *African Studies Review,* Vol. 27, No.2, June 1984.

Freund, W.M., 'Class Conflict, Political Economy and the Struggle for Socialism in Tanzania', *African Affairs,* Vol. 80, No. 321, October 1981.

Friedland, William H., 'African Trade Union Studies: analysis of two decades', *Cahiers d' Etudes Africaines,* Vol. 14, No.55, 1974.

Furedi, Frank, 'The African Crowd in Nairobi: popular movements and elite politics', *Journal of African History,* XIV (2), 1973.

Giliomee, Hermann, 'Eighteenth-century Cape Society and its Historiography: culture, race and class', *Social Dynamics,* 9(1), 1983.

Guha, Ranajeet, 'On Some Aspects of the Historiography of Colonial India', in R. Guha (ed.), *Sub-Altern Studies 1: writings on South Asian history and society,* Oxford University Press, Delhi, 1982.

Guha, Ranajeet, 'The Prose of Counter-insurgency', *Sub-Altern Studies II,* Oxford University Press, Delhi, 1982.

Havnevik, Kjell J., 'Some Observations on the Empirical Foundations of Theories of Underdevelopment with Particular Reference to Tanzania', *Proceedings of the First Annual Conference of the Norwegian Association of Development Research,* Bergen, 6–8 April, 1984.

Henderson, Ian, 'The Origins of Nationalism in East and Central Africa: the Zambian case', *Journal of African History,* XI (4), 1970.

Joseph, Richard, 'Ruben Um Nyobi and the "Kameroun" Rebellion', *African Affairs,* Vol. 73, No. 293, October 1974.

Jubber, Ken, 'Sociology and its Social Context: the case of the rise of Marxist sociology in South Africa', *Social Dynamics,* 9(2), 1983.

Karaus, Jon, 'African Trade Unions: progress or poverty?', *African Studies Review,* Vol. 19, No. 3, December 1976.

Kitching, Gavin, 'Suggestions for a Fresh Start on an Exhausted Debate', *Canadian Journal of African Studies,* special issue, *Mode of Production: the challenge of Africa,* Vol. 19, No. 1, 1985.

Koffi, Tetteh A., 'Peasants and Economic Development: populist lessons for Africa', *African Studies Review,* Vol. 20, No. 3, December 1977.

Legassick, Martin, 'South Africa in Crisis: what route to democracy?', *African Affairs,* Vol. 84, No. 337, October 1985.

Legesse, Lemma, 'The Ethiopian Student Movement, 1960–74: a challenge to the monarchy and imperialism in Ethiopia', *Northeast African Studies,* 1 (1), 1979.

Lonsdale, John, 'States and Social Processes in Africa: a historiographical survey', *African Studies Review,* Vol. XXIV, Nos. 2/3, June–September 1981.

Mafeje, Archie, 'On the Articulation of Models of Production: review article', *Journal of Southern African Studies,* Vol. 8, No. 1, October 1981.

Mafeje, Archie, 'Peasants in Sub-Saharan Africa', *Africa Development,* Vol. X, No. 5, 1985.

Mamdani, Mahmood, 'Peasants and Democracy in Africa', *New Left Review,* No. 156, March–April 1986.

Mohan, Jitendra, 'A Whig Interpretation of African Nationalism', *Journal of Modern African Studies,* 6 (3), 1968.

Mohan, Jitendra, 'Nkrumah and Nkrumahism', *Socialist Register,* 1967.

Nicanor, Njiawue, 'Some Lessons from the History of the Cameroon Revolution', *The Pan-Africanist,* No. 4, July 1972.

Nzongola-Ntalaga, 'Amilcar Cabral and the Theory of the National Liberation Struggle', *Latin American Perspectives,* Vol. 11, Issue 41, No. 2, Spring 1984.

O'Brien, Donal Cruise, 'Modernization, Order and the Erosion of a Democratic Ideal: American political science, 1960–70', *Journal of Development Studies,* Vol. 8, No. 4, July 1972.

Okpewho, Isidore, 'Cheikh Anta Diop: the search for a philosophy of African culture', *Cahiers d'Etudes Africaines,* XXI–4, 1984.

Ottaway, Maria, 'Democracy and New Democracy: the ideological debate in the Ethiopian revolution', *African Studies Review,* Vol. XI, No. 1, April 1978.

Palma, Gabriel, 'Dependency and Development: a critical overview', in Dudley Seers (ed.), *Dependency Theory: a critical assessment,* Frances Pinter, London, 1981.
Posel, Deborah, 'Rethinking the "Race–Class" Debate in South African Historiography', *Social Dynamics,* 9(1), 1983.
Ranger, T.O. 'Connection between "Primary" Resistance Movements and Modern Mass Nationalism in East and Central Africa', Parts 1 and 2, *Journal of African History,* IX (3–4), 1968.
Redmond, Patrick M., 'Maji Maji in Ungoni: a reappraisal of existing historiography', *International Journal of African Historiographical Studies,* VIII, 1975.
Rey, Pierre-Philippe, 'Production et contre-révolution', *Canadian Journal of African Studies,* Vol. 19, No. 1, 1985.
Rhodes, William, 'The Philosophical Underpinnings of the Afro-American Liberation Movement: an interpretative essay', *The Pan-Africanist,* No. 9, January 1982.
Rodney, Walter, 'Marxism in Africa', *Forward,* Kampala, Uganda, Vol. 7, No. 1, 1986.
Said, Edward W., 'Orientalism Reconsidered', *Race and Class,* XXVII (2), 1985.
Scott, Jim, 'Everyday Forms of Peasant Resistance', *Journal of Peasant Studies,* Vol. 13, No. 2, January 1986.
Scotton, James F., 'The First African Press in East Africa: protest and nationalism in Uganda in the 1920s', *International Journal of African Historical Studies,* VI (2), 1973.
Shivji, Issa G., 'The State in the Dominated Social Formations of Africa: some theoretical issues', *International Social Science Journal,* Vol. XXXII, No. 4, 1980.
Shivji, Issa G., 'Working Class Struggles in Tanzania', *Mawazo,* Vol. V, No. 1, June 1983.
Sklar, Richard L., 'Democracy in Africa', *African Studies Review,* Vol. XXVI, Nos. 3–4, September–December 1983.
Southall, Roger, 'Review Article: South African labour studies', *South African Labour Bulletin,* Vol. 9, No. 7, June 1984.
Soyinka, Wole, 'The Writer in an African State', *Transition,* 31.
Spiegel, Andrew R., 'Review of Claude Meillassoux's *Maidens, Meal and Money', Social Dynamics,* 9(2), 1983.
Stichter, Sharon, 'Migrant Labour in Kenya', in *Capitalism and African Response, 1895–1975,* Longman, Harlow, Essex, 1982.
Tamarkin, M., 'Mau Mau in Nakuru', *Journal of African History,* XVII (1) 1976.
Taylor, Fraser D.R., 'The Development of African Studies in Canada', *African Research and Documentation,* No. 34, 1984.
Taylor, G. John, 'From Modernisation of Modes of Production', in *A Critique of the Sociologies of Development and Underdevelopment,* Macmillan, London, 1979.
Thomas, Clive Y., 'The Grenadian Crisis and the Carribbean Left', *IDS Bulletin,* University of Sussex, April 1985.
Throup, D.W., 'The Origins of Mau Mau', *African Affairs,* Vol. 84, No. 336, July 1985.
Tignor, Robert L., 'Kamba Political Protest: the destocking controversy of 1938', *African Historical Studies,* IV (2), 1971.
Van Zwanenberg, Roger, 'Neo-colonialism and the Origin of the National Bourgeoisie in Kenya between 1940 and 1973', *Journal of East African Research and Development,* Vol. 4, No. 2, 1974.
Wamba-dia-Wamba, E., 'History of neo-colonialism or neo-colonialist history?' Working Paper No.5, Africa Research and Publications Project, Trenton, New Jersey, 1983.
Waterman, Peter, 'A New Focus in African Worker Studies: promises, problems, dangers', *Cahiers d'Etudes Africaines,* 95, XXIV–3, 1984.
Wa Thiong'o, Ngugi, 'The Language of African Literature', *New Left Review,* No. 150, March–April, 1985.
Weinstein, Warren, 'Burundi 1972/73: a case study of ethnic conflict and peasant repression', *Pan-African Journal,* Vol. VII, No. 3, Fall 1974.
Wolpe, Harold, 'Capitalism and Cheap Labour Power in South Africa: from segregation to apartheid', *Economy and Society,* 1(4), 1972.
Wolpe, Harold, 'The Theory of Internal Colonialism: the South African case', *Bulletin of the Conference of Socialist Economists,* Autumn 1974.

Zeleza, Yiyambe, 'Colonalism and Internationalism: the case of the British and Kenyan labour movements', *Ufahamu,* Vol. 14, No. 1, 1984.

Unpublished works

Beckman, Bjorn, 'Capitalist State Formations in the Third World', paper presented to Workshop on Democracy and Development at the VIIth Nordic Political Science Congress.

Cohen, Robin, 'Marxism and Africa: old, new and projected', University of Birmingham, Centre for Development Area Studies, Working Paper No. 2, August 1975.

Doornbos, Martin, 'Protest Movements in Western Uganda: some parallels and contrasts', University of East Africa Social Science Conference, December 1966.

ICT, 'Speaking for Ourselves', Members of African Independent Churches Report on their Pilot Study of the History and Theology of their Churches, Box 32407, Braamfontein, South Africa.

Janmohamed, Karim K., 'Labour Protest in Mombasa', Staff Seminar Paper No. 12, Department of History, University of Nairobi, 1978–79.

Nyong'o, Anyang', 'Academic Freedom and Political Power in Africa', Staff Seminar Paper No. 8, Department of History, University of Nairobi, 1978–79.

Ogot, Bethwella and William Ochieng, 'Mumboism: an anticolonial movement?', University of East Africa 5th Social Science Conference, Nairobi, 8–12 December 1969.

Ohaegbulam, F.U., 'The Nadir of African Nationalism', paper presented to African Studies Association 13th Annual Meeting, Boston, Massachusetts, 21–24 October 1970.

O'Meara, Dan, 'Class, Capital and Ideology in the Development of Afrikaner Nationalism: 1934–1948', Ph D. thesis, University of Sussex, 1979.

Rahmato, Desalegn, 'Cabral and the Problem of the African Revolution', IDR Working Paper No. 16, University of Addis Ababa, January 1962.

Ranger, Terence O., 'Religious Movements and Politics in Sub-Saharan Studies', paper for presentation to African Studies Association Annual Meeting, New Orleans, Louisiana, 23–26 November 1985.

Robins, C.E., 'Conversion and Conflict: Christian fundamentalism and the problem of evil in Kigezi District, Uganda', paper presented to the Canadian Association of African Studies Conference, Dalhousie University, Nova Scotia, 1974.

Sembene, Ousmane, 'Man is Culture', African Studies Program, Indiana University (no date).

Steinhart, Edward, 'Marxism and African History: reviews and agenda', Staff Seminar Paper No. 11, Department of History, University of Nairobi, 1979–80.

'Student Unrest in Africa' (no author), May 1970. Source: Scandinavian Institute of African Studies Library, Uppsala.

Sutten, Anne, 'A Preliminary Study of Lugbara Response to Alien Intrusion in West Nile District, 1880–1920', University of East Africa Social Science Conference, 1968–69.

Uzoigwe, G.N., 'The Kyanyangire, 1907: passive revolt against British over-rule', Makerere University papers, Kampala (no date).

Wamba-dia-Wamba, E., 'Struggles for the "Second Independence" in Congo Kinshasa', paper presented to Mawazo workshop 'Which Way Africa?', Kampala, Uganda, 26–28 April 1985.

Wolpe, Harold, 'Draft Notes on (a) Articulation of Modes of Production and the Value of Labour Power, (b) Periodisation and the State', Sussex University seminar paper, 1975.

Working papers

Claude Ake, *Social Science Issues in Nigeria,* COD/SSD/2–1981.

F. Baffoe, *Social Science Politics in Africa: the case of Botswana, Lesotho, and Swaziland,* COD/SSD/3–1981.

Nujra and Mkandawire. *The Evolution of Social Science in Africa: problems and prospects,* COD/SSD/4–1981.

C. Atta-Mills. *The Role of the Social Scientist in Development: the rise, fall and rebirth of social science in Africa,* COD/SSD/5–1981.

S. Koajo, *Social Science and Society.* COD/SSD/6–1981.

Henri Mapolu. *Workers' Participation in the Management of Public Enterprise,* COD/PSD/1–1981.

S. Bedrani. *Le Rôle du secteur public dans la transition du socialisme: le cas algérien,* COD/PSD/2–1981.

K. Botchwey. *The Political Economy of Public Enterprise in Ghana,* COD/PSD/2–1981.

S.H. Elmaihub. *The Role of the Public Sector in a Capital Surplus Economy: the case of Libya,* COD/PSD/5–1981.

Akin Fadahunsi. *A Review of Nigeria's Public Sector Industrial Development Policy: 1960–1978.* COD/PSD/6–1981.

Y. Yachir. *Resources minières africaines at division internationale du travail,* COD/MIN/1–1981.

Akin Fadahunsi. *Transnationals and the Nigerian Oil Industry.* COD/MIN/3–1981.

A.M. Ould Cheikh. *Les Multinationales et l'exploitation du fer mauriatanten,* COD/MIN/5–1981.

T.M.Ocran. *The Proposed United Nations Code of Conduct on Transnational Corporations: an African point of view.* COD/MIN/7–1981.

T. Mkandawire. *The World Bank and Rural Development in Malawi,* COD/IFO/1–1981.

F. Mansour. *Restructuring of the World Bank? An Outsider's View,* COD/IFO/2–1981.

B. Duhamel. *Transfert de technologie et technologie de rapture.* COD/BNT/1–1981.

M. Salem. *Le Contrat 'Clés en main stratégie d' importation de la technologie* COD/BNT/2–1981.

P. Anyang' Nyong'o. *Technology and Basic Needs.* COD/BNT/7–1981.

I.Illunkamba. *L'Etat post-colonial au Zaire: sa nature et son rôle dans le développement.* COD/PSD/2–1981.

E. Barigume. *L' Impact des mesures prises. par les Nations-Unies en faveur des pays les moins développés et enclaves sur leur développement: le cas du Burudi.* COD/LLDCs/1–1982.

L.M. Gakou. *Queques rèflexions relatives aux problèmes de développement du Mali: pays enclave.* COD/LLDCs/2–1982.

T. Kafando. *Coopération économique régionale en Afrique de l'Ouest et problematique du développement des pays enclaves: le cas de la Haute Volta. du Mali et du Niger.* COD/LLDCs/3–1982.

R. Murapa. *Geography. Race, Class and Power in Rhodesia.* COD/L L DCs/4–1982.

N. Shanmuyarna. *Self-Reliance and Internal Mobilization of Landlocked Economies.* COD/LLDCs/5–1982.

G.K. Simwinga. *The Backwash of Landlockedness: the Zambian case,* COD/LLDCs/6–1982.

B. Wanji. *Botswana Landlockedness: the structure of underdevelopment and options for disengagement.* COD/LLDCs/7–1982.

PART TWO

Illustrative Profiles

Introduction

Autonomous social movements are at the centre of people's attempts to participate in the struggle for democracy, development, cultural autonomy, self-determination, justice and rights, and social change. They represent concrete instances of social praxis.

Social movements have diverse origins and agendas depending on historical, social and developmental circumstances that have necessitated autonomous social praxis. They are a vitally important dimension of the experiential reality of the people. A proper evaluation of their intervention, strength and limitations is necessary for the sharpening of our concepts and for refining praxis.

The seven chapters included in this part of the book examine profiles of some social movements in the South. They range from such macro movements as Palestinian mobilization for nationhood to micro-level action groups oriented towards specific issues.

These profiles illustrate some key aspects of social praxis. Mobilization, conscientization and organization for countervailing power are three related themes in these processes. There are also instances where the processes have been spontaneous or catalysed. Yet another dimension is the capacity of the people to view their life in the totality of its existence, survival and transformation.

6. Survival and Democracy: Ecological Struggles in India[1]

Harsh Sethi

Modernization, development and ecological damage

Any search for an alternative democratic theory that accepts the great diversity of human situations—yet provides coherence to them through an active political process, opens up new and creative spaces within the framework of civil society and restructures the state for realizing these ends—must start with a critique of the modern development project. Ecological damage and cultural destruction are central to contemporary change and in extreme cases, alongside militarization, they threaten the very foundation of life, of people and of the planet.

India too is no stranger to this strange mix of human progress with development. While the last four decades of development under an independent nation state have undoubtedly seen an improvement in the social and material environment for a substantial proportion of the population, through the creation of the infrastucture of a modern democracy—free and regular elections at all levels, the rule of a constitution, a free judiciary and press, laws to protect the rights of individuals and property—the very same process has also resulted in a deep dualism that creates for the hitherto excluded not just a crisis of survival, but the prospect of triage.[2]

Rarely have our planners and intellectuals understood that in large, diverse, and predominantly pre-industrial societies like India, basic survival for the poor is deeply dependent upon access to and use of natural resources, what in current literature are referred to as 'the commons'. Any alteration in the institutional mechanisms governing this use not only impacts differentially upon different strata, but also gives rise to conflicts. What this chapter attempts is to trace the evolution of conflicts and struggles around the use and control of natural resources. This evolution is discussed both as discourse and practice in an effort to understand how ecological issues and struggles have been responded to and accommodated within the evolving Indian political system. These issues are crucial not just because they affect the daily life chances of millions, particularly the rural poor, or because the survival of the planet is at stake, but because ecological issues do not permit easy aggregation of interest groups, are only partially admitted in the political discourse, and thus demand responses and strategies—both from the movement and the state—that cut across the simplistic divides of class, rural–urban, etc. In this sense, this chapter traces the hesitant trajectory of a system in evolution.

Conflicts over the ownership, control and mode of use of natural resources are hardly new or recent. As populations grow, new communities are born, markets expand, and new and more productive technologies come into play, alterations take place in the relationships of both man to nature and man to man, and conflicts arise between livelihood patterns and lifestyles. An early record of a struggle of this kind in India is mentioned in the epic *Mahabharata,* where the clash between the Aryas, pastoralists and agriculturists, and the Nishads, forest-dwellers, resulted in the burning down of the Khandava-vana, the site of modern-day Delhi.

It is, however, with the heralding of the modern age, introduced in India through the colonial encounter and the conquest by the British, that the advent of new technology made possible the establishment of modern industry and consequently a different framework for the use of natural resources. Previously, 'the indigenous modes of natural resources utilisation were (relatively more) sensitive to the limits to which these resources could be used' (Shiva and Bandopadhyaya, 1988). The demands of the industrial revolution in Britain imposed new conditions in India. The setting up of indigo plantations in Bengal and Bihar to feed the dye industry, the introduction of cotton in Gujarat and the Deccan, or the large-scale felling of trees in the sensitive mountain ecosystems of the western Ghats and the Himalayas to meet the requirements of the shipbuilding and railway industries—all led to the emergence of new conflicts that induced new forms of poverty and deprivation, resulting in turn in local responses geared to retain control over local natural resources. These conflicts are mentioned in literature as the Indigo movement in eastern India, the Deccan movement for land rights, and the forest movements in the western Ghats, central Indian hills and the Himalayas.

In many ways the independent nation state, which decided to pursue economic development based on modern industry and agriculture, led to a further widening and deepening of these conflicts. Committed to achieve accelerating rates of economic growth, the state placed increasing reliance on a wide-scale application of modern technology, a process to tame nature, 'colonize' newer resources and regions. Ironically, the hope was that, the concomitant disruptions apart, the all-round increase in material production, once appropriately distributed, would lead to a general increase in prosperity. In the first two decades of planned development the base was laid for the widespread modernization of all sectors of productive life—industry, agriculture, forestry, fishing, etc.—with inevitable consequences both for natural resource systems and the communities whose livelihood patterns and lifestyles depended upon these resources.

Accompanying this policy of accelerated economic growth seeking to alter the man–nature relationship was another significant transformation: that of the downgrading and decay of social cohesions, modes of living and belief which had so far helped mediate this relationship. Since the modern nation state provides primary cognitive legitimacy only to the state and the citizen, as a result of the growth of the public (state) and private forms of ownership, control and use of resources, the country suffered a major decline in the commons. It is being neither utopian nor romantic about the living conditions and social systems in pre-colonial rural India to state that during the pre-colonial period, since natural resources were not alienable commodities, village communities had worked out systems of resource management, both of use and maintenace. Even 'crown land' was not owned in the Western sense by the king. With the introduction of alienable property not only did the earlier systems of use and maintenance break down but trends that restricted access to the earlier commons were strengthened. Recent research indicates that a major factor behind India's rural poverty is the decay and destruction of community-held resources—be they grazing lands, forests, water sources, irrigation systems, etc.[3]

It is a queer paradox of history that the early decades of independence, which saw the celebration of the idea of modern development and provided the foreplay to the conflicts and disasters to come, engendered little resistance. The few voices of dissent were either too weak or were arrogantly dismissed as irrelevant impediments in the march to progress. For instance, the powerful critiques against the large dams and river-valley schemes posed by Dr Ram Manohar Lohia, a leader of the Socialist Party, were dismissed by Pandit Nehru as not worthy of consideration. It is indeed instructive that Lohia's essays on these themes find a far more receptive audience today, more than two decades after his death, than they ever did while he was alive. Today, as the idea of development has lost much of its sheen, it is precisely the same sets of issues that have come on to the centre stage of social and political concern.

At one level the country is facing a rapid rate of depletion of forest cover. Not only is the land mass covered by forests now as low as 10–11 per cent, but also much of what gets classified as forest land is only shrub cover. Equally dangerous is the replacement of multi-species forests by mono-species plantations. This use and conversion of a vital resource into the service of the urban–industrial complex has severe consequences, foremost for the communities of forest people who are dependent upon these resources, but also for vital variables such as rainfall and soil degradation in catchment areas leading to siltation in dams and rivers, and for wildlife, etc. Similarly, the popularization of chemicals-based, high-water-intensity agriculture through deep-bore tube wells and canals has led to thousands of hectares of good arable land being lost every year to waterlogging and salinity, desertification, and a drastic lowering of natural soil productivity. Additionally, we are suffering the consequences of a decline of gene diversity, monoculture, the giving-up of older crop rotation practices—leading to the emergence of new crop diseases. The situation regarding water resources is equally dangerous, with pollution affecting almost all surface water systems, and groundwater levels dipping low as deep-bore tube wells are pressed into the service of both the cities and industrial centres and modern agriculture. The coastal regions face a rapid depletion of marine resources as trawlers indulge in reckless over-fishing. And the infamous Bhopal gas leak gave fresh reason to be aware of the dangers of mindless industrialization (CSE, 1985).

The reasons behind the near-breakdown in man–community–nature relationships are not all to be traced to dramatic and large interventions. There is the silent, but all-pervasive, degradation of natural resources caused by an increase in the intensity of resource use beyond the carrying capacity of nature and culture. This is due not just to a demographic explosion, as many conservative and neo-Malthusian experts claim with tiresome regularity, but also to the fact that forces of political economy have forced communities and peoples considered marginal on to poorer resource areas just as their lack of choice forces them to over-exploit what they have. This silent but steady depredation creates an atmosphere of inevitability leading to responses more in the form of adjustments than of struggle by the victim groups. Cutting down trees for fuel and shelter, over-grazing or over-farming in ecologically fragile areas all create serious conflicts, though these may not lead to any struggles.

The sources of conflict, as I have indicated, are many and widespread. What this chapter attempts is a preliminary mapping and typologizing of the struggles, at least the more overt ones that these conflicts have given rise to, and a drawing of some tentative conclusions, about both the future of these struggles and also the different visions of state, society and development encoded in these conflicts. But first some distinctions need to be drawn between struggles and movements on the one hand, and between conflicts with ecological ramifications and ecological struggles on the other.

The specificity of ecological struggles is marked by a combination of both political and moral economy considerations, and an ecological perspective involves a worldview about nature and the positioning of community in this perspective.

Just because tribal peoples or peasants or workers in a forest plantation are involved in a struggle does not imply that we can look upon it as ecological, though it is easily conceivable that shifts in capital–labour relations may well imply techno-organizational changes that would impact differently upon nature. Similarly, demands for a ban or regulation of logging, for the setting up of more greenbelts in urban areas, or for stricter pollution control regulations are at best a reflection of environmental concerns. If, however, there is resistance to the conversion of a multi-species natural forest into a mono-species plantation, a process which would undoubtedly alter, through the food–fodder–fuelwood chain, the relationships of the communities which depend upon this common resource, that resistance may be seen as ecological. Such a struggle operates at the planes of both political and moral economy—seeking to alter the rules governing the rights of use to the forest, implying a different notion of the forest itself. For the struggle to be classified as a movement, it should not only meet the criteria of scale, intensity, temporality, and impact, but should also signify a narrowing of the distance between the actor-participants and the interlocuters. In other words, it is the quality of the sharing of self-consciousness about the means and ends of the struggle that contributes to the making of a movement.

The rise of ecological movements

It was the 1972 Conference on Environment and Development at Stockholm that set the stage for the entry of the concepts of environment and ecology into the mainstream of Indian discourse on both development and social movements. While the Western representatives highlighted the issues of pollution and the depletion of non-renewable natural resources, the official Indian position was that 'poverty is the greatest pollutant'. One concern that the 1972 debate brought to centre stage related to the differential rates of consumption of natural resources by the West and countries such as India, that is, issues of global political economy. Whilst in itself a correct reflection of the stranglehold that the Western countries have over global resources, within the country this line of reasoning had three implications. The first was that the environmental problem was seen essentially as a Western one, arising only in the context of advanced industrial societies. Second, that too great a focus on such issues in a Third World context was seen as reflecting an anti-development bias. More sharply, it was argued that environmentalists were anti-national and anti-people, agents of Western imperialism wedded to blocking the necessary development of industry in India. The third response, partly as an admission of Western concerns, was a reiteration of faith in the miraculous powers of science and technology, that the use of better techno-managerial techniques could keep the negative consequences of developmental intervention in check.[4]

The debate settled at a level of an uneasy consensus which, while accommodating the demands of the conservationist lobbies—for the protection of wildlife, for the setting up of reserved forests and national parks, for building up greenbelts in the cities, for restrictions on the location of industry (particularly polluting industry) in urban concentrations, etc.—reflected its faith in the dominant views on economic progress based on the use of modern technology. At that stage the only partially dissenting view within the dominant paradigm was of the Marxists, who sought to extend the distributional logic of the use of resources and the benefits from that use from the global to the national terrain.

None of this is to argue that alternative views on the man–nature relationship were not part of the Indian discourse. The most prominent of course was the Gandhian view, which from the early years of the twentieth century had consistently argued for a model of state and society based upon the village as the primary unit, and the farmer/peasant as the key productive agent. In *Hind Swaraj,* published in 1908, Gandhi had formulated both a well-worked-out critique of the modern industrial vision and an alternative to it. Both Gandhi and Tagore, drawing upon the traditional wisdom in the country, looked upon nature not as something dead but as the living source of light and air, food and water. They sought to enshrine the diversity in life and nature as the dominant principle in society, that of decentralized, democratic pluralism. Intrinsic to such a viewpoint was a respect for different traditions, cultures and modes of livelihood—arranged not in a hierarchy, but in an interrelationship that respected autonomy. But the so-called makers of modern India, particularly after the death of Gandhi in 1948, could easily afford to dismiss such visions as romantic, rooted in an idyllic notion of the past and fundamentally reactionary: in brief, unsuited for the demands of the present. Similarly too, the weak voices of protest that could be gleaned from popular writings in the vernacular could be safely ignored, first, because they were weak and, second, because it was expected that the strata these views represented were being consciously worked upon to bring them into the mainstream of productive existence.[5]

In the early 1970s, at the time that environmental experts were debating their viewpoints in Stockholm and similar forums, another movement, now famous in developmental literature as Chipko, started making its impact in India. Drawing upon earlier struggles of forest- and hill-based people in the lower regions of the Himalayas, the current phase of Chipko began as a movement to save the local forest resources from commercial exploitation by outside contractors. The initial demands were mainly for local control of local resources. Since the hill regions are highly underdeveloped, most adult males have to migrate to the plains for employment. By demanding a stop to the timber contracts given to outside businessmen, the nationalization of forests and provision of contracts to local cooperatives for the use of forest produce, it was hoped that male outmigration could be substantially reduced since now local resources would be available for local income generation. This struggle, partially successful, could not, however, address itself to the question of an alarming depletion in the forest cover, which was leading to landslides and soil erosion, a drying up of local streams and other water sources, and shortages of fuel and fodder for domestic consumption. These issues, posed most sharply by hill women, led finally to a major ecological tendency emerging in the hills. The new demands were for a complete ban on the felling of green trees (a demand conceded in 1973), for a substantial step-up in afforestation efforts based on tree species that were environmentally suitable and locally useful, and for control of local forests to pass into the hands of local village communities.[6]

The Chipko movement, a classic example of non-violent resistance and struggle by thousands of ordinary hill folk without the guidance and control of any centralized apparatus, recognized leadership or full-time cadre, has in the last decade and a half not only spread across the Himalayas, but also inspired similar struggles in other parts of India. Whilst other consequences of this unique movement will be discussed later, one crucial ideological shift that it implied in the popular discourse on these issues was that it focused attention on the centrality of renewable resources (soil, air, water, trees) in the livelihoods and lives of people in our country. Chipko, as a voice from the margins of Indian civil society, thus managed to demonstrate, quite unlike the concerns of India's elite classes, that the crucial environmental conflicts are not just city-based (pollution) or related to the depletion of non-renewable resources useful for industry, but arise directly from the philosophical premises embedded in the modern Western and capitalist vision that seeks to subjugate and colonize nature via technology in the service of man.

What follows is a quick reconnaissance of the different types of struggles and conflicts over the control and use of natural resources that have come up in the last two decades. In each domain of productive activity, one can discern three types of response/struggle. At the most primary level, the struggle operates in the domain of political economy, that of a redefinition of *rights* of different strata and communities to the resources in question. Such a response does not involve any substantative questioning of either the developmental model or a redefinition of the man–nature relationship. At the second level we can see an *environmental* response, one that seeks correctives through legal and policy-based shifts in the patterns of resource use. This is normally accompanied by a heightened sensitivity towards the depletion and destruction of natural resources, both renewable and non-renewable and thus gives rise to an anti-pollution and conservationist consciousness. Here too, there is no rejection of the philosophic premises underlying resource use within the dominant developmental model. Finally, the struggle may take an *ecological* dimension, one that rejects the dominant development paradigm and seeks to alter the very classification of both man and nature on which notions such as progress are based. No struggle is ever a pure one, nor is the trajectory one of unidirectional movement from a struggle over rights to ecological redefinitions. The actual sparking-off could be on any point of this notional scale, its actual trajectory being shaped by the concrete circumstances within which it is articulated.

In themselves, these struggles (of all three types) could either be clustered around different natural resources—land, water, forest, air, sea—or the symbols around which different struggles coalesce. In what follows, the empirical material has been presented around the resource/activity domains.

Forest-based struggles

As a result both of increased state/elite sensitivity to declining forest cover, with all its attendant implications, and the growing immiserization and pauperization of forest-based communities and people as a result of growing encroachment by industry (both state and private) on dwindling forest resources, small and large struggles have broken out and commanded attention all over India. The Chipko struggles in the Himalayan region, the Appiko movement in the western Ghats which is actively involved in struggles against the illegal over-felling of trees and in replanting forest lands with multipurpose broad-leaf tree species, the struggle against the replacement of sal trees by teak species in the forest areas of Bihar, Orissa and Madhya Pradesh (the Jharkhand–Bastar belt), resistance to the monoculture plantation of commercial chir pine in Himachal Pradesh, the uprooting of eucalyptus plantations pushed primarily by government and industry for the benefit of paper and rayon fibre extraction industries, the dozens of voluntary efforts engaged in massive afforestation (both for employment generation and to protect exposed lands): these struggles command the greatest spread and involvement, and have in turn had the greatest impact.

Each of these struggles has thrown up different demands in different phases. The most common have been struggles to regularize the rights of access to and use of resources for local communities dependent upon them. These may take the shape of regularizations of incursions into state forests for farming purposes, for access to forest produce (fuel, fodder), and for better pricing for minor forest produce (mahua flower, tendu leaves), the collection and sale of which is controlled by either the forest department or contractors. At a second level they may take the form of legal struggles either to regularize the traditional relationships of forest-based communities to the forest or to reclassify forests and wastelands. At a third level they may be fighting for an improvement in the ecological balance to permit a more sustained resource use, that is, for afforestation, bans on tree-felling, a modification in the tree species being planted, etc.

Most crucially these scattered and diverse struggles focused attention on the proposed Forest Bill of 1982 which sought to give greater control of forest resources to industry, and highlighted as never before the need to pass control of forest resources to local communities, who are unarguably in the best position to determine their pattern of use. The scale of the struggles also made clear that if the afforestation programmes, vitally needed to restore the ecological balance, are to be successful, local communities and groups have to be made the centrepiece of the strategy (Fernandez and Kulkarni, 1983).

The agitation against the Forest Bill marked a crucial watershed in ecological politics in India. For the first time many diverse and scattered groups were forced to network at local, regional and national levels. This networking also forged class/support structure organizations. In particular, the success of this effort (the proposed Bill was finally not placed before the Indian Parliament for discussion and ratification) popularized the campaign mode of functioning, not only in the environmental domain but in all areas where social activist groups were trying to make headway. Another significant contribution of the 1982 agitation was the convergence of ecological issues with those of human rights. Since the primary victims of the proposed legislation would have been the tribal communities, state responses and policy towards them become a matter of furious debate.

These struggles also led to a shift in the discourse on forests, to a realization that the equation of forest to timber (an extractable resource for industry) was what had contributed in the previous two and a half centuries to a decline in forest cover, and to a realization also that the allegation that it was local communities in search for fuel and building material who were responsible for deforestation was fundamentally fallacious. This shift in discourse is best epitomized by the slogans that the different struggles threw up. In Chipko the cry was 'What do the forests bear? Soil, water and pure air!' as against the dominant notion, 'What do forests bear? Profit on resin and timber!' Similarily the Jharkhand struggles highlighted the differences between sal (a tree species which gave the forest communities leaves for fodder, nuts and fuelwood) and saqwan (teak).

Struggles over land use

Most land-based struggles have arisen in the context of ownership and control, that is, in the form of movements of landless and poor peasants for tenancy modifications and equitable distribution of this most vital resource. Not surprisingly land reform, at least till the end of the decade of the 1960s, was high on the agenda of political parties. But such struggles have suffered a secular decline, not because land reforms have a lower political salience or rational justifiability, but possibly because with the worst excesses of landlordism now behind us, and land more securely in control of cultivating communities, the possibility of launching successful struggles to alter ownership status is now bleaker. Nevertheless, smaller struggles by marginal agrarian classes continue to break out, as also to lesser degree do struggles to change ownership laws to enable women to own and operate farm land (Agarwal, 1988).

What is new is the recent focus on the impact of both on- and off-farm activities on the quality of the land itself, its rapid degradation. Realization of this impact is now giving rise to demands and struggles with an environmental/ecological dimension alongside the traditional dimension of political economy.

The increasing industrialization of agriculture is forcing an ever larger number of farmers to realize not only that modern agriculture is more resource-intensive, dependent upon inputs from outside the farm or village, but also that the indiscriminate use of modern inputs may well lead to a decline in soil fertility, affect water tables, lead to a decline in gene diversity, etc. Whilst the major demands of farmers centre on the cost-price calculus of inputs and outputs (demands for cheaper or subsidized seeds, fertilizers, pesticides, water, electricity and a higher price of outputs), there is the simultaneous realization that these demands, whilst meeting short-run needs, cannot respond to the emerging threat of non-sustainability (Nadkarni, 1987).

Struggles, mainly localized, have broken out: against the indiscriminate popularization of chemical inputs that negatively affect soil productivity; against new hybrid seeds that are both more dependent upon a controlled and sustained supply of inputs and even more susceptible to new diseases; against mono-cropping practices; against the liberal granting of permission to deep-bore tube wells which lead to a decline in water tables; against faulty irrigation schemes, particularly canals, which lead to waterlogging and salinity; and against farm forestry schemes that affect soil and water, etc.

While in a few cases these struggles have led to major agitations, as in the Tawa Command area of Madhya Pradesh where waterlogging had led to the loss of thousands of acres of good soil, these struggles are efforts to come to terms with industrialized agriculture (Mishra, n.d.). Whether, as exemplified by the Friends Rural Centre, Rasulia, it is a return to Fukuoka-style natural farming practices, or a shift back to traditional seeds and cropping pattern practices, or a greater reliance on organic manure, or efforts at local watershed management, a great disillusionment with the promise held out by modern agriculture can be clearly discerned. Whilst the opposition is currently very weak, and the industrialization of agriculture grows apace, such conflicts are likely to increase. The ecological critique of modern agriculture is slowly acquiring a social base.

A second recent focus of land-based struggles has been the area of mining. Exploitation of mineral resources, in particular the opencast mining in the sensitive watersheds of the Himalayas, western Ghats, and central India, have done a great deal of environmental damage. Probably the most successful of these struggles has been the one against limestone quarrying in the Garhwal region of the Himalayas. Notwithstanding the fact that hundreds of local people were employed in these mines, slowly the adverse ecological impact, particularly on local water sources and land, led thousands of peasants to agitate against quarrying. A recent ban by the Indian Supreme Court on quarrying may have brought immediate relief, but the struggle highlights the contradiction between immediate and long-run, and stable, employment opportunities (Shiva and Bandopadhyaya, 1987).

Struggles have also broken out against the Bharatiya Aluminum Company in the Gandmardhan hills in Orissa, in the coal and iron ore belts in Bihar, and in the coal-rich regions of Singrauli and Baster in Madhya Pradesh. While it is true that most of these struggles have grown out of land takeovers and inadequate compensation and rehabilitation, and issues related to providing the newly created jobs to outsiders rather than locals, and the social consequences (prostitution, alcoholism, gambling, violence) that seem to accompany the development of mining areas, slowly what is also being understood is the longer-run environmental and ecological destruction wreaked in the wake of these activities.

A third focus of land-based struggles is against the recently promulgated Wastelands Development Policy. The basic thrust of this new policy is to classify village commons—used particularly by poorer people for fuel, fodder, housing materials, etc.—as wasteland, and for the state to appropriate them and then put them under plantation of fast-growing tree species. The aim is both to meet environmental objectives (by increasing tree cover) and the needs of industry. This issue has come up most sharply in the state of Karnataka where nearly 75,000 acres of common land has been appropriated and put under eucalyptus plantation. The Manu Rakshna Koota (Save the Soil) agitation has challenged both the choice of tree species and the reclassification of land. The peasant participants in the struggle link the degradation of the soil and decline in water tables to the eucalyptus plantation, and also resent their common resources being taken away to serve, in this case, a polyfibre factory which extracts rayon from eucalyptus (*Lokayan Bulletin*, 1985, 1986).

These struggles within farming, against injudicious land use policy, against classification of commons as wastelands, highlights the need for an environmental sensitivity sorely missing in the current policy mix. As with forest-based struggles, here too one can discern the seeds of a thoroughgoing critique of land use patterns. Though still weak and fragmented, these struggles have widened the base of questioning of the industrialized vision of society and progress.

Struggles against big dams[7]

Once classified by Jawaharlal Nehru as the temples of modern India, large multi-purpose dams and river valley schemes have today become the focus of widespread agitation. The Tehri and Pong dams in the north; the Kosi, Gandhak, Bodhghat and Koel-Karo schemes in the east; the Narmada Valley project in central India; Bedthi, Bhopalpatnam and Ichampalli in the west; the Tungbhadra, Malaprabha and Ghatprabha schemes in the south, all are facing resistance. Each one of these schemes has raised issues of location, design, destruction of natural resources (mainly forests, arable land and wildlife), displacement of local people in the catchment areas, and inadequate compensation to and rehabilitation of those ousted from their homes. And the question has also been raised of whether these schemes actually deliver what they promise, namely, increased irrigation in the command areas, better flood control, and generation of electric power. Equally in question has been the policy of linkage with foreign donors—both governments and multilateral agencies such as the World Bank—for both capital and technology/skill inputs.

An early successful struggle against a proposed dam project was that over Silent Valley. The Kerala government had in the early 1970s proposed the building of a dam on the Kuntipuzha river, ostensibly with the aim of generating electricity to facilitate industrialization in the region. The proposed dam, with a catchment area of 77 square kilometres, would inundate Silent Valley, one of the last surviving natural tropical forests in India. The ensuing agitation was unique because building a dam in this uninhabited area would not involve a displacement of people, and thus was fought primarily on environmental grounds.

Against the complete support given to the proposed scheme not only by the state government but also by all the political parties in the state, the agitation spearheaded by the Kerala Shastra Sahitya Parishad (KSSP), a local people's science movement, managed to involve an entire gamut of counter-experts—botanists, zoologists, economists—and succeeded in arguing that not only would the scheme have adverse environmental impact on a rare ecosystem rich in biological and genetic diversity, but also that the required power generation could as easily take place by setting up thermal power units in other locations and improving the efficiency of the transmission system.

The controversy assumed, for the first time, the character of a genuine public debate, not only in Kerala but all over India. In fact, with organizations like the World Wildlife Fund and the International Union for the Conservation of Nature and Natural Resources jumping in to the defence of the lion-tailed macaque, a rare breed of monkey resident in the Silent Valley, the controversy soon assumed an international dimension. After years of furious debates, campaigns, lobbying through the press, parliament and expert committees, the idea of a dam in Silent Valley was finally shelved, and the region was declared a national biosphere.

The success in Silent Valley thus set the stage for an intense questioning of all such schemes. At one level most of the older river valley projects had turned out to be relative failures. They had been unable to control floods, and in fact often contributed to them because high siltation levels in dam sites due to deforestation in catchment areas led to a raising of river bed levels. High siltation also implied that the projected life span of the dam was cut short by many years. A few of the dams, notably Morvi in Gujarat, burst under the pressure of heavy rains. Others proved susceptible to seismic pressures. In none was the proposed expansion in irrigation ever achieved; this was because of faulty planning of canal systems. Some, like the Tawa project mentioned above, caused waterlogging and salinity, not only creating production losses but also giving rise to a greater incidence of water-borne diseases. And all created serious problems of oustees who, years after the completion of the project, were still awaiting compensation and rehabilitation.

More recently the Narmada Valley project, a gigantic scheme consisting of more than 3,000 major and minor dams and involving an outlay of over 25,000 crores, has generated serious controversy. On one side are ranged the officials and experts of the Union and the concerned state governments (Gujarat, Maharashtra, Madhya Pradesh), plus the rich peasantry in the region which sees possibilities in the scheme for a major boost to irrigation and the power supply, plus construction firms which would reap a bonanza, even many ordinary citizens who believe that the combined benefits of the scheme would lead to an all-round growth in prosperity (through flood control, increased drinking-water supply, new jobs through a spurt in industry and allied activities). On the other side are the potential oustees (it is estimated that the project will displace nearly one million people on completion), voluntary social action groups working with the affected people, environmentalists concerned about the destruction of flora and fauna (nearly 350,000 hectares of forest land and 200,000 hectares of cultivated land will be submerged), and other experts who feel that the benefit–cost figures released by the project authority are misleading. Since this scheme is being co-financed by the World Bank, it has also drawn in sections of the international development community. Northern non-governmental organizations (NGOs) have launched major campaigns in their own countries against finance being made available to such projects. In brief, struggles have broken out at all levels: at the grassroots, at provincial and national levels, and at the global level. The latest entrant in the controversy is the recently formed National Campaign Against Big Dams, a coalition of nearly one hundred groups from across the country, which has generated a heated debate around the policy.

The controversy around dams has also given a fillip to a wide spectrum of creative activity in search for alternatives to both water and energy. The necessity of augmenting sources of irrigation and drinking water has renewed interest in tanks, ponds, dug wells, small bunds, etc. We can see today a fascinating array of both struggles like Pani Chetna in Rajasthan and efforts like the Pani Panchayat in Maharashtra. While the former raises issues related to water scarcity in the arid and semi-arid regions of Rajasthan, in the process highlighting the importance of afforestation, water conservation techniques and water collection modes, the latter has demonstrated the possibility of new cooperative management structures for water harvesting and distribution. The emphasis on flood control has generated efforts at micro watershed management. The search for alternative sources of energy has spawned new research into micro-hydroelectric schemes, windmills, solar energy and the like. And the issues of displacement, rehabilitation and compensation have focused attention on the need for new policies and laws to ensure justice. Equally critical is the recognition of communities as communities: that where displacement does become unavoidable, people need to be settled not as individuals with mere cash compensation but as organic communities, without which they rapidly slide into destitution.

Struggles against pollution

Struggles against pollution *per se* have not been too popular in India. Mostly they have been confined to complaints by the better-off sections in our cities about the quality of the air and water they consume, resulting in some state action of both a regulatory and a provisionary kind. Within cities such action normally takes the shape of new laws to control emission levels in vehicles, regulation of polluting activities—industry, power stations—or their removal from the immediate environs of the city, and provision of potable drinking water. Sometimes irritants such as garbage give rise to civic agitation against the functioning of the local municipality. Another effect of such agitations has normally been to blame the poorer urban citizens—slum- and pavement-dwellers—for polluting the environment, leading to pressure to relocate them on the outskirts of the city. Such arguments provide an easy rationale for slum demolition and development of green belts and parks in the cities.

The living environment of the poorer city-dwellers gets much lower consideration. For them provision of a clean and adequate water supply, sanitation, fuel for domestic consumption and space for recreation, etc., are always given short shrift by the authorities, except when epidemics break out, when there is agitation by the poor for better amenities, or just before elections to ensure votes.

More important in a wider sense is the relatively recent realization that all India's sources of surface water supply—rivers, ponds, wells—are dangerously toxic, posing health hazards not only to those who consume this water, but to all forms of life that it sustains. Industries that pass dangerous effluents into the rivers are now seen as the major culprits, as are the waste disposal systems in all our towns and cities. Rising toxicity levels in our rivers have particularly in the 1980s given rise to many struggles, the most notable of which are the Ganga Mukti Andolan in Bihar, and the struggle against the Harihar polyfibre factory in Karnataka. Both agitations (as also the earlier ones spearheaded by the Vidushak Kharkhana group in Shahdol district, Madhya Pradesh, about the pollution of the Sone river by the Gwalior rayon factory, and by the KSSP which took up the case of the poisoning of the Cheliyar river in Kerala) raise questions that, though beginning from the destruction of the livelihood base of river-based communities—mainly fisherfolk—also relate to issues of dangers to health through waterborne diseases.

Recently reports have started trickling in of how rural farmers too have started protesting about the pollution caused by agro-based industry and allied chemical factories. In Maharashtra, a new organization, the GPJS, has been spearheading the demand for a stricter implementation of the various pollution control acts and also for the writing-off of loans of pollution-affected farmers (EPW, 1988).

The real spurt to all such struggles however came from the mega-disaster in Bhopal, where the leakage of gas from a pesticide plant controlled by the Union Carbide Corporation led to the immediate deaths of nearly 2,500 people, to innumerable illnesses and to the slow death of thousands of others. Bhopal has triggered off groups of concerned citizens and environmentalists in all India's cities and industrial locations, who are questioning the entire gamut of industrial policies, from location of industry to choice of technology and product, machinery to deal with man-made disasters, policies related to medical treatment and rehabilitation, and laws to determine culpability and damages. The furious debate and action that Bhopal has given rise to has shaken, as never before, the near-blind faith that many had in the beneficial impacts of modern industry, science and technology.[8]

Finally, I should also mention the currently weak but growing opposition to the establishment of nuclear power stations in India. Particularly after Three Mile Island and Chernobyl, the claims made by our nuclear estate about the utter infallibility of the safeguards in our nuclear stations are not taken seriously. Thus at all reactor locations, local struggles have broken out objecting to the projects. Joined by those working within a peace framework, plus political economists and energy experts who argue that the costs of generating nuclear energy are prohibitive, and environmentalists who criticize the safety mechanisms and point out to the disastrous consequences of any leak, the anti-nuclear groups are slowly coming into their own. This, in a country whose inhabitants are reminded daily of hostile neighbours with a nuclear capability or intentions, and where information regarding nuclear stations is shrouded under the Official Secrets Act, is no mean achievement.

Against over-exploitation of marine resources[9]

India has a long coastline. For millenia, millions of traditional fisherfolk have subsisted on their catches. A large household-based industry and trade also subsists around marine fishing. Whilst men fish and make and repair fishing craft, women are involved in net-making and the marketing of fish. Earlier struggles of fisherfolk were essentially around the problems of credit and moneylending, storage and marketing facilities. Agencies and groups which work with fisherfolk concentrated on fighting against groups of exploiters and battling the social evils of illiteracy, alcoholism, etc. But during the 1980s, a powerful movement grew, particularly on the western coast, opposing the opening of the traditional fishing places of small fisherfolk to mechanized trawlers. A mode of fishing that should have remained confined to the deep seas has now started poaching in shallow waters, primarily in search of prawns, producing a widespread and intense conflict between the trawler industry and traditional fisherfolk. For the latter, the issue is not simply one of unequal competition, or of destruction of the resources on which their livelihood depends. What concerns them even more is that reckless overfishing is leading to a decimation of young fish and breeding and spawning zones. At this rate, there may well be no fish left to be harvested.

The struggles of the traditional fisherfolk, primarily under the leadership of the National Fishermen's Union, have led to demands including a complete ban on trawling in shallow waters, regulation of the marketing operations of large companies that threaten the livelihoods of women fish-sellers, an economic assistance programme both to meet the consumption requirements of fisherfolk during lean seasons and to upgrade the technology of their fishcraft and gear, and a comprehensive policy to regulate fishing in coastal waters.

The fisherfolk's agitation, whilst currently focusing on the immediate demand for a ban on trawling, has in its complex and troubled trajectory raised issues of both technology and social organization and control. The agitation includes work related to forming cooperatives of fisherfolk, ensuring easier credit and market access; it also includes initiatives for literacy, against alcoholism, and for generation of appropriate technologies that while being ecologically benign would raise the catches.

This struggle is one of two visions. For the modern fishing industry the crucial concern is to maximize the rate of return on capital. For traditional fisherfolk the concern is to ensure a continuation in perpetuity of a natural resource. Like the forest-dwellers, they see the seas, the fish and themselves as part of a cosmological unity in which their role as nurturers of young fish is as important as the income their catches yield to them.

In addition to these major struggles around land, water, forests, pollution and marine resources, the country is racked by dozens of smaller conflicts that arise out of the use and mode of appropriation of natural renewable resources. Each of these struggles, irrespective of the specific issue that sparks it off, develops a complex response: people are fighting against destruction and for preservation, struggling over the distribution of the rewards from resource use, and developing and demanding alternatives in technology and resource use. Whilst discrete and diverse, together these struggles offer a powerful critique of the dominant conception of development and a social organization that through an enforced process of homogenization seems well set to destroy livelihoods, lifestyles and life at the margins.

The nature of new movements and recent struggles

What marks out recent struggles generated by the conflicts over natural renewable resources as both new and different is the mix of actors, modes of intervention, issues that they raise and their eventual impact in terms of redressal, policy shifts and consciousness.

The actors

Unlike earlier and other struggles where the burden of mobilization and agitation is primarily borne by those directly affected, namely wage struggles involving primarily the labourers and their leaders, ecological struggles by their very nature tend to draw in widely disparate and sometimes conflicting actors. At the base, of course, are those most affected by the changes or shifts occurring in the environment: the women who have to work extra hours collecting fuel and water, the tribal people who suffer as a result of losing access to forest produce, the fisherfolk who suffer from excessive trawling, etc. But since many of these conflicts arise in faraway and marginal areas, if protesters are to acquire a hearing space they require allies. The first level of mediation comes through the organizations—voluntary and political—that happen to be working with the affected people or in their areas. Another set of actors active in such struggles are those related to the media—journalists, film-makers, etc.—who are involved in reporting about and communicating the protesters' messages to the world outside. Given the nature of the issues, there is a strong need to involve middle-class professionals—scientists and researchers, doctors, engineers, technologists and lawyers—both to examine the laws governing the resource use and to argue the case in courts; civil and human rights groups may come in as clashes become inevitable and severe. Many of these struggles have also managed to draw in sympathetic and concerned policymakers and bureaucrats. We can, in each struggle, trace a chain of actors, each with their own functional role and removed from the actual struggle to different degrees.

As an example, let us look even at a very small, though successful struggle: against limestone quarrying in the Garhwal region. Whilst at the base of the agitation were the peasant communities and Chipko activists, the struggles acquired a salience only when the elite residents of Dehradun town began worrying about the rising pollution levels from limestone crushers and cement factories, the ugly scars caused by mining in the surrounding hills, the increases in temperature caused by deforestation and mining activity, the decline in water availability as local streams started drying up, etc. Hence a three-pronged strategy was developed—of lobbying, through the press and related institutions, the policymakers and political representatives, of litigation in the Indian Supreme Court for an immediate ban on quarrying-related activities, and of involving scientists both to provide the research-based knowledge necessary to give credibility to the campaign and also to suggest alternatives. Crucial, though not as important as the ground-level struggle, was the report 'Environmental Impact of Mining on the Doon Valley Eco-System', prepared by a group of committed scientists, which provided the major evidence in the litigation. Doon Valley was saved only because diverse actors—though from differing perspectives—were able to discover a common objective and minimally coordinate their actions. Struggles in the adjoining hills of Pithoragarh and Nainital were unable to achieve the same success because they were unable to break out of the constrained, localized environment, within which the opposing forces were too powerful for them to vanquish.

What holds for the struggle against harmful mining in Doon Valley is even more true for more complex and widespread struggles such as that against the big dams, or the campaign against the propogation of eucalyptus. As the nature of issues becomes more complex and non-localized, objectives can be achieved only through a successful coalition of actors and strategies.

For instance, the struggle against the Narmada Valley project has drawn in groups and agencies located outside India. Since the project is being co-financed by the World Bank, help was sought from non-Indian groups to lobby globally against the policies of international donor agencies that support projects with potentially destructive implications. The forging of such an international coalition not only raises serious questions of political ethics, since extra-national actors are being invited to play a role in what are at one level national issues, but also has serious implications for the manner in which issues and strategies are articulated. Similarly the struggle against eucalyptus plantations, particularly in tropical zones, has a strong international involvement. This is not only at the level of struggle against international donor agencies or multinational corporations (MNCs), but also in the scientific expertise that the movement is able to rely on.

The very nature and complexity of ecological struggles, which not only rapidly become non-local but also demand a level of information and expertise often unavailable to those directly affected in socio-economic terms, give rise to a different mix of strategies. It is to this that we now turn.

On modes of intervention

A vital concomitant of organized resistance and protest for this is not only the evolution of organizational forms and strategies that will increase the cohesion amongst those negatively affected, but also the ability to disarm and dissuade those who are likely to benefit from the intervention/activity being opposed. In the Doon Valley agitation, it was vital that the poor and the landless peasants forced to seek employment in the mines that were destroying the ecosystem should not turn hostile. Otherwise, the movement might well have taken an elitist turn.

Since ecological struggles often arise in protest against proposed 'developmental intervention' they are very prone to being classified as Luddite, backward-looking, anti-progress, and hostile to science and technology. They also conjure up visions of extreme localism, ideas that only the 'sons of the soil' have rights over local resources. Consequently, they can also easily end up being painted as anti-national. Such canards can be met only through systematic examination of the conflicts involved, and propagation of rational views about resource use. It is here that middle-class, professional actors have a role to play. Be it through research, the media, or the courts—and each of these modes have been explored—those not directly affected are required to build up a coalition with the direct victims. Networks primarily for 'nationalizing the issue' and building pressure are thus most useful.

Given the anti-development label that accompanies most ecological struggles, the real battle often becomes one of engendering shifts in the public consciousness. After all, we must not forget that conflicts labelled as environmental or ecological acquired a hearing space only after the problem had been legitimized through events like the Stockholm Conference. Consequently, ecological struggles tend to be fought out through the media as much as on the ground. And there the tools are both cognitive and cultural.

The different strategies so far employed, however, display some major weaknesses. The first relates to the relationship of the directly affected communities and their organizers with the removed middle-class professionals. When the issue is taken out of the local environs, it is the latter professionals who become the more crucial in the struggle. This shift not only raises vital questions of the ethics of the struggle, but can lead to a move away from the central question, that of power. Whose rights are primary in such conflicts? Almost invariably, in any coalition between the affected people and their middle-class spokespersons—with the shift in power locus—issues tend to get clouded. While the journalists look for good copy, lawyers for the vital legal points that they will argue in court, and film-makers for their audience, we can easily forget that a grim battle for survival is taking place at the ground. A related problem is that knowledge about ecosystems and how they respond to different interventions is currently inadequate. For instance, technical opinion on the impact of eucalyptus plantations on soil, water tables, undergrowth, etc., is divided. Should such struggles then wait until incontrovertible research evidence is available (Sethi, 1987a)?

Another problem is often created by ecological researchers, particularly those who are theoretically inclined. Answers to concerns such as why destructive development continues to take place in spite of massive evidence now available as to the negative effects, are provided through arguments that trace all current ills to the hegemonic position of modern science. It is argued that the Cartesian worldview leads to a desecration of nature, converts nature into a commodity for use and legitimizes suffering, pain and finally triage—all as a necessary concomitant of the growth of scientific knowledge and progress using it. In this image of the world as being in a continuous downward spiral since the seventeenth century, there is a tendency towards overdetermination and an underplaying of the role of the subject in history. It is the non-recognition of the specificity of the victim, the preference for abstract and generalizable arguments, that leaves the activist worldview somewhat uncomfortable.[10]

Moreover, any media-based strategy (and here I am including the entire spectrum of interventions designed to relate to non-local audiences) tends to emphasize the sensational. Not only does this create distortions, but also, unfortunately, some activities that are best carried out by the outsiders—such as more detailed research into the actual working of the ecosystem, and the search for alternatives—tend to get neglected since they are seen as slow, tedious and non-glamorous. It is thus not surprising that the discourse on conflicts and struggles often abounds in factual inaccuracies and is primarily a trading of idiosyncratic viewpoints.

All such struggles also face a peculiar paradox. At one level they need to become non-localized. For this the urban expert becomes crucial. But this external involvement or coalition, in addition to the shifts in power that it implies, suffers from a cognitive handicap in that the worldviews of communities rooted in nature are at variance with those of their middle-class collaborators. What happens is both a distortion and a downgrading of traditional wisdom and folk and empirical knowledge. Even where attempts are made to resurrect folk wisdom, it comes across often in romantic, ahistorical and idealistic terms instead of as the materially rooted phenomenon of earlier practices.

Issues

Natural resource conflicts around questions of survival raise two sets of issues: those that concern the specific struggle in question, and those related to the nature of the discourse that they give rise to. The struggles themselves are structured around reformist considerations related either to the environmental cost calculus (that is, either working out the tolerance limits of environmental degradation or working out the modes of participation that can best facilitate techno-managerial solutions), or in rare cases to alternative paradigmatic considerations. In practice, since each of these struggle types merge into each other, the general issues that they give rise to—as also the consequent discourse—tend to be fairly jumbled: often confusing more than illuminating. The Indian debate has so far focused primarily on questions of a cost-benefit kind. These relate to both techno-managerial and political economy considerations. The former focus more on ways to reduce negative externalities, while the latter highlight class and distributional questions. Submerged, however, in this otherwise rich and fascinating debate are questions related to lifestyles and life. Why is it that activities and communities located at the margins of the urban industrial complex are invariably at the receiving end? Is the brutal dislocation, even decimation, of these people and their activities a historically foregone conclusion? Is it desirable? In the mad race for development and progress defined in narrow Western ethnocentric terms, are we not only reducing necessary diversity—both social and biological—but also, it may well be, setting the stage for the very destruction of life?[11]

These issues, when seen in conjunction with the set of actors and the modalities of the struggle have also, probably for the first time, raised interesting issues of interconnection, particularly of ecology and feminism, and ecology and human rights. In many of the conflicts, it was mundane, even hidden, issues incorporated within daily routines—for instance, related to the decline in water, fuel and fodder availability—that sparked vociferous protests by women. Why did this happen? Could not the men notice these declines? Can such developments lead us to argue, as some feminist theorists have, that the difference in perception arises from the different relationships that men and women have to nature. While men have a relationship to nature that seeks to dominate and control, so the argument goes, women have a sustenance-nurturing relationship to nature. It is argued that that is why women are the most active in afforestation efforts, in opposing the conversion of mixed natural forests to mono-species plantations.

It has been argued that modern Western science and the theory of economic organization are not only inherently anti-ecological and reductionist, but also patriarchal, downgrading the feminine principle both in nature and in humanity. More specifically, the dominant view, by refusing to consider the activities that peasant and tribal women have been involved in, tends to look upon nature (forests, soil, water) only as a resource for profit.

The resultant implication is deep violence—against women as workers and bearers of knowledge and against nature—creating thereby a crisis of survival (Shiva, 1988).

Similarly, these struggles have raised difficult questions in the area of human rights. Essentially, these relate to the conversion of free community resources in commodities whose use is to be governed by either plan or market criteria. For instance, declaring a forest as a reserved forest, a national resource, takes away the traditional right of local communities to the use of forest produce. Earlier, many of the resources provided by nature did not belong to anyone. There was only a system to regulate the fruits of these resources. Similarly, incidents such as Bhopal, or the decline in gene diversity as a result of modern agricultural practices, or the hazards posed by the nuclear industry and research on genetics, raise questions about the rights of generations still unborn.

More sharply, these struggles have brought to the surface the contradictions between three Indias and three economies: those revolving around the market, the household, and nature. The last, in particular, becomes crucial in tropical zones, where not accounting for the replenishment of resources by nature without the involvement of the labour process, implies missing out a large chunk of both resources and people dependent on them (Shiva, 1986).

In addition to the many questions regarding the tactics and strategy of successful organization and coalition-building, these struggles also raise important questions regarding the understanding of the notion of the 'national'. This is because ecological issues do not respect national boundaries (for example, overfishing in the Indian marine zones affects the neighbouring Sri Lankan fisherfolk too), and because the logic of the nation state, which tends to monopolize the use of resources for ostensibly national purposes, can and does cause much local devastation. Strategically, in say responding to development interventions initiated by agencies such as the World Bank, what is the terrain or terrains on which the struggles ought to be carried out? Should we, as for instance has been done in the struggles against the Narmada Valley scheme, appeal to groups, agencies and states outside the country? Even admitting that the issue has an international dimension, can we be justified in choosing allies that may otherwise be hostile to legitimate national interests?

This issue needs amplification. Those opposing the Narmada Valley project, whether on environmental grounds or on the resettlement-rehabilitation grid, scored their first victory when they managed to convince the World Bank (the co-financing agency) to issue fresh guidelines for the protection both of the people ousted by the project and of nature. The guidelines were then used to put pressure on central and concerned state governments. Whilst in itself representing a major advance since the concerned governments had until then paid no heed to the demands of the victims, this move tended to legitimize the view that the World Bank was the appropriate forum for adjudication. Further, it increased the importance of individuals and groups who had a better access to international fora. Such a shift in importance, common in the environmental domain, slowly saw the very different actors caught up in international politics, where they now willy-nilly became pawns in the justification of new conditionalities, whether fiscal or environmental, on Third World states by various international agencies. In addition to the worrying cognitive shift that is encoded in the shift of 'primary villain status' as environmental destroyer away from First World governments (undeniably the greatest destroyer of natural resources) to Third World states, the shift to the international domain has also trapped local groups into articulating positions defined by Western agencies, both official and non-governmental. An earlier tactical victory has possibly over time led to a strategic defeat.

The distinction between globalization and internationalization is rarely understood. I have argued earlier that, to be successful, ecological struggles need to break out of localism. Unless an issue and concern about it move from the margins to centre stage they are unlikely to be heard, much less responded to. This process of globalization requires the building up of networks and coalitions. Internationalization, however, implies the shifting of the locus of concern and decision-making from the primary victims and their immediate allies to actors and agencies removed from the scene. Premature internationalization, particularly beyond national boundaries, can lead to a serious undermining of the credibility of the activist groups.

Possibly the most significant issue raised by these struggles relates to the realm of the theory of knowledge. In trying to unravel the reasons and causes leading to an ecologically destructive notion of development, researchers linked to these struggles have started challenging the myth of universal, objective and value-free science. What was for decades accepted as true knowledge—with a resultant downgrading if not discounting of alternative knowledge systems, modes of knowing and cognition involving different actor-participants and experts—is now under attack. Science today is seen as ethnocentric (Western), patriarchal (in its conscious exclusion of women and the activities they are involved in) and reductionist. Many go so far as to argue that modern Western science is demonic since it encodes a high degree of violence to both marginal communities (particularly women), and nature. The ecological response to science stresses not only the previously missing and unassimilated elements in a truer system of knowledge, it focuses on life-supporting and regenerative values. Similar debates have sprung up around the previously relatively uncontested notions of surplus, progress, development, etc.

An ecological view of science and society poses a strong challenge to the conventionally received wisdom on the theory of state- and nation-building. Once we grant the move from plurality and diversity in nature to plurality and diversity in society and reject the process of universal homogenization, ethnicity becomes a cardinal principle for the construction of alternative utopias. A rearticulation of the primacy of the commons implies a critique of existing property relations and from that emerges the need to revitalize organic communities based on endogenous principles. The real challenge facing those seeking to resurrect ecology is to build a mode of praxis and discourse which, while recognizing and respecting the autonomy and dignity of different entities, seeks to help them to enter dialogue and influence each other without seeking to order them hierarchically. At this level we can trace most, if not all, problems of the modern age to the near-total victory of an anti-ecological vision (*Lokayan Bulletin,* 1985).

These sets of questions are not only problematic but may well take a purely philosophical turn. Ontological questions can rarely be answered by struggle responses, which are often fated to remain primarily in the terrain of political economy. Nevertheless, many of these conflicts and movements, particularly Chipko and Bhopal, have led to a lively and ongoing debate about the epistemological categories that are employed when talking about science, progress and history. It is to the credit of these struggles that the development debate in India has also incorporated considerations of moral economy.

Impact

What impact have these diverse and scattered struggles and movements had? As discrete struggles they display an uneven, primarily pessimistic history. The Silent Valley agitation may have succeeded, but work on other, much larger schemes continues unabated. The struggles in the Doon Valley may have been partially successful, but that is not true of other struggles in other places, where the potential for destruction is often greater. Bhopal may have directed attention to a wide scatter of issues, but hazardous products and processes continue to multiply in the country. At the gross level, nearly 200,000 people are displaced every year as a result of large development projects alone.

On the other hand, never before has the concern about environment and ecology been as high and intense. This concern is reflected not only in the increased coverage given to such issues in the media, or in the multiplication of institutes and university departments studying the environment, but also in state policy. From 1972 onwards, the official enthusiasm about the environment has seemed staggering. Not only do we have a plethora of policies giving us guidelines about forests, wastelands, water and the like, we have a full-fledged Ministry of Environment, whose clearance has to be sought before any large project is embarked upon. Some of the states even included a system of public hearings before approval may be provided.

While the gains in consciousness are indeed immense, and should not be dismissed lightly or cynically, a number of factors cannot be denied. There remains a deep divide between concern and actual action, particularly on the part of the state, and a greater leaning towards environmental rather than ecological concerns. An environmental view embodies certain assumptions regarding nature, other cultures, and technology: that nature is primarily a commodity or resource which needs to be preserved for reasons of trade, tourism or leisure; that the violence produced through technological obsolescence can be humanized; and that other cultures can be preserved through museumization. An ecological view, running counter to this statist, depoliticized outlook, would argue for the preservation of livelihood, lifestyles and nature—not as museum pieces, but as live organic entities reflecting a plurality of cultures and worldviews. Finally, even though stricter regulation is now sought to be enforced in the context of large projects, dispersed destruction, particularly in the field of agriculture, still goes unnoticed.

Equally surprising is that while the intensity and spread of conflicts has grown, and knowledge and concern about ecological issues has become more widespread, none of the political parties in the country, or their affiliated trade unions and *kisan sabhas* (peasant fronts), have so far raised any of these questions. Whilst in the more right-wing parties concern about these issues, so long as they do not impact upon their direct constituencies, may well be low, to explain the silence or sometimes the hostility of the left-wing parties and groups to these questions is more difficult. Probably the reason is that the party-left in our country, as elsewhere, is still struggling with distributional issues within the earlier framework of progress through industrialization. It thus tends to see ecological issues and struggles as essentially reactionary, as efforts by the erstwhile elite to block the necessary industrialization in the country.

There is probably an associated political reason why the left and progressive elements in India do not take very kindly to the different ecological critiques, particularly those basing themselves on deconstructing the language of modern Western science. Many of the groups who see themselves as ecological fall within one of two camps. The first, epitomized by the Patriotic and People-oriented Science and Technology Foundation (PPST), seeks to discover the Indian roots of science as distinguished from a universalist notion of science. Whilst the PPST has undeniably done path-breaking work in demonstrating that alternative growth paths based on indigenous skills and technologies were available in the colonial and pre-colonial periods and that systematic attempts were made to destroy them, these exercises simultaneously tend to glorify all that was Indian. Some of its leading ideologues rely on ancient scriptures, and the left, seeing all post-Vedic incursions into Indian society as essentially negative, at the practical political level saw the PPST views as colluding with and strengthening religio-fundamentalist groups, with disturbing social implications. A certain lack of sensitivity and finesse on the part of the PPST led to some excellent research being appropriated by socially undesirable forces. The second set of ecology groups falls within the purview of what the Marxists would dub 'foreign-funded groups', who operate on the ideas and strategies derived from Western experience and thus blunt the edge of the nationalist urge against neo-colonialism. More centrally, since both groups view the modern nation state as the central actor in the crisis of survival, their role in international political economy struggles becomes suspect.

Given the diversity of actors and the ideological presuppositions that govern the different modes of intervention in a domain like ecology which is highly internationalized, the real danger lies in the mismatch between what develops as resistance and protest on the ground and the somewhat stratospheric debates that seek to influence policy and consciousness. With environment and ecology having become a popular global concern, the avenues available for the para-professional middle-class experts and agencies too have multiplied manifold. Thus, as in any domain characterized by a mix of high rewards and intense competition, the debates tend to become sharp and polemical, with an eye on approvals from where it matters. Had these debates been contained only at a talking-shop level, such a process might have been disgusting but not disturbing. Unfortunately, polarized and cacaphonic discourse affects not only directions of thought but also policy, as it helps compound the fragmentation on the ground. The current debate about big dams is an excellent example of a situation where the ground-level protest (though limited) has been hijacked, subtly distorted and fed into different circles, many abroad. The feedback loops have now resulted in social-activist groups spending as much time condemning each other as struggling against badly conceived dams or for the rights of the oustees to a life with dignity.

In an arena like ecology where so-called scientific knowledge, particularly for tropical and semi-tropical climes, is very inadequate, even the debate between ostensible experts is plagued with a high degree of uncertainty about the validity of different positions. Given the great divide that exists between the experts and the people, issues of survival tend to get structured within a depoliticized and technicist discourse. This, combined with the fact that often it is victim groups themselves that seek out allies to carve out a hearing space, increases the danger of the victims ending up as manipulable pawns in the fights between different expert groupings.

It is in this sense that, in the long journey (both in the structures of thought and action) from political economy to political ecology, we face tragic struggles that are not only fragmented but amenable to cooptation and distortion by government and other interest groups. At the political economy/rights end of the spectrum, the issues appear better defined and understood and permit better aggregation of victim groups, whilst the modes of struggles are time-tested and attract more stable organizations including political parties. They also do not permit easy internationalization. At the other end of the scale, the issues are not only less understood, but also they often generate only scattered protest and adjustment-based resistance, and attract primarily voluntary and non-party groups and movements. Such a mix rarely adds up to a potent combination for radical and paradigmatic change.

It is thus not surprising that both the perception/understanding of natural resource conflicts and the consequent action remains located dominantly in the framework of rights and justice, with of course somewhat greater sensitivity to environmental concerns. Because the discourse, no matter how confused, garbled and fragmented, is now finding greater space in mainstream concern, the possibility of overcoming the mismatch between debate and gains on the ground has undoubtedly increased.

Future prospects for the ecological movements

How then do we see the future of these struggles and issues in India? Natural resource conflicts, as I have tried to argue, occupy a peculiarly ambiguous and contradictory terrain in both discourse and praxis. At the level of discourse, since the issues raised run counter to the dominant views on development and progress, science and technology, and state- and nation-building, it is to be expected that they are admitted primarily in the form of reformist statements, which also have to meet the criteria of conjunctural viability. That is, even if the destruction being caused by an injudicious use of resources is admitted to be a serious issue, the questions are always reduced to managerial issues. Alongside is the tendency to push even the proposed techno-managerial solutions into the indefinite future.

The controversies related to the strategy of building big dams, or say, of the selection and location of industrial products and processes, are always met with responses such as, 'Is this an alternative? What will be its costs? Who pushes for it? What will we do in the transitional period?' And since the prospects of radically reworking the productive processes and related social institutions appear daunting, current policy-makers and managers leave them for the next generation to sort out. At one level this raises serious questions related to the notion of urgency. Our descriptions of the impending crisis, particularly as faced by marginal sections, are increasingly being painted in more and more horrific terms. Our abilities to do anything about these conflicts are increasingly being pictured as inadequate. Such a mismatch can and does lead to both inertia and amnesia. Second, we face serious problems related to the notion of *irreversibility*. This comes up most sharply when dealing with questions related to gene diversity, nuclear energy and the poisoning of soils and waters. Once the damage in done, can it actually be undone? What is true at the level of natural systems, is equally true at the level of communities, social systems, and systems of thought. The debates on the inevitability of destruction in progress capture this well.

At the level of praxis too, the varied, fragmented and contradictory character of the different ecological struggles creates a lot of confusion. Given the fact that the sections of the populations that get most brutally affected today, and for a long time to come, will not be central to the political process in India, and given that the richer sections can still afford to pass on the costs to others, the chances of cohesive movements based on an ecological worldview appear bleak. In fact, as the struggles for life chances become sharper, the chances are that such issues will get more mystified and the conflicts that will grow in intensity will be those between diferent strata of the have-nots, rather than between the haves and the have-nots. This is true both nationally and globally. How else do we explain the fact that struggles against the poisoning of rivers by industry are often opposed even by trade unions and the workers belonging to the industry—which occurs, even when they themselves suffer as a result of the polluted water? Or that demands to shut down hazardous mining are resisted by mineworkers? For them the choice is often reduced to one between real survival today and potential survival tomorrow. Similarly, at the level of nations, the structures of global political economy dictate an anti-ecological wisdom. Why else do we barter away our valuable natural resources for foreign exchange through IMF conditionalities and the like?

Nevertheless, what is interesting is how even standard issues of political economy—of rights and distributive justice—are slowly being redefined within a broad environmental/ecological perspective. The growing realization that unless the natural resource base on which our culture and civilization has developed is handled more judiciously, the crisis of survival which today affects the marginalized sections will inevitably envelop us all, is what provides a basis for hope. I am informed that, unlike the American Indians who give as much importance to the future as to the past, the dominant Hindu consciousness is more directed to the past. Let us hope that we do not have to wait for an era of acid rain, dead forests and soil-polluted water and air before realizing the folly of our chosen model of development.

Notes

1. I am grateful to Prof. D.L. Sheth, Dr Shiv Visvanathan and Achyut Yanik and colleagues at the Centre for the Study of Developing Societies and Lokayan for helpful comments and ideas. The errors remain mine.

2. That modern development leads to a crisis of survival, in turn weakening the foundations of democracy, is a view that has long found a favourable response in sections of the Indian intelligentsia. For a coherent articulation of this viewpoint for modern India, see Kothari (1988).

3. There is now a rich literature regarding the decline of the commons. The arguments here have been drawn from Singh (1986) and Jodha (1986). Many novels, too, illustrate this trend (for example, Bhairappa, 1986).

4. For a good summary of this debate, see D' Monte (1985) and *Lokayan Bulletin* (1985).

5. For a brief synopsis of the pre-independence debates on environment and ecology, see Visvanathan (1987), Sethi (1987) and Guha (1988). Visvanathan forges the most systematic link between the earlier debates and current thinking.

6. Chipko has long been regarded as the *cause célèbre* in the recent ecological upsurges. Not unexpectedly, the literature on Chipko is vast, confusing and marked with contradictory claims. Partly this is because the trajectory of the movement is different in different regional locations, but greater confusion possibly arises from the sectarian positions taken by the ideologues of the different tendencies that constitute the movement. The material here has been drawn from Bandopadhyaya and Shiva (1987a), Guha (1987) and Bandopadhyaya and Shiva (1987b).

7. The literature on the politico-economic and socio-ecological impacts of large dams and multipurpose river valley projects goes back to the early years of the twentieth century and still remains inconclusive. What cannot be denied is that many more people than ever before, including scientists and planners, are today more sceptical about the beneficial claims made by the proposers of these schemes. For a brief survey see Goldsmith and Hildyard (1984). For the Silent Valley see D'Monte (1985). For information on the Narmada Valley project see Kalpavriksha (1988) and Alvares and Billorey (1988).

8. Bhopal has generated an immense literature. For a good overview see *Lokayan Bulletin* (1988).

9. See Kocherry (1988) and Mathews (1988) for an overview of both the problems of traditional fisheries and fisherfolk and the struggle led by their union.

10. Modern science has occupied pride of place in the imagination of the Indian intelligentsia. Though earlier thinkers like Gandhi and Tagore were often critical of the evils of modern science, the scientific intellectual tendency has in recent years acquired greater legitimacy. For an extremely provocative set of writings see Nandy (1988).

11. This argument has been drawn from Sethi (1987b) and Sharma (1987).

References

Agarwal, Bina, 'Who Sows? Who Reaps? Women and Land Rights in India', *Journal of Peasant Studies,* Vol.15, No.4, July 1988.

Alvares, C. and R. Billorey, *Damming the Narmada,* Third World Network, Penang, 1988.

Bandopadhyaya, J. and V. Shiva, 'The Chipko Movement', *Seminar,* February, 1987a.

Bandopadhyaya, J. and V. Shiva, 'Reply', *Seminar,* August, 1987b.

Bhairappa, *Godhuli* (Hindi), Shabdkar, Delhi, 1986.

CSE, *The State of India's Environment*, Centre for Science and Environment, Delhi, 1985.

D'Monte, Darryl, *Temples or Tombs,* Centre for Science and Environment, Delhi, 1985.

EPW, 'Report', *Economic and Political Weekly,* 12 August 1988.

Fernandez, W. and S. Kulkarni (eds.), *The Forest Policy: a people's response,* Indian Social Institute, Delhi, 1983.

Goldsmith, E. and N. Hildyard (eds.), *The Social and Environmental Effects of Large Dams,* Vol. 2, Wadebridge Ecological Center, Cornell, 1984.

Guha R., 'Communications', *Seminar,* June 1987.

Guha, R., 'Ideological Plurality is Good for the Movement', *Times of India,* 31 May 1988.

Jodha, N.S., 'Market Forces and Erosion of Common Property Resources', mimeo, ICRISAT, Hyderabad, 1986.

Kalpavriksha, *The Narmada Valley Project: a critique,* 1988.

Kocherry, Thomas, 'Mechanisation and Kerala's Fisherfolk', *The Fight for Survival,* Centre for Science and Environment, Delhi, 1988.

Kothari, Rajni, *State Against Democracy,* Ajanta Publications, Delhi, 1988.

Lokayan Bulletin, special issue on survival, Vol. 3:4/5, 1985.

Lokayan Bulletin, 'Report', Vol. 4:3/4, 1986.

Lokayan Bulletin, special issue on Bhopal , Vol. 6:1/2, 1988.

Mathews, Koshy (ed.), *Voices of the Storm,* National Fishermen's Forum, 1988.

Mishra, Anupam, *Mitti Bachao Andolan* (Hindi), Gandhi Press Foundation (no date).

Nadkarni, M.V., *The Farmers' Movement in India,* Allied Publishers, Delhi, 1987.

Nandy, A., *Science, Hegemony and Violence,* Oxford University Press, Delhi, 1988.

Sethi, Harsh, 'Environmentalism, Ecology and the Voluntary Movement', *Indian Journal of Public Administration,* July–September, 1987a.

Sethi, Harsh, *Refocussing Praxis,* UNU South Asian Perspectives Project Report, Colombo, 1987b.

Sharma, Suresh, 'Premodern Proximities', mimeo, United Nations University, Tokyo, 1987.

Shiva, Vandana, 'Ecology Movements in India', *Alternatives,* April 1986.

Shiva, V., *Staying Alive: women, ecology and survival in India,* Kali for Women, Delhi, 1988. Also Zed Books, London, 1988.

Shiva, V. and Jayanta Bandopadhyaya, 'The Chipko Movement Against Limestone Quarrying in Doon Valley', *Lokayan Bulletin,* Vol. 5:3, 1987.

Shiva, V., and J. Bandopadhyaya, 'Political Economy of Ecology Movements', *Economic and Political Weekly,* 11 June 1988.

Singh, Chattrapati, *Common Property and Common Poverty,* Oxford University Press, Delhi, 1986.

Visvanathan, Shiv, 'Of Ancestors and Epigones', *Seminar,* February 1987.

7. Ethnicity and Separatist Movements in Southeast Asia

Teresa S. Encarnacion and *Eduardo C. Tadem*

The consolidation of diverse ethnic groups in Southeast Asia under their respective central governments is a formidable challenge confronting efforts at nation-building in the region. The desired goal is the creation of states where 'collectivities of individuals who feel a sense of belonging based on cultural traits which are usually some combination of religion, language and social mores and a notion of common ancestry' are to be imbued with a strong sense of national identity.[1]

There is no difficulty with the above purpose as far as the dominant ethnic group is concerned. But the minority and other subordinate groups are often at a disadvantage under this arrangement and find themselves compelled to conform to the requirements of the ruling ethnic majority or of its narrow elite component. In some cases, the dominant group does not even comprise a majority of the population of the nation in question.

Thus, the other ethnic groups, in order to preserve their identities as distinct peoples, espouse interests and values contrary to those of central governments and the dominant elite classes. Issues such as the conflict between central and tribal legal systems, the preservation and development of indigenous cultures, and the use and control of natural resources have been longstanding irritants. When compromises are deemed impossible, separatist movements arise. In such a situation:

> Ethnic groups seek to secede or gain autonomy from the control, *de facto* and *de jure,* of a given state. More often than not, the use of force is utilized, i.e., acts of revolutionary violence, to express rejection of the prevailing political and social system and the determination to bring about progressive changes by overthrowing the system.[2]

This chapter examines armed separatist movements in four Southeast Asian countries: Burma, Indonesia, the Philippines and Thailand. The first part will look into the context that gave rise to these movements and the goals they pursue as well as their relative strength and composition. The second part will analyse the problems and issues that emerge from separatist struggles, for example, cooptation into the power structures or outright state repression. We thus attempt to clarify concepts relating to separatist movements in particular and popular movements in general in Southeast Asia and to identify parallels and divergences in the region. Finally, this chapter lays down the bases for the development of alternatives for addressing ethnic-based concerns and issues.

Case studies from Burma, Indonesia, the Philippines and Thailand

During the pre-colonial period, there already existed problems with regard to the integration of minority or dominated ethnic communities under the governance of a ruling group. Nation states as we now know them did not exist. Various kingdoms flourished and, when they acquired enough wealth and military power, brought other ethnic peoples or less powerful or declining kingdoms under their suzerainty. In either case, the paying of tribute and other subservient practices were imposed, which were sources of internal tension often contributing to political instability and sparking off attempts at separation.

But separatism assumed larger and more severe proportions during the colonial period or as a result of attempts by Western colonizers to integrate subjugated economies into the international market. An important prerequisite for this integration was the establishment of a central government directly or indirectly controlled by the colonial power. With few exceptions, indigenous leaders who could politically facilitate the exploitation of natural resources and human labour were coopted and integrated into the colonial bureaucracy.

Bringing together the diverse ethnic people into clearly delineated nations each ruled by a central administration was to prove a near-impossible task. In Southeast Asia alone, there are at least thirty-two major ethno-linguistic groups and the region hosts all the world's major belief systems: Islam, Buddhism, Hinduism, and, later, Christianity.[3] Furthermore, the carving up of Southeast Asia resulted in arbitrarily and callously established national boundaries with no regard for the identity and integrity of ethnic groups. After colonial partitioning, and especially in mainland Southeast Asia, a particular ethnic group would find itself straddling two or more so-called 'national boundaries'. Whenever convenient, the colonial policy of 'divide and rule' was also employed.

This did not augur well with those groups who did not see themselves as part of the nation and who felt strongly about the erosion of their self-identity and the perceived violation of their political and economic rights. Thus there has occurred a continued rise of separatist movements in Southeast Asia.

The Burmese case

There are at present organized rebel groups in twelve population areas (not counting the Chinese) in Burma who identify themselves by some ethnic or regional design.[4] The more active groups are found among the Karen and Shan communities. The Karens found expression for their cause in the creation of the Karen National Union (KNU) formed after Burma won its independence from Britain in 1947. The KNU's objective was to create a federal republic based on parliamentary democracy and granting equal rights to all nationalities.

Together with the Mons, the Karens advocated that this proposed federation be composed of seven states, one each for the Burmese, the Shans, Karens Mons, Chins, and the Arakanese. The KNU later created the Karen National Defence Organization (KNDO) to press for separation from Burma. Another organization formed among the Karens was the Karenni United Liberation Front (KPULF) whose objective is to obtain autonomy within the Burmese Union. It also aims to establish what it calls a 'people's democracy' leading to a Marxist form of socialism.[5]

The Kachins, also, established their own organization, known as the Kachin Independent Organization (KIO), in 1961. Its goal is the creation of a Kachin state independent of Burma. A year after the establishment of the KIO, the Shan State Progress Party (SSPP) was set up after the *coup d'état* staged by General Ne Win. Through the SSPP, the Shans sought to preserve their political rights and cultural identity.

Thus one can see that the non-Burmese groups are concerned with their rights of self-identification and the perceived need for a large degree of autonomy for their region or nationality. Ideological considerations are not primary motivations, as distinguished for example from the aims of the Burmese Communist Party (BCP).

The ethnic insurrections continue. Although they offer no immediate threat to the Union, neither does the central government have the resources or the moral authority completely to stamp out these rebellions. As of 1983, the rebel groups still counted on a considerable number of combatants and mass support.[6] The KNU, for example, is still 3,500 to 4,000 strong. Its military arm, the Karen National Liberation Army (KNLA), is said to be 10,000 to 15,000 strong. Less significant is the Marxist-led KPULF with a reported core of 70 men, 60 of whom are cadres on loan from the Burmese Communist Party. In this manner, the BCP tries to insinuate itself as a force within the ethnic struggle. Another sizeable army is the KIO, which has a strength of 5,000 men, while its armed group, the Kachin Independent Army (KIA) has 3,000 to 4,000 men. The Shan State Army (SSA) has a reported force of 2,000 to 3,000 men and a reserve force of 5,000.

Indonesian secessionist movements

Regional rebellion in Indonesia is of two types. In the first, the central government is challenged merely at the regional level with no attempt at seceding from the nation state. These movements, although considering themselves national in scope, retain the word 'Indonesia' in the names of their organizations. The second type, on the other hand, stresses a distinction from Indonesia in general by proclaiming independence of their regions from the republic.[7]

Examples of the first type are the Darul Islam insurgencies in West Java which began in 1947 and in South Sulawesi in 1950, and the Pemerintah Revolutioner Republik Indonesia (PRRI, or Revolutionary Government of the Republic of Indonesia) which began in Sumatra and North Sulawesi in 1958.[8]

Most of the separatist movements in Indonesia, however, fall into the second category. The Free Papua Organization (OPM) was formed during the country's decolonization process. The OPM's struggle is based in Irian Jaya, formerly West New Guinea (half of the island of New Guinea), which was administered during the colonial period by the Netherlands East Indies Co. through the sultanates of Ternate, Tidore, and Batjan. Its Melanesian culture is completely distinct from the Javanese way of life, which dominates Indonesian society. The leadership of the OPM was composed of intellectuals opposed to Javanese domination over their people. Thus, the OPM seeks separation and independence from the Republic of Indonesia.

Another group is the Free Aceh Movement (GAM). The group's political base was the urban proletariat. Like the OPM, their main grievance is directed at Javanese domination.[9]

A third separatist movement was the South Moluccan Republic (RMS) formed in 1950. Like the Darul Islam, it originated in the decolonization process and was anti-Javanese in orientation. The core group was composed of colonial troops and colonial civil servants who emphasized their ethnic specificity and regionalism.[10]

A fourth movement, and one which has attracted considerable international attention, is the Revolutionary Front for the Liberation of East Timor (FRETILIN) situated in the former Portuguese colony. The group was organized in 1974 shortly after Portugal announced its intention to pull out of East Timor. Previously, the Indonesian government, which had long held the western part of the island, had laid claim to its eastern portion.

FRETILIN's objective is to establish an independent East Timor under a democratic government. Specifically, it is committed to the achievement of social and economic equality and a foreign policy of non-alignment. Initially, it was a moderate group advocating complete and immediate independence from Portugual. Upon the annexation of East Timor by Indonesia however, FRETILIN turned into a radical organization which wages an armed guerrilla war against the new colonizers. Its membership has included young Lisbon-educated intellectuals and elements of the Portuguese-trained colonial armed force.

Muslim secession in the Philippines

Among the more than 100 ethnic groups in the Philippines, the Muslims concentrated in the southern islands have proven to be the most resistant to integration and assimilation. The Moros (a pejorative term coined by Spanish colonizers but now adopted proudly by Muslim militants) comprise about 23 per cent of the population of the southern Philippines (Mindanao and Sulu), or about 7 per cent of the national total. They alone comprise thirteen ethno-linguistic groups, the three major of these being the Tausugs, Maranaos, and Maguindanaos.[11] The three are also the most active in the secessionist movement.

The Muslim separatists contend that their nation has been forcibly incorporated into a politico-economic system dominated by foreign capitalists and their Filipino counterparts.[12] They regard the Manila government's rule as

'Filipino colonialism'. Led by the Moro National Liberation Front (MNLF), the separatists, goal is to establish a Moro republic that would include Muslims, Christians and other ethno-linguistic and religious groups of the southern Philippines.

With the granting of independence to the Philippines in 1946, Muslim leaders petitioned the US government for either independence separate from the north or the retention of the south as a US protectorate. Their main concern was the presence of Christian Filipinos in their territories and the threat that this posed to Islam. But their main grievance was the exploitation by these Christians of the regions's natural resources, which the Muslims regarded as rightfully theirs. The USA ignored this plea, however, and approved the Philippines' independence with the northern and southern regions brought together as one nation.[13]

Following a series of massacres of Muslims by armed Christian groups, the Muslim Independence Movement (MIM) was organized in 1968. This held that only through the establishment of an independent Islamic republic that was sovereign and autonomous could the lot of the Muslim people improve. From this group emerged the more radical Moro National Liberation Front (MNLF) under the charismatic leadership of the former University of the Philippines professor Nur Misuari. During the early years of martial law in the Philippines, the MNLF posed the biggest armed threat to the Marcos government.

The Muslim Malays of Thailand

Ethnic Malays constitute the majority in the four southernmost provinces of Thailand. Some 75 per cent of the country's Muslim population are concentrated in Pattani, Yala, Narathiwat, and Satul. Muslims comprise 3.8 per cent of Thailand's total population. Their strict adherence to Islam has alienated them from the mainstream of Thai society and has made them resentful of the chauvinism of the Bangkok government.[14] An added source of differentiation is their ethnicity and a language similar to that spoken in the Malaysian province of Kelantan.[15]

Economically, the Thai Muslims are engaged in small-scale, inefficient and (by Malay standards) unprofitable rubber, rice and fruit production. Their insignificant presence in middle- and large-scale economic activities compared to the Chinese and Thai Buddhists has led to their continuing marginalization and impoverishment.[16]

The refusal of the Malay Muslims to accept the schemes of Bangkok led to the establishment of their first political organization, the Gagungan Melayu Pattani Raya (GAMPAR, the Association of Malays of Greater Pattani), which was founded in 1948. In order to operate openly within Malay territorial borders and avoid attracting British attention, GAMPAR posed as a social and cultural organization seeking to promote Muslim–Malay interests in Malaya and Thailand.[17] Even as such, the Thai government rejected the group.

The National Liberation Front of Pattani (NLFP) was one of the three major fronts that emerged from the 1947–48 rebellion. Its small armed group, the Pattani People's Liberation Army (PPNLA), numbers around fifty fighters. Although under the PULO umbrella (see page 155), it maintains its autonomy and loose structures.

The 1960s also witnessed the establishment of the Barisan Revolusi National (BRN), the National Revolution Front. The BRN was the first truly political organization launched within the Thai Muslim province. Its ideology is based on the following principles:

1. Malay nationalism on the basis of the oneness of God and humanitarianism.
2. The adoption of the theory and practice of anti-colonialism and anti-capitalism.
3. National ideals which are compatible with the ideology and which promise the development of a just and prosperous society sanctioned by God.[18]

A more conservative Islam-oriented faction of the BRN broke away and established the Barisan Nasional Pembebasan Pattani (BNPP), the Pattani National Liberation Movement, in September 1977. Its broad political objectives include the liberation of all Muslim areas in 'South Thailand' from Bangkok and the establishment of a sovereign and independent Islamic state.[19]

Among the different separatist groups, the Path of God is the only urban-based organization. It is committed to violence against all forms of Thai control of the Malay area. It was founded in 1975.[20]

The reality of Southeast Asian separatism

A common issue that binds together different separatist trends in Burma, Indonesia, the Philippines and Thailand is the socio-political and economic domination in each case of minority ethnic groups by the ruling ethnic group. Thus, one hears of the repression of non-Burmese peoples by the Burmese, the marginalization of the Irianese by the Javanese, the subordination of the Moros by the Hispanized Filipinos and the imposition of Thai rule over the Malay Muslims in southern Thailand.

An important socio-cultural factor that distinguishes the dominant group from the others is religion. In the Philippines and Thailand, Islam is seen as the religion of the minority and in whose name the banner of separatism is unfurled. Religion in Burma also plays a role in highlighting ethnic differences, as in the conflict between the Buddhist Burmese and the Christianized Karens. In Indonesia, the Acehnese GAM had its roots in the Darul Islam movement, whilst traditional Melanesian beliefs in Irian Jaya clash with Jakarta's Westernized concepts.

But socio-cultural differences only serve to highlight the basic cause of separatist movements in Southeast Asia, namely, the economic exploitation of minority ethnic groups. In the four countries studied in this chapter, it was the quest by the more dominant ethnic groups for economic power (for example, control over natural resources and the expansion of trade and commerce), that led to the imposition of politico-military rule over marginalized ethnic communities.

The intrusion of colonialism further intensified majority–minority conflicts. The colonial power pressured the dominant elites in the centre to consolidate their rule over previously autonomous outlying provinces and to integrate forcibly their inhabitants into the mainstream of society in order to facilitate economic exploration and exploitation.

The general response of Southeast Asian separatist movements to these injustices has been to strengthen their resolve to struggle for the establishment of an independent ethnic state responsive to their socio-political and economic concerns. The inability of the region's governments to suppress these movements thoroughly indicates the legitimacy of the issues raised and the relative popular support that these ethnic-based liberation movements enjoy. All these make the issue of separatism a continuing reality in the lives of Southeast Asian peoples.

Strategies of struggle and survival

Although the pre-colonial and colonial contexts present the root causes of separatism in Southeast Asia, it is also important to delve into the factors that serve either to perpetuate or to obstruct these movements.

Foremost among the perpetuating factors is the ability of groups to enter into alliances with one another at the local level. Their combined force makes it more difficult for the central government to deal with them. Also relevant is the external support that some groups receive from either foreign governments or non-governmental organizations sympathetic to their cause. More often than not in such cases, external military and financial assistance to them exceeds their locally generated military supplies and monetary funds.

It appears, however, that the main engine for the resilience of these movements is the popular support they are able to mobilize from their own people, which is usually enhanced by the intensification of government repression.

Alliance-building

The establishment of local alliances among existing separatist movements is more the rule than the exception, particularly during the formative stages of these groups. In Burma, the National Democratic Front (NDF) was organized as a non-communist umbrella organization of the armies of the Karens, Kachins, Shans, Karennis, Was, Pa-os, Palungs, Mons and Arakanese.

Although the groups in the NDF are largely anti-communist, some of them have found it convenient to form alliances with the Burmese Communist Party. The BCP is one of the country's oldest insurgency groups and it went underground in 1948. Its 8,000–15,000 military force draws heavily from the Akah, Lisu, Lahu and Waimin hill tribes for recruitment. An NDF group that has joined forces with the BCP is the Karenni People's United Liberation Front. Some Kachin and Shan insurgents also brought their organizations into tenuous alliances with the BCP during the 1960s.[21]

In Thailand, the Pattani National Liberation Front (PULO) provides a broad and flexible umbrella organization for most of the Muslim Malay separatists. Though a major secessionist group, the National Liberation Front of Pattani is part of the alliance but maintains its autonomy. In recent years, some of the separatist groups have coordinated with the Communist Party of Thailand (CPT) which has expressed support for the groups' call for self-determination.[22]

In Indonesia, FRETILIN, together with its military arm, the 3,000-strong National Liberation Army (FALINTIL), has announced that it will engage in joint military and diplomatic initiatives with the moderate East Timorese Democratic Union (UDT). In the Philippines, the Moro National Liberation Front (MNLF) admitted to the existence of a tacit agreement on the delineation of territorial areas of operation between it and the Communist New People's Army (NPA). In some areas in Lanao province, there were reports of joint MNLF–NPA military operations.[23]

External support

Important in the formation of alliances among separatist groups is their ability to secure various forms of external assistance including economic, military and diplomatic support.

The South Moluccan Republic (RMS) is reported to have received support from the Dutch military.[24] FRETILIN, on the other hand, has opted to shift to a political rather than a purely military campaign and urges states and international organizations to withdraw support and recognition from Jakarta. In the United Nations, where the movement has an accredited ambassador, FRETILIN is trying to forge a peace plan calling for negotiations with the Indonesian government and to include Portugal with Australia as an observer.[25]

The separatist movements in Thailand also receive foreign support. PULO's military wing, the Pattani United Liberation Army (PULA), gets military and political training abroad. PULO supporters include Libya, Syria, Saudi Arabia, Indonesia and the Palestine Liberation Organization (PLO), the latter providing military training. Saudi Arabian financial aid is said to reach US$7–8 million.[26] The group is also loosely allied with the Communist Party of Malaya operating along the Thai–Malaysian borders. This is the major reason why Muslim Malaysia withholds support from PULO.[27]

Muslims in the Philippines also find support from Islamic countries. The MNLF's most ardent supporters are Libya, Malaysia, Iran, Syria, the PLO, Iraq, Pakistan and Saudi Arabia. MNLF leader Misauri admits to basing his office in Libya because, according to him, it is the centre of the front's foreign operations and the Qaddafi government extends all forms of support. Libyan financial aid is said to reach US$250 million annually. While he was chief minister of Sabah, Tun Mustapha was sympathetic to the MNLF and is believed to have provided sanctuary for Muslims fleeing from persecution by the Philippine government. Saudi Arabia is said to have matched Libya's US$250 million aid.[28]

The Organization of Islamic Conference openly urged the Marcos government to stop persecuting Muslims, to freeze Christian migration to the South and to ensure the safety of the Muslim population. It also resolved to raise funds for the Muslims and create a commission composed of the governments of Libya, Saudi Arabia, Senegal and Somalia to discuss the Muslim issue with the Philippines government.

The result was the Tripoli Agreement of 1976 between the concerned parties, which sought to create a provincial government in the south and in particular to grant autonomy to the thirteen provinces defined in the agreement. The pact did not prosper, however, as each side accused the other of violating its principles.[29]

In Burma, some of the Shan and Karen rebel groups are said to be receiving tacit support and moral encouragement from Thai sources. Since the 1950s, the Thai government is said to have indirectly encouraged Burmese insurgent groups to operate along its western borders in order to prevent a tie-up between the Thai Communist Party and the Burmese Communists. On the other hand, ethnic groups who are allies of the Burmese Communist Party are supported by China, since the latter financially aids the BCP. Chin and Maya communities are encouraged by their ethnic relations in India and by their Muslim brethren in Bangladesh, but not by their respective governments.[30]

Local funding sources

Among the four Southeast Asian countries we are considering, only in Burma are separatist movements able to find lucrative internal sources of finance. Profits from the cultivation of opium have become rich sources of insurgent funds in the Shan and Kachin areas.

The Shan plateau, for example, accounts for the major part of the Golden Triangle's opium production of more than 400–500 tons a year. With the use of opium as a source of heroin and growing addiction rates in Western countries, especially in the USA, the Burmese separatist groups are assured of a steady income with which to keep their movements alive.[31]

Keeping the cause alive

Various strategies perpetuate the separatist cause in Burma, Thailand, Indonesia and the Philippines. The formation of tactical as well as strategic alliances, the generation of both material and moral external forms of assistance, and the winning of the loyalty of a significant segment of the people for whom the separatist struggle is advanced—all these help to keep the fires of rebellion burning.

Alliances are sometimes seen as the key to ultimate victory as it is recognised that given the resources at the command of the central government, no single group can overthrow the state apparatus singlehanded. The formation of agreements with communist parties may add new issues that go beyond ethnicity and majority–minority conflicts: such as social class distinctions, poverty and its relation to the distribution of the economic surplus, and strategies for economic development. These larger concerns could be used to gain broader popular support.

With regard to external support for separatism, religion, for example

Islam, plays a central role in securing the sympathy and assistance of foreign governments, as in the cases of the Thai and the Philippines movements. Religion is not only an international rallying point but also a leverage that may be employed in the pursuit of political objectives.

Support from former colonizers, as seen in the soliciting of military assistance by the OPM and RMS in Indonesia from Dutch organizations, appears as an alternative form of external aid. It is interesting that in the Indonesian experience, foreign support comes from right-wing organizations, contrary to the pattern observed in the other Southeast Asian countries.

Obstacles to separatist goals

The factors that contribute to the advance of a movement may also work the other way around. The formation of local alliances may prove to be hazardous due to the presence of conflicting perspectives not only in the strategies of struggle advocated but, more important, in the goals to be achieved.

Also, one cannot disregard the gains that governments have made in confronting the secessionist threat. These are achieved either through military coercion or political and economic incentives to the separatist leaders as well as through diplomatic initiatives in securing assistance from foreign governments that are directly involved or concerned with the cross-country effects of the movements.

Last, the dependence of separatist groups on external support due to the inadequacy of local funds may make them subservient to the dictates of interested foreign powers. This compromises their credibility as indigenous movements and, more crucial, diminishes their capability to establish truly independent ethnic states. An examination of all these factors may throw light on the dynamics of Southeast Asian separatism and also indicate the future status of separatist movements in the region.

Unfortunately for these movements, their alliances have often been characterized by fractious disputes which often lead to organizational splits. These are caused by the irreconcilability of long-term and short-term objectives. Leadership squabbles have added to the problem of disputes.

Government offensives

A major obstacle to separatist aims in the region is the gains made by Southeast Asian governments in confronting the insurgent groups.

In the Philippines, the Marcos government's response to the Moro rebellion was a combination of military offensives, economic measures such as development projects and, probably more effective, financially attractive amnesty programmes for leaders and rank-and-file members. These efforts are partly responsible for the splits within the MNLF. Marcos and now President Aquino have been able to implement a divide-and-rule policy with moderate success. Mrs Aquino seems to be following her predecessor's footsteps in dealing with the MNLF. For instance, she denied a promise made by a personal representative to an MNLF panel on the granting of full autonomy to twenty-three provinces.[32]

The diplomatic overtures of the previous and present regimes have also allowed the Philippine government a certain degree of leverage. The signing of the 1976 Tripoli agreement, for one, while viewed by the MNLF as a diplomatic victory giving tacit recognition of its belligerent status, also gave the central government much-needed breathing space.[33]

Islamic governments were also assiduously courted and cajoled and alternately bullied. Marcos pressured the Malaysian government to seal off the state of Sabah from access to the separatists, that state being the main conduit of arms and other supplies to the rebels. After clear and unmistakable signals were sent by Manila, the Indonesian government declared that the resolution of the Muslim conflict should remain within the context of Philippine sovereignty, a position which clashes with the basic stance of the MNLF. Malaysia and Indonesia, though both Islamic countries, because of their membership in ASEAN were unwilling to antagonize the Philippines unduly, fearing dismemberment of the regional alliance.[34] The Marcos government had also taken advantage of Moro factionalism to parry the peace initiatives of Malaysia and Indonesia.

In addition to appealing for assistance from Islamic countries in the region, the Marcos government had also called on the Organization of Islamic Conference (OIC) to help it. The flamboyant Imelda Marcos feverishly courted Libyan leader Qaddafi and other Arab leaders in order to gain their sympathy. The Aquino government has not only asked the OIC for help, but has also sought the assistance of the World Muslim League.

The Rangoon government handles its separatist problem by seeking a negotiated solution by searching for a degree of accommodation between the demands of the insurgent groups and the political requirements of the central state. Of course, military operations are used equally. And it uses combined psychological, symbolic, and politico-economic and social policies designed to lure both leaders and rank-and-file members.[35]

Perhaps the government model for such accommodations is the 1947 Panglong Agreement under which the Shans joined the government of Aung San's Malay Union on a ten-year trial basis and the Shans' autonomy was guaranteed except in foreign relations. Under this union, the Shan state was represented in the parliament and the first president was a Shan, Sao Shwetalk.[36]

Burma's diplomatic overtures have also been relatively successful. In the 1970s, a Rangoon–Beijing *rapprochement* resulted in a reduction in Chinese material support to the BCP and by 1980 there were signs that this assistance had dropped sharply. This weakened the Shan–BCP alliance and the former turned increasingly to the opium economy to support their activities.[37]

Forging treaties with nations known to be sympathetic to the separatist cause has also proved an effective means of deterring local rebellions. In 1973, Indonesia pressured the government of Papua New Guinea (PNG) to sign a Joint Border Agreement (updated in 1979), which pledged 'that both countries shall consult each other on mutual security problems and... take whatever action is necessary to prevent the border area of one from being used for hostile purposes against the other'.[38] The PNG government showed great reluctance in implementing the agreement, however, as shown by the

1981 hostage incident. The reason is that PNG leaders do not want to risk an expected popular outcry against the use of force against fellow Melanesians, especially in a joint operation with the Suharto government.

Pitfalls of foreign support

The reliance of most Southeast Asian separatist movements on external support, particularly from foreign governments, has led to problematic situations. The dependence of the Moro separatists on the OIC, for example, has subjected the former to the whim of an international body which is far from being a united bloc. Thus, a strong conservative section of the OIC led by Saudi Arabia allowed Marcos to railroad his own version of Muslim autonomy for the southern Philippines.[39]

The other interests of some OIC members, to which they give priority over the concerns of Philippine Muslims, have resulted in decreased assistance to the MNLF. As pointed out above, Malaysia and Indonesia give priority to the unity of the ASEAN regional grouping, of which they are members, and thus limit their support for the Moro movement. National interests also take precedence. Indonesia, for one, fears that if the insurgents in the Philippines succeed, this could catalyse similar movements in its own territory. Malaysia desires peace in Mindanao-Sulu because it wants to send back the 200,000 Philippine Muslim refugees in Sabah.[40]

The difficulty of sustaining external support is especially felt by FRETILIN. As a result, the group has now ruled out a military victory over Indonesia and relies heavily on international diplomacy to resolve the conflict. However, most of the interested governments, including members of the Non-aligned Movement, view Indonesian sovereignty over East Timor as a *fait accompli*.

As for the superpowers, they have always felt that it was more important to maintain good relations with Indonesia, since it is a member of the Organization of Petroleum Exporting Countries (OPEC). Besides, Western powers like the USA have always discouraged any type of rebellion in countries whose governments are perceived as allies and where their global security interests are at stake.

The Non-aligned Movement, on the other hand, has not proved itself effective in fighting for FRETILIN's cause in the absence of any mechanism for implementing its resolutions supporting the East Timor people's right to self-determination. The movement's Arab bloc has thrown its weight behind fellow OPEC member and Islamic brother Indonesia.[41]

The obstacles in review

The difficulties experienced by Southeast Asian separatist movements remain major stumbling blocks to the advancement of their goals. In alliances, sectarianism often prevails and long-term interests are sacrificed for short-term benefits. Sometimes long-term aims clash and prove even more lethal to the movement. Power struggles among the different leaders undermine the ability of the group to lead the overall struggle.

Governments often take advantage of the fragile nature of alliances and even cultivate internal strife among the separatists. There is also the reality that governments run by dominant elites possess a greater leverage particularly in global diplomacy than small separatist groups, for the simple reason that state-to-state or elite-to-elite relations are accorded more importance than the legitimate aspirations of oppressed ethnic populations. Thus *Realpolitik* prevails at the international level.

Power-play in international relations also determines the future of separatist movements. Only when their interests coincide with those of secessionist struggles will powerful nations come to the secessionists' assistance and then only on a temporary and *ad hoc* basis. All these are painful realities which separatism in South Asia and in the rest of the world have to contend with.

The quest for self-determination

An examination of separatist groups in Southeast Asia will uncover the various factors that brought them about as well as the differing strategies employed to achieve established goals. Among the causative factors, the issue of ethnicity is foremost. This may be expressed in the form of upholding one's religious beliefs as with the Muslims of Thailand and the Philippines or of upholding a particular way of life, as with the Melanesians of Irian Jaya and the Shans and Karens of Burma.

But it is not ethnicity *per se* that constitutes the problem since, as a whole, Southeast Asia is composed of hundreds of ethno-linguistic groups. It becomes an issue only when a dominant ethnic group takes control of the state apparatus and proceeds to impose its will on the rest of the population.

The class issue is also intertwined with the ethnic factor whereby the ruling class which appropriates the economic surplus is also the dominant ethnic group in the country. This is not to say, however, that class divisions are absent within the dominated ethnic groups. In the Philippines, there are rich landowning Muslims against whom Misuari's MNLF also contends. They often try to blunt the class issue by raising exclusively ethnic concerns.

A corollary to the ethnic issue is the quest for legitimacy and nationhood. What is desired is recognition of the rights of ethnic communities to exist without being oppressed by other tribes and, more important, the right to determine one's interests and concerns. This coincides with the concept of a nationhood which is reflective of their self-identity.

The situation is complicated further when legitimacy and nationhood are hindered by external factors such as imperialism or colonialism. In this case, exploitation exists not so much because of ethnic distinctions but because local communities are made to play a definite role in the workings of the prevailing international economic order. Because of this, some separatist groups such as the MNLF and PULO raise broader issues like anti-imperialism and anti-capitalism and consequently espouse alternatives based on some form of Islamic socialism.

Differing levels of exploitation also produce different aims and objectives, which affect the viability of alliances. Those groups who merely advocate parliamentary democracy for the whole country in which all nationalities are granted legislative seats may be content with the political participation of its leaders in the centres of power.

Other movements may regard such a form of participation as token representation and push for economic and class equality as well. These groups find it easier to form alliances with communist parties which also seek fundamental socio-economic changes.

But it is important to point out that the integration of broader national issues into separatist struggles will not necessarily downgrade the ethnic factor so as to blur distinctions between, for example, the MNLF and the CPP–NPA, or the SSA and the BCP. Ethnic liberation fronts always make special efforts to distinguish themselves and maintain their distance from communist movements.

From one perspective, these efforts may prove to be disadvantageous to both groups as they split the anti-government cause and breed a permanent atmosphere of distrust between movements. On the other hand, even if communist or left-wing movements were to successfully topple a government, they would still have to confront the ethnic question. If handled improperly, it may pose a thorny problem that will not easily go away.

The Nicaraguan case is particularly instructive. Given the inability of the Sandinista government to address Misquito Indian concerns, the US government took advantage of the situation to arm the Indians to fight Managua. It is thus important that at an early stage, points of convergence must already be determined and the ethnic issues be properly addressed by all popular movements in order to avoid problems in the event of a change in power relations.

While disregarded by nationalist and left movements in the past, it is now becoming clear that ethnicity as an issue is here to stay and has to be included as a primary item in the national agenda. The articulations between class and ethnic issues have to be carefully studied. At what points do they converge and diverge?

Disagreements may arise in the process of delineating priorities and interests, and difficult compromises may have to be made. The success of such efforts will depend on the extent to which separatist groups in particular and popular movements in general are able and willing to set aside narrow sectarian interests for the larger cause.

Notes

1. Joo-Jock Lim and S. Vani (eds.), *Armed Separatism in Southeast Asia,* Institute of Southeast Asian Studies, Singapore, 1985.
2. *ibid.*, p. 32.
3. *ibid.*
4. *ibid.*, p. 52.
5. 'The Karenni Connection', *Far Eastern Economic Review*, 18 June 1982.
6. Lim and Vani, p. 53.
7. *ibid.*, pp. 111–12.
8. *ibid.*

9. *ibid.*, pp.173–5
10. *ibid* ., p.174.
11. *ibid* ., p. 152.
12. *ibid.*
13. Stuart Schlegel, *Muslim–Christian Conflict in the Philippine South.*
14. Kochadum Na Taksin, 'Thai Politics Through Southern Eyes', *Southeast Asia Chronicle* , No. 69.
15. Lim and Vani, p. 217.
16. Chaiwath Satha-Anand, *Islam and Violence: a case study of violent events in the four southern provinces of Thailand, 1976–1981*, Monographs on Religion and Public Policy, Department of Religious Studies, University of Southern Florida, Tampa, USA.
17. Lim and Vani, p. 237.
18. *ibid* ., p. 299.
19. *ibid.*
20. Satha-Anand.
21. Lim and Vani, p. 300.
22. Kochadum Na Taksin.
23. 'Marcos Buys More Time', *Far Eastern Economic Review,* 5 June 1978.
24. Chandran Jeshurum, *Governments and Rebellions in Southeast Asia,* Institute of Southeast Asian Studies, 1985.
25. Denis Freney, 'Fretilin: death and resurrection', *Southeast Asia Chronicle*, No. 14.
26. Paisal Schricharatchanya, 'The Muslims Move In', *Far Eastern Economic Review*, 9 October 1981.
27. John McBeth, 'Separation is the Goal and Religion is the Weapon', *Far Eastern Economic Review*, 20 June 1980.
28. Sheilah Ocampo, 'Calling in the Neighbors', *Far Eastern Economic Review*, 8 February 1980.
29. Resolution No. 4 of the Organization of Islamic Conference (OIC) Foreign Ministers' Meeting.
30. Lim and Vani, p. 61.
31. *ibid.*, p. 66.
32. Amando Doronila, 'Peace Formula: a challenge to the panels', *Manila Chronicle*, April 1987.
33. Lim and Vani, p. 164.
34. Ocampo.
35. Jeshurum.
36. Hikaru Kerns, 'A State of Strife', *Far Eastern Economic Review,* 26 November 1982.
37. Lim and Vani, p. 99.
38. *ibid* ., p. 138.
39. Leila Garner Noble, *Muslim Separatism*.
40. James Clad, 'The Misuari Gamble', *Far Eastern Economic Review*, 11 September 1986.
41. M.A. Browning and Susan Vitka, 'East Timor and Diplomatic Pragmatism', *Southeast Asia Chronicle*, No. 94.

References

Browning, M.A. and Susan Vitka, 'East Timor and Diplomatic Pragmatism', *Southeast Asia Chronicle*, No. 94.

'Centuries of distrust', *Far Eastern Economic Review*, 5 April 1983.

Doronila, Amando, 'Peace Formula: a challenge to the panels', *Manila Chronicle* , April 1987.

Forker, Andrew, 'Legacy of Resentment', *Far Eastern Economic Review*, 20 June 1987.

Freney, Denis, 'Fretilin: death and resurrection', *Southeast Asia Chronicle*, No. 14.

Gunn, Geoffrey, 'Radicalism in Southeast Asia: rhetoric and reality in the Middle Eastern connection', *Journal of Contemporary Asia*, Vol. 16, No. 1, 1986.

Haemindra, Nantawan, *The Problem of Thai Muslims in the Four Southern Provinces of Thailand* .

Jeshurub, Chandran, *Governments and Rebellions in Southeast Asia,* Institute of Southeast Asian Studies, 1985.

Lim, Joo-Jock and S. Vani (eds.), *Armed Separatism in Southeast Asia*, Institute of Southeast Asian Studies, Singapore, 1985.

McBeth, John, 'Separation is the Goal and Religion is the Weapon', *Far Eastern Economic Review*, 20 June 1980.

Manila Chronicle, 9 February 1987.

Noble, Leila Garner, *The Moro National Liberation Front in the Philippines* .

Ocampo, Sheila, 'Calling in the Neighbors', *Far Eastern Economic Review*, 8 February 1980.

Resolution No. 4 of the Organization of Islamic Conference Foreign Ministers' Meeting.

Satha-Anand, Chaiwath, *Islam and Violence: a case study of violent events in the four southern provinces of Thailand, 1976–1981*, Monographs on Religion and Public Policy, Department of Religious Studies, University of Southern Florida, Tampa, USA.

Schlegel, Stuart, *Muslim–Christian Conflict in the Philippine South*.

Schricharatchanya, Paisal, 'The Muslims Move In', *Far Eastern Economic Review*, 9 October 1981.

Schricharatchanya, Paisal, 'Unity is the Raiders' Target', *Far Eastern Economic Review* , 8 October 1982.

Taksin, Kochadum Na, 'Thai Politics Through Southern Eyes', *Southeast Asia Chronicle,* No. 69.

Tasker, Rodney, 'Stepping up the War', *Far Eastern Economic Review,* 16 April 1987.

'The Karenni Connection', *Far Eastern Economic Review,* 18 June 1982.

Untner, Bertil, 'The Shan and Shan State of Burma', *Contemporary Journal of Southeast Asia,* 1984.

Wise, Peter, 'East Timor Offensive', *Far Eastern Economic Review,* 10 April 1986.

8. The Palestinian Social Movement

Bassem Serhan

The context in which the Palestinian movement as a whole has evolved has some unique aspects. First, unlike many other social movements it originated primarily in response to an external factor, namely the Israeli colonization of Palestinian land. Second, political dimensions, rather than purely economic and social factors, are central to the emergence of the various specific Palestinian movements. Third, due to the outmigration and displacement of Palestinian communities, the Palestinian social movement has assumed an extra-territorial character.

The Palestinian movement is an example of an entire populace, forcibly displaced from its traditional land, attempting to recover land, identity, nationhood and territorially located political coherence. The account given in this chapter demonstrates how an initially incoherent, spontaneous and relatively unorganized mass movement developed itself into a major political phenomenon.

The trajectory of Palestinian social movements illustrates some inherent complexities of large-scale mass mobilization. At one level, the identity as well the existence of individual movements depended on their confrontation with Israel and on their relationship with many Arab governments. This relationship has been highly problematic since the frontline Arab states often have had their own political agenda not necessarily in accord with the Palestinian struggle. This was particularly evident in the early 1960s when the concept of 'Arabism' came to challenge the Palestinian notion of 'Palestinism'. This led to the formation of distinctly Palestinian politico-military structures and organizations. At another level, the recurring repression of all political self-assertion by the Palestinian people posed a formidable challenge to the movement. This was particularly the case for Palestinians in Israel, Jordan and Lebanon. Equally crucial is the question of maintaining a national identity among a populace that is territorially dispersed. It is against such a complex backdrop that individual Palestinian movements have played their social and political role.

One of the interesting aspects of the Palestinian social movement is its class dimension. The initial spread of the movement was mainly among the working-class and poor masses. The petty-bourgeois and middle-class elements joined the movement only in the late 1960s. This class dimension gives a genuinely mass character to the Palestinian social movement.

Broad social movements tend to be heterogeneous in their ideologies and immediate goals. The Palestinian movement is no exception. However, what fascinates the student of social movements is the continuity of the spirit of resistance, even though a strictly articulated set of common objectives is not present in the movement. This is also one major distinction between party-based mobilization and mass movements.

The formative years of the new Palestinian social movement

Geographically the Palestinians live in communities, whether refugee or not, in Israel, Gaza Strip, the West Bank, east Jordan, Iraq, Syria, Egypt, Lebanon, the Arab Gulf States and the USA.

Their geo-political fragmentation poses formidable problems for the unity, identity and mass movement of the Palestinian people. During the 1950s at least it could be argued that the only Palestinian institution that remained relatively intact was the family.

This analysis of the roots of the current Palestinian social movement focuses on three areas: Gaza, Jordan and Lebanon. The social movement of Palestinians in Israel will be discussed separately in view of its specific characteristics.

It is worth noting at the outset that Palestinians have not only firmly rejected the loss and dismemberment of their country, but also consider their displacement and the refugee status to be a temporary phenomenon. They have hopes that one way or another they will go back to their homes, villages and towns.

The Western countries which facilitated the establishment of the state of Israel were behind the establishment of United Nations Relief for Palestine on 8 December 1949, which was replaced one year later by the United Nations Relief and Works Agency (UNRWA). Their real aim was to suppress or to end the Palestine problem as soon as possible. Their strategy for that end was the resettlement of refugees.

In June 1953, US Secretary of State John Foster Dulles said that his country favoured the integration of refugees into neighbouring countries.[1] The Arab League agreed in principle to the proposed settlement. UNRWA negotiated specific settlement projects with the Arab governments of Jordan, Syria, Lebanon, Iraq and Egypt. However, all US-sponsored settlement policies had failed by 1960 due to two main factors:

1. Stern resistance and rejection by Palestinian refugees.
2. The poor economies of the host Arab countries and the instability of their political structures.

Arab rulers were very apprehensive about the Palestinian presence in their countries. As Sayigh points out:

> Arab governments considered the refugees a threat to the stability of their regimes. That was the reason behind confining them to certain residential areas—camps—and behind passing certain laws and rules to contain and control their activities as well as their movement.[2]

She also mentions two socio-psychological factors that hindered the integration and assimilation of Palestinians into host Arab societies. These were:

1. Social isolation from the host society caused by being labelled refugees—a connotation which carried a social stigma of inferiority.
2. Loss of social status, which left deep scars in the Palestinian personality, an effect that came close to loss of self-respect.[3]

The only way Palestinian refugees could remedy their loss of status at that time was by regaining their previous status in their country.

Palestinians in various Arab countries rebelled against the settlement project without any sort of central coordination. Palestinians in refugee camps destroyed or threw away all equipment and building materials offered by UNRWA to help them build permanent houses. They insisted on keeping their tents, especially during the first years of refuge. Suleiman notes: 'The Palestinian masses have rejected the settlement projects because they saw in it a real threat to their identity and to their aspirations for return to their country as well as a way of consolidating the Israeli state.'[4]

Another source for the early stirrings of the new Palestinian social movement was UNRWA's educational policy. UNRWA took charge of educating Palestinian refugees, but the curriculum set for UNRWA schools did not include teaching the history and geography of Palestine. UNRWA decided to teach Palestinian children in each community the history and geography of the host country. Palestinians saw that decision as an integral part of the settlement policy that threatened to obliterate their national identity. Student demonstrations and protests initiated and supported by some teachers broke out at the beginning of each school year demanding a modification in the school curricula to include the history and geography of Palestine.

The rise of the new Palestinian social movement was slowly leading to new political organizations. Palestinians in various communities were simultaneously thinking of forming commando groups that would continue the struggle against Zionist Jews in Palestine. However, most of these aspirations did not go beyond indoor discussions, mainly because the Palestinians were relying on Pan-Arab political parties to bring down the defeated Arab regimes and to liberate Palestine. At the end of 1954 the Egyptian government adopted small groups of Palestinian commandos and established bases for them in Gaza and north-east Sinai.

The two major groups participating in the various Palestine social movements were students and teachers. The participation rate was the highest in the refugee camps. The first forms of organization appeared among students. The two main Palestinian student associations were formed in Cairo and Damascus. The Cairo association was established in 1944. Its activities in the years 1944–52 were restricted to social, cultural and union affairs. In 1952, however, it underwent a high degree of politicization. Yasser Arafat was elected as its head, and he kept that position until his graduation in 1956. Many of the leaders-to-be of the Palestinian resistance movement were active members of the Cairo student association. The Palestinian student association of Damascus counted among its goals 'raising the awareness of our people to the Palestine problem and keeping their morale high; explaining the Palestinian problem to international public opinion and preparing our youth for the battle of return'.[5]

The Palestinian social movement in Israel

Palestinians who remained in their homes in 1948 became Israeli citizens as a non-Jewish minority in a Jewish state. However, they did not gain equal rights with Jewish citizens of Israel. They were faced with two major difficulties, which formed the basis of their collective action. First, they had to fight for equal status and equal rights as citizens of Israel and, second, they had to fight to protect their land from Jewish takeover.

Jewish settlers owned 6.6 per cent of the land of Palestine before May 1948. As they won the war they found themselves in control of nearly three-quarters of the area of Palestine.

In 1951 the state property law was passed. Article 2 of this law stated, 'Property of the Palestine authorities, situated in Israel, is property of the state of Israel as from 15 May 1948'.[6] After seizing refugee lands and public lands, the Israeli authorities turned to the lands of Arab citizens of Israel. The principal means of confiscation of such lands was through various provisions of the emergency regulations. These granted the military governor the power to declare specific areas 'closed areas' or 'security zones'. Four days after the establishment of the state of Israel, military rule was imposed on the Arabs living in Israel. It was lifted in December 1966. Arab areas in Israel were divided into three districts, each under a military governor.

In order to defend their lands and their rights in Israel, Palestinians attempted to create their own political organizations. Some local leaders called for a popular conference to be held in Acre on 6 July 1958. A similar conference was held in Nazareth. Both conferences were attended by 120 Palestinians, while 40 were prevented from attending by the orders of military governors. The two conferences saw the birth of the Arab Front, which came to be known as the Popular Front after the Israeli governor refused to register it in its initial name. The front was mainly composed of Arab nationalists and communists. Its declared goals were to work to end military rule, to fight confiscation of Arab lands, to return confiscated land to its owners, to press for the use of Arabic to be allowed in all official dealings and in public departments, and to press for all refugees to be allowed to return home.[7] The front succeeded in establishing six branches within six months.

Although the Israeli authorities fought the Popular Front fiercely, its weakening was in fact the result of internal disputes between nationalists and communists in the Arab world. The nationalists withdrew from the front and decided to work independently, forming the Land Group. The Israeli authorities did not recognize the group and accused it of being Nasserite. By 1964 the group declared itself as a political party called the Land Movement and informed the authorities of its platform as follows: 'Finding a just solution for the Palestinian cause in accordance with the desire of the Palestinian Arabs, the establishment of an Arab Palestinian state, and solidarity with the Arab movement working for liberation, unity and socialism.'[8] The

Israeli authorities banned the new political party and arrested many of its leaders. In a further step, the Minister of Defence dissolved the Land Movement, confiscated its property and threatened its members with ten years' imprisonment if they continued their activities. By 1965 the Israeli authorities had closed down all youth clubs and associations that were sympathetic to the Land Movement.

The struggle of the Palestinians in Israel for equal rights was carried on within the structures of Jewish organizations, mainly the Israeli trade union Histadrot, and through *ad hoc* committees complaining against the condition of Arab schools in Israel. Many Arab activists joined the Israeli Communist Party and presented their demands through that party.

Interaction of the Palestinian and Arab social movements

The struggle of Palestinian nationalists was not isolated from the overall Arab struggle for independence. As part of the Arab world, Palestine was the concern not of the Palestine Arabs alone but of all Arabs. The connection of the Zionist colonialist project in Palestine with imperialist interests in the Arab world had turned the struggle against Zionism into a cause of all Arabs rather than a cause of Palestinians alone. For this reason, Arab armies joined the 1948 war in support of Palestinian Arabs.

During the 1940s the Arab countries witnessed the formation of a multitude of political parties. In addition to existing internationalist parties such as the communist parties and the Muslim Brothers, Pan-Arab nationalist political parties were formed. The Ba'ath party was formed in Damascus in the middle of the decade. It espoused a nationalist Arab ideology that believed in one Arab nation and vowed to realize the unity of the nation in a single state. The Ba'ath also adopted a socialist ideology.

Another Pan-Arab political party was formed in the early 1950s at the American University of Beirut. This party's major goals were to realize Arab unity and liberate Palestine. It considered the loss of Palestine a direct result of Arab disunity or fragmentation and hence saw Arab unity as a precondition for liberating Palestine. Its political programme proposed two stages in Arab struggle, the first being political and the second economic and social. This programme conflicted with that of the Ba'ath party, which proposed that political and social goals could not be achieved separately; Ba'athists sought to struggle on two fronts simultaneously: against imperialism and Zionism, and against Arab reactionary classes and regimes.

A third Pan-Arab political movement, the Nasserite movement, emerged in the mid-1950s. By virtue of Egypt's leadership of the Arab world and Nasser's charismatic leadership, Nasserism became the leading Pan-Arab, anti-imperialist, mass political movement in the Arab world.

All through the 1950s, the Palestinians who sought ways of working for their cause joined the newly formed progressive Arab political parties. They played a key role in the three Pan-Arab political movements. One Palestinian leader described the Palestinian–Arab political interaction of the decade as follows:

> The Palestinian political movement reacted to all events and developments in the Arab world. We shared in many of these events because we believed that they were part of our struggle for Palestine. Our Arab concerns overshadowed our immediate Palestinian concerns. Our people did not hesitate at all to place all their capabilities as individuals or groups at the service of the forces which changed the political scene in the Arab East.[9]

From the mid-1950s until 1961 the Arab mass movement experienced its greatest strength as it fought foreign domination and Arab reactionary governments. The movement under Nasser's leadership fought and won some major political battles: from the Suez war (1956) to the establishment of the United Arab Republic (Egypt and Syria) in 1958 and the overthrow of the Iraqi monarchy by Iraqi Nasserites in the same year.

In September 1961, however, the United Arab Republic collapsed as Syria withdrew from the union. That event was a severe blow to Palestinian aspirations to liberate their country at the hands of a strong and unified Arab army. Palestinians also came to realize that Pan-Arab political parties and movements were unable to offer any clear or convincing conception of how the liberation of Palestine was to be achieved. Palestinians were also disappointed with the bitter conflict among the three major Pan-Arab political movements. This gave rise to a debate over 'Palestinianism' versus 'Arabism'. Palestinianism did not deny Arab identity. It signified that Palestinians had to take the initiative to wage a battle to liberate their country rather than wait for Arab unity and a powerful Arab army, as these might take too long to achieve, or even never happen.

Thus Palestinians, having succeeded in 1964–65 in recreating their own political structure (the Palestine Liberation Organization), and their own political movement, declared it a national liberation movement. That development opened the door for the restructuring of the relationship between Palestinian and Arab social movements. The defeat of the Arab regimes in June 1967 and the rise of the Palestinian resistance movement as a vanguard of the Arab masses leading the struggle against Israel, which was considered by the Arab masses all along as the central mission of Arab struggle, intensified the interaction of Arab and Palestinian mass movements and created higher forms of cooperation between both.

The relationship between Arab national movements and the Palestinian movement from 1968 on has been a highly complex one, varying from one Arab country to another.

Heads of workers' unions in Jordan, Egypt, Lebanon, Syria, Algeria, Palestine, Iraq, Kuwait, Sudan, Yemen Democratic Republic, Libya and Morocco held a meeting in Cairo in March 1970. They decided to work for the establishment of a popular Arab front in every Arab country to mobilize the Arab masses against the USA and Israel. They also decided to organize an annual week of solidarity with Arab workers in the territories occupied by Israel during 1967 war. During that annual event financial contributions are collected. The unions also called upon Arab workers to join the Palestinian revolution as volunteers.

In addition, Arab political parties in Egypt, Syria, Sudan, Lebanon, Jordan and Iraq have announced their absolute support for the Palestinian resistance movement and have called on their governments to protect and support that movement and to be prepared for a major battle against Israel.

These circumstances allowed the development of an advanced relationship between the Palestinian national movement and an Arab national movement, opening the door for unlimited cooperation and coordination between the Palestinian and Lebanese national movements. The Lebanese national movement and oppressed Lebanese masses felt that they had their own army (Palestinian commandos) and thus became more daring in challenging the regime. After the resistance was driven out of Jordan in July 1971, it moved all its forces to southern Lebanon and Syria. However, Syria being sympathetic to the Palestinian movement, was able to establish a working relationship with that movement in which it had the upper hand. Syria and Iraq, on the claim of being Pan-Arab national regimes, soon formed their own (Ba'athist) Palestinian resistance factions, Al-Sal'a and the Arab Liberation Front respectively. Both factions were an integral part of the PLO and of the resistance movement.

The complexity of the relationships between the Palestinian national movement and the various Arab national movements stemmed from the fact that each had to take into account the relation of the concerned Arab national movement to its own government and the position of that government on the Palestinian question in general and the armed struggle specifically.

A radical transformation occurred in the relationship of the Palestinian national movement to Arab social movements after the October 1973 war between the Arabs and Israel. The war enabled the Arab regimes to regain the initiative from the Arab masses and formally to seek a final settlement for their dispute with Israel. The PLO leadership felt the shift and went along with it. By the mid-1970s the Arab national movement was extremely weakened in most Arab countries (except Lebanon). At the same time, the PLO leadership traded its relationship with the Arab masses by adopting the strategy of political settlement rather than confrontation. The Palestinian national movement gave up its motto of revolutionizing the Arab masses and turned itself into a rather conservative force interested in international diplomacy and international solutions.

But despite all the negative developments in relations between the Palestinian and Arab social movements, the developments of late 1987 and early 1988 in Palestine showed unmistakably that the Arab masses had not given up their support of the Palestinian people.

The social movement and Palestinian identity

The major goal of the opponents of the Palestinians has been to eradicate the Palestinian identity of the Arabs of Palestine. If Palestinians could be made to forget that they were Palestinians, they could easily and rapidly be assimilated as Syrians, Lebanese, Jordanians, etc. But what was initially thought to be the easiest strategy has proved the most difficult task to achieve. There was no way that Palestinians would give up their national identity within a few years or decades of the foundation of Israel. But further political developments, two decades later, revived and reaffirmed that identity as a historical reality.

Not only Zionism but also other powers such as the major imperialist countries pinned their hopes on a gradual Palestinian loss of identity and hence in the early 1950s they directed Arab reactionary governments to take steps towards erasing or blurring Palestinian identity. According to Dajani, the biggest threat to Palestinian identity came from Jordan rather than from Israel. Jordan annexed eastern Palestine and bestowed Jordanian nationality on its population, thus turning the majority of the Palestinian people into Jordanians. Dajani adds that, 'Although Jordan's action was the worst, it was not unique or deviant within the Arab context. Most Arab countries attempted to contain Palestinian identity within the framework of their public policy, and through their political parties and organizations.'[10]

In the period extending from 1949 to 1967, Palestinians had to fight really hard against the serious threats to their identity. Several factors, political, economic and socio-psychological, contributed to their success in retaining their national identity. Most prominent among the political factors was the outright repression which took place of Palestinian communities, which was harshest in Israel, Jordan and Lebanon. Another political factor that helped Palestinians remember who they were was the restriction of their movement and travel within Arab countries and from Arab to other countries. This was most true of Palestinian refugees, who were issued with 'travel documents' rather than passports.

Prominent among the economic factors was 'the inability of host societies to formulate comprehensive development plans to integrate the Palestinians into their economic structures. That failure led to the stagnations of Palestinian communities in host societies and thus singled them out as "different" or "strange" communities with negative features or image.'[11] Palestinian identity survived and struck its roots in the refugee camp. One would dare say that if it were not for camp life, Palestinian identity and solidarity would have been immensely weakened. The Arab countries were economically unable to do anything about the refugee camps, and Israel found herself in the same position after June 1967, despite her recognition of the vital importance of camps for the continuity of Palestinian resistance and persistence of the Palestinian cause.

As several studies carried out in the early 1970s on Palestinian children, socialization and aspirations concluded, the Palestinian identity was retained mainly through the family.[12] Through their families, all Palestinian children knew who they were, where they were from and why they were in a camp, that they would be going back to Palestine one day and that they should be prepared to fight for the liberation of Palestine. This knowledge or conception was reaffirmed by teachers in UNRWA schools (unofficially of course). One Palestinian researcher gave the following impressive description of the social–psychological state of Palestinian refugees in Gaza:

> The uprooted refugee could not forget his uprootedness. If he tended to forget that for one moment his tin roof would immediately remind him. Despite long years of refuge he speaks of his house as if he just left it.

> Children have memorized the geography of Palestine as a result of reputed talks about it by their parents and relatives. The refugees did not only carry along with them their traditions but they carried the geography of their homeland as well. Thus expulsion to the uprooted was a mere 'temporary' period in their 'definite' return. To Palestinian refugees, 'return' was a matter of absolute conviction. It became a social norm which nobody can violate.[13]

The rise of the Palestine Liberation Organization in 1964 was a step in the direction of retaining the national identity of the Palestinian people. That identity was finally affirmed or reaffirmed even among Palestinians dispersed all over the world with the rise of Palestinian armed struggle and when the command groups took charge of the PLO in 1967. Al-Khatib believes that until the rise of the resistance movement:

> Palestinian identity was still torn and defeated, unable to face herself or the outside world. The Palestinian personality used to run away from herself by hiding behind the nationality of the host country, by immigration, or by joining Arab political parties. The foremost achievement of the Palestinian armed struggle is the revival of dignity and the will to live to the average Palestinian.[14]

Some years later Dajani wrote:

> The revolutionary practice of the Palestinian Resistance Movement has activated and revived the stagnant Palestinian reality. That was achieved through establishing several Palestinian unions and associations for workers, women, students, writers and teachers. Added to this was the launching of several educational and social programs for the Palestinians in the camps.[15]

From henceforth, Palestinians had their own national institutions within which they could work for their goals. The culmination of the revival of Palestinian identity was reached in 1974 when the Arab summit meeting of all Arab leaders recognized the PLO as the sole legitimate representative of the Palestinian people.

The class dimension of the social movement

No comprehensive study exists of Palestinian class structure after 1948. However, general descriptions of such a structure are available in more than one work on Palestinian politics and economic conditions.[16]

It is not easy to speak of one Palestinian class structure after 1948. There emerged at least two class structures: one for the refugees who lost their means of production and dwelt mainly in camps in Gaza Strip, the West Bank and in neighbouring Arab countries, and the other for non-refugees, mainly Gaza residents and West Bankers who retained their original residence and property.

The total number of Palestinians in 1948 is estimated by Sayigh and Dajani to have been 1,500,000, more than half of whom later became refugees.

Hilal speaks of three social classes in the West Bank and Gaza Strip, each composed of several strata.[17] The big bourgeoisie includes four strata, namely the agricultural, industrial, bureaucratic and commercial bourgeoisie. The small bourgeoisie includes small landowners, owners of small industrial firms, professionals, civil servants and small merchants. The working class includes skilled, semi-skilled and unskilled labourers.

The class structure of Palestinians in the diaspora did not include a big bourgeoisie, not at least until the late 1960s or early 1970s. Palestinian communities in the diaspora were composed mainly of poor, unemployed refugees and a small stratum of the working class and a very narrow layer of the small bourgeoisie composed of UNRWA employees and schoolteachers and shopkeepers.

The dismemberment of Palestine and the displacement of the majority of its population exposed the Palestinian class structure to external forces, thereby generating a certain dynamic towards change. This was due to two forces, namely education–immigration and occupation. Meanwhile, changes in the class structure in the diaspora were facilitated by education–immigration.

Members of the Palestinian big bourgeoisie who had suffered at the hands of the British-protected Zionist bourgeoisie thought that they would find their chance for development in alliance with the less developed East Bank bourgeoisie after the kingdom of Jordan annexed the West Bank. For that reason they supported the annexation. However, their wishes did not come true, because the Jordanian regime followed a discriminatory policy in favour of the East Jordanian bourgeoisie.

The social stratum that benefited most from Israeli occupation was the commercial bourgeoisie, which was able to accumulate wealth at a fast rate and was granted many facilities by the occupation authorities in order to enable it to market Israeli products in the West Bank and the Arab countries.

The small bourgeoisie suffered because of the occupation as a result of its inability to compete with its Israeli counterpart. Many small farmers, shopkeepers and workshop owners were forced to give up their businesses and work as hired labourers themselves. The Palestinian working class suffered most from the occupation. Most of the workforce had no alternative but to work in Israel. They were given menial jobs and hard manual work at lower wages than Israeli workers.

Several Palestinian researchers agree that the Palestinian masses in the camps formed the backbone of the Palestinian social movement. This contrasts with the role of Palestinian city-dwellers. Sirhan found in a study of the records of the martyrs of the Palestinian revolution that 82 per cent of the martyrs up to 1972 were camp-dwellers.[18] The camps formed easy targets for the Israeli army as well as for Arab armies.[19] Palestinian city-dwellers were a less obvious target. Due to their better economic conditions they were able to escape most of the pressures and oppression faced by camp-dwellers. Hammoud notes that 'the Palestinian masses in the camps bore the brunt of uprootedness, poverty and oppression'. However, despite their state of utmost despair they remained most ready to respond to the slightest revolutionary initiative which promised radical changes.[20]

Sayigh writes of a radical difference in the experiences of the Palestinian bourgeoisie and the Palestine working class in the diaspora: 'The Palestinian bourgeoisie, by virtue of its qualifications and property, was exposed to a minor condition of discrimination and enmity in the Arab countries. The working class and the poor carried the full load.'[21] Dajani quotes Issa and Hawatmeh as saying that 'before 1967 the Palestinian bourgeoisie tended to reach an understanding with the bourgeoisie of the host or administering country, and attempted to be integrated with that bourgeoisie. During that period the Palestinian bourgeoisie helped to control the Palestinian masses.'[22]

Although the Palestinian camp-dwellers and working class formed the backbone of the Palestinian social movement all along, since 1968 there has been wide-scale participation in the movement by the small bourgeoisie. That development was encouraged by an overall upsurge in national awareness and feeling coupled with the rise of armed resistance in Jordan and Lebanon. The Palestinian small bourgeoisie and middle classes were soon able to take command of the Palestinian social movement and to control trade unions and popular organizations. That control was facilitated by the PLO leadership and the skills possessed by the middle class. As the movement developed its own structure and leadership by the late 1960s, its class dimensions too became clear. It was mainly working-class-based and controlled and directed by the middle class. The middle class was generally satisfied by running or administering various institutions and organizations of the movement while the working class took the brunt of confrontation, both militarily and politically. As the Palestinian social movement was hard hit in Jordan and Lebanon, many segments of the middle class dissociated themselves from the movement or limited their role to offering financial contributions.

The resistance movement and social movement

The Arab defeat in the June war of 1967 paved the way for the rapid rise of the Palestinian resistance movement. Defeated Arab regimes were unable to obstruct the popular armed struggle as the Arab masses rejected defeat and refused to surrender.

Another significant and unintended by-product of Israel's victory was the 're-unification' of Palestine and 'non-diaspora' Palestinians. This occurred when Israel subjugated Palestinians to a single political authority by excluding Jordan and Egypt from authority over the West Bank and Gaza Strip.

Only two national popular organizations were formed before the rise of the resistance movement, and they were led by students and workers. The General Union of Palestinian Students (GUPS) was formed in Cairo in 1959 with the merger of three student leagues (based in Cairo, Damascus and Beirut). Currently it has thirty branches all over the world. The General Union of Palestinian Labourers (GUPL) was also founded in Cairo, in August 1963. It is an extension of the union established in Haifa in 1925 under the title Arab Palestinian Workers Association.

All the other popular organizations were formed after 1967–68. The General Union of Palestinian Women (GUPW) was formed in 1968 as an organizational framework for Palestinian women all over the world. The General Union of Palestinian Teachers (GUPT) was formed in 1969, the General Union of Palestinian Jurists (GUPJ) in 1971 and the General Union of Palestinian Artists (GUPA) in 1979. The General Union of Palestinian Writers and Journalists (GUPWJ) was established in Beirut in September 1972 after the PLO's Executive Committee named a preparatory committee of twenty-two writers. The General Union of Palestinian Engineers (GUPE) was formed in Iraq in 1973 by representatives of Palestinian engineers in Kuwait, Syria, Algeria and Libya. Currently it has branches in most Arab countries.

Among the PLO-sponsored institutions is the Association for the Development of the Palestinian Camp founded in Beirut in February 1969 by Lebanese and Palestinian women.

The third PLO-sponsored institution is the Palestinian Red Crescent Society (PRCS) established in 1969 to cater for the increasing need for medical and general health services. In addition to dispensaries in all Palestinian camps, the PRCS runs nine hospitals in Lebanon and five in Syria.

As for the social institutions sponsored by PLO factions, it is noteworthy that every Palestinian political organization has its own services designed to cater for the particular needs of the youth and young adults. These service organizations cover scouts and cub scouts, sports and physical education, political and paramilitary training, and sponsorship of educational and vocational training centres.[23] As there are nine PLO factions, ranging from Fatah to the Popular Front for the Liberation of Palestine, there are easily more than 200 social institutions offering social services, mainly in the camps in Lebanon and Syria where the PLO could operate freely.

Palestinian armed struggle against Israeli occupation and the massive Israeli retaliatory attacks on the undefended and unprotected Palestinian camps created the need for mobilization in all Palestinian communities. This was true even of the newly formed Palestinian community in the USA. This is composed mainly of West Bankers who were forced to immigrate due to unemployment and lack of educational opportunities after the Israeli occupation of June 1967. The Palestinian community in the USA currently numbers approximately 150,000 Palestinians who have gained immigrant status or citizenship.

A Palestinian social movement emerged in the USA having as its main concern solidarity with the overall social movement of the Palestinian people. It attempts to influence the US position on the Palestine question in favour of the Arabs. Despite US citizenship and the diaspora, the Palestinian identity of Palestinian Americans has remained dominant. Freedom of organization in the USA has enabled Palestinian Americans to be better organized than Palestinian communities in the Arab countries. However, one should keep in mind that the weight of Palestinian Americans in the Palestinian social movement remains relatively weak. The real weight belongs to the communities of Gaza, West Bank, Jordan and Lebanon.

Palestinian political organizations involved in armed struggle have varied widely in ideology. They may be grouped in three ideological categories:

1. The nationalists, who wanted to regain their country and adhered to Arab unity, yet worked for no specific social system.
2. The socialists, who wanted to free the Palestinian human being while struggling to liberate the land. They proposed a socialist social system in liberated Palestine and proposed that social and national liberation should go hand in hand. They called for strategic alliance with the Soviet Union and considered the Palestinian national movement to be part of the international progressive front. They mobilized the Palestinian masses accordingly. Such organizations include the Popular Front for the Liberation of Palestine and all its socialist and Marxist offshoots.
3. The conservatives, who wanted to regain their country and to establish an independent capitalist state that could maintain good relations with the Arab countries and with both Western and Eastern blocs. The conservatives did not have their own organization. They formed a political current or trend mainly within the Fatah movement. Adherents of this trend did not care much about mobilizing the Arab masses, favoured relations with Arab regimes and sought to create an official Arab position on Palestine.

In general one can speak of two stages in the relationship of the resistance movement to the Palestinian masses. The first stage extended from 1967 to 1973 and could be called the 'democratic stage', as it was characterized by non-coercion of the political leadership over the masses. The PLO factions needed the full support of the masses politically and even financially. During this stage the leadership did not attempt to control the Palestinian social or mass movement. Interaction within popular organizations and trade unions was more or less left to its own course. During these years the internal dynamics and vitality of the mass movement and mass organizations reached its peak. One does not exaggerate by saying that Palestinian communities were like beehives of social, educational and political activity. The political leadership and some of its policies were often publicly criticized in the camps and in meetings of popular organizations. One can even go so far as saying that the mass movement had the upper hand over the political leadership.

That situation changed drastically after 1974 as the PLO leadership changed its strategic aim from liberation to the reaching of a compromise or a 'just political settlement'. During this second stage the leadership was interested no longer in high-level mobilization of the masses, and found it necessary to bring the popular social movement under control. The leadership (the Fatah leadership specifically) used all the means at its disposal to place men loyal to it in charge of most popular organizations. Within a few years these efforts succeeded and social movement became well under control. Freedom of criticism was largely curtailed and all popular projects had to receive the approval of the leadership. The same faces dominated the popular organizations from 1974 to 1987, despite loss of support within their organizations. Palestinian popular organizations hold elections every year or every couple of years, but lists of the new steering committees were prepared beforehand by the political leadership. This was done not only at the level of national committees, but even at the level of small branches in various Palestinian communities. As Palestinian popular organizations lost their democracy, mass participation retreated, and the popular movement in the diaspora lost its vitality, became paralysed and stagnated.

The Palestinian social movement in Kuwait is a good example of what happened. Participation in popular organizations was restricted to small groups who carried no weight numerically or with the masses. For instance, out of 1,000 Palestinians working in the medical professions in Kuwait only 15 attended the 1987 convention to elect a new steering committee of nine. Out of 6,000 teachers only 140 attended the 1987 general assembly of the teachers' union. In April 1977 the leadership of the General Union of Palestinian Writers and Journalists was undemocratically toppled through imposing a large number of new members who were neither writers nor journalists nor even 'readers', as one political cadre put it.

The social movement in occupied Palestine

When Israel so easily occupied the West Bank and the Gaza Strip it found one extremely favourable condition that any foreign occupier would envy. The Palestinian social movement had been crushed and weakened by seventeen years of oppressive Jordanian rule. Israel thus had a golden time in those areas from 1967 to 1973. Israel took its time to set up a long-term comprehensive policy aiming at keeping those territories under its long-term control.

The Palestinian National Council in its eleventh session held in August 1973 called for the formation of the so-called Palestinian National Front in occupied territories. That front considered itself an integral part of the Palestinian national movement and of the Arab liberation movement. Its comprehensive programme stressed the following: resisting Zionist occupation, securing the right of return and of self-determination, defending Arab lands in the face of Zionist seizure, protecting the Arab economy, protecting Arab culture and history, and supporting popular organizations.[24]

The big boost to the newly formed front came from the October War (1973). That war represented a watershed to the Palestinian national movement in occupied territories as it tore apart the legend of undefeatable Israel. The front called upon Palestinians in the occupied territories to participate in the war effort. It also called upon Palestinian workers to stop working in Israeli establishments and to boycott the Histadrot elections in Jerusalem as well as municipal elections.

November 1974 witnessed the beginning of a massive popular uprising, which lasted ten days. The uprising was triggered by stringent Israeli economic measures and restrictions. The social strata who participated in that uprising included students, workers, teachers and merchants. The Israeli authorities brutally crushed the uprising through beatings, arrests, deportations, fines and other economic penalties.

By early 1975 two major developments were helping to fuel the Palestinian national movement in the occupied territories. Economically, Israel was no longer able to sustain its relative prosperity. In fact, the Israeli economy began to rely on a high degree of exploitation of the occupied territories. Second, the Israeli government adopted an aggressive wide-scale settlement programme in the occupied territories. Seizure of Arab lands became a permanent policy of the occupying power. At that point Israel presented Palestinians under occupation with a single political option when it called upon them to accept 'civil self-administration' as their ultimate destiny. On 6 October 1975 students in Ramallah and El-Bireh went on strike against that proposal. Strikes spread to Bier-Zeit University and then to several cities and villages in the occupied territories. Severe clashes took place between demonstrators and occupying forces. The masses in Nablus formed a committee to discuss matters concerning the Israeli proposal. The committee included representatives of the municipal council, the chamber of commerce, workers' unions and women's organizations. Four mayors presented a memorandum to the Israeli governor denouncing and rejecting the civil self-administration proposal.

The Israeli government opened another front by disclosing its plans to seize vast areas of land from its Arab citizens. In August 1975 the Israeli head of state announced that he was wholeheartedly in favour of the Judaization of the Galilee. Palestinians living within Israel proper held a popular conference in Nazareth in October 1975 to discuss ways of defending their lands. Under the slogan 'In defence of our lands' several popular conferences were held within Israel.

Popular Palestinian resistance forced Israel to freeze its settlement plans in Sabastia near Nablus. This encouraged villagers to attack settlers in another village, Kfar Kaddoum. Simultaneously, women organized massive demonstrations demanding the release of all administrative detainees.

At that time the USA put a veto on a UN Security Council resolution denouncing Israeli settlements in the occupied territories as illegal. Massive student demonstrations against the US veto broke out in Nablus and spread to Ramallah and Jerusalem. Heads of municipalities denounced the US veto. Israel again brutally crushed the demonstrations.

On 29 January 1976 the Israeli High Court in Jerusalem passed a rule giving Jews the right to pray in Al-Aqsa Mosque. That rule triggered massive popular protests all over the occupied territories. Violent clashes followed between Palestinians and occupation forces. Israeli brutality led the staff of a school in Nablus collectively to resign. The municipal council resigned in a move of solidarity with the teachers. Other municipalities followed suit as violence continued. The Israeli authorities imposed a curfew on Ramallah and El-Bireh for ten days starting on 16 March 1976. On 19 March Jerusalem witnessed a massive strike by merchants.

As preparations were made for a Day of the Land protest, set to be on 30 March 1976, by Palestinian citizens of Israel, the occupied territories were flooded with leaflets calling for a general strike on that day. The occupied territories responded favourably and, for the first time since 1948, Palestinians took a coordinated, unified stand. Life in Palestine stood still, and Israel used the utmost brutality to break up the strike. In all, 6 Palestinians were shot dead, 69 were wounded and 250 arrested. The Day of the Land became a national landmark to be celebrated annually by Palestinians under occupation and in the diaspora.

Jawad cites four major aspects in the development of the Palestinian social movement in the occupied territories from 1975 on.[25] These are as follows:

1. There was a widening of the social base of the movement. In addition to students, workers and women, the rural poor and middle peasants increased their participation. The merchants and municipal heads also joined the movement.
2. There was a higher degree of clarity and specificity in the demands of the movement.
3. Confrontations between the Palestinian masses and the Israeli forces became increasingly violent.
4. A noticeable 'offensive spirit' emerged in the Palestinian national movement and among its leaders.

These developments and their cumulative impact made it perhaps inevitable that the Palestinian social movement would reach the highest levels of mass mobilization expressed in the 'whole population' uprising that has been going on since December 1987. The Israelis have been continuously raising their level of oppression only to be matched by continuously higher levels of popular Palestinian resistance.

Which way ahead?

Some general conclusions can be drawn about the major features of the Palestinian social movement.

First, the Palestinian social movement was triggered by an external factor (Zionist colonialism) rather than by internal dynamics of social interaction among the Palestinians, such as class struggle and modernization.

Second, the Palestinian social movement is basically a political movement in the sense that all its efforts over the past seventy years have been directed towards one central goal, namely achieving national liberation and independence.

Third, being a national liberation movement meant that achieving the usual union demands in the form of higher wages, better working conditions, better education, improvement of women's status, etc., was and is irrelevant to that movement. These demands were sacrificed or even bluntly delayed and suppressed for the sake of achieving the strategic national goal. Although all Palestinian unions and popular organizations called in their charters for the advancement of union demands, none of them actually had the time or the funds to do so. Women and students were told bluntly that they would have to sacrifice or 'freeze' most of their collective demands until national victory was achieved. Nevertheless, a certain degree of progress in that area did occur.

Fourth, Palestinians living in various communities in the diaspora who found themselves marginal to the political and economical systems of the host countries were not called upon or even allowed (except in Jordan, through to a limited extent) to struggle for or to come up with answers to social issues such as health, education, wages, and social security. As Musa puts it,[26] 'the Palestinian Social Movement found itself literally outside the local dialectical movement in host societies'.

Fifth, Palestinians participated mainly in Arab political parties rather than in Arab trade unions and popular organizations. Even where they belonged to Pan-Arab trade unions all they wanted from these unions were political demands and stands or positions on the Palestinian question.

Sixth, although the Palestinian social movement is broad-based, historically its backbone has been the refugee camp-dwellers.

Seventh, the Palestinian social movement has alternatively taken both spontaneous and organized forms. Whenever the organized structure was hit or crushed, the spontaneous popular movement carried on creating new organized forms that placed the Palestinian social movement at a higher level of struggle.

Eighth, the Palestinian social movement centred on four strategic national goals, namely protection of the land, preservation of national identity, return, and the achievement of national independence. As these goals remain unachieved, there is no way the Palestinian social movement could come to a halt internally or be stopped by external pressures or force. This is evident in the current uprising in occupied Palestine. For this reason Palestinians have a well-known popular belief that the uniqueness of their social movement rests in the fact that the people have always been ahead of their leadership.

Ninth, the Palestinian social movement is so genuine that it has contained the energy capable of carrying it for three-quarters of a century. As the Zionist challenge persists there is no way the Palestinian social movement could subside. It is a highly experienced and rich social movement.

Notes

1. Suleiman, Mohammad, 'Settlement Projects of the Palestinians', *SAMED*, Vol. 3, No. 17, June 1980, p. 10.
2. Sayigh, Rosemary, 'Palestinian Peasants', *SAMED*, Vol. 4, No. 24, January 1981, p. 39.
3. *ibid*, pp. 54–6.
4. Suleiman, p. 20.
5. Shehada, Musa, 'The Experience of the General Union of Palestinian Students', *Palestinian Affairs*, No. 5, November 1971, p. 180.
6. Jiryis, Sabri, 'Settler's Law: seizure of Palestinian lands', *Palestine Yearbook of International Law* , Vol. II, 1985, p. 21.
7. Jiryis, Sabri, *The Arabs in Israel*, Institute of Palestine Studies, Beirut, 1973, p. 316.
8. *ibid*, pp. 322–23.
9. Al-Hassan, Hani, 'Faith Between Theory and Practice', *Journal of Palestine Studies*, February 1972.
10. Dajani, Ahmed Sidki et al., *Palestinians in the Arab World*, Institute for Arab Studies and Research, Tunis, 1978, pp. 159–60.
11. *ibid*, p. 306.
12. Sirhan, Bassem, 'Palestinian Children', *Journal of Palestine Studies,* No. 1, March 1971, pp. 95–106.

13. Abu Al-Namel, Hussein, *Gaza Strip 1948–1967*, PLO Research Centre, Beirut, 1979, p. 332.

14. Al-Khatib, Hussam, 'The Palestinian Revolution: where to?', *Journal of Palestine Studies*, No. 4, September 1971, pp. 5–30.

15. Dajani, p. 257.

16. Works by Hilal, Abu-Namel, Ayyoub, Dajani and others.

17. Hilal, Jamil, *The Socio-economic Structure of the West Bank and Gaza Strip: 1948–1974* (Beirut: PLO Research Centre), pp. 298–301.

18. Sirhan, Bassem, 'Martyrs of the Palestinian Revolution', *Journal of Palestine Studies* , 1972, p. 81.

19. Sayigh, p. 34.

20. Dajani, p. 300.

21. Sayigh, p. 33.

22. Dajani, p. 249.

23. TEAM International, *PLO-affiliated Institutions*, Beirut, 1981, p. 13.

24. *Al-Tali'a*, Cairo, No.11, November 1973, pp. 142–44.

25. Jawad, Sa'id, *National Palestinian Upsurge in the West Bank, Gaza and the Galilee: 1974–1978* , Ibn Khaldoun Publishing House, Beirut, 1979, pp. 180–81.

26. Musa, Shehadeh, 'On the Experience of GUPS', *Palestine Affairs*, No. 5, November 1971, pp. 178–79.

9. Swadhyaya: Values and Message

Ramashray Roy

In about 1960, Goa, Gujarat and Maharashtra in western India saw the beginning of a silent revolution. Initially the effort of a single man, Sri Panduranga Vaijanath Athavale Shastri, this silent revolution has now grown into a massive movement. Geographically, it has now extended to fourteen Indian states with the greatest density in Goa, Gujarat, Maharashtra, Madhya Pradesh, Andhra Pradesh and Haryana. It is also very active in the Gulf states, some pockets of Africa, England, the USA and Canada. In social terms, its adherents come from diverse and heterogeneous socio-economic groups: fishermen, tribals, Vagdis, Kharvas, Mirs, farmers, businessmen, intellectuals and professionals.

The movement is silent because it shuns publicity and avoids public relations. Very few beyond the circle of its adherents know about it, at least intimately. It is a revolution because it aspires to root out the disturbance that is within and that has laid hold of men's minds. This silent revolution is Swadhyaya, which aims to reorient individual perspectives on life and, through this, to reorder collective existence. Its objective is to transform people so that they are able to forge an abiding sense of brotherhood among the children of God and, through this, improve their earthly existence and ennoble their spiritual outlook. Its central thrust is to restore the rule of *dharma* and, by making it the basis of action, shape individuality in such a way that, whilst it retains its uniqueness, acquires self-confidence and manifests self-reliance and self-effort, it also values sociality and cooperative action.

What is Swadhyaya?

Swadhyaya emphasizes the need for self-surrender to God and employs religious idioms and symbols for reorienting individual motivation and action. It is not a religious sect since it neither advocates a search for relief in religion separated from everydayness nor claims a privileged status and therefore a distinct existence for what it considers to be fundamental religious principles. Drawing upon the rich ancient Indian tradition, picking up its elemental ideas and weaving them into a coherent perspective, Swadhyaya calls for the fusion of religion and everyday life. But its reliance on tradition does not make it backward-looking either.

Although Swadhyaya calls for people to render service to society, it is not a service society. In its concept of *purtadharma,* the traditional notion of social service as well as the modern concept of social service are fused through voluntary action. *Purtadharma,* with its origin in charity or piety, points to the inadequacy of performing sacrifices, *tapas,* austerity and purificatory rites for individual salvation, and emphasizes the need to do good to others as a means of attaining the highest merit. It is expressed through works of public utility, charitable work, social service and rendering relief to the poor and the distressed. Even while *purtadharma* may take a public form, it is not directed towards modifying or changing social institutional arrangements. Its thrust is religious rather than social or political.

Swadhyaya rejects the concept of social service. In its view, that smacks of elitist bias in the sense that, on the one hand, it assumes the common man to be ignorant of and unconcerned with his own situation and, on the other, it attributes to a few privileged higher-class individuals a privileged access to knowledge and the right to spread it around. Within this framework, the poor, the destitute and the unexerting represent human puppets with waxen minds and watery wills. To guide the motions of human puppets, there are the 'doctors of morality' (a term used by Helvetius) who know the wires by which these puppets are moved. This in itself implies denial of the equality and dignity of the common man. What compounds this denial further is that, in the name of helping the deprived to overcome their disabilities, modern social service agencies make them passive, dependent and pliable. Swadhyaya, in contrast, strives to instil in the individual a sense of self-confidence, self-reliance and self-effort. It is only through the cultivation of these qualities that individuals can serve themselves as well as the society.

Swadhyaya is often equated with a reform movement. It is not, however, a reform movement if by reform what is meant is social engineering.

The meaning of Swadhyaya

The central idea behind Swadhyaya is the age-old concept of *lokasamgraha* (maintenance and sustenance of the living and working as a unified approach to life). Constituting the concept of *lokasamgraha* are three important dimensions: the individual, the society he or she lives in, and his or her relationship with God. Swadhyaya recognizes that the individual is subject to the ordinary frailties of desires and attachments. Whilst not questioning that these desires must be satisfied and the attachments acknowledged, what is important is the way the individual goes about satisfying individual desires. He can go about this in a destructive way, but then *matsnayaya* (the law of the shark) will prevail, endangering not only his well-being but also his survival. He must therefore discriminate among his desires and satisfy them in such a way that the good of the larger society is also served, since his own good is inexorably linked with the good of the society. But this may entail the submergence of individuality in the all-powerful society. In order, therefore, to protect his individuality from the encroachments and ravages of society, he must strengthen his self by anchoring himself in the all-pervading presence, namely God. Drawing its inspiration from the *Gita*, Swadhyaya emphasizes the need for the individual to lead the normal life of duties and responsibilities that his phenomenal existence imposes on him—a normal life that contributes to the enrichment of his society and allows him to be in peace and contentment in a state of equanimity and in communion with God.

The interconnection between material needs and spiritual requirements becomes life-invigorating only when the pursuit of *artha* and *kama* is brought under the suzerainty of *dharma.* This is possible when *dharma* becomes an active principle in structuring and organizing personal experience and social relations. It requires the liberation of *dharma* from lifeless rituals on the one hand and for it to become the regulator of personal and social conduct on the other. This further means the demolition of the artificial division separating the material from the spiritual. But how is that possible in a society which is increasingly turning towards materiality?

For Swadhyaya, this question has two aspects, personal and social. The personal is, however, the key to the social. That people have to relate with each other itself assumes importance. The notion that individual good can be secured only by sacrificing the good of others or that individual good is possible only on the basis of subordination of the individual to the society at large must be rejected. Individual good compatible with social good is possible if the character of *aham,* the ego, is changed. This is desirable since its eradication or suppression destroys self-identity and self-respect.[1]

Swadhyaya as praxis

Swadhyaya thus signifies self-cultivation. It pertains to the journeying self, the self-exploring individual who, taking stock of his or her passions, appetites and desires, directs them towards devotion to God by sublimating them and, turning inward, mobilizes his or her own internal resources.[2] Thus Swadhyaya calls for sincere efforts to transform the self into something divine.[3] The practice of Swadhyaya brings the realization that the individual is not an ordinary being; concentrated in the individual are all the powers of God. This awareness produces a higher and more effective ego-sense and initiates a process first of withdrawal from and then of relating once again to the object world of hitching one's destiny with God.[4] This higher and nobler sense of ego produces self-respect, self-confidence and self-existence.[5]

Swadhyaya, as a process of self-cultivation for realizing higher values in personal life, also conduces an orientation that makes the individual realize his or her own limitations and check any self-aggrandizing tendency. In this sense, Swadhyaya has purely a personal significance. But it also has a larger import, which is conveyed through the concept of '*Ishavasyam*' interpreted in a novel way. *Ishavasyam* signifies the pervasive presence of God in this world and points to an integral identity among the objects—both sensate and insensate—of this world. Swadhyaya adds to this concept yet another dimension, that is, *Ishavasyam* also implies that the devotees of God must cover this world with the love of God.[6]

Interpreted in this way, Swadhyaya signifies, at one and the same time, that a genuine knowledge of the self entails more than a transforming act upon the self; it entails the realization that to know in this sense is not only to reflect and comprehend, but also to shape and create. For to know oneself is simultaneously to perfect oneself and to help others to perfect themselves.

Committed to the principle that the test of the truth lies in action, Swadhyaya attributes central significance to action as a medium not only of self-development for establishing communion with God but also of enriching and ennobling collective existence. In this sense, though action remains personal, it does not imply the Weberian idea of the ethics of responsibility which excludes critical examination of the basic value premises either in the realm of action or in the realm of science. In order to escape the flaw of Weberian ethics of responsibility, Swadhyaya emphasizes the offering to God of efficiency with which the individual is endowed.

Action with knowledge and devotion is what Swadhyaya emphasizes. It signifies that action must be offered to God and that it must result in the good of others. Acknowledging this, man must express his gratefulness to God by offering his *nipunata,* the efficiency he has been endowed with. To offer one's efficiency to God means the performance of one's inherited or acquired worldly vocation with skill, proficiency and dedication. This implies the enrichment of both personal life and social existence.This is what, in Swadhyaya parlance, is known as *kritishil bhakti,* that is, devotion through work. *Kritishil bhakti,* then, becomes the foundation of *lokasamgraha* which aims at removing animality in man, restraining him from seeking pleasure alone, leading him to compassion and transforming compassion into virtue.[7] It implies *dharma*-impregnated and morality-regulated action.

Yokasamgraha cannot be realized through the supposedly natural process of the concentration of individual actions—actions undertaken by individuals without any reference to their consequence for others. On the contrary, it requires a conscious choice of action which has as its end the good of others. In this sense, *lokasamgraha* is an active and dynamic force which stresses personal responsibility. It signifies actions that are instrumental in awakening consciousness, conscience, compassion and vital life forces in man. To be committed to *lokasamgraha* is to accept the life-invigorating, regulative principle of *dharma.* This means the subjection of the pursuit of *artha* and *kama* to the suzerainty of *dharma.* By this subjection, individuals would rise above their own narrow self-interest, relate themselves to the larger order, and contribute to the enrichment of personal life and social relations.

The structure of Swadhyaya: people and programmes

Swadhyaya as self-development implies not only co-development but also active participation by individuals in stimulating the development of others and the community as a whole. It represents a praxis in its original sense symbolizing more than the identity of thought and action; it signifies a dialectical relationship between them, a relationship in which consciousness becomes instrumental in shaping, directing and regulating practice, with practice in turn deepening and raising consciousness. Various activities launched, sustained and institutionalized by Swadhyaya reflect this dynamic principle. At the root of all these activities is the central idea of divine brotherhood. Individuals may differ in certain specific characteristics, may be located in a highly differentiated factual order, and may have different life experiences. All of them, however, partake in a shareable commonality. There may be distinctions but no differences among them.

The second important element in Swadhyaya is its accent on community-building. The ossification of the traditional social order and the accentuation of individualistic tendencies creating social distances, sharpening social differences and aggravating social cleavages—all these factors have dissipated the idea of the divine brotherhood of human beings. Consequently, social relations are marked with discord, dissension and disruption. Community-building, therefore, receives special attention in Swadhyaya movement.

Swadhyaya has, since its inception, been working intensively and systematically among the tribals and such depressed groups within the Hindu fold as fishermen, Vagdis and other neglected castes.[8] Relegated to the status of socio-cultural pariahs, denied better economic opportunities and exploited by the vested interests in the society, these groups evince what Oscar Lewis calls the 'culture of poverty' both as an adaptation and a reaction of the poor to their marginal position in a highly stratified society.

Faced with this situation characteristic of many social groups in different regions, Swadhyaya aims to break their cultural isolation and, through this, to instil in them a sense of self-esteem and a greater awareness of their important place in the larger society. The breaking of cultural isolation is attempted through making the deprived aware and appreciative of the rich religio-cultural heritage they have been deprived of. By awakening in them the realization of the presence of God within them, Swadhyaya becomes instrumental in instilling in them a feeling of self-respect and self-confidence. This results in the improvement of personal conduct and family relations. The adoption of Swadhyaya as a means of elevating personal life breeds self-reliance which, because of altered consciousness, paves the way for collective self-reliance for improving the economic condition of the group.

It is not only the deprived who live an alienated existence; alienation affects even other, advanced and privileged, socio-economic groups that, in the arrogance of their privilege, have treated the deprived as slaves or servants, useful mainly for their own economic and social ascendance. Farmers, tradesmen, intellectuals and other occupational groups display, in varying degrees, their contempt and disdain towards those who are condemned by society to live a precarious social, cultural and economic existence. Swadhyaya therefore works to rid these groups of their arrogance and their mistaken views about others and about themselves. Swadhyaya attempts to bring everyone into its fold and lay the foundation of an intimate community based on the equality[9] and dignity of the individual.

Two facets of community-building effort noticeable in Swadhyaya deserve special mention. First is the idea of *apaurusheya Lakshmi,* impersonal wealth. This signifies that, since man owes everything to God, he must pay his debt to him in a suitable manner. This consists primarily in the best use of his *nipunata,* expertise and efficiency, in producing whatever he is capable of and good at and offering part of his earnings at God's feet. Second, Swadhyayees engage in certain productive enterprises that are communal in nature and whose products do not belong to a particular individual since the community as a whole has contributed its skill, labour and resources in producing that wealth. It is in this sense that the wealth so produced is *apaurusheya*.

The substratum of Swadhyaya activities, whether personal or collective, is *bhakti* . For Swadhyayees, *bhakti* is a means not only of self-transformation but also of community-building. It conjoins the individual with the supreme, perennial principle, namely God. It is devotional in the sense that the individual makes offering of himself, a self-surrender, and becomes a devotee. As a devotee, he sees the presence of God in everything around him; that is, imbued with the feeling of *Ishavasyam* (the world as the abode of God) he is duty-bound to cover this world with the love of God (*Ishavasyam*). Through a subtle change in the meaning of *Ishavasyam*, a passive principle has, in Swadhyaya, been transformed into a dynamic force of community-building. One of the critical elements of this dynamic force is *bhaktipheri*, devotional tours.

Bhaktipheris are undertaken by small groups of individuals primarily to discuss cultural and spiritual matters with people and to spread the message of Swadhyaya.[10] During these *bhaktipheris,* devotees carry their own food and other essentials and do not accept any hospitality from the village folk. This establishes their credentials and good, disinterested motives. Once rapport is well established, discussions move on to socio-economic problems of the community and then concrete action programmes are launched depending on the number of devotees in a particular community.

Bhaktipheri thus constitutes the first step towards self-development as co-development. It is not only indicative of a person's resolve to take some time out from his busy life and use it for God's work. It also reflects the person's willingness to explore, consolidate, and enrich his self-knowledge and, at the same time, to make others partners in this process. It is through *bhaktipheris* that the circle of divine brotherhood is formed, expanded and consolidated. Every Swadhyayee must at the least do two *bhaktipheris* a month, that is, on the eleventh day of each fortnight, namely *ekadashi.*[11]

The social face of Swadhyaya

Broadly speaking, three types of activities with economic content are generally pursued by Swadhyaya. One type of activity is *Yogeshwar Krishi* (farming) meant specially for farmers. The second is *Matsyagandha* (launching of fishing trawlers) for fishermen communities, and the third is *Yogeshwar Upayana* (orchards) for a local community as a whole. Each of these activities represents community effort and is aimed at generating both *apaurusheya Lakshmi* and reinforcing community solidarity. The central idea behind all these activities is selfless social action aimed at creating common impersonal wealth for the use of the local Swadhyaya community as a whole.

The launching of *Yogeshwar Krishi* about a decade ago was the result of persistent requests by farmers to know how best they could offer their *nipunata* to God. Already, since the mid-1970s, Swadhyaya farmers of Dabjhoi

Taluka in Baroda district (Gujarat) were operating a large farm on their own. Athavale Shastri agreed to extend the experiment elsewhere but only gradually. Swadhyayees in a particular locality take on lease from the government a plot of usually barren land of between three to five acres and engage in collective farming. In cultivating this plot, Swadhyayees contribute their *shramabhakti* (devotion through labour). Every day in a cropping season six to ten Swadhyayees work on the plot.[12] Persons working on the plot are called *pujaris* (worshippers).

The harvested crop belongs to no one in particular but to Lord Yogeshwar, since the produce is the result of the offering of labour by peasant priests. The wealth created by the sale of the produce belongs to God and is therefore called *apaurusheya.* One-third of this wealth is used to meet short-term requirements of the needy Swadhyayees. The help is neither a loan nor charity; it is given as a *prasad* (offerings to God distributed among devotees). The recipient is under no obligation to pay it back; if it is returned, no interest is charged. The giving and receiving are done discreetly and gracefully to obviate any inferiority complex on the part of the recipient. The remaining two-thirds of the income is deposited in a non-interest-earning trust fund called Madhavi Raksha Samkalpa, with different accounts in the name of different communities. The accumulated fund in this trust is used to buy agricultural and other equipment and input needs for Yogeshwar farms from time to time. Four thousand Yogeshwar farms are currently being operated by Swadhyayees.

From the very outset, Swadhyaya recognized the need to bring peripheral and perhaps sullen groups into the fold of the larger society so that they could rediscover their religio-cultural roots and become truly integrated into the cultural mainstream, not by force but by choice. Swadhyaya began to work among tribals, fishermen and other such groups not to proselytize them but to raise their self-esteem and brighten their consciousness of a superior cultural heritage. One such group, the fishermen in coastal Gujarat, Maharashtra and Goa, with a reputation for aggressiveness, drinking, gambling, smuggling and other criminal activities, were approached in the mid-1960s. The fishermen took time to be convinced. But once they overcame their suspicion, they identified themselves with everything that Swadhyaya stands for.

Rechristened as *sagarputras* (sons of the sea), they began offering a part of their earnings to Lord Yogeshwar. When enough funds accumulated, they were used to construct motorized fishing boats. These boats, called *matsyagandhas,* represent floating temples and carry a crew of six to ten Swadhyayee fishermen working as *pujaris.* Fishing goes on almost around the year except for a three-month pause during the monsoon for repairs and refitting. As in the case of farming, no fisherman gets a chance for more than one trip in a year. Again, similar to farming, one-third of the sale proceeds is distributed among needy fishermen, with two-thirds deposited in the account of the local fishermen's community in the Madhavi Raksha Samkalpa. Eighteen *matsyagandhas* have so far been launched.

Both *Yogeshwar Krishi* and *Matsaygandha* are instrumental in evoking pride in the inherited callings of farmers and fishermen. In both cases there are neither employers nor employees and no one has any claim over what is produced by his *shramabhakti.* The work on farms and *matsyagandhas* is influenced by neither the money motive nor the search for pleasure; it is performed in a sense of filial duty and as a means of strengthening the ties of divine brotherhood.

There is yet another important experiment that serves to restore the traditional orientation of respect for the natural environment. This is *Yogeshwar Upayana* (orchard), which symbolizes the living presence of God in non-human objects too. Swadhyayees take on lease from the government large plots of barren land and turn these plots into *upayana.* Each of these *upayana* is named after an ancient sage. After acquiring a plot, Swadhyayees from fifteen to twenty neighbouring villages or towns rehabilitate the land, dig irrigation wells and prepare pits for planting saplings. On the day of the planting, hundreds of thousands of people from far and near gather and planting is finished in quick time amidst the chanting of *mantras.* Eight *upayana* have so far been planted and the amount of impersonal wealth they are going to yield is staggering. Interestingly, survival rates of the plants is 100 per cent. In the case of the *upayana* too, a batch of fifteen to twenty Swadhyayees work daily as *pujaris.*

Another interesting symbol of community effort and solidarity is the *Amritalayam.* It serves as an instrument to regenerate the social, cultural, intellectual and spiritual life of the people. A village where Swadhyaya work has taken deeper roots is allowed to build an *Amritalayam.* A simple structure using locally available materials is made through *shramabhakti* of the villagers in which are installed idols of gods. Each village household gets the chance of working as *pujaris* for a few days in a year. An *Amritalayam* is a public temple where people remember God and offer their prayers, but it is also a community centre where they deliberate on their problems, debate ways and means of solving them, and arrive at consensual decisions. *Amritalayam* is significant in yet another sense. Swadhyaya insists on expressing gratefulness to God by making him a sharer in one's earnings. Offerings made to God in the *Amritalayam* are distributed among the needy in the form of *prasad.*

The *Amritalayam* also functions as a centre for transmitting traditional culture. It is here that the individual ego sheds its aggressive 'I'-ness and merges into the collective We by subjecting itself to the discipline of the community based on *dharma. Amritalayam* becomes the means of this disciplining as well as of personal renewal. More than one hundred *Amritalayams* have been built since the first was erected in April 1980.

After a few years of *bhaktipheri,* a village gets a *Swadhyaya Kendra,* an embryonic *Amritalayam.* Subsequently, when 50 per cent of villagers turn Swadhyayees, the village can have a Yogeshwar farm and graduate to *Arjun Sabha Ghar,* a stage prior to *Amritalayam.* When more than 90 per cent of the village population become Swadhyayees, a regular *Amritalayam* is built.

As well as these activities, there are others that become the source of cultural regeneration and of reinforcement of personal commitment. Swadhyaya emphasizes the need for continuous ego moderation, connectedness, creativity and love. It therefore creates occasions when a large number of Swadhyayees participate and renew their commitment. To facilitate participation, Swadhyaya picks up elements from Indian tradition, which are then adapted to new purposes. *Utsavas* (festivals), *teerth-yatras* (pilgrimage), *yajnas,* etc., illustrate this well. All of them combine sacred and not so sacred elements in which the expression of personal devotion turns into joyous collective celebrations. In addition, there are *vayaska sanchalan* camps (reorientation camps for maturer Swadhyayees in the age group 18–40) which are organized each year at the district or the regional headquarters. As Swadhyayees move from one encounter to another, they advance in their search for purity and deepen their awareness that they are engaged in creating a better community.

In addition, Swadhyaya engages in numerous socio-economic, educational and cultural activities for disseminating appropriate cultural, moral and spiritual values on the one hand, and expanding the space of shareable commonality on the other. One such example is what is called 'divine brains trust', which is the focal point for children and adolescents of both sexes to discuss spiritual and cultural matters. However, neither profit nor the creation and expansion of material resources is the objective of Swadhyaya. Its main thrust is ideational and inward change so that the tradition-sanctified patterns of behaviour may enrich and strengthen socially propitious urges of the people and help them in coping with the problems of modern times. It aims at changing outlook and orientation for a better relationship between the individual and the society he or she is a part of. In the words of Athavale Shastri:

> Religion is the means through which every individual should attain a moral level ... where his self-discipline may render the government and the laws unnecessary....The basic revolution should be of human mind.... People's outlook on life must be changed.[13]

Organization and finance

It is surprising that a fast-expanding movement like Swadhyaya lacks all visible signs of a well-articulated, centralized and rule-bound organizational structure which keeps in touch with individuals and field offices through a well-developed and elaborate communications system. Swadhyaya does not in any sense exemplify a modern organization of Weberian type based on impersonal rules, division of functions, hierarchy and specialization. Yet it has been successful in organizing large assemblies attended by thousands of people, implementing programmes and communicating effectively with distant Swadhyaya centres. Swadhyaya deliberately spurns the structure of modern organization. Instead, it aims at inculcating family feeling and fostering community solidarity among its followers without the claptrap of hierarchical ordering of functions, authority, and power.

However, its dense and extensive networks require information, coordination and review. In order to prevent hierarchical principles from creeping in, Swadhyaya has given effect to an organizational structure which is decentralized but not ineffective on that count. At the district level, an informal group of activists and eminent Swadhyayees coordinates various activities in its area and is in constant touch with the Bombay headquarters. The numbers of these groups vary from one district to another. Called *Mota Bhais* (elder brothers), they organize, supervise and coordinate different Swadhyaya activities in the district. At the *taluk* level, a smaller group of Swadhyayees, called *Kshetrapal* (local guardians), coordinate Swadhyaya activities at the village level.

With the expansion of modern means of communication, it has become comparatively easy to spread word of the happenings in Swadhyaya, collect information and keep an eye on things in general. If such means are lacking, messages are spread by word of mouth. At each level, it is sought to resolve problems through democratic discussion and consensus. Frequent meetings of active workers are organized at *taluk,* district and regional levels. These meetings serve three vital purposes. First, Athavale Shastri himself attends, whenever he can, most of these meetings and delivers discourses. Second, *Mota Bhais* from different areas report on the activities. And, last, they return from these meetings to their own areas with new guidelines, decisions and future plans. In so far as the accounts are concerned, each community makes statements of income and expenditure, and on a fixed day in the year such accounts are placed at the feet of Lord Yogeshwar, breeding thereby a sense of responsibility and integrity.

Swadhyaya does not have a budgeting process, nor a fixed income, nor any operating funds for administrative purposes. All its activities are run by selfless workers who, instead of charging Swadhyaya for their labours, do Swadhyaya work free, spending their own money. The funds deposited in the Madhavi Raksha Samkalpa, in fact, do not belong to Swadhyaya as a whole; the *Samkalpa* itself is the concentration of deposits made by different communities and these are used by them for purposes determined by them alone. It is interesting to note that there are more than 125,000 active workers in Swadhyaya who devote much of their time to Swadhyaya work without being paid.

Overview

What accounts for the effectiveness of Swadhyaya as a social movement? Swadhyaya, as indicated earlier, is committed to the idea that individuals must live a normal life of duties and responsibilities, a life that reflects sociality and allows them to be content in a state of equanimity and communion with God. This is a very old and revered ideal. Its contemporary significance is heightened by the growing individual alienation and social discord in society. Modern social movements and social service agencies too are concerned with these problems. But their solution and ways of working tend to aggregate those factors which have given rise to the problems in the first place. In contradistinction, Swadhyaya promises to emancipate human beings from the pervasive despair caused by the aggressive pursuit of self-interest. What aids Swadhyaya in realizing this promise is its creative and imaginative renovation of the traditional worldview. Buried deep down in the psyche of the Indian people under several layers of modern sensibilities and orientations, their traditional consciousness is resurrected and reactivated by the message of Swadhyaya.

However, Swadhyaya does not aim at proselytization. It leaves the people themselves to decide whether they want to tread the path of Swadhyaya. Nor does it seek to hasten the pace of transformation. What Swadhyaya aims at is to make it possible for the people to reorient their consciousness through dialogues. Once this happens, people become aware of the need not only to reorganize their personal lives but also to reshape their social and natural environments. Out of this awareness are born various Swadhyaya activities catalysed by the particular problems facing a particular community. There is no planning machinery, no blueprints and no central command to impose on the people decisions on what ought to be done and in what ways. People themselves are the initiators and implementers of Swadhyaya activities, although suggestions from others and blessings from Athavale Shastri, the founder of Swadhyaya, may have shaped decisions. This is instrumental in protecting the 'public space' from the encroachment of the 'bureaucratic space'.

The feeling that people themselves are the authors as well as practitioners of Swadhyaya ideas and activities, even while the main inspirations may come from Shastri, lends to Swadhyaya the quality of being *apaurusheya*. This feeling is further reinforced by the lack of a modern, bureaucratic organization where central command and coordination play a crucial role in articulating and realizing organizational objectives. The organizational structure of Swadhyaya resembles that of a joint family where the sense not of right but of duty inspires people gladly to undertake responsibilities not for any financial gain but in order to realize collective purposes since their own welfare is inexorably tied up with it.

In short, what Swadhyaya is engaged in, on a very large scale, is the creation of a symbolic and social world in which men and women acquire their fundamental character (*saamskar*) and which reflects, through human adaptation (*laukik anukaran*), an eternal ideal world. Through this, Swadhyaya aims at conjoining certain eternal values with material practices. Put differently, its efforts are directed towards bringing civilization, as an external system of work and leisure and concerned primarily with the organization of material life, closer to culture as the internal meaning structure of civilization. Swadhyaya attempts to bring together civilization denoting fundamentally the acquisition and coordination of means from the perspective of social utility and culture symbolizing the search for freedom. In this, Swadhyaya draws heavily on the traditional Indian worldview, to be sure; but it also reinterprets and renovates tradition.

Notes

1. *Ishavasyam,* Sadvichar Dharshan Trust, Samvat 2042, Bombay, p.158 and *Gita Ke Panchaprana,* Sadvichar Dharshan Trust, Bombay, 1983, p.17.

2. *Esha Pantha, Etatkarma,* compilation of P.V. Athavale Shastri's *Pravachans,* Sadvichar Dharshan Trust, Saṁvat 2041, Bombay, p. 1 (in Hindi).

3. *Swadhyaya Se Pancharangi Kranti,* Sadvichar Dharshan Trust, Bombay, 1986, p.15.

4. *Esha Pantha, Etatkarma*, p. 6.

5. *ibid,* p. 15.

6. *Ishavasyam,* p. 10.

7. *Gita Ke Panchaprana,* p. 21.

8. It is not possible to provide here a complete statistical break-down of the Swadhyayees, their diverse socio-economic background and their regional spread. This chapter therefore does no more than indicate broad social categories of people participating in the Swadhyaya movement.

9. By equality Swadhyaya does not mean equality in its modern sense. The Swadhyaya interpretation of equality comes closer to Rousseau's meaning, that is, equality of dependence.

10. The first *bhaktipheri* was undertaken by a group of nineteen Bombay-based intellectuals, professionals and businessmen in a part of Saurashtra in around 1970. These persons, influenced by Athavale Shastri's discourses, would engage him in discussions about man and society every evening on the Chowppatty beach. They would propose several methods, including the Marxist one, of changing village life in India. Realizing that they had little knowledge and experience of village life, Athavale Shastri suggested that they go on a picnic, not to any amusement park but to a village. This was the beginning of *bhaktipheri.*

11. This has a special significance. Man is endowed with ten senses over which mind as the eleventh faculty presides. It is to orient mind to God's work and to accept God as the Supreme Lord that *ekadashi* is symbolically chosen for *bhaktipheris.*

12. Every Swadhyayee is keen to work on the plot and contribute his *shramabhakti.* However, an individual gets a chance to work on the plot only once or twice in a cropping season.

13. Quoted in Mohammad Vazeeruddin, 'Taking Man Closer to Man', *Sunday Tribune,* 11 March 1984.

10. Building Countervailing Power in Nicaragua, Mexico and Colombia

Orlando Fals Borda

Introduction

The purpose of this chapter is to contribute to a better understanding of peasants and the furthering of their participation in the development processes through self-reliant forms of organization.[1] The processes are examined in the light of the knowledge-making efforts and methodology known as participatory action research (PAR), which is opening up encouraging perspectives.

The five years following the Cartagena World Symposium of 1977, which launched the methodology now known as participatory action research, were an intense period of trial and error for both revolutionary and developmentalist policies. The results of these years have been submitted to international criticism and the practical consideration of grassroots organizations. From Asia and Africa to Latin America, PAR has made its presence felt both scientifically and politically and is recognized dialectically in both spheres. In the process of determining its specific components, it has tested in practice the techniques and guidelines that distinguish it from those other activities that seek to combine knowledge with efficacy in the task of social transformation.

Numerous field reports were made by those of us who carried out these experiments, and national, international and regional meetings were organized for this purpose. Several theoretical works were published, and an initial attempt was made at systematization with the compilation of one or two manuals of procedure.[2]

Although our cultures and political systems as well as the premises of our research and ideologies were very different, we managed to achieve a conceptual and technical consensus in a way we had never expected. Perhaps the common problems of the poverty, exploitation and oppression of our nations brought us together as dependent peoples of the peripheral Third World where the PAR idea was originally conceived. Such preoccupations served to unite us. For all these reasons it can now be said that PAR has acquired a certain consistency and that it seeks to achieve even greater acceptance as an open and creative alternative towards the political and scientific goals that we saw as the challenge facing us in Cartagena.

PAR has shown itself to be an endogenous intellectual and practical creation of the peoples of the Third World. Neither its appearance nor its significance in Latin America can be understood outside the specific context of the economic, social and scientific development of the region during the 1960s. Its main components derive from the regional appearance and diffusion of theories of dependence (Cardoso, Furtado) and exploitation (Gonzalez, Casanova), the counter-theory of subversion (Camillo Torres) and the theology of liberation (Gutierrez), dialogical techniques (Freire) and the reinterpretation of theses on scientists' commitment and neutrality taken from Marx and Gramsci, among others.

Indeed, we view PAR as a methodology within a total experiential process (ensuring a satisfactory productive cycle of life and labour in human communities). Its aim is to achieve 'power' and not merely 'growth' for the grassroots population. This total process simultaneously encompasses adult education, scientific research and political action in which critical theory, situation analyses and practice are seen as sources of knowledge. PAR implies the acquisition of experience and valid data for the construction of a special kind of power—people's power—which belongs to the oppressed and exploited classes and groups and their organizations, and the defence of their just interests to enable them to advance towards shared goals of social change within a participatory political system. People's power is expressed through external and internal mechanisms that monitor and supervise these processes of change and the leaders who bring them about, in the forms that we have called 'countervailing power', the most complex expressions of which are the regional socio-political movements.

The PAR studies carried out up to now have been based almost exclusively on small local cases and individual regions. The approach has been necessary in order to identify and understand clearly the mechanisms of this complicated research process. The attempts at systematization have reflected simply the overall results of the cases examined and led to the paradox (counter-productive, in my view) of giving the impression that PAR is an already finished product. This, of course, is not so and was not the goal sought by those of us who put forward the idea. On the contrary, we wish to preserve the original freshness and spontaneity of PAR as we advance towards the necessary methodological clarity.

However, among the tasks that were not completed during these difficult and decisive years of struggle was one that concerns the direct comparative use of the same conceptual and technical guide for working with PAR in different contexts, countries and cultures. Such a step—which at first sight seems to contradict the autonomous parameters of the method—could not be taken without the support of local participatory bodies. Nor could it be done without national teams of researchers who were able to carry out the work responsibly and carefully in the allotted time without losing sight of the philosophy of action or the quest for knowledge that had stimulated all of us from the beginning.

In Colombia, four private institutions that had been working with peasants for a number of years offered their collaboration. In addition to the Punta de Lanza Foundation in Bogota, the Development Co-operation Enterprise (EMCODES) and the People's Communication Foundation, both in Cali, provided staff and resources for work in the south of the country. Local coordination was the responsibility of Alvaro Velasco Alvarez, a lawyer, and John Jairo Cardenas, an educator. They chose Puerto Tejada as the site for the participatory experience in view of the interesting history of research and action that their organization had been pursuing there since 1978.

In northern Colombia, the Sinu Foundation at Monteria organized corresponding activities with its directors, Victor Negrete and Jose Galeano, both educators. It was decided to provide participatory support for fieldwork that they had been carrying out in El Cerrito, a hamlet on the shores of a lagoon, where peasants had been waging a struggle to defend their land rights.

In Mexico, cooperation was provided on behalf of the Centre for Studies and Assistance to People's Science and Education by Felix Cadena Barquin, Bertha Barragan, Carlos Cadena and Roberto Cubas, who are educators and social scientists with links to the Mixteco community of San Agustin Atenango (Oaxaca), which had been chosen for the participatory experience. Salvador Garcia Angulo, a social worker with considerable experience with the Otomi peasants in the valley of Mezquital, also provided valuable assistance.

In Nicaragua, we first made contact with the National Planning Department, where Malena de Montis, a sociologist, was entrusted with the fieldwork in El Regadio, which had been selected because it was a 'vanguard community' in Region No. 1, Esteli, close to Honduras. Subsequently, support came form the Vice-Ministry of Adult Education and the National Union of Farmers and Cattlemen (UNAG).[3]

One question which united us all was the problem of people's power and countervailing political mechanisms, and their relation to the search for and accumulation of knowledge to bring about necessary social changes. Such a collective study of the problem of people's power and knowledge could be carried out in many ways: for example, we could have chosen a sociological approach, with all its working hypotheses, variables and matrices, or formal anthropology. This would undoubtedly have led to long and interesting studies, full of statistical tables, excellent photographs and drawings, and presented in a heavy and ponderous style. But this learned knowledge would have been limited to a small group of readers, to an intellectual and disciplined elite. It would not have reached the communities themselves, and probably none of the local people would have been aware of the existence of such monographs or if they had been, they would not have been able to understand them.

Our objective was quite different: to examine and test, in a comparative and critical manner, the idea that it was possible to produce a serious analytical work, based on practical knowledge of the reality of both the ordinary population and of the activists, that would enrich not only the general fund of science but also the people's own knowledge and wisdom. Our idea was to take grassroots knowledge as a starting point and then to systematize and amplify it through action in collaboration with external agents to change—such as ourselves—in order to build and strengthen the power of formal and informal rural workers' organizations.

Our aim was not to carry out purely scientific or 'integrated rural development' work, objectives that no longer really satisfied us, but to fashion intellectual tools for the ordinary working classes—those who have unjustly borne on their shoulders the weight of the development and social and economic enrichment of other classes—and to establish or promote grassroots organizations such as cooperatives, trade unions, handicraft and cultural centres, education and health brigades, which would allow the people to cope with real-life situations through recourse to justified popular mobilization, create new employment opportunities, increase incomes and improve the standard of living in the communities studied. Indeed, these processes and changes were witnessed in the field during these years, as described in the following sections. There was a real process of transformation and congruent material and intellectual progress without personal and institutional aims. This process is still alive, and it has sometimes gone beyond our expectations.

If such were our intellectual, social and economic objectives, they were nevertheless subordinated to another general goal of a more practical kind. Our referents were and still are the representatives of the interests of the people with their capacity for becoming (if they are not so already) efficient and enlightened leaders, members of a new type of service vanguard who would be non-sectarian and non-messianic, and who would not impose their views vertically from above. Together with them, we wanted to contribute in our own way and within the limits of our abilities to change the unjust and violent society that we have inherited, so that together we could initiate the necessary transformations.

Thus the intellectual and practical aspirations of all of us were rooted in a single and shared experience, in which distinctions between leaders and subordinates had no part. With this philosophy as our spiritual anchor, we tested the different techniques for creating and communicating knowledge, with the appropriate adjustments being made in attitudes and values. These techniques are described in the following sections. Nor did we forget the problems of organization and interaction implied in the popular struggles, or the need to support and reinforce the workers' own organizations.

As participatory researchers sharing the land and life of the people, we met several times in the three countries to compare experiences and information, discuss ideas and techniques and to clarify our positions. Of course these meetings, which sometimes included colleagues from other parts of the world, strengthened the comparative approach of our work and, as noted above, led us to a fruitful consensus at the theoretical, practical and ideological levels. We saw that these problems could indeed be tackled by PAR in a coordinated manner in different cultural and political contexts. The principal categories with which we started (chosen on the basis of former participatory experiences) were gradually confirmed; others passed to a secondary rank or were rejected. The resulting consensus is expressed in this summary study.

It was important to understand the different stages of economic, social, cultural and political development of the three countries at the time of the studies. In Colombia some PAR experiences had been carried out during the 1970s with peasants and labourers. They were part of a powerful wave of political activism by the major peasant organization and trade unions of the time. The ups and downs of this process affected the development of PAR in the Caribbean coastal regions of the country. However, following the partial destruction of the initiatives launched in the 1970s, the participatory methodology was gradually resurrected later in the same communities and locations, until the appearance of the present El Cerrito project. El Cerrito is thus a serious and careful continuation of those pioneer ventures. It is therefore not surprising that this experience not only served to strengthen the aspirations and civic and cultural struggles of the people of the coast but also led to the publication of interesting regional studies of scientific calibre.

Something similar had been happening, in an independent way, in the same years in southern Colombia, where an active group of intellectuals and political cadres made use of existing organizations to work with the peasants. The result was a research-oriented popular movement that influenced the struggles of the local black communities, especially in the towns of Puerto Tejada and Caloto. The PAR approach was formalized precisely during one of these active periods of the movement, and for this reason it was included in the present project.

In Mexico, in the valley of Mezquital to the north of the capital, there had been a similar development of PAR-related methods during the 1970s, which were the subject of a number of theses, analyses and studies. The local Otomi Indians and mestizo peasants of this valley were—and still are—searching for economic and cultural avenues of development independent of the dominant classes which have exploited them. Like the Oaxaca Mixtecas in San Agustin Atenango (where the process of methodical action was initiated by us), the Otomis have attempted valuable participatory experiences with external cadres. These are also described in the present study.

As for Nicaragua, PAR was introduced as an experimental idea following the overthrow of the regime of Anastasio Somoza and the establishment of the National Reconstruction Junta in 1979. Some of the junta's advisers (including a noted action research epistemologist) began to talk about PAR in official documents and government seminars.

Thus the PAR approach was taken to Nicaragua and actively used for the first time in a revolutionary context, in a 'vanguard community' involved in national defence and food production. Following the confirmation of its suitability and congruence with the national revolutionary process, the experience reached a crucial stage involving its generalized application to other parts of the country. The extension of the El Regadio experiment to seventeen other rural communities in the same and other regions was decided by the Nicaraguan government in 1984 in association with the FAO and the National Union of Farmers and Cattlemen.

In Mexico and Colombia the continuity of our projects was assured by various non-governmental organizations as well as through local support.

As was anticipated in the conceptual and technical guide, fieldwork was flexible in each country and subject to the criteria of the national teams as regards programming, procedures, tactics and aims. Each community defined its own tasks and techniques with the collaboration and encouragement of the outside researchers. Other related activities were carried out, which cannot be described in the present study, such as meetings, marches, festivals, workshops, and other complementary tasks designed to foster employment and raise the standard of living and culture of the people. Moreover, we tried to encourage and maintain self-reliance and people's power in existing workers' organizations and in the new ones being formed, because this seemed indispensable in creating permanent and stable structures to implement action.

Since the five communities chosen in the three countries were and are our reference groups, the present study was conceived and written for them (in Spanish) in a simple and direct manner, in line with the techniques governing the diffusion of knowledge adopted by PAR researchers. It will be recalled that four levels of communications have been established: '0', when the information is without printed words and is based only on symbols and pictures; '1', when the same information is given by combining both visual and written signs, as in an illustrated booklet; '2', when the information is prepared with a view to training community leaders or cadres who have already received some conceptual initiation; and '3', when the same material is carried to a more complex analytical, conceptual and theoretical stage, for advanced cadres and intellectuals.

The first lesson from this study deals with 'learning to interact and organize' in order to attain our aims, with account being taken not only of participatory experience but also of the urgent need to bring about significant changes in the structure of our societies. In this connection we believe it is essential to break the relationship of submission (and the related modes of production of knowledge) found in most types of work and life in our societies and elsewhere, and to induce stable forms of organization for action.

The second lesson—'learning to recognize oneself'—emphasizes the actual components of the PAR approach and the means for producing and diffusing the acquired knowledge. Here emphasis is placed on the centrality of the collective work undertaken, the recovery of our awareness of regional history and the use of, and respect for, popular cultural elements. Both lessons are preceded by a description, in the form of a dialogue, of the five communities we studied and which sets the tone of the text which follows. Finally, after a theoretical and conceptual section (level 3) and suggested further reading, we have included summaries of each participatory experience.

Some positive consequences of the studies were observed in the life and culture of the rural populations and in the creation of new work and income opportunities in the organized communities, as stated above. This can be seen in the field as well as in the detailed partial reports. There were also other immediate practical results, especially in Colombia: the reinforcement of local networks of independent political, civic and cultural movements.

An association was established between dispersed participatory initiatives within a new context of study and action focused on the establishment of people's power or countervailing power. This context has now acquired a national dimension. The regions are represented in this national network from the base upwards and from the periphery to the centre, a situation that may allow the communities to regain the power that is their original and constitutional right, so that more participatory forms of democracy can be developed.

The articulate national system of people's power, with its countervailing political mechanisms (action groups and committees, trade unions, cooperatives, community boards, etc.) is now also spreading through the world. It has been discovered that PAR works well even in countries governed by dictatorships, if prudent and imaginative procedures are applied. Moreover, many interesting participatory experiences have been carried out not only in countries of the Third World but also in Austria, Belgium, Canada, Italy, the Netherlands, Sweden and the USA. Several coordination and exchange bodies have been established in cities such as Santiago de Chile, Toronto, Rome, Helsinki, Colombo, New Delhi, Geneva, Mexico City and Bogota. The general PAR process is now culminating in the establishment of convergent networks of international institutions that lend their support to the struggle for people's power, such as the International Group on Grass Roots Initiatives (IGGRI). This is necessary because the problems of the groups and classes concerned often go beyond national frontiers.

The time has thus come in which the mechanisms of countervailing power provided by PAR in any given place are being given multiple forms of support at the regional, national and international levels. Much has been achieved since the first World Symposium in Cartagena.

Field experiences[4]

Potential for people's education in the social transformation of rural areas: the case of El Regadio (Nicaragua)[5]

El Regadio is a village of small farmers, agricultural tenants and sharecroppers dedicated to the growing of basic staple foods (maize, beans, coffee, sugar cane, sorghum). It is situated to the north east of Managua, near the frontier with Honduras, 23 kilometres from Esteli, the departmental capital, with which it is connected by an unpaved road.

It has a population of 759 (363 men and 396 women, according to the local census of 1982), the majority of whom are natives of the village. There are a total of 110 houses, with an average of seven people to a house. The village is divided into two hamlets: Valle Arriba and Valle Abajo, separated by a steep rocky path. Out of the 110 houses of the community, 71 have direct access to the land, of which 260 *manzanas* were sown in the agricultural year 1981–1982 (each *manzana* equals four-fifths of a hectare). The rest of the people cultivate small plots and also work for a wage, especially in the agricultural cooperatives and in the reserve infantry battalion that operates locally for territorial defence.

Of the homes at El Regadio, 44 possess a total of 790 head of cattle and 115 transport animals. Almost everyone has pigs and poultry. There were only 87 illiterate people in 1982 (47 men and 40 women) equal to 10 per cent of the population, following the intense educational campaigns of the previous years; 263 persons had already completed their primary education and another 53 their secondary education. In addition, 83 persons were attending the People's Education Collectives (CEPs) in the year.

Besides the local primary school, the community also boasts a Catholic chapel, a public telephone and a telegraph service. A health centre was also being built. There is no electricity. The houses are of sun-dried brick, some with latrines.

At the time of the study there was a Sandinista agricultural cooperative (CAS), as well as a credit and service cooperative. Another CAS was recently formed on lands recovered from local estates, now considered areas of public property. The two CAS cooperatives decided to unite once their respective debts contracted with banks during the past production years were settled. The National Agrarian Reform programme was giving them the ownership titles of approximately 1,000 *manzanas* (800 hectares) to form a mixed cooperative for grain and cattle comprising 28 members, all from the region.

There is a high level of organization in the community, as shown by the existence of the Luisa Amanda Espinoza Association of Nicaraguan Women (AMNLAE), the Committees for Sandinista Defence (CDS), the National Union of Farmers and Cattlemen (UNAG), the Sandinista Popular Militias (MPS), the Reserve Infantry Battalion (BIR) and the Christian Youth. Membership in these organizations varies between 27 and 67 per cent of the local population. There is a large female participation in all these fronts, especially the CEPs, where the women act as coordinators and constitute the absolute majority. This acceptable level of activity in the processes of popular participation in a community situated in a region of strategic importance to national defence was the reason why El Regadio was chosen as the first place in which to try out the PAR methodology in Nicaragua, as proposed by the central government.

The first efforts to organize the community had started in 1977 when a Catholic priest encouraged the people as a whole to reflect on the injustices of the Somoza regime. He contacted young people to whom he gave sporadic courses on how to assume their responsibilities as 'delegates of the Word'. Some of these young people are still active in the field of adult education.

On entering the United Peoples' Movement in 1978, the community formed its first civil defence committees, in which the hero and martyr Pedro Barrientos played an important part. During the war of liberation, El Regadio helped the fighting vanguards by providing them with food, clothing and medicine. Some peasants joined the nearby war camps at Los Encinos and elsewhere. Twenty-one fell in battle.

The first inhabitants of the region were Chorotega Indians, descendants of the Nahuatl Indians of Mexico. During the period of Spanish colonization beginning in the sixteenth century, these Indians were forced into a servile relationship or exterminated, while *encomiendas*[6] and estates were established for the whites. Between 1680 and 1690 Esteli was founded as a stopping place on the way towards the gold mines in the north.

Approximately six generations ago, El Regadio started as a large estate. Its first owner, Juana Evangelista Castellon, was from Matagalpa. The original estate was successively divided between its heirs until it was reduced to medium-sized plots.

Towards 1930 a shoemaker called Jose Maria Briones came to the region selling miscellaneous goods on his way to Limay. Little by little he bought up plots of land until he was able to consolidate them into another estate, part of which had been the property of Juana Evangelista Castellon. He eventually set up a shop in Valle Abajo, where he gave credit on usurious terms to the peasants. He established sugar plantations and cattle-farming and became very rich.

The prosperity of the Briones family led Jose Maria to become a senator of the Republic and to support the Somoza regime then in power. Somoza reciprocated by helping him to improve the road from El Regadio to Esteli to make it accessible to vehicles.

During the revolution, the Briones dispersed, and Jose Maria died. The triumphant revolutionaries confiscated the lands of the estate and founded the first cooperative. Some local institutions such as the school, the chapel, the estate house and the principal shop still remain from the Briones period. The shop today belongs to the peasant who used to be Briones's overseer; he now shares his house with the local command.

Recognizing that the poor peasantry of the country constituted the principal force of the Sandinista revolution, the present study focused on the problem of how to develop a peasant and cooperative movement that would be congruent with and encourage the social changes necessary to the construction of a new society. The objective was to stimulate the conscious and organized participation of the working classes in political, economic, social and cultural affairs, and in the management of businesses, farms, cooperatives and cultural centres, in other words, to form and consolidate people's power. To this end it was necessary to know, to investigate, to systematize and to reflect in order to make appropriate decisions.

The adult education programme that had already been initiated, in the form of basic popular units, was a driving force in this process. It was important to understand how the people could teach themselves without negative interventions by teachers trained under the earlier system. This process was essentially one of social change, designed to give power to the common people and provide instruments of production and action such as cooperatives, mass organizations, and community, municipal and regional institutions of the state, in such a way that technical knowledge could be harmoniously combined with the common people's wisdom and experience.

It was with these aims in mind that the participatory study of El Regadio started in 1982. From the beginning it included collective sessions and study groups. There were two stages in this fieldwork. The first comprised interviews with key informants and leaders of the community (promoters and coordinators of the adult education programme, directors of mass organizations and cooperatives) in order to establish a working relationship and to get to know community activities.

During the second stage, a local team was set up to undertake the work jointly with the outsiders. This team was called the Temporary Coordination Commission of the participatory investigation and its research principles were fully accepted. The commission prepared a survey–census with a community profile instrument, which made it possible to identify the basic characteristics of El Regadio, as well as its levels of organization. Practical workshops were held to prepare for the inquiry. A detailed map of the community was drawn and the survey work was planned on this basis. The results of the profile were tabulated and examined in the same community, whose members corrected and amplified the data in general assemblies (about 100 people were present in such meetings).

It was then decided to socialize the data through a pamphlet and an audio-visual aid. A wooden mimeograph was made. The audio-visual aid was converted into a technical production instrument that could be shared with people from outside the community and from other countries.

Finally, the history of the community was recovered by means of documents, and the use of archives and interviews with the elders of the community and key informants. An effort was made to understand local production problems better, through specific research on aspects of the local agriculture. The experience of the local CEPs was also critically assessed.

The war with counter-revolutionary forces stationed nearby prevented the culmination of this experience. Half of the Coordinated Commissions were mobilized on war and self-defence fronts. Nevertheless, the positive development of the participatory methodology carried out for the first time in El Regadio suggested not only that it could be useful in such moments of national crisis, but also that it could eventually be extended constructively and in support of the revolution to other parts of the country. Indeed, the National Union of Farmers and Cattlemen (UNAG) subsequently decided to continue this experience and extend it to seventeen other rural communities in the country, with support from the FAO and a Belgian non-governmental organization and with the full approval of the revolutionary government.

People's contervailing power and the Mixteca cooperative in San Agustin Atenango (Mexico)[7]

The Mixteco village of San Agustin Atenango is situated in the state of Oaxaca in the district of Silacayoapan, to the south of Mexico City. The name originally meant 'wall between two rivers' which reflects the reality of its geographical position in the Cerro del Clavo not far from the mestizo village of Tonala.

Its 2,411 inhabitants (1,177 women and 1,234 men) live from irrigation and dry farming, palm weaving and similar handicraft activities. They grow maize, beans, tomatoes, watermelons, red peppers and vegetables; their rudimentary methods of tilling the land with hoes and ploughing with oxen are gradually being modernized. There are many goats. The land is partly private and partly communal and is already insufficient to support the population. As a result many people (especially the young) are migrating to the northern Mexican states and the USA from where many return with money and new ideas about agricultural and livestock techniques. In San Agustin Atenango the minimum facilities of an ordinary peasant town exist, with communal institutions, guilds, street vendors, shopkeepers, musicians, butchers, shoemakers and rural teachers.

As in other parts of Latin America, the recent history of the Indians in Oaxaca has been one of exploitation. In the Mixteca language the equivalent of the word 'servant' did not exist. The Indian people gradually adopted Spanish institutions (the church was built between 1810 and 1825) and actively participated in the main movements of the Mexican nation: independence, reform and revolution. During this last period they joined the Zapatista forces (followers of Emiliano Zapata), which made the most radical demands concerning land tenure, the reclamation of common lands and struggle against the large estates.

In all the processes, San Agustin Atenango, like many other Indian villages, managed to preserve a good part of its cultural heritage as reflected in animist beliefs in the Mixteca deities, costumes, agricultural practices, music, language, and collective labour practices such as *tequio* (voluntary community assistance) and *topil* (civic service).

The cultural heritage is represented by one of the elders of the village: the Tata Yiva or 'Lord of the powers', whose authority is widely accepted and recognized. The force of tradition in community vigilance and control was demonstrated a few years ago when a young man who became the mayor tried to end the annual festivities and ancient celebrations. He was sacked by the people (the women played a major role) and expelled from the village; subsequently the authorities were more cautious and respectful. 'Custom must prevail,' as the leaders said.

With the outbreak of the Mexican revolution, some local wealthy families managed to keep part of their land and went into other activities such as the production and marketing of eggs and poultry, while peasants continued to depend on traditional farming. As a result, they developed other forms of dependency on the dominant families, especially in relation to credit. One of these families has taken the role of dominance recently, by giving loans 'without interest' (in fact really to defend what is left of their land, in the opinion of local peasants) to peasants who want to grow tomatoes, although such a venture requires much greater investment and modern technical know-how.

The idea of growing tomatoes had come from the migrants (the 'swallows' or 'wetbacks') who returned to the village after having seen production on a commercial scale in the north. The idea was also related to the pressure of the new monetary economy reaching the village. Some of the people decided to form a cooperative, and started to organize and sell their products with relative success once the water for irrigation started to flow in 1972. The contradictions of the economic system, the dangers of the coopting and corruption of leaders, and failures in communication with the outside world led this cooperative into successive crises, from which it was barely rescued with the 'help' of some of the dominant families. In this way, the tomato business could not prosper.

The arrival of participatory researchers from Mexico City brought some solutions to these difficulties. The community had been chosen precisely because it offered typical regional conditions. There were personal links with local families, which made it easier to introduce the participatory methodology.

One initial possibility was to rationalize the management of the tomato cooperative with a simple, practical accountancy manual prepared by the Indian peasants themselves and written in their own language. Collective analytical sessions were also held as a way of understanding the cooperative experience and planning what subsequent steps should be taken.

These tasks were considered valid since they could be integrated into specific local processes and interests, which were of vital importance to the people and their organizations, especially as regards production cycles. A need was felt in San Agustin Atenango to 'do the accounts properly' both as concerned the administering of loans and in order for the peasants to defend themselves against middlemen. Other tasks were subsequently pursued: the struggle for access to irrigation facilities and the local recovery of history so that the young people could reinforce their ethnic and cultural identity in such a critical period.

The worsening of local, regional and national problems during this participatory experience led to the autonomous development of interesting initiatives in which the people were able to combine the needs they felt with the recovery of their history in the local training councils. Thus it was decided to revive forgotten crafts like pottery, for which the old people rediscovered ancient suitable clay deposits. They wanted to manufacture the local products as before, without having to pay hard cash for mass-produced versions manufactured elsewhere. Barter once again began to flourish in the search for communal autonomy.

At the same time, the researchers worked at several levels of communication in order to inform the community of the results of the investigation. There were collective discussions and workshops on various topics, and several audio-visual productions proved effective. A pamphlet prepared jointly with base groups on the history of the village was completed 'so that the young people would be able to know how it was', to quote the words of the Tata Yiva.

In this manner, the embryonic forms of contemporary people's power appeared enmeshed within the ancient Indian traditions. Several institutions—religious, educational, political, and economic—were involved in the process. Traditional control and vigilance mechanisms can, if the appropriate adjustments are made, help to produce better things for the progress of all.

Other promotional activities were undertaken, as well as practical errands for the functioning of the cooperative van, and organized support to obtain financial aid from various authorities or for the holding of some festivity or meeting.

All these initiatives went through several discussions and were submitted to a new training centre, which was set up when one of the leaders asked what would happen in Mexico if the peasants should decide not to sow cash crops but only crops for their own use. This introspective trend, observable also in other parts of Mexico, is slowing the commercial production of tomatoes and intensifying once again the traditional production of maize and beans.

Self-subsistence, independence and communal autonomy are thus stimulated in the face of external modernizing influences. They are trends that show not only the vitality of the Mexican Indian peasant culture but also the contradictions of the system and the alternative ideas and actions that could benefit this immense and rich nation in the short or long term.

People's countervailing power in the valley of El Mezquital (Mexico)[8]

El Mezquital is a series of valleys and low hills with a temperate climate located on the central Mexican plateau (Hidalgo state) in the Tula river basin, some five hours to the north of Mexico City by paved highway. There are 29 villages in the area and 54 communities of Otomi origin with 416,000 inhabitants who have a rich cultural tradition which has managed to resist the successive Nahuatl and Spanish invasions. Their culture includes precious codices and stable communal forms of social and economic organization.

The 1910 revolution succeeded in redistributing the land of the local estates but preserved a mixed system of private and community-held property. For this reason conflicts, land invasions and endless litigation are still persistent features in El Mezquital. Capitalism has spread and is now dominant thanks to the extensive irrigation system of the valley, despite the fact that the canals are contaminated by detergents and other waste products from the great metropolis.

El Mezquital has been the subject of almost constant study over the last fifteen years. This research has not, however, been sufficiently respectful of the Otomi nor has it allowed them any participation. In 1975 another type of research was initiated to help the people of the valley to rediscover their cultural roots and acquire the wisdom and the spirit necessary to improve their conditions of life.

This research effort began by proposing the need for a collective learning model in the form of meetings for the exchange of views and information. These meetings have proved fruitful in several fields of knowledge: agriculture, health, recreation and applied sciences. Questions were answered and doubtful concepts and meanings of words were made clear in such groups. This method, known as 'collective self-teaching', is still being used in the valley and includes self-training and self-evaluation.

In such a method it is the group that analyses the problems of the community and that is trained to take action to resolve them; this leads to the organized participation of the group. Discussion of matters such as the village shop or the village mill are a concrete expression of this kind of work.

These mobilized groups have acquired the capacity to involve the community through the use of different means of social communication to inform the various neighbourhoods. This often causes jealousy and anger on the part of the authorities. The groups have also sought to finance themselves with their own funds, and standards of living have tended to improve.

Such research experiences have also been conducted with, and on behalf of, the local communities of San Pablo Oxototipan, Maguey Blanco, and Puerto del Dexthi: collective mills have been established, literacy campaigns launched and primary schools opened. In these efforts, study and action were never very far from one another, on the insistence of the Indian peasants themselves. Near Ixmiquilpan, the main mestizo towns of the region, similar experiments were carried out.

In general, apprenticeship in the solidary self-teaching model is a collective creative act. Acceptable levels are reached in the systematization of knowledge, as occurred in San Pablo Oxototipan on an experimental cactus plantation where an attempt was made to control erosion. The same is true in the field of health (with the use of medicinal plants and experiments with homeopathic kits), in the sowing and use of soy beans, in maize mills and forage ovens, and in the joint purchase of household articles and construction materials.

A useful technique has been the use of 'social trees', which are drawings showing society in the form of a tree with three branches: the economic, the political and the ideological. They are used as a means of increasing community awareness and enabling the Indians of the valley to overcome their fragmentary and native vision of reality.

In the past, there have been exchanges of experiences among the communities, with mutual visits and direct observation, although there has been very little systematic return of the information acquired. Even so, note has been taken of various expressions of the people's struggles such as the songs of the revolution, which continue to be used as elements for popular mobilization. Pamphlets and leaflets have been printed in several communities and radio programmes have been devised. However, it has been seen that the best way to make a peasant sensitive to political issues is to acquaint him with another peasant who has been politicized; hence the importance of horizontal communication.

Especially during the early years, external activists tended to slow down this process at in appropriate times or to accelerate it beyond what objective or subjective conditions of the struggle could support. The fact that the external agents did not share the experiential problems of the people, since they belonged to other social classes and lived in different environments, made them incapable of devising appropriate strategies to promote or sustain the people's struggle.

The present stage of the work of El Mezquital leads one to believe that there are now adequate bases for popular mobilization in which due account will be taken of the decisive role of the working classes, together with the catalytic role of the people's organic intellectuals. There is a greater awareness of the potential contribution of these cadres ('resource persons') as regards tools and techniques that the people do not have at their disposal, such as the knowledge of history and other means for systematizing their struggles.

A new experience in participatory research and action: the case of El Cerrito (Colombia)[9]

El Cerrito is a hamlet situated 15 kilometres to the southeast of Monteria (the capital city of the department of Cordoba) in the torrid Caribbean coastal region of Colombia. The hamlet has 120 families (720 persons) living in three clusters of 90 houses. Eighty-five per cent of the people are illiterate, but there is a radio in each house and some have television sets.

The hamlet was founded in 1800 on what used to be an island of a big marshy lagoon. The lagoon was a source of food for the peasants who lived on its banks from their small plots of semi-seasonal crops (rice, bananas, coconuts, yucca, yams, maize). The people are in general of a tri-racial ethnic origin (Indian, black and white).

The peaceful peasant occupation of this marshy region was first threatened at the beginning of the twentieth century, when the owners of the large estates started to expand their properties, put up barbed wire around dried banks of the lagoon and introduced cattle. Such conflicts worsened in 1966 when the Colombian Institute of Agrarian Reform (INCORA) drained the lagoon and declared the 1,590 resulting hectares to be common land.

Although the agrarian law (as well as the national constitution) stipulates that such lands are for the exclusive use of poor peasant communities, today after fifteen years, 1,000 hectares of El Cerrito continue to be in the hands of the rich cattlemen and politicians of the region. There is a possibility that INCORA might legalize the cattlemen's tenure. Thus the social and economic situation of the people has deteriorated and today the local peasants have almost no land or marshy plain. This leads them to ask themselves what action they can take to defend their rights over their lands.

When INCORA started to give the marshy plains to the rich, the inhabitants of El Cerrito appealed to experienced cadres who had been involved in previous peasant struggles (with the national peasant association, ANUC) since 1971. They decided to take defensive action in three stages: the compilation of information with the people of the hamlet; the seizure or partial recuperation of the land in question; and the consolidation and widening of their experience. These steps were taken with positive and lasting results.

In the first stage, agreement was reached with the leaders of the community to work in two closely coordinated ways: research and organization. Contact was made with older persons and key informants who were well versed in the history of the community: they told their story. Private and official archives and some secondary sources were examined. A promotional campaign for the defence of the hamlet was launched through a radio programme and a newspaper in Monteria. An attempt was made to use a common language for this purpose, without theoretical or technical jargon and using the local form of narrative or story-telling in which the coastal peasants excel.

There was some initial apathy in the organization of action. This was caused by the former failures of ANUC, the negative influence of certain religious beliefs, feelings of helplessness in the face of the power of landowners and the government, and the migration resulting from the lack of work, as well as machismo and paternalism among local political bosses.

Nevertheless, people's assemblies were held and proved to be useful. The old and recent history of the hamlet was related, pertinent experiences of similar peasant groups involved elsewhere in the struggle for land were evaluated, photographs of the region were shown, and tales and legends based on the culture of the marshy area were related. The consensus in the assemblies fully and morally justified the effort to recuperate the people's ancient rights over the area.

Action was finally taken in February 1982. It was the first time that this had occurred in El Cerrito, but the peasants with their practical wisdom and sharp sense of observation and experimentation gradually solved all the problems so as to stay on the land, in spite of successive police raids sent by the landowners.

The peasants' effort to regain the land was affected by the arrival of a group of activists who did not share the participative method, but who wanted to impose themselves as a typical vanguard. The inevitable discussions that ensued distracted the attention of the base groups and thwarted the self-expression of the community. But the free debate that followed in what was called 'meetings of friends' clearly showed who was right in this ideological and practical confrontation. The newly arrived cadres lost their influence and withdrew from the area.

During June and July the peasants dedicated themselves to consolidating their organization and ensuring the greatest possible participation in the land takeover. Additional advanced training was given to leaders in local skill programmes.

Meanwhile, the drafting of the history of the hamlet was finished, based on testimonies and documents of the local people ('trunk archives'). The resulting text was read and discussed at assemblies. On these occasions activities were enlarged to include artistic and cultural expression, such as folk music. Shortly afterwards, a complete booklet on the history of the hamlet was published for the use of the community and for general distribution.

The techniques employed covered aspects of communication, organization, research and education, simultaneously or by stages.

The mass media (radio and newspapers) were used from the beginning to create a widespread feeling of solidarity and collective pride. As the number of tape recorders had increased, a programme of cassettes was devised dealing with the history of the village, based on the published pamphlet. There were slides and photographic exhibitions and ample use of popular songs adapted to the circumstances of the struggle for the land, as had occurred before during the emergence of ANUC.

The investigation of the community profile was carried out by sifting data in different archives, through discussions in the 'meetings of friends', and the recovery of oral tradition with the elders of the hamlet and in meetings on the exchange of experiences. Communal work was fundamental. A friendly dialogue with the community was essential to the discovery of hidden aspects of the people's culture.

The main organizational aspects have been mentioned. External animators acted as advisers more than anything else and tried to support and promote the natural leadership of the community, but without stimulating the traditional charisma that leads to the manipulation of grassroots groups (and which involves some degree of machismo). This was difficult but highly instructive. The resulting organization allowed the peasants to keep up the pressure on the recuperated land through a group of about forty who have so far remained there.

It is evident that this methodology requires persons who are completely identified with PAR ideals, and who have a clear and critical political position. It is also evident that academic learning combined with the people's own understanding make for a type of knowledge that is more complete and closer to reality, all of which is more appropriate to investigators and grassroots alike. The people of El Cerrito have the ability to create knowledge and possess sufficient historical, social and cultural values to allow them to propose alternatives for change and people's power.

People's power: genesis of a social and political movement in Puerto Tejada (Colombia)[10]

Puerto Tejada is a town of 50,000 inhabitants located in the northern part of the department of Cauca, near the city of Cali. The vast majority of the town's inhabitants are black, descendants of the slaves and runaway slaves who occupied the region from the seventeenth century onwards in farms and in small free settlements.

The local people traditionally lived from the cultivation of cocoa, bananas, coffee and other staples of the Colombian countryside, until it was discovered that the lands of the valley of the Cauca river (to which Puerto Tejada belongs) were ideal for the commercial cultivation of sugar cane. From 1940 there was a great expansion of sugar cane cultivation in twenty plantations, which eventually occupied all the land up to the town limits of Puerto Tejada. The owners took over small peasant farms by coercion and added them to the plantations. Sugar cane, which covers 60,000 hectares in this part of the valley, has induced radical changes in the economy as well as in the ecology of the area. Puerto Tejada has been transformed into what is today just a strictly regulated camp of black wage-earners.

A characteristic of the sugar cane expansion was that it left the boundary of the town completely fixed, imprisoning it by a 'green enclosure', which reached as far as the last houses. Meanwhile the local population was growing. There were cases of fifty people or more living in one house, with all the problems that such a situation involved, without any action or interest being taken by the departmental or municipal authorities.

Inevitably, the people finally exploded. On 22 March 1981 more than 1,000 families forcibly took possession of some of the land of a neighbouring sugar plantation, cut down the cane and built huts. This process of direct action was supported by another process, namely, the collective investigation and reflection that eventually culminated in a social and political movement: the People's Civic Movement of Northern Cauca, which is still active in the region.

The fact that the families are matrifocal in this area gave the local women an important role in the entire process. Without them, there would have been no investigation or action. The research was directed towards discovering from the past those elements of popular mobilization that would serve the cause of the present struggles. Indeed, the community elders and key informants who were interviewed made an important contribution to the community profile because their memory was good: events were reconstructed and the black heroes of the people, hitherto forgotten or despised through ignorance, were once again brought to life in the popular imagination. Also, studies were made of the present housing situation, the public services, and other aspects of life, which were presented in a communal form covering the entire region. There it was decided to recover the past and to affirm the identity of the blacks, so as to show what their positive role was in the creation of Colombia as a nation.

The local political and social action had dramatic ups and downs, from the moment when the soldiers and police tried to expel the people from the seized land and destroy the huts. The authorities relented and discussed alternatives with the people to solve the problem, because it was clear to everybody that the people were right. A massacre was avoided when the military yielded to common sense. And so a new neighbourhood for the common people was born.

The historical recovery of the profile of Puerto Tejada and its people led to an understanding of the role of two cultural symbols: the sugar cane as a symbol of evil; and the cocoa as an embodiment of freedom, a traditional value held by the escaped slaves that had been lost after the development of capitalism. These symbols allowed the work to be undertaken on the basis of popular feelings, shared not only by those who took over the land but also by the rest of the people. This created widespread solidarity, which in part allowed the slow and counter-productive work of some leaders of the political left and right, who had remained in the area, to be neutralized.

There were assemblies every Friday, which took as a starting point the community action boards. There the moral aspects of action and concepts like 'sin' and 'crime' were discussed. The fear of action was conquered, once the conviction of justice had been acquired.

The struggle against such fears led to the emergence of a new consciousness and the acquisition of a new knowledge. The search for reasons to act confirmed that the people were right.The process of investigation also had a specific objective: to prove the justice of the demands. Hence commissions of people's researchers were formed. This created interest in knowing other local realities, for example in the districts of Cali taken over by the people and in the Indian communities of the southern regions of Cauca and Narino.

With the idea of invasion ripening, the leadership passed from the community action boards to other more directly concerned bodies, principally the Association of the Homeless, which organized the takeover and negotiated with the government. The success of the association went beyond all expectations and convinced thousands of people. Unfortunately, it also attracted the forces of repression, so that it had to apply the old tactics of survival. However, in the end the departmental government had to yield before the clear decisions of the people, and those lands remain occupied even today.

The success in Puerto Tejada opened up possibilities for action in other neighbouring areas. In Caloto a foreign company wanted to build a sulphuric acid plant that would pollute the environment. The people of Caloto organized themselves into a special committee for study and analysis similar to that of Puerto Tejada, and acted decisively with the help of advisers from the Civic Movement.

The dynamics of social and educational movements of this kind made people look for ways to support one another. Thus the Regional Forum, already mentioned, discussed such topics as the following: 'Our region is rich but our people are poor' (an analysis of the causes of poverty); 'The public services' (judgement of the state); 'The black people of northern Cauca' (a search for historical, ethnic and cultural identity); and 'Environmental problems' (ecology and society). They were useful for developing people's thought and action in northern Cauca. As a result, the regional movement became stronger.

Action continued in another neighbourhood of Puerto Tejada where a flood had occurred that the traditional politicians tried to exploit. Reflection and action workshops were organized on infant population problems, and plays, songs and so on were presented.

Something similar as regards people's organization, study and action occurred in the nearby town of Santander de Quilichao as a result of an act of police repression. The initial local protest was organized by the young people who were acquainted with the experience of Puerto Tejada. They published a small newspaper and participated in the local elections in unusual ways: the objective was to 'give people back their voice'. They organized songs, plays, masquerades and carnivals. The people and their culture were the protagonists of this campaign. Their town councillors were elected.

The regional movement of northern Cauca has kept its course. Its leaders and animators continue to work in spite of difficulties. They believe that it is necessary to go on designing an alternative model for the exercise of politics, that is for 'genuine, good politics'. They want a movement that values people's knowledge, that knows how to orient the mobilization of the masses, and that can build alternative ways of producing useful knowledge that will eventually lead to true people's power.

Notes

1. The study of PAR in Nicaragua, Mexico and Colombia was conceived within the framework of the Participatory Organizations of the Rural Poor (PORP) Programme of the International Labour Office, and is embodied in an ILO study by the author entitled *Knowledge and People's Power*, Indian Social Institute, 1985.
2. See the bibliography.
3. The present study is a synthesis or global methodological and conceptual vision of

this collective enterprise. In order for our work to be a truly comparative endeavour towards this common goal, we based our tasks on a previously prepared technical guide or conceptual frame of reference, which reflected the regional problems that went beyond the local context with which in principle we identified ourselves, as well as on the basic concerns shared by participatory researchers in general. The test of its effectiveness came with practice, a challenge which the guide met successfully. The fieldwork was done between 1982 and 1984 in the five peasant communities (mestizo, black and Indian) selected according to the conditions and contexts explained below.

4. These summaries were prepared by the coordinator on the basis of partial detailed reports from the national teams.

5. Malena de Montis in Fals Borda (1985).

6. Systems of Indian labour held in trust for the Spanish Crown.

7. Bertha M. Barragan and Felix Cadena Barquin in collaboration with Carlos Cadena and Roberto Cubas in Fals Borda (1985).

8. Salvador Garcia Angulo, in Fals Borda (1985).

9. Victor Negrete and Jose Galeano, in Fals Borda (1985).

10. Alvaro Velasco Alvarez in collaboration with John Jairo Cardenas, in Fals Borda (1985).

References

Aviles Solis, C., *Medios de communicacion en la educacion rural: una experiencia en el valle del Mezquital*, Universidad Nacional Autonoma de Mexica, Mexico, 1981.

Barraclough, S., *A Preliminary Analysis of the Nicaraguan Food System*, UNRISD, Geneva, 1982.

Bhaduri, A. and M.A. Rahman, *Studies in Rural Participation*, Oxford and IBH Publishing Co., New Delhi, 1982.

Brandao, C.R., *Pesquisa participante*, Editora Brasiliense, Sao Paulo, 1981.

Brandao, C.R., *O ardil da ordem*, Papirus, Campinas, 1983.

Buijs, H.Y., *Access and Participation*, University of Leiden, Leiden, 1979.

Cadena Barquin, F., *Capacitacion campesina y cambio social*, Programa de Desarollo Rural, Mexico, 1980.

Castillo, G.T., *How Participatory is Participatory Development? A review of the Philippine experience*, Institute of Development Studies, Manila, 1983.

Centro de Estudios y Accion Popular, *Conocimiento y accion popular*, Pozo de Rosas, Venezuela, 1981.

Comstock, D.E., *Participatory Research as Critical Theory: the North Bonneville, USA experience*, Evergreen State College, Olympia, Washington, 1982.

De Castille, M.V., *La contradiccion: objectivos de la educacion–producto educativo, el caso de Nicaragua*, Asociacion Nicaraguense de Cientificos Sociales, Managua, 1983.

De Shutter, A., *Investigacion participativa: una opcion metodologica para la educacion de adultos*, CREFAL, Patzcuaro, Mexico, 1981.

De Silva, G.V.S., N. Mehta, M.A. Rahman and P.Wignaraja, 'Bhoomi Sena, a struggle for People's Power', in *Development Dialogue*, No. 2, pp. 3–70, Uppsala, 1979.

De Vries, J., *Science as Human Behaviour: on the epistemology of participatory research approach*, Studiecentrum, Amersfoort, Netherlands, 1980.

Erasmie, T. and F. Dubell (eds.), *Adult Education II—Research for the People, Research by the People: an introduction to participatory research,* University of Linkoping, Linkoping, 1980.

Falabella, G., *Highlights of the Development of Participatory Research in Latin America*, Institute of Latin American Studies, University of London, London, 1981.

Fals Borda, O., *La ciencia y el pueblo: nuevas reflexiones sobre la investigacion–accion*, Asociacion Colombiana de Sociologia, Bogota, 1981.

Fals Borda, O., 'Science and Common People', in *Journal of Social Studies*, No. 11, Dacca, 1981.

Fals Borda, O.,'Die Bedeuting der Sozialwissenschaft und die praktische Produktion von Wissen in der Dritten Welt: die Herausforderung der Aktionsforschung'. in *Osterreichische Zeitschrift für Politikwissenschaft* , No. 2, Vienna, 1981.

Fals Borda, O., 'Participatory Action Research', in *Development*, Society for International Development, No. 2, Rome, 1984.

Fernandez, Walter and R.Tandon, *Participatory Research and Evaluation: experiments in research as a process of liberation*, Indian Social Institute, New Delhi, 1981.

Forum International d'Action Communautaire, 'La Recherche Action: enjeux et pratiques', *Review Internationale d'Action Communautaire*, No. 5/45, Montreal, Spring 1981.

Freire, P., *Pedagogia del oprimido*, Editorial America Latina, Bogota, 1970.

Fuentes Morua, J., *La organizacion de los campesinos y los problemas de la investigacion participativa*, IMISAC, Morelia, Mexico, 1983.

Fundacion Punta de Lanza, *Critica y politica en ciencias sociales*, Bogota, 1978.

Gajardo, M., *Evolucion situacion actual y perspectivas de las estrategias de investigacion participativa en America Latina*, Facultad Latino-americano de Ciencias Sociales, International Development Research Centre, Ford Foundation, Santiago, 1982.

Gajardo, M., J.J. Silva and V. Edwards, *Primer encuentro de investigacion-accion y educacion popular en Chile*, PIIE, Santiago, 1980.

Galeano, J.S. and V. Negrete, *El Cerrito,* Fundacion del Sinu, Monteria, Colombia, 1982.

Galjart, B., *Participatory Rural Development Projects: some conclusions from field research*, University of Leiden, Leiden, 1981.

Gamez, J.A., *Evaluacion del modelo de autodidactismo solidario*, Centro de Estudios Economicos y Sociales del Tercer Mundo, Mexico, 1981.

Garcia Angulo, S., *Autodidactismo solidario: uno experiencia de education de adultos en el valle del Mezquital*, Centro de Educacion de Adultos, Izmiquilpan, Mexico, 1980.

Garcia Angulo, S., *La educacion de grupos marginados en Mexico,* Centro de Educacion de Adultos, Mexico, 1983.

Gaventa, J., *Power and Powerlessness: quiescence and rebellion in an Appalachian valley*, University of Illinois Press, Urbana, Illinois, 1980.

Gianotten, V. and T. de Wit, *Universidad y pueblo: teoria y practica del Centro de Capacitacion en Educacion de Adultos y Desarrollo Rural,* Universidad Nacional de Huamanga, Ayacucho, Peru, 1980.

Gomes, S. 'Participation Experience in the Countryside: a case study in Chile' (mimeographed World Employed Programme Research Working Paper; restricted), ILO, Geneva, 1981.

Gould, J., *Needs, Participation and Local Development*, University of Helsinki, Helsinki, 1981.

Hall, B. and A. Gillette, *Participation Research*, International Council for Adult Education, Toronto, 1977.

Huizer, G., *Peasant Participation in Latin America and its Obstacles*, Hague Institute of Social Studies, 1980.

International Council for Adult Education, 'Participatory Research: development and issues', *Convergence*, Vol. XIIV, No. 3, Toronto, 1981.

LeBoterf, C., *L'Enquête participation en question*, Ch. Corlet, Conde-sur-Noireau, France, 1981.

Max-Neef, M., *From the Outside Looking In: experiences in barefoot economics*, Dag Hammerskjold Foundation, Uppsala, 1982.

Moser, H., *The Participatory Research Approach on Village Level: theoretical and practical implications*, University of Munster, Munster, 1982.

Moser, H. and Ornauer (eds.), *Internationale Aspekte der Aktionsforschung*, Kosel-Verlag, Munich, 1978.

Mustafa, K., *Participatory Research and Popular Education in Africa*, African Participatory Network, Dar es Salaam, 1983.
Negrete, V., *La investigacion-accion en Cordoba*, Fundacion del Sinu, Monteria, Colombia, 1983.
Nelson, C. and S. Arafa, *Problems and Prospects of Participatory Action Research: an Egyptian rural community*, American University, Cairo, 1982.
Oakley, P. and D. Marsden, *Approaches to Participation in Rural Development*, ILO, Geneva, 1984.
Oquist, R., *Epistemologia de la investigacion-accion*, Punta de Lanza, Bogota, 1978.
Orefice, P. (ed.), 'La ricerca participativa', in *Quaderni delle Societa delle Autonomie Locali per l'Educazione Adulti*, No. 3–4, Rome, 1982.
Paakkanen, L. (ed.), *Participation, Needs and Village-level Development (Jipemoyo)*, University of Helsinki, Helsinki, 1981.
Paranjape, P.V. et al., *Grass Roots Self-reliance in Shramik Sangathana (Dhulia, India)* (mimeographed World Employment Programme research working paper; restricted), ILO, Geneva, 1981.
Park, P., *Social Research and Radical Change*, University of Massachusetts, Amherst, Massachusetts, 1978.
Parra Escobar, E., *La investigacion-accion en la Costa Atlantica: evaluacion de la Rosca, 1972–1974*, Fundacion para la Communicacion Popular, Cali, 1983.
Pearse, A. and M. Stiefel, *Inquiry into Participation: a research approach*, UNRISD, Geneva, 1980.
Peek, P., *Agrarian Reforms and Development in Nicaragua* (mimeographed World Employment Programme research working paper; restricted), ILO, Geneva, 1981.
Pozas, R., *La construccion de un sistema de terrazas en los altos del estado de Chiapas*, Centro de Estudios del Desarrollo, Universidad Nacional Autonoma de Mexico, Mexico, 1979.
Rahman, M.A. (ed.), *Grass-roots Participation and Self-reliance*, Oxford and IBH Publishing Co., New Delhi, 1984.
Rahman, M.A., *The Theory and Practice of Participatory Action Research* (mimeographed World Employment Programme research working paper; restricted), ILO, Geneva, 1982; reproduced in O. Fals Borda (ed.), *The Challenge of Social Change,* Sage Publications, London, 1985.
Regional Centre for Adult Education and Functional Literacy for Latin America—International Council for Adult Education, *Informe final del Segundo Seminario Latinoamericano de investigacion participativa*, Patzcuaro, Mexico, 1982.
Sanguinetti Vargas, Y., *La investigacion participativa en los procesos de desarrollo de America Latina* , Facultad de Psicologia, Universidad Nacional Autonoma de Mexico, Mexico, 1980.
Sevilla Casas, E., *Atraso y desarrollo indigena en Tierradentro*, Universidad de los Andes, Bogota, 1976.
Sheth, D.L., 'Grass-roots Stirrings and the Future of Politics', in *Alternatives*, IX, New Delhi, 1983.
Society for International Development, 'Participation of the Rural in Development', in *Development*, No. 1, Rome, 1981.
Sole, M., *Three False Dichotomies in Action Research: theory vs. practice, quantitative vs. qualitative, science vs. politics,* University of Uppsala, 1982.
Sotelo, L., *Una experiencia de comercializacion: la huerta de Comapan*, PRODER, Mexico, 1981.
Stronquist, N., 'La investigacion participativa: un nuevoenfoque sociologico', in *Revista Colombiana de Educacion*, No. 11, Bogota, 1983.
Swantz, M.L., *Rejoinder to Research: methodology and the participatory research approach*, Ministry of Culture and Youth, Dar es Salaam, 1980.
Swedner, H., *Human Welfare and Action Research in Urban Settings,* Delegation for Social Research, Stockholm, 1983.
Velasco Alvarez, A., *Genesis y desarrollo de un movimiento social en Puerto Tejada, Colombia*, Empresa de Cooperacion para el Desarrollo, Cali, 1983.

Vilas, C., *Entre la produccion de lo nuevo y la reproduccion de lo viejo: educacion, ideologia y poder popular en Nicaragua*, Ministry of Education, Managua, 1982.

Vio Grossi, F., V. Giannotten and T. de Wit (eds.), *Investigacion Participativa y praxis rural*, Mosca Azul, Lima, 1981.

Volken, H., A. Kumar and S. Kaithathara, *Learning from the Rural Poor*, Indian Social Institute, New Delhi, 1982.

Werdelin, I., *Participatory Research in Education*, University of Linkoping, Linkoping, 1979.

Wignaraja, P., *Women, Poverty and Resources*, Sage Publications, New Delhi/Newbury Park/London, 1990.

Wignaraja, P., A. Hussain, H. Sethi and G. Wignaraja, *Participatory Development: learning from South Asia*, Oxford University Press, Karachi/Oxford, 1990.

11. Brazilian Crossroads: People's Groups, Walls and Bridges*

Leilah Landim

Some three years ago, a meeting held in London by agencies of the North allowed me to make contact, for the first time, with people from NGOs (non-governmental organizations) coming from worlds that are more distant from my life in Brazil than are those of western Europe. (There are various worlds in the Third World, and it is surprising how our 'horizontal' meetings are still restricted; even in this, the North has the privilege of being throughout the globe....) My Indian colleagues energetically raised the question of culture. 'You in Brazil are already lost; you no longer have a cultural identity,' one of them provoked me. This pessimistic vision made me indignant for a moment, but he did have a point. The differences between our worlds are really, and happily, very great.

None the less, at the same time and paradoxically, I was surprised by the familiarity and ease with which we from the South were able to discuss and understand one another with regard to a series of questions: from the paths our lives had taken to the problems we encounter in our work at the grassroots. There was a common language, there were common categories, common references and common basic commitments. We shared, fundamentally, the same values. The debate ran freely from the moment of first contact.

This reflects both the strength and weakness of NGOs, and it is in their delicate equilibrium that we have faced our challenge: to work with the tension between the universal and the particular, between Westernized language and the pluralism of different cultures, between the values of citizens, individualism, autonomy and equality on the one hand, and values of membership, holism, hierarchy, and complementarity on the other. Our journey with the grassroots of society has brought us to walk on a tightrope that establishes commitments between innovating and conserving, transforming and respecting, overcoming and redeeming.

In an attempt to outline the trajectory of the current challenges that we face in our work in Brazil, I will be relating experiences that recur in a similar way in various parts of the world. This is proof of the universality that

* Translated by William D. Savedoff.

certain forms of exploitation, ideologies and social relations have assumed in the wake of Western domination; the Third World is an organic part of a single contemporary scene. But one also sees revealed in this the universality of discourse and the problematic that the activities of the development agencies have forged since the 1960s in various parts of the world. Even at the risk of sounding repetitive, I prefer to embark on a brief report of Brazil's experience and reality. I will try to arrive at the grand problems without leaving aside the particularities.

Origins and trajectories

The term 'NGO' is a new one which has come to be applied to social phenomena which are not so new in Brazil. It serves to designate an immense group of entities that have established themselves, *sui generis,* since the end of the 1960s, embedded in the dynamic and the interests of popular groups and movements. One could say that it designates a field of initiatives and agents who specialize in work with the bases of society. It is an inappropriate name, as has been said. But its imprecision may be useful for designating something whose profile is fluid, changing, open.

Until a few years ago in Brazil, 'non-governmental organization' signified nothing in particular to the academic community, public opinion in general, or even to those active in these entities themselves. The lack of awareness, or the absence of the term itself, certainly indicated a lack of recognition of a common identity among this grouping of organizations and initiatives.

In fact, it was only a few years ago that the organizations which today we call Brazilian NGOs began to meet and form permanent networks to debate their common problems and perspectives. 'Who are we?' or 'what is our role?' is the basic fabric of these debates, which have spread more and more, joining and creating ties between people who were dispersed during all those previous years to the four corners of the country, dedicated to the most varied work at the bottom of society. The present moment is one of evaluation, of discovery and consolidation of an identity (and there the ghosts of corporatism must be well exorcized) beyond the enormous plurality of experiences.

One of the reasons for the low profile and fragmentation of NGOs in Brazil during a major part of the country's history can be sought in their origins. The organizations were born and consolidated during the harshest times of the authoritarian regime that imposed itself on the country with the military coup of 1964. Under the stifling climate of the dictatorship of the 1970s the Popular Education Centres, and Social Promotion Centres and Advice and Support Centres knew how to develop a creativity and flexibility which allowed them to survive and to grow.

At that time, molecular and discrete forms of action—the so-called 'work of the ants'—were consolidated, associated with a wide range of socially subordinate groups, in the city and in the country, and radically turned their backs on the state. Although the state appeared clearly as an opponent, the political choice made by the Centres in this period was to avoid direct confrontation with it, and to maintain themselves on the margin. Their position was to stimulate parallel initiatives outside the grand institutions—which were all in crisis, eviscerated or under rigid government control—such as unions, parties and universities. It was a period of small economic projects of a 'communitarian' or 'participatory' kind, of the work of 'animation', 'base education' and 'self-help' to find solutions to problems from the community's own resources. During the 1970s, the Centres offered support in the opening up of small spaces for resistance and participation, in direct contact with popular groups, as a basic characteristic of their work. In the face of an authoritarian state that at the same time completely lacked any social policies to provide even minimal benefits for the popular strata, the formula was to create nuclei, cells of popular organization: A counter-society.

What are the ideological sources of this work? Where do their agents come from and what social space is available for them to reach popular groups? Many ideals are combined in the diversity of micro initiatives, of micro mediators spread out through the bases of society. The history of the 'roots' of the current NGOs—the point of reference from which they create their style of work—is still to be told.

Certainly during this period they were much more aware than today of the history of development agencies in the 1950s, with their assistance programmes dominated by an aid mentality. The NGOs of the 1970s established themselves precisely within the climate of a break with this past, inspired in large part by dependency theory, which was influential throughout Latin America at the time.

The Catholic Church played a fundamental role in this process through its sectors engaged in popular pastoral work, under the inspiration of Liberation Theology. The Church was able to maintain its space in a civil society destructured by authoritarianism. For years, the Church filled an important function of assistance and support for the movements that resisted the regime. The popular pastoral work of priests penetrated the most diverse areas of the social life of dominated sectors. It was in these spaces that the new work of 'popular education', inspired by Freire, germinated. It attracted new recruits—lay people, religious people, atheists—committed to the construction of new social practices through daily living with popular groups. The Centres that were created at that time were autonomous with respect to the ecclesiastical hierarchy and this was not without its consequences. However, the social bases with which they carried out their work were groups fundamentally linked to the popular religious movement.

Since that time, many things have changed. The NGOs became secularized, steadily more autonomous, and increasingly diverse in their work. But their origins left their marks. Certainly the Catholic Church and, to a lesser degree, some Protestant denominations continue to be important mediators in the field of base work in Brazil. The international cooperation agencies linked to the Christian world in the North similarly have a fundamental role in supporting projects in this field in Brazil.

Little by little, a diverse contingent of activists came together in the Centres producing a special concoction: new generations of Christians (religious and lay) inspired by Liberation Theology with its 'option for the poor'; militant Marxists disenchanted with the political practices of traditional vanguard parties (and, further, prevented in large part from continuing them); old agents of community development who had become critical of the aid mentality; and intellectuals discontented with the ivory towers of their universities and wanting now to produce 'committed' knowledge. Later, with the political amnesty, many former exiles also found space for themselves within the NGOs and so returned, in new ways, to their former commitments, bringing along with them their experience acquired during the long years of residence in the North.

The NGOs consolidated themselves, therefore, in alternative spaces, accustomed to mixtures and to the challenge of living with differences. As has been observed, they are spaces where one can make politics without being a party, research without being a university. Autonomy, then, is the keyword, although it certainly accommodates a certain structural ambiguity between moments of approximation/distance, dependence/independence, in relation to the poles set by the grand institutions, the different political and ideological currents, and the different social movements. NGOs live on a knife edge between being an institution and being a movement, between profession and militancy. They must know how to live in tension, free of anxiety to try to resolve it.

Born under authoritarianism, the NGOs expanded even more with the democratization of the 1980s. The recent vitality of an enormous group of civil organizations that have multiplied themselves throughout the country, geared to very diverse forms of social transformation, is impressive. Despite the basic fact of ongoing economic crisis, misery and marginalization, it is also a time of pluralism, new paradigms for social and political practices, and affirmation of cultural identities hitherto submerged in Brazil's extreme and glaring modernization. It is a time of consolidation of a strategy characterized by the restructuring of popular representative groups and a time for the emergence of other worlds among traditional social movements.

In a society where the state is strong and authoritarian, the NGOs emerged with a radical vocation for civil society. They were, in the first instance, strongholds for initiatives characterized by resistance to the military dictatorship; in the second instance they were spaces oriented towards pluralism and the construction of popular civil society. This is how the role of NGOs in Brazil came to be defined.

Brazil 1990

To break with secular self-denigration before the so-called authorities, expressed in the logic of bosses and clientelism; to promote horizontal solidarity, self-reliance, and autonomous initiatives in which popular groups take account of their lives and their interests; to encourage citizenship and participation; to forget the vanguardism that reproduces schemes of domination, and to incorporate the ends in the means; so the transformation is made in daily life, bit by bit, in a dynamic that gives voice to the silenced, that respects their culture, that valorizes and affirms their understanding, that follows their rhythm, without missing the wood for the trees. It is a slow transformation from the roots. The Centres affirm themselves with this ideal. The words are 'popular education', 'conscientization'.

The first winds of political opening brought with them another magic word: 'organization'. The armies of NGOs joined their strength and will to the movement for organizing and restructuring the unions, neighbourhood associations, cooperatives, consumer groups, small traders, and peasant associations of all kinds. Projects in economic action, communication, human rights, participant research, health, and education all proliferated. The partnerships between non-governmental agencies in the North and Centres of the South developed and consolidated the channels by which funding, ideas and people circulated. The state—authoritarian, clientelist, inefficient in its functions—remained always the opponent.

And now? The organized popular movements have been able to impose themselves as actors on the national political scene. The military dictatorship ended. The process of democratic transition—even if controlled from above—has concluded in institutional terms. Brazil's democracy is insecure and handicapped, but reasonably distant from the suffocating climate of 'Brazil, love it or leave it'—the slogan of the repressive military governments. Those who lived under it, know.

And the Centres, the utopias of popular education, the micro-level work, what path have they taken?

One could say that the Centres became NGOs. They became visible; they became politicized; and they have had to reverse their posture with regard to the state, the unions, the political parties and the universities, which are all reorganizing. It not always easy to adapt oneself to new times—which, furthermore, they helped to create. The original generation of the Centres learned to do their work in the shadows, seeing the world in stark black and white, and with a clear principal opponent. 'They aren't very used to the various shades of colours of the country and current world,' as Lopezllera says. A certain clandestine syndrome insists on surviving because of the fact—which has its rationale—that liberty here is fragile. But events swarm and overrun efforts to keep the base work in belljars. The NGOs learn more and more that their strength comes today from their very visibility and legitimacy in the new political and social scene of Brazil. And they must learn, crucially, to link the local with the global—in order to forestall any threat of seeing their efforts dissipate at the first breath of the big bad wolf returning. Global transformations will not wait for changes at the roots. We must link together in diverse terms.

These questions are the order of the day in the debates, networks, and meetings that are spreading and proving the continuing vitality of this world of civic entities, today, in Brazil. I shall discuss only a few of the multiple challenges facing us.

Is the time of the NGOs past?

This question appears strange, in view of the proliferation of advisory groups and entities. Perhaps it is being placed on the agenda rather insensitively—like many other themes and questions—by the international financial agencies posing the question: will it still be profitable to invest in Brazil, an industrialized, modern and democratized country? Be that as it may, the question has been raised among NGOs who define themselves as being at the service of the movements and popular groups. And it certainly refers to a more profound questioning of the identity of the NGOs.

There are those who consider the advisory and support groups as a necessary evil, which have their purposes so long as popular organizations are not solid enough to stand on their own feet, forging their own intellectuals or contracting their own advisors, educators, etc. This rationale, alas, is akin to that which considers the NGOs dispensable as soon as the state assumes responsibility for its social functions, along with the popular groups. According to this conception, the NGOs would only be a substitute for work that the state neglects. In the march of history for societies that do take popular class interests into consideration, the NGOs would have only a temporary existence.

This discussion does not in fact have any practical effect since no one believes that this utopian moment has arrived. But it does permit a better explication of the character and role of NGOs. Although it places them at the service of popular movements, the NGOs, or the advisers, are not to be confused with those movements, possessing their own institutional purposes. At least in Brazil, in addition to being sources of support for these movements, the NGOs have come to play a more complex role, emerging also as actors in strengthening the path towards democracy and towards a popular civil society. By their nature, the NGOs have also fulfilled the functions of micro mediators, or articulators, between the groups and movements on the one hand, and churches, state, universities, etc., on the other.

The NGOs' role goes beyond the conjunctural. Their time is not confined to specific forms of government, since their vocation is not toward transformations conceived in terms of state power (which clearly does not mean that they cannot work in cooperation with the state—a possibility that is of current importance so long as the movement for democratization deepens). Their inclination is towards putting down roots at the bases, towards encouraging autonomy of popular initiatives and participatory democracy. In this way they seek to redeem diverse cultural contributions and to move towards the utopia of new social relations, beyond the dilemma of reform or revolution.

Other words: the ecological and the popular

In Brazil, we have conducted an appraisal of the civic entities involved in building and supporting various social movements. The results show that there are more things between heaven and earth than our vain philosophy can imagine, when we enquire beyond the NGOs dedicated to organized popular movements of which we have basically spoken until now. For those who like numbers: in 1988 we had in Brazil 447 entities that defined themselves as being 'at the service of popular groups and movements'; 565 entities that struggled with the question of blacks; 196 entities dedicated to women; and 402 entities linked to ecology.

The number of organizations that have arisen in the late 1980s is impressive, above all in the ecological field (which, it may be noted, lends itself to much piracy by fashion, the media and the market). The gulf between these worlds is rather extraordinary. Each kind forms a subgroup that is reasonably sealed off from the others in terms of organizational forms and styles of action. Each comprises its own separate clan of activists with its own myths and totems, where the social world appears fragmented between the categories 'people', 'blacks', 'women', 'humanity'. Daily contacts, articulations, meetings, joint action are carried on in a rather distinct fashion within each of these groups, and the areas where their activities intersect across these boundaries are rather small. They devote themselves to distinct practices, to different conceptions about the legitimate questions of the political arena, and to diverse institutional forms.

How is it possible to transcend these preconceptions and competition? The growth of the ecological movement in Brazil has generated some stimulating challenges.

The groups classified as ecological NGOs in Brazil are characterized by a high degree of informality, voluntarism, and fragmentation into minute and localized groups. What they focus on is significantly diverse: preservation of the environment, defence of flora and fauna, organic agriculture, appropriate technology, alternative medicine, alternative agricultural communities, esoteric knowledge, alternative journalism, meditation, struggle against giant dams, defence of indigenous communities, the anti-nuclear struggle, alternative physical therapies.... They present a huge mosaic of activities, which gain meaning as a whole only because they share common sources of thought and action.

Although profoundly differentiated, the ecological NGOs have in common a perspective that sees contemporary social questions in terms of the crisis of modernity and civilization. They bring to the political sphere questions of transformative models of life, of habits and values, of a search for equilibrium between body and mind, between humanity and the cosmos—where spiritual practices have their place. The dichotomies oppressor/oppressed, exploiter/exploited, man/woman, black/white are replaced by the relationship humanity/nature, where present dislocation must transform itself into harmony. If 'development' is a traditional word for the universe of international agencies and NGOs, the ecological world is going to reconstruct it through a critique of the basic ideas and values connected with development. To the dilemmas of democracy versus authoritarianism, capitalism versus socialism, they add one more: a predatory society versus an ecological society. The axis of life versus death is placed at the centre of the problems, which are planetary. What is in crisis is our own paradigms.

What are the possibilities for effective articulation and communication between the matrices of ecology and the matrices which are traditionally thought of as popular movements?

There is certainly a divergence. Many of the activists involved in the popular movements suggest that the ecological field is a cluster of 'out-of-place ideas'—generated in countries of the North—that do not apply to Brazilian reality, marked as it is by dramatic impoverishment and marginalization of immense popular sectors. Before criticizing the values linked to the consumer society, they say, we simply have to provide for consumption. How can we think about the ozone layer if we are oppressed and dying from hunger? Even if the ecological questions are meaningful, they disperse energy from the key struggles.

Already, the 'ecological tribe' has criticized the traditional left for its conception of 'economic people', which reduces human beings to only one of their many facets and impoverishes their potential. But this view of the ecological movements constructs an unrealistic image of a poor worker imprisoned by the domination of material necessities, and it therefore underestimates the complexity of the system of symbolic representation of popular culture. The economic crisis, exploitation and misery do not exclude the discussion of life models that stunt the will and the imagination, which are macho and violent. And Brazil is a country where the social problems of affluence and of misery are equally present.

Both sides certainly have their logic, and our road will be indicated for us by the real dynamic between these groups and movements in society.

In a sense, a question arises for which we still have no answer, and it is the following: if it is true that the ecological ideal and ecological struggles were born in the countries of the North, in what form do these questions and practices occur in a social context like our own? How are they being effectively appropriated, or retranslated, within Brazilian society in its diverse movements, groups and social classes?

The question makes us return again to the bases of society, to the dominated groups and their cultural universes. Tribal societies, Afro-Brazilian religions and peasant traditions are some of the elements that strongly mark our culture. In these cultural sub-systems, very particular and specific forms of representation of nature and effective relations with natural forces occupy an important place. What kind of links can be found between the imaginary and popular values of a worldview and the proposals brought by the winds of ecology? What specific dialogue can be established there? We already know that the old-style social movements (trade unions, political parties), with their modern and universalistic Western ideals, do not always ensure the establishment of effective bridges with the cultural specificities of large sectors of the population. We can ask ourselves whether the ecological ideals will be able to open new means for the manifestation of cultural identities in the range of Brazilian social movements.

It was the assassination of Chico Mendes—union leader and ecologist—that tragically brought forward an example of the possibilities of convergence between ecology and social justice in Brazil. Rubber workers, Indians and peasants in the Amazon certainly have much to share—if we are disposed to listen—about the familiarity the *enchanted ones* (the beings that inhabit the forests and rivers) have with their struggles. Many are the paths discerned when one escapes the world of reason during the *miracoes* (visions) obtained from the teas made from native plants. The People of the Forest—as these social groups call themselves in their current struggles of resistance—have the remarkable capacity of harmonizing visions of the world that for us are frequently irreconcilable.

Culture: convergence and divergence—the NGOs on a tightrope

The question of ethnic and cultural diversity is the current issue the world over. Predictions of an inexorable march toward a uniform world have not come true. And, more than this, the developed world has discovered itself to be dissatisfied with the forms that progress took, even for itself, the prime beneficiary. The search for other values, other world-views, curiosity about those strange ways of life which dare to resist the calls or pressures for Westernization, these are the so-called post-material questions.

The non-governmental development agencies are propitious places, by virtue of the type of practices and sensitivity that they stimulate, for these questions to be raised. Some voices are beginning to ask themselves in what way the NGOs come to function as heralds of Westernization, virtual Trojan horses, in the four corners of the world.

Certainly equivalent questions are being posed in Brazil, a country significantly lost to Westernization. But in the Brazilian NGOs this is still quite an incipient debate, restricted to a few people and entities. I believe, none the less, that we have only to gain by revising our old ways.

We construct our practices of popular education and our projects for economic action according to the principle of respect for knowledge and for the cultural groups reached by this work. Daily living with the bases ensures the success of these intentions. In this way we distinguish ourselves not only from vanguardism, but also from academia (the participant observer must ensure the production of the new understanding useful to and on the side of those involved).

The balance of the past two decades has been positive and original, above all in the area of building popular organizations and associations of all kinds. Now we can undertake an evaluation of certain impasses and limits.

People talk in Brazil of a crisis in the growth of the trade union and neighbourhood association movements. The proportion of workers who participate in these organizations (generally divided internally into dogmatic subgroups) is relatively small. The masses of marginalized people accumulate in the *favelas* (squatter settlements) and peripheral areas of the big cities, in large part—which is not to say completely—unreached by the work of the NGOs. The groups linked to the work of the Popular Church are weakening in the face of the onslaught of the proliferating fundamentalist and spiritualist groups, and also are isolated themselves in relation to the popular Catholicism lived by the poorest ranks of the population. Our feminist discourse has not been able to excite attention among the articulate parts of the popular classes. The black movement has had enormous difficulties in reaching the masses of a mestizo society where, as a popular and sarcastic expression goes, 'blacks know their place'.

The causes of these impasses are various and complex. I would like to focus on merely one aspect of the question: the divergence and misunderstanding between our language (the language of the NGOs, of projects, of conscientization) and the vast areas of cultural life of the popular sectors. In the face of popular non-adherence to the proposals we support, we must expand our analysis and go beyond explanations that rely on 'alienation' or 'ideological domination' (which are, none the less, real).

It would be worthwhile to analyse the reasons for the blindness of agents at the base with respect to whole dimensions of the social life of the groups who benefit from projects—despite the agents' experiential contact of living with them. The image that seems to dominate is of people who have only positive qualities and whose life is summarized in their suffering from lack of material goods.

For example, analysing the results of participant research done in Brazil, we see many important contributions, but they have not succeeded in surpassing certain limits. Normally infused with common sense, their analyses rely on the verification only of problems experienced in work, production, exploitation and the economic activities undertaken by the groups.

The participant researcher and the popular educator hear the people, but one has the impression that their hearing is selective in terms of the symbolic and social universe of those whom they contact. Where are the Afro-Brazilian cults, with their supernatural entities that inhabit and interfere in daily life? Where are the saint worship, the votives, the festivals of patron saints? Where is carnival, whose preparations in some cities mobilize some of the poorest sectors for the better part of a year, for which they weave a complete network of informal economy, loyalties and costumes, and in which the suggestion of luxury and wealth makes up a key part of the grand popular theatre that is carried on to the streets? Where is the *funk* culture, which has been modified here in specific Brazilian ways, and which has spread through the suburbs in clubs and via pirated records that are not aired on the radio? In the area of work with women, where is the *pomba-giru,* an African cult strongly present in the behaviour and definition of feminine identities? And so on.

The agents of the NGOs because of their formation, their origins, and the frameworks of thought to which they refer, are unfamiliar with these branches of popular culture. It is extremely rare to find these themes raised in papers or debates in the NGOs' world; their engagement is left largely restricted to the academic community, as if they were a topic for those with 'idle time' in their 'ivory towers'.

None the less, we must face more profoundly certain short-circuits in communication with popular sectors: how to raise the discourse of human rights, citizenship, liberal judicial principles, with the rank and file of the population, as with the people of the squatter settlements, where the law of the hill rules. Many times, our discourse becomes a kind of choir of angels. In the area of negritude, for example, our rhetoric is dualistic: black versus white. But Brazilian racism deals with the mixture, with the variety of colours. The difference between the sexes passes in Brazil through the complexity of Afro–Caboclo–Mediterranean customs; and our feminist discourse is in large part inspired by the egalitarian traditions of the Afro-Saxons. Egalitarian and collectivizing spiritual projects in the country run aground on social systems based on relations that are traditionally hierarchical, having the family unit of production and consumption as their basic unit of logic.

Many examples could be analysed, where we suddenly find a divergence between our discourse—which is Cartesian, universalist and pure—and the popular logic of syncretism, mixture, hierarchy and reciprocity.

This is our great challenge: how to articulate values of citizenship, so absent and so fundamental in our society, with the attitudes in existence. We appear to place ourselves, in this moment, in the tension between transforming and respecting. How can we establish bridges, dialogues, new paths? This is the important goal. At least we must remain clear that our place is in this tension, our path is on the tightrope.

Finally, note that we are not dealing here with the danger, which is so common, of trying in some purist fashion to encounter an untouched and submerged non-Western quality in everything as if it were utterly sacrosanct. I believe that the best point of departure for thinking about cultural diversity is the recognition that, since the nineteenth century, there has been an ineluctable development of civilizing integration. This integration has happened simultaneously, but with locally differentiated movements. Or rather, the specific effects of material global forces depend on the diverse ways in which they are mediated by local cultural frameworks. These persist, but they are always transformed in some way or other, developing their subjects by virtue of cohabitation and mixture between diverse frames of reference and forms of logic. We must remind ourselves, finally, that the people of Western capitalism's periphery also affect their social order, by their diverse ways of culturally articulating what has happened to them. And we can also ask ourselves: is the West as uniform as at times we want to believe?

North, South, East, West: paths that cross

The debate among Brazilian NGOs has been widespread in the climate of change with which we have begun the 1990s, at home and abroad.

Some internal questions can be cited. How to confront the new relations in a democratic constitutional system with its popular state administrations and local municipalities? There is the great problem of how to reach marginalized groups with our projects, including here the dramatic situation of minors, the street kids.There are the questions of urban violence and police violence against subordinated sectors of the population, the question of material projects with greater reach, to confront the problem of absolute poverty; or is this a return to an aid mentality? And what should be the function of the NGOs?

One debate has taken shape and, in its generality, it deserves to be briefly outlined here. This is the discussion about international cooperation. I highlight only two of the main issues below.

First, there is the problem of how best to politicize the relations between the NGOs of the South and the agencies of the North, so that we need no longer face the agencies as mere sources of funding. What are the possibilities for effective influence over the agencies' policies? What are the possibilities for two-way activities, in which we would play a role in supporting the forces that, in the North, are fighting for a new economic and political order? What are the possibilities for stimulating our partners in terms of specific questions, such as are occurring in relation to the campaign over the external debt? What chance is there to decentralize decisions, or to stimulate the creation of political and cultural mechanisms on the part of the agencies of the North, so that the problems that affect us have greater international repercussions?

The NGOs open space for a new style of internationalism, with informal networks in which autonomy, pluralism and mutually trusting relations are preserved. It is time for us to reflect together on the long term, reviewing horizons and impasses, at the international as well as the micro level.

Our speech and conceptions must respond creatively to the new challenges set by the unification of Europe, by a time of severe crisis in the Third World, and by changes in the countries of Eastern Europe.

Some experiences of articulation between South and East are beginning, which should be stimulated. Whatever efforts the European NGOs make toward establishing activities in the East should open and stimulate dialogue with them, the newest partners in the East, and with their older partners in the South.

South/South relations are extremely precarious, and it is urgent that they be encouraged.

Second, the question of direct partnerships with government or multilateral agencies of the North—among which the World Bank should be emphasized—is becoming more and more important. Brazilian NGOs have sought to treat this matter with the care it requires, creating meetings and even networks around this discussion. More aware and concerted action is sought in this area, between groups of various sizes and from various regions.

There would be advantages in concerted action, for example, in terms of resources, which continue to be scarce relative to the quantity of applications which appear and the complexity of social movements. Embarking on material projects of a more large-scale character has particular possibilities.

This issue must be discussed carefully, however, so as to avoid problems such as the great risks of political control and financial dependence. The difficulty of relationships with the bureaucracies of multilateral and governmental organs must also be evaluated.

The question of the World Bank in Brazil is above all delicate because the NGOs have accustomed themselves, by force of circumstances, to a role of continuing to criticize the bank's activities in terms of sustaining military regimes, co-responsibility for administrative corruption, and the destruction of nature. The World Bank's policy of support for NGOs—above all in the ecological field—appears contradicted by experiences that are not of the ancient past, but rather are very much current.

In sum, the question is complex and demands serious discussion so that our work, built up over years and years, should not run the risk of being compromised.

We have many walls to topple and many bridges to build. The decade of the 1990s begins under the sign of novelty and perplexity, obliging even the most intractable among us to reconsider old frameworks and old words to which so many of us still cling. In Brazil—and in Latin America—the rising tide of democratization brings new hopes. Let us confront the shadow of economic crisis and marginalization fed by these new energies.

12. Action Groups in the New Politics

Harsh Sethi

Despite a great deal of concern in India about development and the problems of the rural and urban poor, conditions in the country are deteriorating, and the position of the lower strata is worsening.[1] Politically there has been both an increase in the power of the urban-based educated elite and the alliance of this elite structure with the upper and middle castes in the rural areas. On the whole, 'development' is more rhetoric than reality and on present indications (with concentration of economic power and a continuous narrowing of the base of the political system) there seems little chance of matters improving.[2]

These and various other trends of increasing poverty and inequality, and growing landlessness and unemployment, on the one hand, and a growing centralization of power on the other, coupled with a more frequent and intense use of the repressive machinery by the state to crush any local movements, have been clearly in evidence for some time now. What is more shocking is the incapacity of the macro organizations of the poor—the communist parties, the *kisan sabhas* (peasant fronts, attached as mass fronts to communist or socialist parties), the trade unions—to act effectively against these trends.[3]

It is in response to the continuing negative trends and failures of the macro organizations to initiate positive developmental and participative tendencies that, of late, attention has begun to be focused on organizations and activities outside the purview of both the government and the political parties. Variously called voluntary agencies (VAs), non-governmental organizations (NGOs) or non-party political formations (NPPFs), these organizations have been the focus of a concerted and heated debate in India over the last decade. This chapter is an attempt to intervene in the debate about the role, responsibility, functions and limitations of these groups and activities.

The debate derives its legitimacy from an increasingly popular conviction that the conventional forums through which the masses attempt to participate in decision-making, as well as to vent their discontent—namely, the state and its development agencies, political parties and their mass fronts—are fast being devalued. We even have a clear admission by the state that the official agencies are by themselves unable to plan and implement officially stated development objectives. Therefore the involvement of VAs and NGOs in government programmes, ranging from adult education centres and rural health services to facilitating the organization of the rural and urban poor, becomes important even to the state, as documents of the Planning Commission show.

At the more formal political level, a myriad small and large struggles have erupted outside the confines of the traditional political organizations. Prominent amongst these have been the Gujarat and Bihar agitations in 1973–74; the struggles against the Emergency in 1975–77; the farmers' agitations in Tamil Nadu, Karnataka, and Maharashtra during 1980–81; and most recently the textile strike in Bombay.[4] In addition, hundreds of efforts by local and regional-level organizations—in both urban and rural areas, with different strata, and displaying different degrees of militancy—are attempting to articulate the interests of the popular classes.

Some issues regarding classification

VAs, NGOs or action groups (AGs) are loose categories. The examples referred to above represent a bewildering mix of ideologies, objectives, working styles, social composition, funding and support sources, size of organization and operation, which precludes any possibility of putting this heterogeneous collection under a single rubric.

At the formal level, the only common characteristic of such organizations is that they are registered under the Societies Registration Act (1861), are not expected to make any profit on their activities, and are considered non-governmental and non-political: non-governmental only in their not being part of the official machinery, and non-political only in their non-participation in any direct manner in electoral processes. This, however, is only a juridical classification, not an analytical one.

Leaving apart juridical concerns, these activities spring from a similar context, a similar concern, and in many ways represent a common tendency. Most of the groups and activities that I will be discussing emerged after 1965, having internalized the experiences and critiques of official development strategies as well as the more political of the movements led by the Left parties. These groups are organizations composed mainly of sensitized/radicalized middle-class youth, working for and with the oppressed and exploited strata with a view to transform society. They are involved in a range of activities from development with a political perspective to militant organization of the masses. These activities take place outside the control of the government and political parties. There is no primary focus on the capture of state power.

Whilst the above definition provides a broad organizing umbrella, a better way to develop a classification is to look at activities and the organizations behind them. The activities may be classified in a number of broad domains: relief and charity, development, mobilization and organization, politics, and political education.

The organizational classification would be as follows: development and charity groups; action groups involved primarily in the processes of conscientization, mobilization and organization of the oppressed without an explicitly stated political perspective (very often, posing as non-political or even anti-political bodies); political groups carrying out tasks very similar to action groups but formed with reasonably clearly defined political perspectives and goals; pre-party political formations formed with the purpose of graduating on to the level of political parties; and support groups carrying out specialized tasks of bringing out journals, creating documentation and resource centres, lawyers' forums, etc., working in tandem with other groups and political parties.

The nature of the activities under consideration

I shall attempt to present the dynamics of various groups within each activity domain listed above, indicate how different sectors view these organizations and activities, attempt to demonstrate the linkages across the domains, and finally examine the strengths, weaknesses and possibilities indicated by the history of these groups within the current context.

Much of my work has been made easier by earlier work of Roy and Aftab. Roy, in a series of papers written in the 1980s, has analysed the historical emergence and role of these groups in relation to the major shifts that took place in Indian society and polity. Aftab has concentrated primarily on the more political of these groups. I shall also indicate my areas of agreement and disagreement with the analyses offered by these two scholars.[5]

Further, most of my observations are based on the experience of a very specific substratum within these groups—ones that I consider have the potential to contribute to the development of participative polity. My observations are also coloured by my own experience of working at the fringes of some of the Left political parties, and having had the opportunity to participate in the debates being held within these groups.

Relief and charity

The charity organizations are the most established of all the VAs. By definition, they are only ameliorative organizations, very often working under religious inspiration, and drawing upon the innate qualities of altruism present in all human beings. There are many examples of this kind of organization, which are considered useful by both the state and political parties—presuming that they work honestly.

Even when considering such organizations, problems with the official definition of VAs immediately arise. Are these organizations or such activities non-political? This would very much depend upon where they draw their funds from and to what use they put their resources. A substantial number of the larger organizations draw their resources from foreign agencies. Whilst this may not in itself be objectionable, it constantly gives rise to the fear that these organizations are operating at the behest of some foreign power. Very often they are accused of proselytization, particularly if they are non-Hindu, or of being part of the Central Intelligence Agency (CIA) of the US government. Organized charity has always been big business, which permits some of these organizations to use the goodwill they have built up for activities other than those for which they were founded.

Individual or group charity, carried out with the noblest of purposes and with all honesty, does little to change the situations and processes that give rise to the necessity of these activities. Altruism, self-sacrifice and the prospect of being rewarded in heaven do not carry sensitive individuals very far. Having confronted misery in its starkest forms, they are forced to ask the questions 'Is all this suffering necessary? What causes it? How come it is only the poor who suffer? Can social problems be dealt with by charity?' Then starts the process of internal turbulence and debate. Very often individuals and organizations change through a process of open-ended questioning. The pressure is to push them towards developmental activity, as illustrated by the history and experiences of organizations such as Oxfam, Christian Aid and the Ramkrishna Mission.[6]

It is interesting to note that as the nature of internal debate and activity mix undergoes a change, so does the nature of external criticism. If earlier, the charity agencies were accused of helping to contain the contradictions that became apparent in disaster situations, they are now, if they start questioning the political economy of disasters, accused of making political capital out of human misery. From charity-merchants they are converted into death-merchants. Irrespective of how this debate is resolved, it is now clear, even to most charity practitioners, that their activity is not politically neutral.

Development[7]

Development activities begin where charity ends. These groups attempt, essentially, to provide the basic social and economic infrastructure to facilitate the development of productive forces. Shying away from political involvement, they supplement the state effort for development in areas where such effort is non-existent, insufficient or inefficient. So we have groups digging wells, doing farm extension work, running schools and hospitals, setting up credit and marketing agencies—all with a view to helping the target population reach income and social self-sufficiency.

The major strength of these groups lies in their ability to draw in motivated middle-class professionals willing to provide their expertise at rates lower than those they would otherwise command in the market. Combine this with their relatively more flexible organizational structure and approach, and you are likely to get results that are far more spectacular than the government's, at least in the specific area of their operation.

The fact that such groups are 'non-political' encourages state support to an extent that some governmental plan documents have based a number of their programmes on such agencies (namely, the NAEP during 1977–79; the Antyodaya programme in Rajasthan; the Lok Jumbish programme in the same state, etc.).[8] These groups also serve the interests of business houses and banks who view such efforts very favourably, because they help integrate newer sections into the modern market spectrum.

These groups also receive support from the clientele for whom they work because they are so much more efficient and less arrogant than the lower echelons of the bureaucracy that the vast masses of our populace have to deal with. What is important to remember is that these groups have no retaliatory power, and cannot tax, harass, imprison and otherwise trouble the poor, as the bureaucracy so often does.

The reaction of the political parties, particularly of the Left, is also predictable. At best, these activities are dismissed as reformist, do-gooder attempts, which can never solve the basic problems confronting society. At worst, there is direct hostility towards these groups, because their work allegedly defuses tensions and delays the much-awaited revolution. The fact that such activities receive liberal support from state and non-state (including foreign) sources makes it easier to dismiss them as part of an official conspiracy to weaken the Left.

But no matter how committed or innovative these groups may be, they still have to face serious limitations. Most of them are small and operate in restricted areas. Whilst this facilitates flexibility and deeper knowledge of the local area and people, it also limits the range and type of activity they can engage in. The fact that most groups depend upon external funding very often forces them into accepting programmes that are designed to suit funding agency requirements and end up being irrelevant to the local population.

The major limitation, however, is inherent in the nature of development activity. Very few development groups start their work with any explicit understanding of the political environment. As long as they view development as a neutral process depending primarily on technical skills, they survive. But no group, if sensitive and dedicated to its original charter, can escape the brutal reality. The local bigwigs, the bureaucracy, the politicians—all serve to frustrate any attempt at honest work. And then begins the tussle of ideologies, not as empty abstractions but as concrete reflections of actual working styles, and the groups start entering a crisis phase.

Individual members accuse each other of being more or less political. Involvement in technical activity declines. Funding agencies become a little chary of extending support to a group that spouts radical phraseology. Local vested interests become hostile as they sense that the organization will no longer toe the line. Increasingly, there is a dissonance between the inherited organizational structure and the professed ideology.

The more politicized group members see their activity as futile and become either cynical and disheartened, leave to join another, more explicitly political, group or continue where they are, ineffectual. The technicists too lose out in the process, and very often return to more conventional jobs where they can turn this brief exposure to concrete reality into a paying asset.

This loss of cadre finishes off most organizations. Some make feverish attempts to replace the external middle-class professionals with local cadre, but this does not necessarily solve the problem. While local cadres provide a greater link with the local environment, the group starts facing additional problems. The first relates to the relative inability of such local cadres to attract funds from external sources to continue the programme: and programmes of this sort, with salaried personnel, can rarely be funded out of local resources. One must not forget that the target population that such groups are working for rarely has the surpluses to support such a group.

A second and greater danger is that of localism: the group loses its ability to stay out of local factional fights and very often ceases to have the wider perspective that impelled it to undertake its activity in the first place.

This, in brief, is the story of most development groups that are not organized as a business. But does this mean that such activities are useless? I would plead otherwise.

Constructive work activity has a value not only in itself, or in providing an entry point for more radical work, or in generating cadres for organizational and political activity, or in supporting the work done by more overtly political action groups and parties, but very much because such groups offer the possibility of experimentation with alternative styles of doing things, and with different organizational models and processes.

Of the potential roles suggested above, the first four do not require much elaboration. The entry point argument is now well accepted, not only as a tactical move, but also as a gradual process of learning, which takes place in each group, which permits the transcending and converting of a non-political activity into a political one. Sometimes these activities are also considered useful in consolidating the gains made during the process of 'struggle'. Not all phases are war phases, and any long-term revolutionary activity has to plan for times of 'peace'. If carried out with a different consciousness, development activity helps tide over and consolidate the periods of lull that trade unions and *kisan sabhas* find so difficult to deal with.

The fifth position requires some elaboration. As an example, Rajnikant Arole's work in the area of health care in Jamkhed[9] is useful and meaningful not only because the population covered gets better health care, but also because we learn how alternative health care delivery systems can be designed and run. We put into operation systems that challenge the conventional notions of health care, explore the possibility of alternative doctor–patient relationships, demonstrate the superior value of preventive and social medicine over hospital-based curative techniques and, above all, convert an ostensibly neutral technical profession and task into a political one. And Arole not only becomes a symbol for others in the profession, but also, the work at Jamkhed challenges the very basis on which medical mystification is based. The values and the operating style of the profession get a jolt. Even if such work cannot be replicated or extended, it is a constant reminder of what is possible, even within the existing structures, and this to my understanding is an extremely important political task.

This needs to be elaborated. What I am arguing is that work such as that of Arole in the field of health care, or of ASTRA[10] in the field of appropriate technology, creates two kinds of political tension. The first relates to the delivering capacity of the existing structures and system. If Arole's work can alter the health statistics of his project area, then pressure naturally builds upon the official health machinery to perform as well, if not better. The other, and more important, political tension arises within the profession itself, where the norms of the profession themselves get challenged.

Now, it is no longer a question of working more efficiently, but of its ability to work differently. The profession is forced to contend with the charge that either it too should follow the initiative of the innovating group or, if this is not feasible within current systemic constraints, then part of the professional concerns have to be with facing up to and changing these constraints.

Mobilization, organization, politics and political education

Activities in this sphere take on a far more intense form. Much has been written in the past on the role of action groups. Aftab's article referred to earlier is the most detailed analysis of organizations in this area. Whilst he has explained the inherent limitations of action groups in a variety of situations—slums, factories, tribal areas, with fishermen, etc.—he does not explore a number of possibilities. Aftab's formulations follow a classical Marxist position, and he sees the possibility of combating the present political crises only through the mediation of a macro working-class organization. Consequently, he views the actions of the numerous action groups at best only as a feeder into larger political formations—and at worst as diversionary and counter-revolutionary.

Political involvement and action, more than any other activity, brings home the macro constraints inherent in the Indian situation. So what if a group succeeds in mobilizing and organizing a bunch of workers, or peasants, or tribals, or slum dwellers? Does it change anything? Is it not a weakening of the existing macro formations that are attempting to challenge the system? A recent CPI(M) Central Committee resolution on action groups[11] would have us believe so. And the existing scenario wherein a number of the groups are non-Marxist, or even anti-Marxist, supported by a variety of internal and external sources, linked to religious bodies, etc., only tends to strengthen this formulation.

But we forget that the existing Left parties, though the major carriers of the tradition of struggle against colonial and feudal oppression in India, are beset with problems. If only we remember that most of the action groups emerged as a result of the continuous limitations and failures of the Left parties, we are forced to come to a slightly different conclusion.

The strength of most action groups comes from their local character, the fact that they are where the action is. They are aware of the local environment, responsive and responsible to it. Unlike that of the political parties, their relationship with the masses is not one of making use of them. Their size permits flexibility, and a possibility of innovation, that larger parties lack. Their selection of issues, the processes of mobilization and organization, the relative stress on empowering the people rather than the organization, all tend to mark them out as different from the political parties, including the parties of the Left.

It is possible to illustrate this through a few examples. In both the Shramik Sanghatana in Dhulia and the Bhoomi Sena in Thana, the full-time cadres of the organization sit along with the Tarun and Mahila Mandals to examine each of the decisions taken.[12] Not infrequently, the cadres admit their errors and decisions get revised. Each decision has to be constantly explained to and ratified by the mass bodies, not as in periodic party plenums, but on a frequent and regular basis. It is because of such frequent interactions and because the notion of accountability to the masses is put into practice that the groups display a greater degree of involvement with issues of daily concern. An example of fairly extreme accountability may be cited from an independent trade union working with powerloom workers in Belgaum, where even the interpersonal relations of a cadre couple were discussed collectively.

The involvement of a Chattisgarh Mazdoor Shramik Sangha (CMSS)[13] in issues of health care, in children's recreation and education, in fighting the tendency towards alcoholism, etc.—issues that rarely excite the attention of the normal trade unions—to my mind springs from their ability to make a break from the kind of patron–client, leader–led relationships that other organizations suffer from. A similar tendency is evident in the Bihar Colliery Kamgar Union (BCKU) for which such issues as tribal people, deforestation, or regional development are as important as issues relating to wages and bonuses.

But action groups too are facing a crisis of survival, of growth, of identity. How does a small group survive the onslaughts of the local vested interests? What if repression is also from the forces of the state? Where does one make links and forge alliances? There are dangers of localism, of lapsing into a parochial and reactionary fold. Can they survive without the active support of the Left parties? These are some of the key questions that form part of an intensive ongoing debate.

I think most of these questions and fears are valid, and many action groups have in fact broken up because of them. The attempt to combat localism has basically taken three forms:

1. To join with a major political party. This provides an all-India perspective, of having allies one can count upon. The ability to withstand repression increases and the problem of identity gets partly resolved. However, and this has been borne out in all such attempts, the group and the activity lose whatever distinctive character they had, that had marked them out as an effort worth watching. It is rarely that the larger political party will change its style just because a group, or a number of groups, has been included within its fold. However, this process may strengthen the anti-bureaucratic tendency within the party.
2. To try to form an autonomous federation with other non-party action groups. This move has succeeded only at a regional level when the ideology and objectives of the groups have been similar. Even then, as the experiments of Jabaran Jot (tribal groups in Maharashtra getting together to press for the restoration of cultivation rights to tribal people on cleared forest land), or the Jharkhand Mukti Morcha (a federation of tribal and local groups in Bihar, Bengal and Orissa to demand a separate state in the Indian Union) clearly indicate, these federations work only for a limited period to attain or attempt to attain a specific objective.
3. To remain autonomous but have a working relationship with one or a number of political parties. The major limitation in this strategy emerges

from the difference in the relative strengths of the two parties trying to enter a contract. Because most action groups have a popular base, and do not have electoral ambitions, sometimes larger parties are interested in forming alliances with them during elections—but only then.

These three variations have been mentioned only to indicate that the action groups are aware of some of their existential weaknesses, and are trying to overcome them. The value to their experience is not, however, insignificant. Again, like the developmental groups, not only do these groups select areas and issues neglected by political parties, but also their relative success in these areas indicates that groups and strata considered unorganizable for social transformation, both in conventional Marxist theory and in practice (because of their relative unimportance in decisive struggles for the capture of state power), cannot so easily be denied their roles in the struggle for change. The experience of a Bhoomi Sena or a Shramik Sanghatana, a Swadeshi workers' collective or a Chattisgarh Mazdoor Shramik Sangh, underlines the importance of different organizational models and processes. More important, and this will be argued a little later, their very existence challenges the notion of a macro Bolshevik Party as the only viable agency for social transformation. What we learn is that whilst the politics of capture of power, the *raison d'être* of political parties, may be a necessary condition for transformation, it definitely is not a sufficient one.[14]

Protest groups and related activities[15]

I have still not touched upon the activities of the environmental groups, lawyers' collectives, alternative professional associations, groups fighting for civil liberties and democratic rights, radical journals, theatre groups, etc. These too have contributed significantly to both our understanding of and attempts at social transformation. The functioning of such groups raises issues about both developmental and conventional political organizations. These protest groups contribute to the development of a heightened sensitivity and debate that draws conventionally apolitical citizens into expressing and fighting for their basic right to participate in the country's decision-making processes.

Equally important, these are also assertions by professionals that question the role and functions of their own professions. They demonstrate, among other things, that a doctor to be political does not necessarily have to be a *Datta Samant* (a doctor turned trade-unionist) but can still fight to transform the medical profession (through organizations such as the Medico Friends Circle or the Voluntary Health Association of India); that theatre groups can not only serve the interests of the paying public (read, commercial establishment) but may also work for underprivileged sections and, equally important, challenge the established understanding and practice of relations between art and society (Samudaya, Jan Natya Manch, etc.);[16] that natural wealth cannot be exploited rapaciously (Chipko). All these activities represent the right of citizens to take the initiative, to know and to act, and in the process to contribute to the development of a generalized sensibility that challenges the right of any minority to rule over others.

Some general comments: problems, crises[17]

Having discussed the role of action groups in different activity domains, we are now in a position to make a few general observations though, as has been stated earlier, generalization is not without its hazards.

The first major point to underscore is that irrespective of the activity domain, the groups are in a position, and have demonstrated the capacity, to make some significant contributions. The major contributions of such formations are:

- responsiveness to the local situation and population;
- a mass democratic method of operation;
- work with neglected sections and issues;
- a political approach to many spheres of life traditionally considered non-political.

But the groups also reflect, and not surprisingly, the fratricidal divisions that characterize their larger and better organized compatriots, the political parties. They too seem in a state of shock, with events constantly overtaking them, creating in turn an incapacity for effective intervention, even at the micro level. What is more important and interesting is that the validity of political action at this level is itself being seriously questioned, in the absence of a larger ideological and programmatic framework.

This internal debate has ideological, organizational and personal dimensions, which get reflected in different kinds of conflicts manifesting themselves at the level of the individual, the activity, and the organization.

Ideological problems

The major ideological problem facing the groups comes from their accent on the 'people' and the 'masses'. This emphasis on people and not on a class is part of a strong populist streak which 'idealises the wisdom and innate qualities of the people and all spontaneous actions are seen as transformative with some hope for future'. Part of the leaning towards the 'people' is a direct result of the Gandhian legacy, but equally it is due to the rigid denial by the Left of any central and political role to the non-industrial working classes. 'In a country where the organised working class sector is small, and will continue to remain so for the foreseeable future, this theoretic and strategic bias is, to say the least, misplaced.'[18]

But who are the people? It almost appears that the people comprises anybody who catches the fancy of the groups. Even if we add 'oppressed', 'exploited', 'deprived', 'marginalized', etc., as qualifying adjectives to the 'people', we are still left with a loose category that blurs the reality of class.

An accent on the 'people' pushes the groups towards a strategy of organization commonly referred to in the relevant literature as Community

Organization (CO). The CO strategy, drawing its inspiration essentially from the writings of Paulo Freire and Saul Alinski, is based upon attempts to organize the community on issues that the community identifies as crucial to its existence. Whilst the CO strategy provides a much-needed weightage to the concerns and beliefs of the group being organized (which a large number of the Left organizations seemed to have conveniently forgotten in their mistaken belief that as professional revolutionaries in vanguard organizations, they have grasped the 'true' nature of working-class consciousness and can inject it into the class in the movement for social transformation), it makes the mistake of seeing the community as one. It disregards the objective material forces and idealizes whatever may be the current concern of the people.

A combination of the populist streak and the CO strategy serves to confuse the analyses and organizational activity of groups. The notions of 'people power' and a 'people's movement' are most relevant when political power is held by a small coterie who have lost all legitimacy in the eyes of the people. In a struggle against a foreign power, or against an illegitimate dictatorship with a narrow social base and excessive reliance on repressive mechanisms, a multi-class alliance with well-defined, narrow objectives, as in China or more recently in Nicaragua, may have some meaning. Otherwise, this ideological orientation by itself cannot resolve the contradictions of a class society.

Of course, in the concrete case of India, many have characterized the country as a 'spoils society', where the Indian state has been confused with an individual and a small coterie. Whilst not underplaying the importance of the increased 'privatization of the state', I do feel that it would be wrong to present the Indian reality as simply that. The ruling coterie has its autonomy, but only in a limited terrain. The spoils system may ensure a particular kind of loyalty, so necessary for the survival of a populist regime, but it cannot ensure the implementation of stated objectives.

The preceding discussion refers to two sets of problems, both operating at different levels. The first relates to giving primacy to any single category of analysis. In our kind of situation where no societal category (class, caste, community, sex, religious or linguistic identity, citizen, etc.) can emerge as a pure and sharp category, to pose the analytical framework in terms of either class or citizen (the basic categories used by the Left parties and groups) necessarily turns out to be inadequate. Rarely is it realized that each issue is, in a sense, a multi-category issue and has to be seen in a context where each category of analysis is itself constantly undergoing transformation.

The second problem arises before all those groups or parties, operating within any of the frameworks (Marxist or otherwise), who want not only to understand and analyse, but also to make positive interventions. The problem now changes from deciding the categories of analysis to one of giving relative weight to different strata. Specifically, even if the primacy of class analysis is accepted over other frameworks of categorization, how does one decide that not only a stratum can be identified but also its role can be designated.

It is therefore not surprising that there are frequent swings in both the choice of categories of analysis as well as in the strategic importance given to different strata (namely, working class over peasantry, or *dalits* over *non-dalits* , etc.).[19]

Organizational problems

A second set of problems facing the action groups relates to the organizational question—the form and content of the organization, inner organizational democracy, the relationship between the leaders, cadres and masses.

Intrinsic to the group psyche is an ideal of a mass, participative, democratic and unifying activity. The political parties, particularly those of the Left, were criticized strongly for their substitutionalist tendencies. So were their mass fronts. This tendency becomes even more galling when each party claims to be the sole, legitimate voice of the working class, with complete disregard for the reality of the fragmentation of the class. The groups have absorbed a strong sense of suspicion against vanguardist proclamations.

This dislike for authority and hierarchy within the organization, and for a leadership role vis-à-vis the working class, often pushes groups into adopting loose organizational models that in practice may become ineffective. Rarely is it realized that the hierarchical and authoritarian tendencies so evident in the political parties, while not to be eulogized, are not merely a result of the personal aberrations of some leaders. Nor is it the case that all organizations beyond a certain size fall prey to Michel's Iron Law of Oligarchy—irrespective of ideology, aims and objectives. Shaping an organization in both its internal and external relations is strongly conditioned by both its aims and objectives, as also by the nature and consciousness of the groups the organization works with.

In addition to sorting out ticklish theoretical and practical questions relating to the inner organizational mode of working, groups have also to contend with their small size and localized character. This issue is inherent in their evolution and structure. Groups are not macro organizations spanning the country. Their effectiveness stems from their ability to respond to the specificities of the local situation, an ability sorely lacking in the local units of larger organizations, tied as they are to concerns of a different order. This effectiveness becomes also the source of their weakness, because issues are not always local, and dealing with them requires a perspective and an organization that goes beyond local concerns. This becomes evident both in developmental and politico-organizational tasks.

The small size of the groups raises the perennial questions, both financial and organizational, regarding stability. Where does the group draw cadre from? Can it survive the cooptative or repressive strategies of the state? Survival becomes a key question, and when this issue becomes acute, inner organizational democracy is one of the first values to be sacrificed. Most groups started around a key individual or individuals. They display a cultish character, for it is this fanatical obsession with themselves, their group and their leader that gives them the ability to survive the tensions created by their size. But what happens when the original leadership departs? Just as, within the developmental groups, local cadre are rarely a workable replacement for the external middle-class cadre, the new leadership is rarely able to replace the old. The range of tasks and the small size of the groups normally heighten the division of skills within the groups, with an important range of decisions being made exclusively by the leadership. This practice is rarely questioned as the groups in a sense formed themselves around a charismatic leader. Rarely, therefore, are groups able to survive a leadership transition.

Finally, this brings us to issues related to attempts to overcome the limitation of smallness. By this, I am referring to the debate about linking up with other groups and/or political parties. I am deliberately not discussing the possibilities of and attempts at lateral expansion: first, because this tendency is not empirically prominent, and, second, because larger groups necessitate a more formal organizational structure with well-defined roles and responsibilities at different levels of the organizational hierarchy, which as a model, is very different from those of smaller groups.

I have already discussed the possibilities and problems encountered in the process of federating groups, whether on an issue basis or on a regional basis. Issue-based link-ups have succeeded temporarily, as for example in opposition to the Rape Bill, or the proposed Forest Act, but they tend to have a strong negative orientation. So long as the issue is live and important, groups can disregard their differences of ideology and approach, but as soon as it loses force, the alliance breaks down. This is not necessarily a bleak picture, however, because more stable alliances can develop only through the social practice of working together, and at least there is always the possibility of a mass protest on the specific issue in question.

Regional federations have also emerged in India, and in many ways they have a better chance of success because the issues that the groups in a region face are more likely to be common. But such organization, too, tends to slur over some of the fundamental differences between the various organizations participating in the alliance.

The fate of the Jharkhand Mukti Morcha, a multi-group/party alliance fighting for the formation of a new state within the Indian Union, is a case in point. Though the alliance did serve the twin purpose of highlighting both the exploitation of the region by other regions and the exploitation of the majority community—the tribal people—by non-tribals, the cohesive nature of the struggle very soon started developing cracks. Personal rivalry considerations apart, it became difficult for the local exploiters (the backward castes, in this context), and the exploited (the tribal people) to forget their differences because of the cultural contradictions relating to sub-nationalism.

Both forms of alliance, issue-based and regional, are at best temporary and depend upon a strong and emotive resentment about a specific issue. We have as yet to see this kind of social practice emerging with an alternative stable and programmatic focus.

Relations with political parties, particularly those of the Left, have been major bugbear of groups and parties. This is only to be expected because many groups either consciously emerged out of criticism of these parties, or their very existence is a critique of parties. They hurl accusations at each other, the groups accusing the parties of dogmatism, monolithic structures, big-brother attitudes, non-democratic and manipulative practices and bureaucratism. The counter-accusations are equally vicious: groups are accused of considering the Left parties as the major enemies, dividing the progressive forces, entering into dubious alliances with right-wing forces, and playing into the hands of the state. This spree of mutual accusations has so vitiated the ideological space that their coming-together seems almost impossible.

Examples of collaboration are not unknown, however, and organizational difficulties have nudged many a group into applying for membership or partnership status with political parties. This is only to be expected as the survival crisis of the groups becomes more intense in response to a more repressive policy by the state.

In my view, this debate, though very vociferous, is sterile. Groups are not parties, and the reverse is also true. Both operate in different domains and the clash comes out of mistaken perception that they are organizations vying for control of the same political and ideological space. So long as groups continue to operate with parameters similar to those of political parties, and engage in similar practices, there is bound to be a clash of interests. They have to realize that their relations, though contradictory, do not have to be antagonistic. I am not arguing that groups should cease to be political, but that their forte lies in operating outside the considerations of capture of state power.

One issue in this debate retains a degree of seriousness. In a situation of increasing resort to repressive acts by the Indian state, and a general right-wing resurgence in the country, how far is it correct or desirable to continue to identify the Left parties as a major enemy? True, similar bogeys have often been raised by the Left parties and their unions when their rule was threatened, but an all-out attack on the Left, without constantly keeping in mind the institutions and strategies of capital, can very easily lead the action group into providing the rationale for the attack on Left parties and their mass fronts.

Personal problems

In addition to the ideological and organizational dilemmas facing the action groups, the range of their personal problems is not insignificant. A major section in the groups, as has been repeatedly stressed, comprises middle-class activists, a stratum that has its own peculiar problems. One important sentiment governing the psyche of these activists is sacrifice and self-denial. There is a feeling of having given up what might have been theirs, in their work with the poor. This process of class- and self-denial can express itself in a variety of ways when the overall conditions turn difficult.

There are the constant pressures to settle down, to take up a stable job, to display responsibility towards one's family. These are routine. What is a little more difficult to express, but probably more serious, is the tension that results from the desire at one level to develop as a person, and the sacrifices and self-denial constantly demanded in the name of the cause. The cause, however, is elusive, and creates a nagging feeling of somehow having been cheated.

This tension arises primarily out of the apocalyptic vision of politics that most middle-class cadres have. The revolution is imagined as a spectacular event and its imminence is felt very personally. Thus, when the pace of change is not to one's liking, and the much-awaited revolution is a little long in coming, there is a strong sense of disappointment leading sometimes to a resolve for further work but, more frequently, to cynicism and withdrawal.

A specific expression of this tension emerges in the case of professionals involved in political work. A major criticism of political parties relates to their inability to design appropriate politico-professional tasks for their professional cadres. Most groups suffer from the same handicap. The general tendency is to view professional work, that is, work relating to theatre, art, medicine, law, research, etc., either in conventional professional terms or as merely feeding into the political programmes. Either outlook tends to be dissatisfying, even in conventional terms, resulting in neither good professional nor good political work. Both outlooks tend to strengthen the view that politics is a specialized activity to be monopolized by the specialist politicians.

Another expression of this tension between the growth of the individual as a person and meeting the requirements of the cause emerges in dissatisfaction with being effective 'only' at the local level. Radicalized middle-class cadres often suffer from what one might be tempted to call delusions of grandeur—an aspiration to play a role on a larger stage. Their so-called sacrifice and self-denial further strengthen this delusion, having now armed it with a moral imperative. The resultant feeling is one of being trapped into an activity and role that is felt to be much below one's capacities and talents.

The small size of most groups creates its own tensions. Isolation, lack of companionship, paucity of intellectual stimulus are some of the common complaints. To draw strength from the masses is an easy slogan, not an easy task. These issues are not easy to discuss openly, and this is sad, because frank and open discussion could definitely resolve some of the tensions.

The crises

The various issues and dilemmas discussed above generate a strong sense of crisis and helplessness in most groups. The alarming rate of fatality of groups can, for the most part, be explained by their relative inability to resolve these dilemmas to any satisfactory level. This crisis is partly one of specification: at two levels. At one level it is that of micro groups (both developmental and political) confusing themselves with macro agencies—borrowing their range of organizational objectives—which, as we have argued, they are structurally incapable of meeting. The second relates to a more generic question, a question that affects every organization, large or small, which sets up its objective function and constraints in such a manner that no preferred solution is possible. What I am referring to is the tendency to set up absolute objectives—say, the desire to usher in an egalitarian, exploitation-free, non-scarcity society, using democratic, open-ended and participatory means—without reference to the socio-historical context within which the attempt is being made. Thus every success towards the achieving of a partial goal is seen not as a success, but only as a failure. It almost appears that there is a desire to prove unsuccessful.

This crisis has different manifestations and gets reflected at different levels:

The individual

The most commonly felt conflict is at the level of individual, mainly the external middle-class cadre. The range of personal dilemmas that we have described very often results in the expression of a strong feeling of dissatisfaction. This results in deep introspection, which often ends up in the external middle-class cadre looking for new options. While this loss of cadre is serious, and may cause the group to fold, it cannot by itself be taken as a proof of the invalidity of group activity. Dissatisfaction of the middle-class cadres, with its consequent impact on the groups and activity, does not imply that the group was not serving a useful purpose. All it implies is that the activity should be designed keeping in mind that the involvement of the external middle-class cadre is likely to be transitory.

The activity

A second and a different kind of conflict arises from the nature of the target population most groups work with. As has been stressed earlier, most groups work with the poor—the oppressed and marginalized—in sectors of production and existence that can best be described as precarious. It is not totally without reason that those areas have so far remained unorganized—though not unorganizable. Working with shifting populations or artisans in a declining trade, in slums and far-off villages generates pressures difficult for small groups to handle. More often than not, the target population is linked in a patron–client relationship with exactly the same forces and individuals that the groups want to struggle against. It is not surprising that success is a little elusive (though the work done by the Self-employed Women's Association, SEWA, in Ahmedabad, or the organization of domestic workers in Pune, gives cause for hope). We call this an activity-based conflict.

The organization

By far the most serious conflict groups face is from forces that are not local in character and cannot be resolved or tackled locally. In situations of riots—caste, language, communal or revivalist upsurges, etc.—small groups get swamped by the tide generated. Years of dedicated work can be wiped away in such a situation, and in the current state of India, it is this limitation that is brought home most sharply to groups. We call this a crisis of the organization. The fact that macro organizations, too, seem incapacitated in such a situation does not absolve the groups of this charge.

It is this combination of dilemmas and conflicts that gives rise to what one may term the 'structural crisis of the groups': an inherent inability to overcome and resolve macro contradictions in a micro frame, leading in turn to a high degree of mortality in all such efforts.

There have, of course, been attempts to respond to this structural crisis, arising mainly out of the local character and small size of the groups. As discussed earlier, one response has been to set up regional and/or national federations of groups and agencies. There are obvious problems connected with this approach. In our understanding, it is neither useful nor feasible to bring together groups characterized by a large variation in ideologies, activities, operating style and organizational strength. Most of such attempts only end up in creating debating forums, which likewise rarely get off the ground.

More fundamental is the error of presupposing that groups which arose in response to local questions can, just by being brought together, play a positive role on an altogether different plane. Regional federations, however, have a better chance of success, mainly because the issues groups face in a given region are more likely to be common. With a commonness of shared reality, it should be easier to design a common response.

For similar reasons, issue-based federations will continue to have a future, though a limited one, and that too of protest. The furore over the proposed changes in the Rape Law and the Forest Act are adequate testimony to this. Though limited, this role for such federations must not be slurred over. Protests at least serve to demonstrate the wide base of resentment to specific actions of the government, and it is only through many such experiences that the capacity to focus on more complex problems can develop.

Another equally significant tendency empirically is the attempt to link up with the macro organizations. Even though the experience of such moves has not always been very happy, this tendency demonstrates that the search for new answers and organizational responses is not limited to groups alone. Political parties too are willing to shed some of their older inhibitions and come together with smaller, local groups.

Groping for a new tradition

While new organizational models are a necessary requirement, we do, very often, spend far too much time attempting to unify the existing individuals, groups and parties. An equally critical and urgent task is the search for a new unifying tradition. This is not to argue that we disregard the deep and fundamental schisms that divide our society, but only that no fragmentary ideology, based on sectional interests, can serve a transformative function.

In a country such as India, we confront a dual problem posed both by our fragmented reality and by the nature of our intellectual tradition(s). The requirement, simply stated, is to draw from one or many of our traditions and concepts an analytical framework that can explain both the concrete and the general, and can link up our past with our future. In more formal terms, as Saberwal so elegantly states, can we combine the sociologist's and social anthropologist's tools, with those of the historian?[20] The anthropologists and sociologists, who have worked with the traditional concepts—caste, kinship, family, ritual, status—have ended up explaining only how individuals and groups relate to each other. The historians, who attempt a subcontinental analysis, work with concepts—nationalism, secularism, socialism—that are not rooted in the traditions. How, if at all, can we reconcile the demands and the opportunities of our two, possibly disparate, worlds? Is it possible to move to a more general analytical ground, in which we can consider both layers simultaneously?

In my view, none of our existing traditions offers us more than a partial answer. If the Gandhians serve to remind us of the essential unity of ends and means, of having a morality in politics, their social practice and theory leaves much to be desired. Their Luddite rejection of science and technology binds them to a rural vision not only of low productivity, but also of all the ramifications of caste, class and sex oppression that go with the glorification of our villages. More disturbing is their tendency to defuse all antagonisms and appeal to the goodwill of those in power to effect social transformation. Reconstructive activities can hardly be built upon by neglecting the fundamental inequalities that characterize our system.

The Lohia socialist tradition[21] is only a variant of the Gandhian theme. While it constantly points towards the necessity of evolving a native tradition, and has a legacy of struggle against Brahmin hegemony, it carries its anti-Western attitude towards an anti-urban one, leading its protagonists into the blind alley of pronouncing the rural–urban conflict as central to the Indian polity. Their social practice thus leads them into unqualified support for the rich farmer, as for instance is evident in their stand on the recent farmers' agitation.

The Marxists too are not without their failings. Their dogged perseverance with concepts and theories derived from nineteenth-century Europe often leads them into a class-reductionist attitude. Having classified Marxism as scientific truth, they are convinced that their reading of history cannot be wrong:

> If the masses at the moment are unable to comprehend the movement's line and language, the movement itself must not lose heart. It has to be continuously at it, until comprehension dawns on the people, and they embrace the red flag.[22]

True, the Marxist parties have a heroic record of being in the forefront of the anti-feudal struggle, and have rarely fallen prey to caste and religious chauvinism, but their excessive preoccupation with the leading revolutionary role of the industrial proletariat serves to create barriers between them and the struggles of the *dalits* and tribals. If the Gandhians and the Lohiaites serve to glorify all that is 'Bharat',[23] the Marxist tradition, tied as it is to the visions of a Western industrial society (the deep crises of those societies notwithstanding), cannot without serious modifications help us to understand and discover forces of change in a predominantly agrarian society.

The search for a new unifying tradition, or at least for its essential preconditions, can lead us down many a blind alley. The answers are not self-evident, living as we are in a world characterized by disintegrating visions. The task becomes more difficult, in ex-colonial countries like ours, because all versions, as present today, are both informed and distorted by our colonial encounter. A critical necessity is to decolonize our minds. 'Only when the intellectual doors of our perception are cleaned shall we be able to grapple with the fundamental reality.'[24] The answers, if any, can only be sought in the attempt to overcome both biases: of seeking answers in our past (the mythical Ram Rajya)[25] or of mistakenly believing that the West of today or tomorrow offers us a vision of our future. Only multiplication of many autonomous and different attempts towards the synthesis of a new praxis can create a dialectic complex enough to unify our diverse strands. We should strive towards such a vision.

An assessment, auto-critique and some possibilities: moves towards a reconstructive politics

What situation do action groups find themselves in the beginning of the 1990s? The overall situation can only be described as bleak, crisis-ridden, and displaying little or no possibility for a radical transformation. The current centralizing tendencies; the state's increasing resort to violence; the slow dismantling of the economic planning system; large areas of the country left completely at the mercy of local vested interests; increasing neocolonialization of the state; the growth of fissiparous regional, linguistic, communal and caste tendencies; and above all the almost complete exclusion of the vast majority of our people from the benefits of growth: all have been documented in great detail.[26]

What we seem to have at the top are the twin tendencies of *erosion*—of institutions, values, frameworks and ideas—and a corresponding *insecurity* that governs the actions of everybody, from the very top to the bottom. In brief, we face the prospect of a fragmenting state and society. The situation may be summed up in this remark by Kothari:

> Slowly and imperceptibly we are moving towards a new political dispensation, backed by a new political ideology which if not countered decisively and through the united intervention of all those who care for the country, will end not only Indian democracy but possibly the Indian State as well.[27]

This state is not, contrary to the arguments put forward by many analysts, the result of the vagaries of certain individuals and groups in power. Rather, the roots of the current crisis have to be traced to the functioning of the very system we have inherited and attempted to run. The crisis is not one of management, which would imply in some way that the problem is only of sub-optimal decisions, and that in principle, 'right' decisions can be taken. Instead, what we confront today is a structural crisis, where all options are between 'wrong' decisions that weaken the system and increase its strains. 'Politicians no longer have options between policies which will enhance the crisis and others which will lessen it. They only have the lesser option of deepening it in different ways.'[28]

It is not as if this steady degeneration has gone unchallenged. If one dominant tendency in our recent history has been the steady dismantling of our institutions, the other has been that of protests: at all levels, from the electoral to mass movements and ethno-regional upsurges. Whichever way we look, the nation is in turmoil. Caste tensions have aggravated, implying among other things that the *dalits* are no longer passive. The nationalities, or rather the subnationalities, question has come to the forefront with agitation gripping regions as far away and diverse as Assam, Punjab, Jharkhand or Chattisgarh. Equally important is the continuing struggle of the textile workers in Bombay, where thousands of workers have resorted to prolonged strike action.

Far more significant than large and spectacular movements has been the mushrooming of small, sporadic, individualized and group protests. The emergence of non-party political formations has to be seen within this context.It is not as if the various movements do not have glaring inadequacies. They have them in abundance. What is heartening is that they represent a mass stirring against the cynical manipulation of the people. A new spirit of questioning is slowly overtaking our normally passive and apathetic society.

One significant factor that has emerged through all these movements and counter-movements is the devaluation of political parties as instruments of social transformation. This should not, however, be interpreted as an argument against politics. The state has always supported the tendency towards depoliticization in its attempt to convert every problem into a techno-managerial one. This move finds much favour with the traditional middle-class view, strongly upheld and propagated by all our institutions, that says that 'good and honest citizens should concentrate on their work, leaving the business of politics to politicians'.

Ironically, the crusading sections of our press have, perhaps unwittingly, helped to consolidate this feeling. Their valiant exposures of the gross misdeeds of our elected representatives have created a confusion between politics and politicking. Disgust at the activities of politicians and political parties, in the absence of a cohesive critique of the processes that give sustenance to such activities, very often only strengthens the feelings of apathy and depoliticization that the state desires.

The critique of the Indian parties should not be confused with a condemnation of politics as such. The solution lies not in being non-political, but in understanding the functioning of the formal political sphere of which the parties are an integral component. It is my contention that the very functioning of our formal political sphere is populist, plebiscitary and manipulative, and offers little or no space for genuine participatory involvement of the people in deciding affairs crucial to their own existence. By confining themselves to the formal political sphere, all political parties are open to the charge that they alienate the common people from the political process. By setting themselves up as exclusive and specialized mediators, they only serve to institutionalize popular feelings of helplessness, of leaving one's fate in the hands of the specialist, the politician bureaucrat.

If the political parties are in a state of crisis, in many ways so too are the action groups, the non-party political formations that are the focus of my analysis. I have argued at some length that the groups too face serious dilemmas and conflicts—at the ideological, organizational and personal level—

which not only limit their effectiveness, but very often pose stark questions of survival. The solutions, if any, will have to be sought in the concrete histories of the myriad parties and groups and their experiments.

As a start, we will have to rethink and redefine the dominant views about politics and power. The social democratic view presupposes that the parliament and allied electoral activity are the sole legitimate ground for politics. Politics becomes that which is done by political parties. Underpinning this view is the belief that political power resides in electoral institutions. Periodically, at election times, this power is momentarily dispersed amongst the citizens before it becomes reconstituted into a new unity. Hence, according to this view, the entire energies of the political parties should be polarized towards that supreme moment when power is dissolved and resolved.

Ironically, the conventional Marxist–Leninist view is a mirror image of this viewpoint. It dismisses parliament as a facade to be participated in only for tactical reasons, and insists that power resides in the central core of the state apparatus that monopolizes the legal use of coercion. The capture of this inner citadel by some political or quasi-military manoeuvre organized by the party then becomes the ultimate objective of political activity, to which everything else is secondary.[29]

Both viewpoints have been presented in a highly schematized manner. All social democratic parties also function outside the electoral framework, just as all Marxist parties work for aims other than the ultimate revolution. But both these visions focus on the capture of state power, without controlling which it is considered impossible to effect societal changes. Little, if any, importance is given to spontaneous and autonomous actions of individuals, groups and strata. Politics is constantly reduced to a specialized activity, reserved for the specialist politician.

Both views may disagree as to the specific location of political power, but they are one in regarding power as the exclusive preserve of a narrow range of institutions. Neither view appreciates that dominance is exercised by a web of interlocking structures, including many not recognized as political. Both end up restricting our strategic perspective unnecessarily.

Rarely is it realized that unless part of the new societal vision is translated into actual reality in the course of the struggle itself, we are likely to end up with a social formation similar to Khomeini's Iran. The focus on the capture of state power, the smashing of the bourgeois state, does not by itself help fill the void created after a revolution. The tendency then is to revert to tried and tested methods, and continuing old social practices necessarily give rise over time to old social relations. This is in many ways the trap that all post-revolutionary societies have fallen into.

What we are arguing for is not the creation of a modern Yenan, a new revolutionary base from which sorties are made into existing society. This, to start with, is hardly feasible in the present conditions. Instead, what we are advocating are attempts to inculcate new social practices, individual and institutional, that constantly strain existing social barriers. The future has to be encapsulated into the present, if the future itself is to have a reality different from the present.

New frontiers of struggle

What we require is to go beyond old traditions, concepts and models of organized practice. A key element to be underscored is that in a country like India, where power is exercised through a web of interlocking institutions and structures, and no single set of issues can be isolated to which all attention can be directed, the focus on capturing one or the other institution may be necessary for social transformation, but it definitely is not sufficient. Our plea is for the 'politics of hegemony',[30] or what Bahro calls 'the new historic compromise': 'We must transcend the old divisions to set into motion an overwhelming majority for the "peaceful conquest" of the State machine in all its levels and departments. Nothing short of this will do.'[31]

The task, therefore, is long and arduous. It demands the winning of the diverse structures of power. The struggle will have to be carried out wherever it is feasible, not only in the arena of formal politics. The key emphasis is on the relative importance given to the *processes* of social action, rather than only to the *structures* of the exercise of power.

Fortunately for us, India still has a democratic legacy, and a number of working institutions that are not very easy to wipe out. This offers us space for action in all spheres of social activity, and our energies must be concentrated on maintaining, deepening and extending the spaces for democratic and collective action.

Is it that we are over-reading the level and nature of the institutionalization of democratic tendencies in our system? In reacting to the narrowly political perspective of the revolutionary Left, are we committing the obvious error of minimizing the reality of the coercive apparatus? Do we believe that the ruling classes will permit a slow and peaceful dismantling of their state apparatus? These doubts are all valid and gain sustenance from the historical fact that no revolution has so far been peaceful.

My plea for the politics of hegemony does not imply that the coercive power relations backed by the state will just wither away as a result of positional skirmishes in different institutions. It stems more from a reading that in societies like ours, violent revolutions resulting in the overthrow of the state are more a chance than a necessity.

I do not visualize any short-term or even medium-term possibility of the working class establishing its will over society through force. There is also a nagging feeling, based on the experience of 'post-revolutionary societies', that violent revolutions result in the imposition of a new authoritarian logic, undoubtedly different from the earlier capitalist system, maybe even better, but nowhere near what we are striving for.[32] Large heterogeneous and multicultural societies can only transform themselves over a long period of learning how to accommodate their differences. This transformative process may be interspersed with shorter periods of violent change and realignment of societal and class forces, which may facilitate long-term transformation, but the process in its essence has to be long-drawn-out and peaceful.

Calls for social transformation very often take an idealist turn, and we are overcome by despair and hopelessness, the tendency then being either to give up or to wallow in voluntarist euphoria. In his 'Reasons for Hope',[33]

Shourie points to the countless acts of heroism, both great and small, that individuals have displayed in their rejection of the present system. It is his understanding that it is the acts of betrayal by the many that have brought us to the present state of affairs, and it is only when the individual, the common man, refuses to acquiesce in the vagaries of our rulers, that the change will come.

Be that as it may, a greater sign of hope lies in the very existence and activities of the groups and individuals we have characterized as non-party political formations. These groups are in a flux. Charity and welfare groups are displaying a development consciousness, whilst development groups are moving towards a struggle orientation. The more political groups are seeking new allies. These recent changes in the various developmental, non-political transformative, and semi-political groups, and the growing interaction among them indicates that they have a potential for moving towards a new politics of the future.

For a start, these groups are not structured in the image of a party. Politics, for them, is not a professional activity, but only a means to a larger social transformation. They work on issues directly concerning the poor, not *for* them but *with* them. This opens up for them a whole range of neglected human and cultural issues not evident when people are viewed, not as subjects of change, but as mere objects to be mobilized for an external vision. The same empathy brings them into contact with strata—the *dalits* and tribals—that are rarely in the forefront of political discussion about transformation. Finally, they are not constrained by the logic of capture of state power. This allows them flexibility and open-endedness, experimentation and innovation in devising their programmes and picking issues. Taken together, the potentiality of these several types of non-party groups lies in their growing recognition of the non-political and non-economic aspects of the contemporary structures of power and domination embedded in the culture of modern politics.[34]

Whilst this capacity to learn gives a definite edge to the micro movements under consideration, they have yet to address themselves to another equally important task, that of combining the new micro practice with the creation of a new social knowledge. Without the creation of an alternative macro structure of thought and institutions, the movements are likely to be absorbed only as pressure groups to correct local anomalies. They may of course survive as anachronisms, to be admired and studied but hardly the focal points for social transformation.

It is therefore necessary to recognize new issues, contradictions and challenges that our changing polity continuously throws up. This is not easy in a society where issues related to survival still reign paramount. Given our degrading poverty and deep-rooted inequality, struggles will for some time revolve around issues of livelihood, land, wages and dignity.

We shall thus have to learn to handle these issues differently. How do we handle the issue of 'land to the tiller' in the face of an extremely adverse land–man ratio? Can cooperatives be thought of and put into practice, not as a vision for a far-off future, but as a practical alternative to individualized peasant production or capitalist farming dependent upon wage labour? The tribal struggles in Dhanbad in the early 1970s combined opposition to moneylenders with the simultaneous creation of 'grain goals' to meet consumption needs during the lean season. They also initiated cooperative farming to raise productivity.[35] The Bhoomi Sena experiences provide indications for combining the social and the economic. Their handling of bondage with changes in marriage rituals is the kind of innovative step we should be looking for.

What of issues related to ecology? These encompass not only problems related to the changing structure and rapid depletion of our forest resources, or the complex problems related to water management and building dams in the seismologically sensitive Himalayan regions, but also the hazards millions of our slum- and pavement-dwellers face in daily living. The demand for eco-development is not just a cry of the middle-class nature lover, but forces us to question and revise the very basis of our understanding and application of modern science and technology in the creation of an industrial civilization.

To be relevant, action groups have to face these and many other challenges. They must continue to engage in a wide range of social practice, and simultaneously strive for the creation of alternative macro theories and institutions. It is only through the dialectic of micro practice and micro thinking, grounded in the objective forces of change, that we can visualize the promise of a new politics.

Notes

1. This chapter is a part of, and an intervention into, a much larger and ongoing debate between individuals, groups and political parties seeking to find ways of social mobilization and transformation. Many stances taken are only tentative, designed as much to provoke reaction as to place on record the current understanding. Parts of this chapter were presented in the Inter-disciplinary Research Methodology Workshop organized by the Madras Institute of Development Studies at Coimbatore in June 1982. I am grateful to Professor Kurien and other participants for helpful comments. I would also like to thank friends at LOKAYAN and BUILD. This chapter has developed as a result of a running dialogue with them.

2.Rajni Kothari, 'An Alternative Framework for Rural Development', in *Another Development: approaches and strategies,* Dag Hammarskjold Foundation, Uppsala, 1977.

3. Making such a statement immediately raises a few problems. First, it is argued, 'Why single out the Left for criticism? Is the record of any of the non-Left unions (both rural and urban) and parties any better?' Such a concern can partly be met by a counter-argument that, vis-à-vis the others, one never had any illusions or hope. It was and is only the Left, which had or has the ability to create 'illusion' about its potential. Thus the fact that the comment has been directed to the Left is only symptomatic of the relative regard in which it is held.

Second, the issue is raised that such a criticism is hardly fair. After all, the Left exists, but in a scattered manner, barring the few states where it enjoyed or still enjoys electoral power. This too, in my view, is only begging the question. If, in a city such as Kanpur, where the Left for years controlled the unions in the textile industry, it was still possible for a Swadeshi Mills massacre to occur, with hardly any upheaval taking place in the city, or if in West Bengal it was possible for urban slum-dwellers or rickshaw-pullers to be brutalized in the same manner as by the Congress regime in Bombay, then it is, in my view, fair for us to raise questions about the ability of the Left parties, as currently constituted, to handle the problems thrown up by our distorted society.

4. The Gujarat agitation, referred to in the literature as the Nav Nirman Movement (Movement to Create a New Society), was a student-based movement directed against corruption in the provincial government. It finally led to the Chief Minister of the state being dismissed and replaced. This Bihar agitation, also referred to as the J.P. (Jai Prakash Narain—an important Gandhian leader) Movement, quite like the Gujarat agitation, also based itself amongst students and youth against the rampant corruption in the state machinery. It was finally crushed by the imposition of a state of emergency on 26 June 1975. Many of the leading activists of these two agitations were jailed, and after the 1977 elections, with the victory of the Janata Party, they emerged as important regional political figures.

5. Dunu Roy, 'The Problem of Communication between Groups and Individuals Engaged in Social Development and Change', report submitted to the ICSSR, 1982. See also Aftab, 'Crisis, Action-Groups and Political Action, A Note', Background Papers, BUILD Documentation Centre, Bombay, March 1981.

6. The Ramkrishna Mission is a sect comprising the followers of Sri Ramkrishna Paramhansa, a leading nineteenth-century mystic–saint, and his disciple Swami Vivekananda. The mission has set up numerous foundations running schools, hospitals and general welfare and development works.

7. Some of the points raised in this section have earlier been discussed in Dunu Roy, 'The Structure of Interventions', unpublished manuscript, 1975; and 'Cadres and Cadre Formation', unpublished manuscript, 1976. Also, see H. Sethi, 'Alternative Development Strategies: a look at some micro-experiments', *Economic and Political Weekly,* special number, 1978; and 'Between Myth and Uncertainty: the making of a vision', mimeo, ICSSR, 1979.

8. The National Adult Education Programme (NAEP) was a major programme to eradicate adult illiteracy initiated during the Janata regime. The Antyodaya programme, literally meaning 'Lift the Bottom-most', consisted of identifying the five poorest families in a village and organizing schemes and activities for their economic upliftment. The Lok Jumbish was an innovative programme that focused on energizing existing development programmes meant for the poor through seeking an active involvement of voluntary agencies.

9. Rajnikant Arole was director of the Comprehensive Rural Health Care Project, a programme marked by tremendous innovation in the training and use of illiterate village *dais* (midwives) as health delivery agents.

10. ASTRA, or Application of Science and Technology for Rural Areas, is a department of the prestigious Indian Institute of Science, Bangalore, which since the mid–1970s has done pioneering work in the generation and dissemination of appropriate technology for rural areas.

11. This resolution (1982), amplified in an article 'Action Groups/Voluntary Agencies: a factor in imperialist strategy', Prakash Karat, *The Marxist* (1983), lays out the party line on the voluntary sector. Basically it argues for stringent state control on foreign funding for the voluntary sector, within a framework that sees the phenomenon as an anti-national/anti-communist fifth column.

12. The Shramik Sanghatana is a Marxist action group organizing tribal landless labour in Dhulia district, Maharashtra. It became very important in the late 1970s and early 1980s since its organizational base was substantial enough to threaten political parties and the state. Later the organization split; some of the leading activists joined the CPI(M), whilst others preferred to maintain their independent organization. The Bhoomi Sena is a tribal organization working on issues of bondage, wages and employment in the Thana District of Maharashtra. Mahila and Tarun Mandals are women's and youth groups, respectively.

13. The CMSS is a militant and independent trade union of informal mine-workers in the Dalli-Rajhara mines attached to the Bokaro Steel Plant in Chattisgarh, Madhya Pradesh.

The union charted out new paths in organizing the workers into cooperatives and using the surpluses to run schools and a hospital.

14. H. Sethi, 'Lok Chetna Jagaran', unpublished mimeo for the ICSSR, January 1978.

15. This discussion has drawn upon S. Sarkar, 'Citizens' Initiative Movements', unpublished manuscript, 1978; and M. Bookchin, *Post-scarcity Anarchism,* Ramparts Press, New York, 1978.

16. Samudaya is a theatre group in Karnataka that received public recognition through its innovative campaigning against Mrs Gandhi in the 1978 by-election in Chickmaglur. The Jan Natya Manch is a street theatre group active in Delhi, and loosely affiliated with the CPI(M).

17. This section is based on the discussion that took place in the UNRISD-LOKAYAN Workshop on Non-Party Political Formations in India, 21–23 December 1982.

18. Can this criticism be handled by diluting the role of the working class to one which primarily is that of providing leadership as, for instance, in the concept of a 'democratic revolution'? I do not think so, because the notion of the 'working class' and 'working-class consciousness' is itself in a flux. The worker is a complex and contradictory human, who like everyone else operates on multiple concerns, with different concerns and identities taking primacy in different situations. Merely converting this complexity to clichés and slogans only reduces the 'working class' to the factory workers and the appeal in the name of its consciousness to whatever may be the current fancy of theoreticians and leaders of the working class. For further elaborations on this argument see *Human Futures,* special issue on trade unions and the labouring poor in India, New Delhi, 1982. Also see Arvind Das, 'Working Class Movement: straws in the wind', *Probe,* June 1983.

19. *Dalit* is the political term to denote scheduled castes.

20. S. Saberwal, 'Societal Designs in History: the West and India', Occasional Papers on History and Society, No. 1, Nehru Memorial Museum and Library, New Delhi, 1983.

21. This refers to a political tendency initiated by Ram Manohar Lohia, a prominent socialist leader.

22. A.M., 'Calcutta Diary', *Economic and Political Weekly,* 29 January 1983.

23. The Hindi term for India, 'Bharat', denotes a nature-oriented, political category, distinguishing those who talk of 'Bharat' from the urban, Westernized Indians. It fits well into the Michael Lipton urban bias thesis.

24. *South,* January 1983.

25. This is a metaphoric allusion to the mythical golden age of the past, the rule of Lord Rama. The phrase was popularized by Gandhi during the struggle for independence.

26. As a small sample, see Rajni Kothari, 'Democracy and Fascism in India', mimeo, 1981; 'Towards Intervention', *Seminar,* January 1982; and Arun Shourie, 'Reasons for Hope', *Indian Express*, 15 August 1982.

27. Kothari, 1981.

28. S. Kaviraj, 'Economic Development and the Political System', paper presented at the Vienna Colloquium on Contemporary India, University of Vienna, 1982.

29. For a good discussion on this theme, see M. Prior and D. Purdy, 'Out of the Ghetto', *Spokesman*, 1979.

30. *Ibid.*

31. R. Bahro, *Socialism and Survival,* Heretic Books, London, 1982.

32. S. Banerjee, 'The Island of Dr Marx', *Economic and Political Weekly,* January 1982.

33. Arun Shourie, 'Reasons for Hope', *Indian Express,* 15 August 1982.

34. D. L. Sheth, 'Movements and the Future of Politics', paper presented at the Seventh World Conference on Future Studies, Stockholm, 1982.

35. K.G. Iyer and R.N. Maharaj, 'Agrarian Struggle in Dhanbad', mimeo, National Labour Institute, Delhi, 1976.

Select Bibliography

Abu Al-Namel, Hussein, *Gaza Strip 1948–1967,* PLO Research Centre, Beirut, 1979.

Adkin, Laurie and Catherine Hyett, 'The Chilean left and the question of democratic transition', *IDS Bulletin,* University of Sussex, April 1985.

Afigbo, A.E., *The Poverty of African Historiography,* Nigeria Industrial Arts and Crafts, Lagos, 1977.

Aftab, 'Crisis, Action-Groups and Political Action, A Note', Background Papers, BUILD Documentation Centre, Bombay, March 1981.

Agarwal, Bina, 'Who Sows? Who Reaps? Women and Land Rights in India', *Journal of Peasant Studies,* Vol. 15, No. 4, July 1988.

Alas, Higinio, *El Salvador, por que la insurreccion?,* first edition, Secretariado Permanente de la Comision para la Defensa de los Derechos Humanos en Centroamerica, San Jose, Costa Rica, 1982.

Al-Hassan, Hani, 'Faith Between Theory and Practice', *Journal of Palestine Studies,* February 1972.

Al-Khatib, Hussam, 'The Palestinian Revolution: where to?', *Journal of Palestine Studies,* No. 4, September 1971.

Alvares, C. and R. Billorey, *Damming the Narmada,* Third World Network, Penang, 1988.

Amin, S., *Unequal Development*, Monthly Review Press, New York, 1976.

Amin, S., *Eurocentrism,* Zed Books, 1988.

Amin, S., *L'Egypte nassérienne,* Minuit, 1964; *The Arab Nation,* Zed Books, 1978; *The Crisis of Arab Society* (in Arabic), Cairo, 1985; *The Arab Nation,* Cairo, 1989.

Amin, S., *L'Afrique de l'Ouest bloquée,* Minuit, 1971; *Impérialisme et sous développement en Afrique,* Anthropos-Economica, 1988; *The Maghreb in the Modern World*, Penguin, 1970; *La Faillite du développement,* Harmattan, 1989.

Amin, S. and F. Yachir, *La Méditerranée dans le système mondial,* La Découverte, 1988; preface in Y. Sertal, *Nord–Sud, crise et immigration, le case turc,* Publisud, 1987.

Arias, Arturo, 'El movimiento indigena en Guatemala 1970–1983', in Daniel Camacho and Rafeal Menjivar (eds.), *Movimientos populares en Centroamerica,* Editorial Universitaria Centroamericana (EDUCA), San Jose, Costa Rica, 1985.

Arrighi, G. and J.S. Saul, *Essays on the Political Economy of East Africa,* Heinemann, London, 1973.

Aviles Solis, C., *Medios de communicacion en la educacion rural: una experiencia en el valle del Mezquital,* Universidad Nacional Autonoma de Mexica, Mexico, 1981.

Babassana, Hilaire, *Travail force, expropriation et formation du salariat en Afrique Noire,* Presses Universitaires de Grenoble, Grenoble, 1978.

Badiou, Alain, *Théorie du sujet,* Seuil, Paris, 1982.

Bandopadhyaya, J. and V. Shiva, 'The Chipko Movement', *Seminar,* February 1987.

Bandopadhyaya, J. and V. Shiva, 'Reply', *Seminar,* August 1987.

Banerjee, S., 'The Island of Dr Marx', *Economic and Political Weekly,* January 1982.

Barraclough, S., *A Preliminary Analysis of the Nicaraguan Food System,* UNRISD, Geneva, 1982.

Beaud, Michel, *A History of Capitalism, 1500–1980,* Macmillan Press, London, 1984.

Benton, Ted, *The Rise and Fall of Structural Marxism: Althusser and his influence,* Macmillan Press, London, 1984.

Bernstein, Henry and Bonnie K. Campbell (eds.), *Contradictions of Accumulation in Africa: studies in economy and state,* Sage Publications, Beverly Hills and London, 1985.

Bhaduri, A. and M.A. Rahman, *Studies in Rural Participation,* Oxford and IBH Publishing Co., New Delhi, 1982.

Bhairappa, *Godhuli* (in Hindi), Shabdkar, Delhi, 1986.

Bisbergen, William Van and Mattew Schofeleers (eds.), *Theoretical Explorations in African Religions*, KPI, London, 1985.

Blomstrom, Magnus and Bjorn Hettne, *Development Theory in Transition: the dependency debate and beyond: Third World responses,* Zed Press, London, 1984.

Bodenheimer, Susanne J., 'The Ideology of Developmentalism: American political science's paradigm-surrogate for Latin American studies', *Berkeley Journal of Sociology,* 1970.

Bookchin, M., *Post-scarcity Anarchism,* Ramparts Press, New York, 1978.

Brandao, C.R., *Pesquisa participante,* Editora Brasiliense, Sao Paulo, 1981.

Brandao, C.R., *O ardil da ordem,* Papirus, Campinas, 1983.

Browning, M.A. and Susan Vitka, 'East Timor and Diplomatic Pragmatism', *Southeast Asia Chronicle,* Issue No. 94.

Buijs, H.Y., *Access and Participation,* University of Leiden, Leiden, 1979.

Cadena Barquin, F., *Capacitacion campesina y cambio social,* Programa de Desarollo Rural, Mexico, 1980.

Calla Ortega, Ricado, *La encrucijada de la COB,* mimeo, La Paz, Bolivia.

Camacho, Daniel and Rafeal Menjivar, *Movimientos populares en Centroamerica,* Editorial Universitaria Centroamericana (EDUCA), San Jose, Costa Rica, 1985.

Castells, Manuel, *Movimientos sociales y urbanos,* sixth edition, Siglo XXI Editores, Mexico, DF, 1980.

Castillo, G.T., *How Participatory is Participatory Development? A review of the Philippine experience,* Institute of Development Studies, Manila, 1983.

Centro de Estudios y Accion Popular, *Conocimiento y accion popular,* Pozo de Rosas Venezuela, 1981.

Cezar, Maria do Ceu, 'As organizacoes populares do Recife: trajectoria e articulacao politica (1955–1964)', in *Cadernos de Estudos Sociais,* Vol. 1, No. 2, July/December 1985.

Chegge, Michael, 'The Revolution Betrayed', *Journal of Modern African Studies,* 17(3), 1979.

Chen, Martha Alter, *A Quiet Revolution,* BRAC Prokashana, Dhaka, Bangladesh, 1986.

Chilcote, Ronald H., *Dependency and Marxism: toward a resolution of a debate,* Latin American Perspectives Series No. 1, Westview Press, Colorado and London, 1982.

Chilcote, Ronald H. and Dale L. Johnson, *Theories of Development: mode of production or dependency?,* Sage Publications, Beverly Hills, 1983.

Chiriboga, Manuel, 'Crisis economica y movimiento campesino e indigena', unpublished mimeo.

Chomsky, Noam, *The New Mandarins,* Vintage Books, New York, 1974.

Clayton, Anthony, 'The General Strike in Zanzibar, 1948', *Journal of African History,* XVII (3), 1976.

Cohen, Robin, 'Marxism and Africa: old, new and projected', University of Birmingham, Centre for Development Area Studies, Working Paper No. 2, August 1975.

Comstock, D.E., *Participatory Research as Critical Theory: the North Bonneville, USA experience,* Evergreen State College, Olympia, Washington, 1982.

Concha Malo, Miguel et al., *La participacion de los cristianos en el proceso popular de liberacion en Mexico (1968–1983),* first edition, Siglo XXI Editores, Mexico, D.F., 1986.

Cooke, Peter and Martin Doornbos, 'Ruwenzururu Protest Songs', *Africa*, Vol. 52, No. 1, 1982.

Crisp, Jeff, *The Story of an African Working Class: Ghanaian miners struggles, 1970–1980,* Zed Press, London.

CSE, *The State of India's Environment,* Centre for Science and Environment, Delhi, 1985.

Dajani, Ahmed Sidki et al., *Palestinians in the Arab World,* Institute for Arab Studies and Research, Tunis, 1978.

Das, Arvind, 'Working Class Movement: straws in the wind', *Probe,* June 1983.

Davidson, Basil, 'On Revolutionary Nationalism: the legacy of Cabral', *Latin American Perspectives,* Vol. 11, Issue 41, No. 2, April 1984.

De Castille, M.V., *La contradiccion: objectivos de la educacion-producto educativo, el caso de Nicaragua,* Asociacion Nicaraguense de Cientificos Sociales, Managua, 1983.

Depelchin, Jacques, 'The Transformation of the Petty Bourgeoisie and the State in Post-colonial Zaire', *Review of African Political Economy,* No. 22, 1981.

De Shutter, A., *Investigacion participativa: una opcion metodologica para la educacion de adultos,* CREFAL, Patzcuaro, Mexico, 1981.

De Silva, G.V.S., Wahidul Haque, Niranjan Mehta, Anisur Rahman and Ponna Wignaraja, *Towards a Theory of Rural Development,* Progressive Publishers, Lahore, 1988.

De Vries, J., *Science as Human Behaviour: on the epistemology of participatory research approach,* Studiecentrum, Amersfoort, Netherlands, 1980.

Diaz Coelho, F., 'Identidade e' diferencas. O movimento de bairros no Rio de Janeiro', unpublished mimeo.

D' Monte, Darryl, *Temples or Tombs,* Centre for Science and Environment, Delhi, 1985.

Doble Jornada, supplement to *La Jornada,* Mexico D.F., 2 August 1987.

Doornbos, Martin, 'Protest Movements in Western Uganda: some parallels and contrasts', University of East Africa Social Science Conference, December 1966.

Doornbos, Martin, 'Land Tenure and Political Conflict in Ankole, Uganda', *Journal of Development Studies,* Vol. 12, No. 1, October 1975.

Drake, St Clair, 'Democracy on Trial in Africa', *Annals of the American Academy of Political and Social Sciences,* July 1964.

Elam, Yitzchak, 'Nomadism in Ankole as a Substitute for Rebellion', *Africa,* 49(2), 1979.

Ellis, Diana, 'The Nandi Protest of 1923 in the Context of African Resistance to Colonial Rule in Kenya', *Journal of African History,* XVII (4), 1976.

Erasmie, T. and F. Dubell (eds.), *Adult Education II – Research for the People, Research by the People: an introduction to participatory research,* University of Linkoping, Linkoping, 1980.

Eriksen, Tore Linne, 'Modern African History: some historiographical observations', *Scandinavian Journal of History,* No. 4, 1979.

Falabella, G., *Highlights of the Development of Participatory Research in Latin America,* Institute of Latin American Studies, University of London, London, 1981.

Fals Borda, O., *La ciencia y el pueblo: nuevas reflexiones sobre la investigacion-accion,* Asociacion Colombiana de Sociologia, Bogota, 1981.

Fals Borda, O., 'Science and Common People,' in *Journal of Social Studies,* No. 11, Dacca, 1981.

Fals Borda, O., 'Die Bedeutung der Sozialwissenschaft und die praktische Producktion von Wissen in der Dritten Welt: die Herausforderung der Aktionsforschung', in *Osterreichische Zeitschrift für Politikwissenschaft,* No. 2, Vienna, 1981.

Fals Borda, O., 'Participatory Action Research', in *Development,* Society for International Development, No. 2, Rome, 1984.

Fals Borda, Orlando, *Knowledge and People's Power,* Indian Social Institute, 1988.

Fernandez, W. and S. Kulkarni (eds.), *The Forest Policy: a people's response,* Indian Social Institute, Delhi, 1983.

Fernandez, Walter and R. Tandon, *Participatory Research and Evaluation: experiments in research as a process of liberation,* Indian Social Institute, New Delhi, 1981.

Fields, Karen E., *Revival and Rebellion in Colonial Central Africa,* Princeton University Press, Princeton, 1985.

Flores, Graciela, Luisa Pane, and Sergio Sarmiento, 'Muto Campesino y politica agraria. 1976–1984. Tendencias actuales y perspectivas', unpublished mimeo.

Forker, Andrew, 'Legacy of Resentment', *Far Eastern Economic Review*, 20 June 1987.

Forum International d'Action Communautaire, 'La Recherche action: enjeux et pratiques', *Revue Internationale d'Action Communautaire*, No. 5/45, Montreal, Spring 1981.

Fougeyrollas, Pierre, *Les Processus sociaux contemporains*, Payot, Paris, 1980.

Fougeyrollas, Pierre, *Sciences sociales et marxisme*, Payot, Paris, 1980.

Freire, P., *Pedagogia del oprimido*, Editoral America Latina, Bogota, 1970.

Freney, Denis, 'Fretilin: death and resurrection', *Southeast Asia Chronicle*, No. 14.

Freund, Bill, *The Making of Contemporary Africa: the development of African society since 1800*, Macmillan Press, London, 1984.

Freund, Bill, 'Labour and Labour Studies in Africa: a review of the literature', *African Studies Review*, Vol. 27, No. 2, June 1984.

Freund, W.M., 'Class Conflict, Political Economy and the Struggle for Socialism in Tanzania, *African Affairs*, Vol. 80, No. 321, October 1981.

Friedland, William H., 'African Trade Union Studies: analysis of two decades', *Cahiers d'Etudes Africaines*, Vol. 14, No. 55, 1974.

Fuentes Morua, J., *La organizacion de los campesinos y los problemas de la investigacion participativa*, IMISAC, Morelia, Mexico, 1983.

Fuglesang, Andreas and Dale Chandler, *Participation As Process* (case study of Grameen Bank), NORAD, Norway, 1986.

Fundacion Punta de Lanza, *Critica y politica en ciencias sociales*, Bogota, 1978.

Furedi, Frank, 'The African Crowd in Nairobi: popular movements and elite politics', *Journal of African History*, XIV (2), 1973.

Gajardo, M., J.J. Silva and V. Edwards, *Primer encuentro de investigacion-accion y education popular en Chile*, PIIE, Santiago, 1980.

Gajardo, M., *Evolucion situacion actual y perspectivas de las estrategias de investigacion participativa en America Latina*, Facultad Latino-americano de Ciencias Sociales, International Development Research Centre, Ford Foundation, Santiago, 1982.

Galeano, J.S. and V. Negrete, *El Cerrito*, Fundacion del Sinu, Monteria, Colombia, 1982.

Galeano, Luis A., 'Entre la protesta y la lucha urbana. Dos estudios de casos', in Domingo Rivarola (ed.), *Los movimientos sociales en Paraguay*, Centro Paraguayo de Estudios Sociologicos, Asuncion, 1986.

Galjart, B., *Participatory Rural Development Projects: some conclusions from field research*, University of Leiden, Leiden, 1981.

Gamez, J.A., *Evaluacion del modelo de autodidactismo solidario*, Centro de Estudios Economicos y Sociales del Tercer Mundo, Mexico, 1981.

Gandhi, Mahatma, *Non-violence in Peace and War* (2 volumes), Navajivan Publishing House, Ahmedabad, 1962.

Garcia Angulo, S., *Autodidactismo solidario: uno experiencia de education de adultos en el valle del Mezquital*, Centro de Educacion de Adultos, Izmiquilpan, Mexico, 1980.

Garcia Angulo, S., *La education de grupos marginados en Mexico*, Centro de Educacion de Adultos, Mexico, 1983.

Gaventa, J., *Power and Powerlessness: quiescence and rebellion in an Appalachian valley*, University of Illinois Press, Urbana, Illinois, 1980.

Gendzier, Irene L., *Managing Political Change: social scientists and the Third World*, Westview Press, Boulder, Colorado and London, 1985.

Gianotten, V. and T. de Wit, *Universidad y pueblo: teoria y practica del Centro de Capacitacion en Educacion de Adultos y Desarrollo Rural*, Universidad Nacional de Huamanga, Ayacucho, Peru, 1980.

Giliomee, Hermann, 'Eighteenth–century Cape Society and its Historiography: culture, race and class', *Social Dynamics*, 9(1), 1983.

Goldsmith, E. and N. Hildyard (eds.), *The Social and Environmental Effects of Large Dams*, Vol. 2, Wadebridge Ecological Center, Cornell, 1984.

Gomes, S., 'Participation Experience in the Countryside: a case study in Chile' (mimeographed World Employed Programme Research Working Paper; restricted), ILO, Geneva, 1981.

Gould, J., *Needs, Participation and Local Development,* University of Helsinki, Helsinki, 1981.

Gouldner, Alvin W., *The Coming Crisis of Western Sociology,* Hearst Corporation, Avon Books, New York, 1970.

Guha, R., 'On Some Aspects of the Historiography of Colonial India', in Guha (ed.), *Sub-Altern Studies 1: writings on South Asian history and society,* Oxford University Press, Delhi, 1982.

Guha, R., 'The Prose of Counter-insurgency', *Sub-Altern Studies II,* Oxford University Press, Delhi, 1982.

Guha, R., *Elementary Aspects of Peasant Insurgency in Colonial India,* Oxford University Press, New Delhi, 1983.

Guha, R., 'Communications', *Seminar,* June 1987.

Guha, R., 'Ideological Plurality is Good for the Movement', *Times of India,* 31 May 1988.

Gunn, Geoffrey, 'Radicalism in Southeast Asia: rhetoric and reality in the Middle Eastern connection', *Journal of Contemporary Asia,* Vol. 16, No. 1. 1986.

Gutkind, Peter C.W., Robin Cohen and Jean Copans, *African Labor History,* Sage Publications, Beverly Hills and London, 1978.

Gutkind, Peter C.W., and Immanuel Wallerstein (eds.), *The Political Economy of Contemporary Africa,* Sage Publications, Beverly Hills and London, 1976.

Hall, B. and A. Gillette, *Participation Research,* International Council for Adult Education, Toronto, 1977.

Havnevik, Kjell J., 'Some Observations on the Empirical Foundations of Theories of Under-development with Particular Reference to Tanzania', *Proceedings of the First Annual Conference of the Norwegian Association of Development Research,* Bergen, 6–8 April, 1984.

Henderson, Ian, 'The Origins of Nationalism in East and Central Africa: the Zambian case', *Journal of African History,* XI(4), 1970.

Hilal, Jamil, *The Socio-economic Structure of the West Bank and Gaza Strip: 1948–1974,* Beirut, PLO Research Centre.

Hilton, Rodney, *The Transition from Feudalism to Capitalism,* New Left Books, London, 1976.

Huizer, G., *Peasant Participation in Latin America and its Obstacles,* Institute of Social Studies, The Hague, 1980.

Huntington, S.P., *Political Order in Changing Societies,* Yale University Press, New Haven, Connecticut.

ICT, 'Speaking for Ourselves', Members of African Independent Churches Report on their Pilot Study of the History and Theology of their Churches, Box 32407, Braamfontein, South Africa.

International Council for Adult Education, 'Participatory Research: development and issues', *Convergence,* XIIV (3), Toronto, 1981.

Iyer, K.G. and R.N. Maharaj, 'Agrarian Struggle in Dhanbad', mimeo, National Labour Institute, Delhi, 1976.

Jaffe, Hosea, *A History of Africa,* Zed Press, London, 1985.

Janmohamed, Karim K., 'Labour Protest in Mombasa', Staff Seminar Paper No. 12, Department of History, University of Nairobi, 1978/79.

Jawad, Sa'id, *National Palestinian Upsurge in the West Bank, Gaza and the Galilee: 1974–1978,* Ibn Khaldoun Publishing House, Beirut, 1979.

Jeshurun, Chandran, *Governments and Rebellions in Southeast Asia,* Institute of Southeast Asian Studies, 1985.

Jiryis, Sabri, *The Arabs in Israel,* Institute of Palestine Studies, Beirut, 1973.

Jiryis, Sabri, 'Settler's Law: seizure of Palestinian lands', *Palestine Yearbook of International Law,* Vol. II, 1985.

Jodha, N.S., 'Market Forces and Erosion of Common Property Resources', mimeo, ICRISAT, Hyderabad, 1986.

Joseph, Richard, 'Ruben Um Nyobi and the "Kameroun" Rebellion', *African Affairs,* Vol. 73, No. 293, October 1974.

Joseph, Richard, *Radical Nationalism in Cameroun: social origins of the UPC rebellion,* Clarendon Press, Oxford, 1977.

Jubber, Ken, 'Sociology and its Social Context: the case of the rise of Marxist sociology in South Africa', *Social Dynamics,* 9(2), 1983.

Kalpavriksha, *The Narmada Valley Project: a critique,* 1988.

Karaus, Jon, 'African Trade Unions: progress or poverty?' *African Studies Review,* Vol. 19, No. 3, December 1976.

Kaviraj, S., 'Economic Development and the Political System', paper presented at the Vienna Colloquium on Contemporary India, University of Vienna, 1982.

Kitching, Gavin, 'Suggestions for a Fresh Start on an Exhausted Debate', *Canadian Journal of African Studies,* special number entitled *Mode of Production: the challenge of Africa,* Vol. 19, No. 1, 1985.

Kocherry, Thomas, 'Mechanisation and Kerala's Fisherfolk', *The Fight for Survival,* Centre for Science and Environment, Delhi, 1988.

Koffi, Tetteh A., 'Peasants and Economic Development: populist lessons for Africa', *African Studies Review,* Vol. 20, No. 3, December 1977.

Kothari, Rajni, 'An Alternative Framework for Rural Development', in *Another Development: approaches and strategies,* Dag Hammarskjold Foundation, Uppsala, 1977.

Kothari, R., 'Democracy and Fascism in India', mimeo, 1981.

Kothari, R., 'Towards Intervention', *Seminar,* January 1982.

Kothari, R., *State Against Democracy,* Ajanta Publications, Delhi, 1988.

Kowarick, Lucio and Nabil Bounduky, 'Sao Paulo. Espacio urbano y espacio polatico: del populismo a la redemocratizacon', *Estudios Sociales Centroamericanos,* No. 44, May–August 1987.

Kries, Rafael, 'Confiar en si mismos. Las organizaciones de base en Chile', *Nueva Sociedad,* No. 64, Editorial Nueva Sociedad, San Jose, Costa Rica, January–February 1983.

Lampe, Armando, 'Los nuevos movimientos religiosos en el Caribe', unpublished mimeo.

LeBoterf, C., *L'Enquête participation en question,* Ch. Corlet, Conde-sur-Noireau, France, 1981.

Legassick, Martin, 'South Africa in Crisis: what route to democracy?', *African Affairs,* Vol. 84, No. 337, October 1985.

Legesse, Lemma, 'The Ethiopian Student Movement, 1960–74: a challenge to the monarchy and imperialism in Ethiopia', *Northeast African Studies,* 1(1), 1979.

Leon, S. and I. Marvan, 'Movimientos sociales en Mexico (1968–1983): panorama y perspectivas', mimeo, Mexico, DF, 1987.

Lewis, John Wilson, *Peasant Rebellion and Communist Revolution in Asia,* Stanford University Press, Stanford, California, 1974.

Leys, Colin, *Under-development in Kenya: the political economy of neo-colonialism,* Heinemann, London, 1975.

Lim, Joo-Jock and S. Vani (eds.), *Armed Separatism in Southeast Asia,* Institute of Southeast Asian Studies, 1985.

Ling, Trevor, *Buddha,* Sharma, Jagdish.

Lonsdale, John, 'States and Social Processes in Africa: a historiographical survey', *African Studies Review,* Vol. XXIV, Nos. 2/3, June–September 1981.

Luke, David Fashola, *Labour and Parastatal Politics in Sierra Leone: a study of African working-class ambivalence,* University Press of America, Lanham, New York and London, 1984.

Mafeje, Archie, 'On the Articulation of Models of Production: review article', *Journal of Southern African Studies,* Vol. 8, No. 1, October 1981.

Mafeje, Archie, 'Peasants in Sub-Saharan Africa', *Africa Development,* Vol. X, No. 5, 1985.

Mamdani, Mahmood, 'Peasants and Democracy in Africa', *New Left Review,* No. 156, March/April, 1986.

Marini, Ruy Mauro, 'O movimiento operario no Brasil', *Movimientos Sociais no Brasil,* Politica e Administracauo, No. 2, Edicion especial FESP, Rio de Janeiro, 1985.

Marx, K., *El Capital,* Vol. I, Editorial Cartago, Buenos Aires, 1965.

Mathews, Koshy (ed.), *Voices of the Storm,* National Fishermen's Forum, 1988.

Max-Neef, M., *From the Outside Looking In: experiences in barefoot economics,* Dag Hammerskjold Foundation, Uppsala, 1982.

McBeth, John, 'Separation is the Goal and Religion is the Weapon', *Far Eastern Economic Review,* 20 June 1980.

Meillassoux, Claude, *Maidens, Meal and Money: capitalism and the domestic community,* Cambridge University Press, Cambridge and New York, 1981.

Mejia, M.C. and S. Sarmiento, *La lucha indigena: un reto a la ortodixia,* Siglo XXI Editores, Mexico, DF, 1987.

Mejia, M.C. and S. Sarmiento, 'La lucha indigena en Mexico 1970–1983', Mexico, unpublished mimeo.

Menjivar, Rafeal, *Acumulacion orginaria y desarrollo del capitalismo en El Salvador,* Editorial Universitaria Centroamericana (EDUCA), San Jose, Costa Rica, 1981.

Miller, Christopher L., *Blank Darkness, Africanist Discourse in French,* University of Chicago Press, Chicago and London, 1985.

Mishra, Anupam, *Mitti Bachao Andolan* (in Hindi), Gandhi Press Foundation (undated).

Mohan, Jitendra, 'Nkrumah and Nkrumahism', *Socialist Register,* 1967.

Mohan, Jitendra, 'A Whig Interpretation of African Nationalism', *Journal of Modern African Studies,* 6 (3), 1968.

Moser, H., *The Participatory Research Approach on Village Level: theoretical and practical implications,* University of Munster, Munster, 1982.

Moser, H. and Ornauer (eds.), *Internationale Aspekte der Aktionsforschung,* Kosel-Verlag, Munich, 1978.

Munshi, K.K. and R.R. Widakar, *Kural, The Great Book of Tiru-Valluvar,* Bharatiya Vidya Bhawan, Bombay, 1965.

Munslow, B. and H. Finch, *Proletarianisation in the Third World,* Croom Helm, London, 1984.

Musa, Shehadeh, 'On the Experience of GUPS', *Palestine Affairs,* No. 5, November 1971.

Mustafa, K., *Participatory Research and Popular Education in Africa,* African Participatory Network, Dar es Salaam, 1983.

Nadkarni, M.V., *The Farmers' Movement in India,* Allied Publishers, Delhi, 1987.

Nandy, A., *Science, Hegemony and Violence,* Oxford University Press, Delhi, 1988.

Negrete, V., *La investigacion-accion en Cordoba,* Fundacion del Sinu, Monteria, Colombia, 1983.

Nelson, C. and S. Arafa, *Problems and Prospects of Participatory Action Research: an Egyptian rural community,* American University, Cairo, 1982.

Nicanor, Njiawue, 'Some Lessons from the History of the Cameroon Revolution', *The Pan-Africanist,* No. 4, July 1972.

Nieto Montesinos, Jorge, 'El sindicalismo obrero industrial', mimeo, Lima, Peru.

Nunez, Orlando, 'Los sujetos de la revolucion', unpublished original, Managua, September 1986.

Nyong'o, Anyang', 'Academic Freedom and Political Power in Africa', Staff Seminar Paper No. 8, Department of History, University of Nairobi, 1978–79.

Nzongola-Ntalaga, 'Amilcar Cabral and the Theory of the National Liberation Struggle', *Latin American Perspectives,* Vol. 11, Issue 41, No. 2, Spring 1984.

Oakley, P. and D. Marsden, *Approaches to Participation in Rural Development,* ILO, Geneva, 1984.

O'Brien, Donal Cruise, 'Modernization, Order and the Erosion of a Democratic Ideal: American political science, 1960–70', *Journal of Development Studies,* Vol. 8, No. 4, July 1972.

Ocampo, Sheilah, 'Calling in the Neighbours', *Far Eastern Economic Review,* 8 February 1980.

Ogot, Bethwella and William Ochieng, 'Mumboism: an anticolonial movement?', University of East Africa 5th Social Science Conference, Nairobi, 8–12 December 1969.

Ohaegbulam, F.U., 'The Nadir of African Nationalism', paper presented to African Studies Association, 13th Annual Meeting, Boston, Massachusetts, 21–24 October 1970.

Okpewho, Isidore, 'Cheikh Anta Diop: the search for a philosophy of African culture', *Cahiers d'Etudes Africaines,* XXI–4, 1984.

O'Meara, Dan, 'Class, Capital and Ideology in the Development of Afrikaner Nationalism: 1934–1948', PhD thesis, University of Sussex, 1979.

Oquist, P., *Epistemologia de la investigacion-accion,* Punta de Lanza, Bogota, 1978.

Orefice, P. (ed.), 'La ricerca participativa', *Quaderni delle Societa delle Autonomie Locali per l'Educazione Adulti,* No. 3–4, Rome, 1982.

Ottaway, Maria, 'Democracy and New Democracy: the ideological debate in the Ethiopian revolution', *African Studies Review,* Vol. XI, No. 1, April 1978.

Oxaal, Ivan, Tony Barnett and David Booth, *Beyond the Sociology of Development: economy and society in Latin America and Africa,* Routledge and Kegan Paul, Boston and Henley, 1975.

Oxhorn, Philip, 'Organizaciones poblacionales, la reconstitucion de la sociedad y la interaccion elite–base', unpublished mimeo, Santiago de Chile.

Paakkanen, L. (ed.), *Participation, Needs and Village-Level Development (Jipemoyo),* University of Helsinki, Helsinki, 1981.

Palma, Gabriel, 'Dependency and Development: a critical overview', in Dudley Seers (ed.), *Dependency Theory: a critical assessment,* Frances Pinter, London, 1981.

Paranjape, P.V. et al., *Grass Roots Self-reliance in Shramik Sangathana (Dhulia, India)* (mimeographed World Employment Programme research working paper; restricted), ILO, Geneva, 1981.

Park, P., *Social Research and Radical Change,* University of Massachusetts, Amherst, 1978.

Parra Escobar, E., *La investigacion-accion en la Costa Atlantica: evaluacion de la Rosca, 1972–1974,* Fundacion para la Communicacion Popular, Cali, 1983.

Parsons, Talcott, *The Structure of Social Action,* Free Press, Illinois, 1949.

Pearse, A. and M. Stiefel, *Inquiry into Participation: a research approach,* UNRISD, Geneva, 1980.

Pease, H. and E. Ballon, 'Limites y posibilidades de los movimientos populares: impacto politico', in *Dialogo sobre la participacion,* Geneva, UNRISD, No. 2, April 1982.

Peek, P., 'Agrarian Reforms and Development in Nicaragua' (mimeographed World Employment Programme research working paper; restricted), ILO, Geneva, 1981.

Posel, Deborah, 'Rethinking the "Race–Class" Debate in South African Historiography', *Social Dynamics,* 9(1), 1983.

Pozas, R., *La construccion de un sistema de terrazas en los altos del estado de Chiapas,* Centro de Estudios del Desarrollo, Universidad Nacional Autonoma de Mexico, Mexico, 1979.

Prior, M. and D. Purdy, 'Out of the Ghetto', *Spokesman,* 1979.

Rahman, M.A. (ed.), *Grass-roots Participation and Self-reliance,* Oxford and IBH Publishing Co., New Delhi, 1984.

Rahman, M.A., 'The Theory and Practice of Participatory Action Research' (mimeographed World Employment Programme research working paper; restricted), ILO, Geneva, 1982; reproduced in O. Fals Borda (ed.), *The Challenge of Social Change,* Sage Publications, London, 1985.

Rahmato, Desalegn, 'Cabral and the Problem of the African Revolution', IDR Working Paper No. 16, University of Addis Ababa, January 1962.

Rahro, R., *Socialism and Survival,* Heretic Books, London, 1982.

Rajagophalachari, C., *Mahabharata,* Bharatiya Vidya Bhavan, Bombay, 1968.

Ramirez, Juan Manuel, *El movimiento urbano popular en Mexico* (first edition). Siglo XXI Editores, Mexico, DF, 1986.

Ranger, Terence O., 'Connection between "Primary" Resistance Movements and Modern Mass Nationalism in East and Central Africa', Parts 1 and 2, *Journal of African History,* IX (3–4), 1968.

Ranger, Terence O., 'Religious Movements and Politics in Sub-Saharan Studies', paper for presentation to African Studies Association Annual Meeting, New Orleans, Louisiana, 23–26 November 1985.

Ranger, Terence O., *Peasant Consciousness and Guerrilla War in Zimbabwe: a comparative study,* James Currey, London, 1985.

Redmond, Patrick M., 'Maji Maji in Ungoni: a reappraisal of existing historiography', *International Journal of African Historiographical Studies,* VIII, 1975.

Regional Centre for Adult Education and Functional Literacy for Latin America—International Council for Adult Education, *Informe final del Segundo Seminario Latinoamericano de investigacion participativa,* Patzcuaro, Mexico, 1982.

Rey, Pierre-Philippe, *Colonialisme, néo-colonialisme et transition au capitalisme,* Maspero, Paris, 1971.

Rey, Pierre-Philippe, *Les Alliances de classes,* Maspero, Paris, 1973.

Rey, Pierre-Philippe, *Capitalisme négrier: la marche des paysans vers le prolétariat,* Maspero, Paris, 1976.

Rey, Pierre-Philippe, 'Production et contre-révolution', *Canadian Journal of African Studies,* Vol. 19, No. 1, 1985.

Rhodes, William, 'The Philosophical Underpinnings of the Afro-American Liberation Movement: an interpretative essay', *The Pan-Africanist,* No. 9, January 1982.

Robins, C.E., 'Conversion and Conflict: Christian fundamentalism and the problem of evil in Kigezi District, Uganda', paper presented to the Canadian Association of African Studies Conference, Dalhousie University, Nova Scotia, 1974.

Rodney, Walter, *How Europe Underdeveloped Africa,* Bogle-L'Ouverture, London, 1972.

Rodney, Walter, 'Marxism in Africa', *Forward,* Kampala, Uganda, Vol. 7, No. 1, 1986.

Rostow, W.W., *The Stages of Economic Growth: a non-communist manifesto,* Cambridge University Press, Cambridge, 1960.

Roy, Dunu, 'The Problem of Communication between Groups and Individuals Engaged in Social Development and Change', report submitted to the ICSSR, 1982.

Rweyemamu, Justinian, *Underdevelopment and Industrialisation in Tanzania,* Oxford University Press, Nairobi, 1973.

Saberwal, S., 'Societal Designs in History: the West and India', Occasional Papers on History and Society, No. 1, Nehru Memorial Museum and Library, New Delhi, 1983.

Sadvichar Darshan Trust, *Ishavasyam,* Bombay, Samvat 2042.

Sadvichar Darshan Trust, *Gita Ke Panchaprana,* Bombay, 1983.

Sadvichar Dharshan Trust, *Swadhyaya Se Pancharangi Kranti,* Bombay, 1986.

Said, Edward W., *Orientalism,* Vintage Books, New York, 1979.

Said, Edward W., 'Orientalism Reconsidered', *Race and Class,* XXVII (2), 1985.

Sandbrook, Richard and Robin Cohen (eds.), *The Development of an African Working Class: studies in class formation and action,* University of Toronto Press, Toronto and Buffalo, 1975.

Sanguinetti Vargas, Y., *La investigacion participativa en los procesos de desarrollo de America Latina,* Facultad de Psicologia, Universidad Nacional Autonoma de Mexico, Mexico, 1980.

Sarkar, S., 'Citizens' Initiative Movements', unpublished manuscript, 1978.

Satha-Anand, Chaiwath, *Islam and Violence: a case study of violent events in the four southern provinces of Thailand, 1976–1981,* Monographs on Religion and Public Policy, Department of Religious Studies, University of Southern Florida, Tampa, USA.

Sayigh, Rosemary, 'Palestinian Peasants', *SAMED,* Vol. 4, No. 24, January 1981.

Schricharatchanya, Paisal, 'The Muslims Move In', *Far Eastern Economic Review,* 9 October 1981.

Schricharatchanya, Paisal, 'Unity is the Raiders' Target', *Far Eastern Economic Review,* 8 October 1982.

Scott, Jim, 'Everyday Forms of Peasant Resistance', *Journal of Peasant Studies,* Vol. 13, No. 2, January 1986.

Scotton, James F., 'The First African Press in East Africa: protest and nationalism in Uganda in the 1920s', *International Journal of African Historical Studies,* VI (2), 1973.

Sectas Protestantes en Centroamerica, 'La Santa contra-insurgencia', in *El Parcial,* April 1984, No. 12.

Sembene, Ousmane, 'Man is Culture', African Studies Program, Indiana University (no date).

Sethi, H., 'Lok Chetna Jagaran', unpublished mimeo for the ICSSR, January 1978.

Sethi, H., 'Alternative Development Strategies: a look at some micro-experiments', *Economic and Political Weekly,* special number, 1978; and 'Between Myth and Uncertainty: the making of a vision', mimeo, ICSSR, 1979.

Sethi, H., 'Environmentalism, Ecology and the Voluntary Movement', *Indian Journal of Public Administration,* July–September 1987.

Sethi, H., *Refocussing Praxis,* UNU South Asian Perspectives Project Report, Colombo, 1987.

Sevilla Casas, E., *Atraso y desarrollo indigena en Tierradentro,* Universidad de los Andes, Bogota, 1976.

Sharma, Suresh, 'Premodern Proximities', mimeo, United Nations University, Tokyo, 1987.

Shastri, P.V. Athàvale (ed.), *Pravachans* in *Esha Pantha, Etatkarma,* Sadvichar Darshan Trust, Bombay, Samvat 2041 (in Hindi).

Shehada, Musa, 'The Experience of the General Union of Palestinian Students', *Palestinian Affairs,* No. 5, November 1971.

Sheth, D.L., 'Movements and the Future of Politics', paper presented at the Seventh World Conference on Future Studies, Stockholm, 1982.

Sheth, D.L., 'Grass-roots Stirrings and the Future of Politics', *Alternatives,* IX, New Delhi, 1983.

Shiva, Vandana, 'Ecology Movements in India', *Alternatives,* April 1986.

Shiva, V., *Staying Alive,* Zed Books, London, New Jersey and New Delhi, 1989.

Shiva, V. and J. Bandopadhyaya, 'The Chipko Movement Against Limestone Quarrying in Doon Valley', *Lokayan Bulletin,* Vol. 5:3, 1987.

Shiva, V. and J. Bandopadhyaya, 'Political Economy of Ecology Movements', *Economic and Political Weekly,* 11 June 1988.

Shivji, Issa G., 'The State in the Dominated Social Formations of Africa: some theoretical issues', *International Social Science Journal,* Vol. XXXII, No. 4, 1980.

Shivji, Issa G., 'Working Class Struggles in Tanzania', *Mawazo,* Vol. V, No. 1, June 1983.

Shivji, Issa G. (ed.), *The State and the Working People in Tanzania,* CODESRIA, Dakar, 1985.

Shourie, Arun, 'Reasons for Hope', *Indian Express,* 15 August 1982.

Singh, Chattrapati, *Common Property and Common Poverty,* Oxford University Press, Delhi, 1986.

Sirhan, Bassem, 'Palestinian Children', *Journal of Palestine Studies,* No. 1, March 1971.

Sirhan, Bassem, 'Martyrs of the Palestinian Revolution', *Journal of Palestine Studies,* 1972.

Sklar, Richard L., 'Democracy in Africa', *African Studies Review,* Vol. XXVI, Nos. 3–4, September–December 1983.

Smith, Alan K. and Claude E. Welch, *Peasants in Africa,* African Studies Association, USA, 1978.

Society for International Development, 'Participation of the Rural in Development', *Development,* No. 1, Rome, 1981.

Sole, M., *Three False Dichotomies in Action Research: theory vs. practice, quantative vs. qualitative, science vs. politics,* University of Uppsala, Uppsala, 1982.

Sosa, Arturo, *Communidades eclesiales de base en Venezuela,* Centro Gumilla, Caracas, February 1985.

Sotelo, L., *Una experiencia de comercializacion: la huerta de Comapan,* PRODER, Mexico, 1981.

Southall, Roger, 'Review Article: South African Labour Studies', *South African Labour Bulletin,* Vol. 9, No. 7, June 1984.

Soyinka, Wole, 'The Writer in an African State', *Transition,* 31.

Spiegel, Andrew R., 'Review of Claude Meillassoux's *Maidens, Meal and Money', Social Dynamics,* 9(2), 1983.

Steinhart, Edward, 'Marxism and African History: reviews and agenda', Staff Seminar Paper No. 11, Department of History, University of Nairobi, 1979/80.

Stichter, Sharon, 'Migrant Labour in Kenya', in *Capitalism and African Response, 1895–1975,* Longman, Harlow, 1982.

Stronquist, N., 'La investigacion participativa: un nuevoenfoque sociologico', in *Revista Colombiana de Educacion,* No. 11, Bogota, 1983.

'Student Unrest in Africa' (no author), May 1970. Source: Scandinavian Institute of African Studies Library, Uppsala.

Suarez, Isauro, 'Trayectoria y actualidad de las luchas agrarias en Colombia', unpublished mimeo.

Sudarshan, R., 'Theory, Ideology and Action in Economics and Law', *Lokayan Bulletin,* 6.6, New Delhi, 1988.

Suleiman, Mohammad, 'Settlement Projects of the Palestinians', *SAMED,* Vol. 3, No. 17, June 1980.

Sutten, Anne, 'A Preliminary Study of Lugbara Response to Alien Intrusion in West Nile District, 1880–1920', University of East Africa Social Science Conference, 1968/69.

Swantz, M.L., *Rejoinder to Research: methodology and the participatory research approach,* Ministry of Culture and Youth, Dar es Salaam, 1980.

Swedner, H., *Human Welfare and Action Research in Urban Settings,* Delegation for Social Research, Stockholm, 1983.

Taksin, Kochadum Na, 'Thai Politics Through Southern Eyes', *Southeast Asia Chronicle,* No. 69.

Tamarkin, M., 'Mau Mau in Nakuru', *Journal of African History,* XVII (1), 1976.

Tasker, Rodney, 'Stepping up the War', *Far Eastern Economic Review,* 16 April 1987.

Taylor, Fraser D.R., 'The Development of African Studies in Canada', *African Research and Documentation,* No. 34, 1984.

Taylor, G. John, 'From Modernisation of Modes of Production' in *A Critique of the Sociologies of Development and Under-development,* Macmillan Press, London, 1979.

Thomas, Clive Y., 'The Grenadian Crisis and the Carribbean Left', *IDS Bulletin,* University of Sussex, April 1985.

Throup, D.W., 'The Origins of Mau Mau', *African Affairs,* Vol. 84, No. 336, July 1985.

Tignor, Robert L., 'Kamba Political Protest: the destocking controversy of 1938', *African Historical Studies,* IV(2), 1971.

Tovar, T., 'Barrios, ciudad, democracia y politica', mimeo.

Unda, Mario, 'Que hay de nuevo bajo el sol? Barrios Populares y sistema politico en El Ecuador', mimeo, Quito.

Untner, Bertil, 'The Shan and Shan State of Burma', *Contemporary Journal of Southeast Asia,* 1984.

Uzoigwe, G.N., 'The Kyanyangire, 1907: passive revolt against British over-rule', Makerere University papers, Kampala (no date).

Valverde, Jaime, 'Sectarismo religioso y conflicto social en Costa Rica', unpublished mimeo.

Van Zwanenberg, Roger, 'Neo-colonialism and the Origin of the National Bourgeoisie in Kenya between 1940 and 1973', *Journal of East African Research and Development,* Vol. 4, No. 2, 1974.

Vargas, J., 'Movimientos barriales', in *Movimientos sociales y participacion communitaria,* Nuevos cuadernos CELATS, Lima, 1985.

Vazeeruddin, Mohammad, 'Taking Man Closer to Man', *Sunday Tribune,* 11 March 1984.

Velasco Alvarez, A., *Genesis y desarrollo de un movimiento social en Puerto Tejada, Colombia,* Empresa de Cooperacion para el Desarrollo, Cali, 1983.

Vilas, C., *Entre la produccion de lo nuevo y la reproduccion de lo viejo: educacion, ideologia y poder popular en Nicaragua,* Ministry of Education, Managua, 1982.

Vio Grossi, F., V. Giannotten and T. de Wit (eds.), *Investigacion Participativa y praxis rural,* Mosca Azul, Lima, 1981.

Visvanathan, Shiv, 'Of Ancestors and Epigones', *Seminar,* February 1987.

Vives, Cristian, 'El Pueblo Napuche: elementos para comprenderlo como movimiento social', unpublished mimeo, Santiago, December 1984.

Volken, H., A. Kumar and S. Kaithathara, *Learning from the Rural Poor,* Indian Social Institute, New Delhi, 1982.

Wamba-dia-Wamba, E., 'History of Neo-colonialism or Neo-colonialist History?', Working Paper No.5, Africa Research and Publications Project, Trenton, New Jersey, 1983.

Wamba-dia-Wamba, E., 'Struggles for the "Second Independence" in Congo Kinshasa', paper presented to Mawazo workshop 'Which Way Africa?', Kampala, Uganda, 26–28 April 1985.

Waterman, Peter, 'A New Focus in African Worker Studies: promises, problems, dangers', *Cahiers d'Etudes Africaines*, 95, XXIV-3, 1984.

Wa Thiong'o, Ngugi, 'The Language of African Literature', *New Left Review*, No. 150, March–April, 1985.

Weinstein, Warren, 'Burundi 1972–73: a case study of ethnic conflict and peasant repression', *Pan-African Journal*, Vol. VII, No. 3, Fall 1974.

Werdelin, I,. *Participatory Research in Education*, University of Linkoping, Linkoping, 1979.

Wignaraja, P. and A. Hussain (eds.), *The Challenge in South Asia: development, democracy and regional cooperation,* first edition, Sage Publications, New Delhi/Newbury Park/London, 1989; second edition, Oxford University Press, Karachi/Oxford, 1989.

Wignaraja, P., *Women, Poverty and Resources,* Sage Publications, New Delhi/Newbury Park/London, 1990.

Wignaraja, P., A. Hussain, H. Sethi, and G. Wignaraja, *Participatory Development: learning from South Asia,* Oxford University Press, Karachi and Oxford, 1990.

Wise, Peter, 'East Timor Offensive', *Far Eastern Economic Review,* 10 April 1986.

Wolf, Eric, *Europe and the People Without History,* University of California Press, Berkeley, Los Angeles and London, 1982.

Wolpe, Harold, 'Capitalism and Cheap Labour Power in South Africa: from segregation to apartheid', *Economy and Society,* 1(4), 1972.

Wolpe, Harold, 'The Theory of Internal Colonialism: the South African case', *Bulletin of the Conference of Socialist Economists,* Autumn 1974.

Wolpe, Harold, 'Draft Notes on (a) Articulation of Modes of Production and the Value of Labour Power, (b) Periodisation and the State', Sussex University seminar paper, 1975.

Zanotta Machado, Lia and Custodia Selma S. do Amaral, *Movimientos religiosos no centro oeste,* Centro Latino de Altos Estudos (CLAE), Brasilia, 1986.

Zeleza, Yiyambe, 'Colonialism and Internationalism: the case of the British and Kenyan labour movements', *Ufahamu,* Vol. 14, No. 1, 1984.

Index